SUN, MOON AND PLANET SIGNS

You know that your Sun is in Taurus, but do you know that your Moon
is in Sagittarius, your Mercury in Aries, your Venus in Gemini, your
Mars in Libra, your Jupiter in Scorpio and your Saturn in Pisces?
And do you know what all that means, and how you can use it to
change your life?
This is the first astrology book to give details of *all* the planetary
influences at work at the time of your birth – on any date from
1 January 1930 to 31 December 1995.
Clear, user-friendly tables indicate in which sign of the zodiac your
Sun, Moon, Mercury, Venus, Mars, Jupiter and Saturn lie. Every
possible combination of Sun, Moon or Planet and zodiacal sign is
given its own individual character-revealing analysis, together with
a unique "Transformer", a flow chart suggesting how you can turn your
negative traits into positive ones.

Lyn Birkbeck has been a professional astrological consultant since
1979. His interest in astrology began at a time when his life had
reached crisis point, and it is in part his own experience that has
inspired and enabled him to help others to enrich and transform their
lives through astrological analysis.
As well as giving personal consultations, Lyn is featured frequently
on radio and television and in the press. He lives in Cumbria.

SUN, MOON AND PLANET SIGNS

An Astrological Guide to
Self-Discovery and Transformation

LYN BIRKBECK

BLOOMSBURY

First published in Great Britain 1990
Bloomsbury Publishing Limited, 2 Soho Square, London W1V 5DE

Line drawings by Paul Birkbeck

A CIP catalogue record for this book
is available from the British Library

ISBN 0-7475-0659-0

10 9 8 7 6 5 4 3 2 1

Typeset by Bookworm Typesetting, Manchester
Printed by Butler and Tanner Limited,
Frome and London

To Isabelle, with beautiful eyes and voice so clear —
for your help and love.

To all those who further and assist
astrological understanding.

To my mother —
and her Jupiter in Cancer.

CONTENTS

Introduction

The Sun, the Moon and the Planets through the twelve Signs of the Zodiac

Tables for Planet-Sign positions for all birth dates from 1 January 1930 to 31 December 1995

Index for Sun, Moon and Planets through the Signs

INTRODUCTION

HOW YOU AND THIS WORLD WORK

THE OUTSIDE WORLD IS CREATED BY WHAT IS INSIDE ALL OF US. YOUR OUTSIDE WORLD IS CREATED BY WHAT IS INSIDE YOU. CHANGE WHAT IS ON THE INSIDE AND YOU CHANGE WHAT IS ON THE OUTSIDE.

Your outside world is a reflection of what is inside you, that is, how you think and feel and act. A negative thought or feeling or action creates a negative outer effect – a problem – which itself becomes a thought or feeling, or a physical condition. This makes it into a vicious circle that is hard to break. But if we look at the situation from a different angle or a higher point of view – as if seen from above, from an aeroplane, or from the Planets! – we can then begin to approach life with a new idea or action. In so doing, a negative personality trait may be transformed into a positive one, and, consequently, a more creative and problem-free lifestyle may evolve.

By the same token, positively transforming yourself helps positively to transform the world – for you are a part of this world. Conversely, the negative condition of the outside world in general offers no relief to any negative condition of your own. On the contrary, it should be seen as a challenge to transform it! Even though it might be relieving temporarily to blame it, this does absolutely nothing towards finding a lasting solution.

Everything on this Earth that was made by a human being began inside, with either a seed, an idea, or a feeling. What we have made the world into, and what we can change it into, can and has been done in exactly the same way – beginning, most importantly, with YOU.

SUN, MOON AND PLANET SIGNS is an astrological guide to discovering who that YOU is, solving its problems, and transforming it by giving it a more positive sense of itself – YOUR self.

HOW THIS BOOK WORKS

This book looks at the essential parts of your personality and the various positive and negative traits that characterize them. These are astrologically determined, not just by the Sign in which the Sun was placed when you were born (your Sun-Sign), but also by the Sign positions of the Moon, Mercury, Venus, Mars, Jupiter and Saturn. All these Planetary positions are to be found in the easy-to-read Tables (no sums or symbols) at the back of this book, beginning with simple instructions on how to read them on page 205.

After you have looked up the Sign positions for the Sun, Moon and Planets for your date of birth (or anyone else's), you may then, after consulting the Index at the back of the book, turn to the relevant double-page spread for each of these Planet-Sign positions.

Note: For the sake of convenience the Sun and Moon are also referred to as Planets.

This is what you will find:-

LEFT-HAND PAGE

<1> The top left-hand corner gives the name and a picture of the Planet in question; the top right-hand corner gives the name and a picture of the Sign in which that Planet is placed. These pictures have been drawn specially to illustrate the symbolic qualities of the Planets and Signs.

<2> The central panel, headed "ESSENCE", contains a description of the essential meaning of the Planet-Sign position. It aims to reveal to you the heart or root of that part of your being that is symbolized by that Planet-Sign combination. It is through contacting such a dynamic and fundamental part of you that all your comparatively minor characteristics and apparent difficulties may be drawn into perspective – just as the extremities of your body draw life from your heart, or as a tree is supported and sustained by its roots. In short, by going to the root you find meaning and sustenance; and by coming from the heart you find truth and vitality. Reading ESSENCE, you will find, speaks for itself.

<3> Between the word "ESSENCE" and <2> are two smaller panels. The upper one gives the general key phrase for that Planet-Sign combination. This is always compiled simply by coupling the keyword of the Planet and the keyword of the Sign with the word "through" or "in", for example, Moon in Sagittarius = Security (Moon) through Seeking (Sagittarius). (See Index for Sun, Moon and Planets through the Signs for all keywords.) The lower panel gives two other phrases, epithets or sayings. These serve as personal mottoes or handles, giving a readily remembered direction or sentiment with regard to that attribute of your personality.

<4> Two panels at the bottom of the page, headed "LIKES" and "DISLIKES". Your Likes and Dislikes are highly indicative of your fundamental being, and thereby reveal much about you – or about whoever you are looking at. This can be appreciated through realizing that the oldest part of the brain (the limbic system) is the part that says simply "Like it" or "Don't like it", which, if you think about it, is how we got by in the first place!

So, as a rule, you may go for the Likes as they indicate your natural flow of urges and needs. However, although your Dislikes are usually best avoided, in some cases it might be worth re-evaluating what you think of as dislikable – unless it is obviously negative. This is because what once may have seemed bad for you may now actually be beneficial to you.

RIGHT-HAND PAGE

This page, which is headed in the same way as the left-hand page, is the "TRANSFORMER". It comprises four sections which flow into one another: "POSITIVE" traits and "NEGATIVE" traits (of the Planet-Sign position in question), "PROBLEM" (problems arising from negative traits) and "SOLUTION" (solutions to those problems).

If, on perusing the POSITIVE traits, you reckon to be in possession of some (or all!) of them, then well and good. You can also take it a step further by seeing how one positive trait fits into the whole perspective given by the others, thereby making it even more positive!

Secondly, you may simply observe how the NEGATIVE traits are revealing mirror-opposites or negative expressions of the POSITIVE traits. This can be very helpful in understanding how a bright side exists to every dark side – and vice versa – both in yourself and in others.

But the main use and purpose of the TRANSFORMER is PROBLEM-SOLVING. This is done, not merely by sitting on a problem and hoping it will go away, but by transforming the NEGATIVE traits behind the PROBLEM into POSITIVE traits. So, by following the ARROWS along the relevant channels you can see how a PROBLEM springs from NEGATIVE traits; and by continuing to follow the arrows see how a given SOLUTION to a PROBLEM effectively TRANSFORMS the original NEGATIVE traits into POSITIVE ones.

As you begin to apply the TRANSFORMER to yourself, or to someone else, it may be productive to look first at the PROBLEM section and note which problems you identify with. You may then trace the arrows backwards to the originating cause, or NEGATIVE trait.

On reading the SOLUTION, you will possibly have to ponder its meaning and significance – after all, as a rule, nothing worthwhile is achieved without some effort. On the other hand, reading a SOLUTION may cause something just to fall into place in your mind, or may simply confirm and agree with an idea that had already occurred to you.

Furthermore, you will see that the solutions often take the form of questions, quips or suggestions aimed at provoking greater clarity and shedding light on problems. Overall, the solutions are intended to prompt or stimulate you into looking at life, yourself and others in a more creative and positive fashion.

The TRANSFORMER has many uses. Apart from helping you gain a deeper understanding of how you and others tick, it also illustrates graphically the cyclical patterns and geometrical symmetry of life, which is what astrology is truly about.

Finally, in the bottom left-hand corner you will see the astrological glyph for the Planet, and in the bottom right-hand corner, the glyph for the Sign.

TAKING IT FURTHER

Here we go a little further into the complexities of the vastness of astrology, which will enable you to get even more out of this book. It is suggested that you look initially at your seven Planet-Sign combinations, and then, if you feel up to it, take it further . . .

Look at Fig 1 on page 17 to see how the Sun, Moon and Planets, the Zodiac and the Earth are related in physical reality. The Sun, Moon and Planets are seen, from the point of view of the Earth, to travel progressively through the Signs of the Zodiac in an anti-clockwise direction (although every so often they appear to wander backwards – the word "planet" means "wanderer"). Interestingly, however, the Earth's own *faster* anti-clockwise rotation creates the illusion of the Planets' revolving around us in a *clock*wise direction. So, at any given moment, most particularly at the time of birth in question, each Planet will be positioned in a certain Zodiacal Sign. These positions are given in the Planet-Sign Tables.

Each Sign belongs to a specific ELEMENT: FIRE, AIR, WATER or EARTH, and MODE: CARDINAL, FIXED and MUTABLE. Fig 1 shows which belongs to which.

If you wish, you may now pencil on to Fig 1 your Sun-, Moon- and Planet-Sign positions.

COMPATIBILITY

By using Fig 1 you may determine both your Internal Compatibility – how the various dimensions of your personality co-exist – and your External Compatibility – how you get on with others, and what kind of people or experiences you will attract, or be attracted to. You will also observe that your External Compatibility has a lot to do with your Internal Compatibility.

Internal Compatibility

First of all, it is important to understand that the seven dimensions of your being – as symbolized by the Sun, Moon and Planets – really go to make up ONE WHOLE BEING. Internal Compatibility shows how these parts interact to comprise that whole, like this ...

<1> A Planet in the same Sign as another is UNITED with it in such a way as greatly to emphasize in your personality the quality of that Sign. Also, the quality of one Planet will bind together with another Planet in such a way as to make them operate together – with ease and/or difficulty, depending on the nature of the two Planets involved. For example, if you had both the Sun and Mercury in Virgo, the ANALYTICAL quality of Virgo would be intensified, and the manner of your LIVING (Sun) would be inextricably bound up with your way of THINKING (Mercury).

In any case, by reading the two Planet-Sign positions one after the other, you will get a clearer idea of how they can be united positively in their expression.

If more than two Planets are placed in the same Sign, then that Sign's qualities will be even more strongly emphasized, and the group of Planets will give rise to quite an intense personality complex.

<2> Planets placed in the same MODE, but not the same Sign, will be challenging or in conflict with each other. However, this can work in one of two ways. Firstly, when the Planets are in Signs that are OPPOSING each other, you will probably express the characteristics of the one that you feel most at home with, and PROJECT the characteristics of the other on to someone else. Yet really you are trying to incorporate both into your being, and are forcing the other Planet's qualities into AWARENESS through seeing them embodied in another being. For example, with Sun in Virgo (Mutable) and Mars in Pisces (also Mutable), you would probably express the Sun in that ANALYTICAL and critical way of Virgo, but encounter others who FORCE (Mars) you to ACCEPT (Pisces) things more.

In the second case, when Planets are in Signs at right angles or SQUARE to one another, you will feel the conflict as something more internal and self-generated. For example, Sun in Virgo (Mutable) square to Saturn in Sagittarius (Mutable) could mean that the Virgo-Sun ANALYTICAL nature, and the importance of WORK, would be challenged by the TEST in SEEKING or BELIEF that Saturn in Sagittarius poses. In other words, you would have to have a job that you believed in to satisfy both the Sun in Virgo and Saturn in Sagittarius, or there would be a conflict between the two.

<3> Planets in the same ELEMENT but in different Signs will flow and harmonize with one another. Again, for example, Moon in Aries (Fire Sign) and Saturn in Sagittarius (another Fire Sign) would suggest that the restless NEED to look for NEW FRONTIERS that is characteristic of Moon in Aries, would greatly assist the NECESSITY of SEEKING something in which you BELIEVE, symbolized by Saturn in Sagittarius.

To a lesser extent, Planets placed in compatible Elements (Fire and Air, or Water and Earth) will also harmonize with one another, but more conscious effort is needed. For example, the NEED to find NEW FRONTIERS of Moon in Aries (Fire) could be helped by the broad sweep of contacts created by Jupiter in Gemini (Air).

It is very important to appreciate that although – or rather because – <1> and <2> above are harder to deal with, they are more dynamic and have more power of expression, for the simple reason that they cannot co-exist unless something is DONE about it! And, although <3> is easier, such Planet-Sign interaction does not necessarily provoke or stimulate you into making anything out of it.

The above is only a sketchy outline of how ASPECTS work in astrology, that is, how one Planet aspects another from Sign to Sign. However, by studying your Planet-Sign positions you will become increasingly able to understand your Internal Compatibility. In the simplest terms, you will find that the more consciously and positively you express any Planet-Sign combination, the more easily it will support, harmonize and co-operate with any other Planet-Sign combination in your chart.

External Compatibility

Relationships are really just the externalization of ourselves. We are attracted to certain people because they reflect or stimulate parts of our being. Through growing to know, like and love another we come to know, like and love ourselves. Similarly, the parts of us that we do not like or know well will attract relationships that include dislike, confusion, fascination and even hate – although at times mixed up with loving feelings – which, again, reflect and project those parts within us. So, using Fig 1, you can see what you attract and are attracted to, and why, like this . . .

<1> Someone with a Planet in the same Sign or in the opposite Sign as a Planet of yours will strongly affect you according to the qualities of the two Planets in question. (And so, to a lesser extent, will someone with a Planet at right angles or square to one of yours.) For example, if you had Sun in Virgo and were involved with someone with Saturn in Virgo or Pisces, your EGO (Sun) would feel TESTED (Saturn) by him/her, and his/her sense of AUTHORITY (Saturn) would be ILLUMINATED (Sun) by you. Your Ego could feel either CONSOLIDATED or RESTRICTED, and his/her sense of Authority could feel either VITALIZED or OVER-SHADOWED.

<2> A Planet in the same ELEMENT as a Planet of someone else would be in harmony – again, according to the nature of the Planets involved. For example, the SENSITIVE DESIRE of Mars in Pisces (Water) would be comfortable with the SYMPATHETIC LOVING of Venus in Cancer (Water). Additionally, Planet-to-Planet contacts between Signs of compatible Elements (Fire to Air, or Water to Earth) can be quite harmonious with some conscious effort.

Note: As with Internal Compatibility, <1> is more dynamic and would elicit a more magnetic attraction, yet at the same time possibly create tension and conflict.

Obviously there are many combinations here, and the whole subject of astrological Compatibility (or Synastry, as it is called) is pretty complex. However, here is a general guide together with the more important Planet-to-Planet contacts and their meanings.

*> Any Planet to Sun: The Sun-person will feel that he/she is a strong or even ruling influence, whereas the other person's Planet will feet Vitalized and Strengthened by the Sun-person.

Sun to Sun: Ego conflict or support, challenge or harmony.

Sun to Moon: A very good interchange when in similar Elements. In the same Sign it is very powerful, with the Sun Warming the Moon Feelings or, alternatively, making those Feelings uncomfortably Exposed. Conversely, the Moon Reflects or Secures the Ego-expression of the Sun.

*> Any Planet to Moon: The Moon-person feels very Emotional about the quality of the Planet it is contacting in the other person. The other person feels that the Moon-person Reflects that Planet's qualities.

Moon to Moon: Emotional/Domestic harmony or conflict. Feeling comfortably or uncomfortably familiar with each other.

Moon to Venus: This contact creates an affectionate and sympathetic feeling for each other, or a clash of needs and values.

Moon to Saturn: This has been called a "Fated contact", because the Moon-person's Feelings are strongly affected through being both/either Consolidated and/or Inhibited by the Saturn-person's Authority or Fear (of Feeling). And the Saturn-person's Fears can feel either assuaged by the Nurturing of the Moon-person, or rather inadequate and rigid by comparison.

⋆> Any Planet to Mercury: The Mercury-person will give Voice and Mental Awareness in response to the nature of the Planet-person in question. Verbal/Mental harmony or conflict. The other Planet-person will stimulate the Mercury-person's Thought processes.

⋆> Any Planet to Venus: The Venus-person will apply Love and Harmony to the other Planet-person – or will Indulge them. The Venus-person will feel very Attracted to the quality of the Planet in the other person. Venus-Mars contacts are very sensual or sensuous.

⋆> Any Planet to Mars: The Mars-person will Stimulate – Sexually, Aggressively or just Energetically – the Planet of the other person. In the case of the Receptive Moon, for example, the Mars-person could be experienced as exciting but threatening. The Mars-person's manner of Assertion is affected according to the nature of the other Planet. The Inhibition or Authority of Saturn, for instance, can be particularly irresistible to Desirous or Impulsive Mars.

⋆> Any Planet to Jupiter: The Jupiter-person encourages the other Planet-person with their Enthusiasm and Faith, or, alternatively, the Jupiter-person can be experienced as too Optimistic and Overbearing. If Saturn, for instance, came into same Sign or opposing Sign contact with Jupiter, it would Limit its Enthusiasm and make it more aware of Concrete Reality. Conversely, Jupiter could lend some Faith and Opportunity to the Doubts of Saturn.

⋆> Any Planet to Saturn: These contacts are very important because Doubts and Fears not only are a stumbling block in relationships, but it is through love and understanding that such Fears can be lessened or eliminated – and this is why Saturn will be attracted to the Planet in someone else which the Saturn-person is not particularly good at expressing. So, any Planet contacting Saturn will be Tested – but hopefully passing that test will make the Saturn-person more confident and less repressed.

Through carefully observing the Planets and the people with whom you are closely involved, your skill in relating – and "astrologizing" – will steadily increase.

PLANETS IN THE SIGNS OF THEIR DIGNITY OR DETRIMENT, EXALTATION OR FALL

When you see [crown symbol] on the left-hand page immediately above LIKES and DISLIKES, it means that this Planet is in the Sign of its Dignity (or the Sign that it is said to Rule). This indicates that the Planet's nature is expressed well in that Sign. Example: Moon in Cancer.

When you see [symbol] on the left-hand page immediately above LIKES and DISLIKES, it means that this Planet is in the Sign of its Detriment (or the Sign opposite to the one it Rules). This indicates that the Planet's nature is difficult to express in that Sign, and therefore has to be worked on. Example: Moon in Capricorn.

When you see [star symbol] on the left-hand page immediately above LIKES and DISLIKES, it means that this Planet is in the Sign of its Exaltation. This indicates that the Planet's nature can potentially be expressed in its highest, most spiritual, way. Example: Mercury in Aquarius.

When you see [star symbol] on the left-hand page immediately above LIKES and DISLIKES, it means that this Planet is in the Sign of its Fall. This indicates that in order to express positively that Planet's nature, the old way of expressing it has to "die" in order to be reborn. Example: Moon in Scorpio.

	DIGNITY	DETRIMENT	EXALTATION	FALL
SUN	LEO	AQU	ARI	LIB
MOON	CAN	CAP	TAU	SCO
MERCURY	GEM + VIR	SAG + PIS	AQU	LEO
VENUS	TAU + LIB	SCO + ARI	PIS	VIR
MARS	ARI + SCO	LIB + TAU	CAP	CAN
JUPITER	SAG + PIS	GEM + VIR	CAN	CAP
SATURN	CAP + AQU	CAN + LEO	LIB	ARI

URANUS, NEPTUNE AND PLUTO

These, the Trans-Saturnian Planets, are not included in SUN, MOON AND PLANET SIGNS as their influence is felt not so much through the Signs as through the Houses and *precise* Aspects, which are not within the scope of this book. These Planets symbolize Forces of Evolutionary Change: Uranus works through Awakening or Disruption, Neptune works through Sensitizing or Undermining and Pluto works through Intensification or Elimination. They lie beyond the Limits set by Saturn, and therefore the limits of this book, but they are still very much with us.

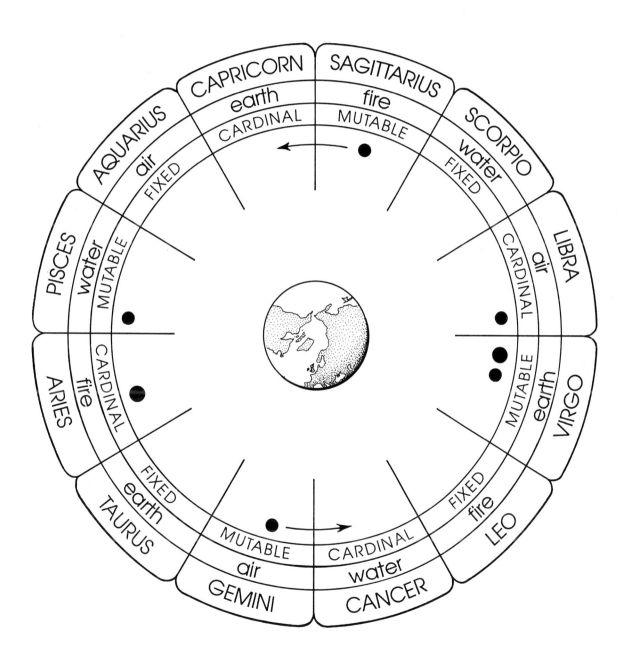

FIG 1

THE SUN, THE MOON AND THE PLANETS THROUGH THE TWELVE SIGNS OF THE ZODIAC

THE SUN

Keyword: LIVING

The Sun is the CENTRE, HEART and LIFE-GIVING FORCE of our Solar System. So, astrologically, your Sun-Sign describes the CENTRE OF YOUR BEING – your WILL; what dwells in or lies close to your HEART and what gives your LIFE a SENSE OF CREATIVE PURPOSE. The Sun is symbolic of your SPIRIT.

Negative expressions of the Sun are traits such as CONCEIT and EGOTISM, according to which you attach too much or the wrong sort of importance to the qualities of the Sign in which your Sun is placed.

The Sun is the most important astrological energy because all of the Planets (including the Moon) revolve around It and draw their life from It. And so your Sun-Sign nature affects and VITALIZES your Moon-Sign and all your Planet-Sign positions. Expressing the Solar Will comes more naturally to males, so if you are female you may be attracted to males who embody your Sun-Sign qualities. Sooner or later, through life's experiences and relationships, you come to realize and to express consciously the power and nature of your OWN INDIVIDUALITY.

THE SUN IN ARIES

ESSENCE

LIVING THROUGH DOING

THE PIONEER   THE CHAMPION

As the first Sign of the Zodiac, your role as an Arian is simply to get something started, which is why the Sun is Exalted in Aries, for here the Will has free rein to express itself. You could be doing this in some form of leadership, or by forcing others to look at themselves in a new way. You could accomplish this either consciously, by carrying out a deliberate act in the name of some cause, or unconsciously, by making it hard for others to relate to you as you are.

It is preferable to be consciously aware of your pioneering streak, for in this way not only do you enjoy life more, but you avoid feeling pushed around by others. And with Aries it's more or less a case of push or be pushed. This can be objectionable to others at times, but you must have the freedom to act, rather than just thinking about it and getting pent-up in the process. At all costs you need to avoid negative emotions like resentment, regret and self-pity, for they would deny you what is essential to your Arian nature: Straightforwardness.

As an Arian, you like a challenge that will stir you to action. This challenge may just be frustration; or at a more evolved and conscious level, you may know what or whom you're fighting for. If you don't, then ask yourself until you have an answer. An Arian without a direction in which to head or a cause to champion is more like a sheep than a Ram. The quest is all.

You should not be afraid to be forceful, for this is central to your nature. If you are afraid, then look for negative examples of force in your personal history, such as violence or abuse from others, or a tradition that negated independence and personal initiative, for this could have inhibited your natural urge to go forward into life in a direct and uncomplicated fashion. Conversely, such bad influences could also have led you to be overly forceful, or to be unsympathetic to your own needs and sensitivity. Much as you are the Ram, there is still the Lamb in you, which means that at times you would attain your goals more easily by gently falling in with the demands of a given social situation, rather than getting your horns entangled in something bigger and more powerful than yourself. This of course takes patience, the acquiring of which is definitely your greatest achievement – along with a sense of the strength of your inner softness.

You like extremes – physical, emotional and mental – and are all the better for experiencing them; but if your extremism goes too far beyond social acceptability, then expect to be extremely lonely. At your Arian best, you can inject new life into relationships and enterprises. Ever emerging like a fountain-head into the arena of life, you lead others from darkness into light.

LIKES
Action · Coming first
Challenges · Championing causes
The spur of the moment

DISLIKES
Waiting around · Admitting defeat
Lack of opposition · Tyranny
Taking advice

If you are a woman, this could be the kind of man to whom you are attracted – but it is really you, so realize it and express it.

THE SUN IN ARIES

TRANSFORMER

POSITIVE	NEGATIVE
Assertive Go-getting Crusading Enthusiastic	Aggressive Unreflective Fanatical Arrogant
Direct Frank One-pointed Straightforward	Blunt Tactless Blind to side-issues Simplistic
Spontaneous Energetic Stimulating Courageous	Impatient Restless Irritating Foolhardy
Good starter Warrior caste Leader type Confident	Bad finisher Argumentative Unco-operative Pompous
Independent Strong willed Single-minded Original being	Self-centred Headstrong Thoughtless Intolerant
Know that freedom and individuality are found in the narrowest passes and the loneliest places.	Feeling alone, with no external point of reference or source of comfort.
See your role as the ideas person, then inspire the other(s) to carry them through.	Projects that come to nothing. Partnerships that come to blows.
What springs from your body or mind is only as good as what dwells in your heart.	Lacking coherence and direction. Failing to contemplate posing as decisiveness.
If you truly have a point, then they'll come back for more. If you don't – they won't!	Being deserted by others because they cannot make you notice them and their feelings any other way.
Learn to look before you leap, which means first finding out what you wish to make happen.	Always tripping over yourself, inviting conflict and harsh treatment. Getting deflated.
SOLUTION	PROBLEM

23

If you find yourself on the receiving end of negative traits, it is because you are not expressing the opposing positive traits.

THE SUN IN TAURUS

ESSENCE

LIVING THROUGH STABILIZING

MOTHER NATURE'S OWN   BEAUTY AND THE BEAST

No sign is closer to the Earth than Taurus the Bull. It is as if the whole purpose of your Taurean Life is to maintain the Stability of Earthly things. However, you can go wrong by interpreting this only to mean having a substantial amount of money and possessions, or being assured of a predictable future in a purely tangible world. In fact, your main possession as a Taurean is your sense of Earthly harmony and wholesomeness. When you truly get in touch with this sense, you need worry no longer about blindly reassuring yourself with external possessions and securities, for you will then know and feel that this sense, this art, attracts these very things.

Another of your solid virtues is the ability to endure change, while at the same time conserving those habits and traditions that are so important to a healthy and wholesome physical life. You have to be careful not to let this talent become blunted merely into the ability to resist change – even when it is for the good. Your broad Taurean back can carry more than you sometimes believe.

Taurus is the great provider. This is not just in the material sense, but more essentially it is your calm and unruffled vibration, along with a well-vitalized body, that can work wonders on the physical and emotional state of others, be it through sensuous affection, massage, good living, artistic expression, or just your sheer physical presence that emanates that aura of stability, that feeling that the Earth and Heaven are in their respective and proper places.

However, the other side of your Earthy wisdom and natural docility is probably your most dangerous state, that of sluggishness, inertia and grossness – the Beast – born of a fear of change or of what you cannot handle. When you fall into this state, it is only a matter of time before you attract someone or something that will make such immobility uncomfortable and compromising. It is then that a change has to be made, and something let go of. When you make such a change, you then discover how much more stable things become as a result!

Ultimately, as a Taurean, you have to discover your truest, deepest and highest values. This is symbolized by ascending terraces of sweeter and sweeter clover. When you know what is truly valuable, you are no longer chained to people and to things that have to do with lesser values. The greatest indication of value is beauty, which cannot be owned, but only appreciated. And as a Taurean you certainly know how to appreciate beauty, not only in the sense of being aware of its value, but also through implanting and increasing its value in the hearts and minds of others.

LIKES
Stability · Being attracted
Things natural · Time to ponder
Comfort and pleasure

DISLIKES
Disruption · Being pushed
Synthetics · Being hurried
Sensory deprivation

If you are a woman, this could be the kind of man to whom you are attracted – but it is really you, so realize it and express it.

THE SUN IN TAURUS

TRANSFORMER

POSITIVE	NEGATIVE
Earthy Sensuous/artistic Productive Practical provider	Materialistic Hedonistic Gross and extravagant Prodigal
Steadfast and stable Unruffled and calm Even-tempered Soothing	Plodding and ponderous Sluggish and lazy Boneheaded Boring
Self-trusting Loyal Persevering Trustworthy	Self-satisfied Possessive Stubborn Bigoted/fanatical
Appreciative Admiring Affectionate Aesthetic	Self-gratifying Idolatrous Lecherous Aloof
Physically comforting Magnetically healing Attractive	Unaware of "unseen" Sucker for good looks Easily attached
You are not just a body, but a set of vibrations that both attracts and is attracted.	Feeling that you are being manipulated, led a dance, taken for what you've got.
Discover your truest and highest values, then realize how well you can express them physically.	The world of the senses feels less and less appealing and more and more appalling.
You have the power to attract faithfulness, but being unable to let go signifies a lack of faith.	Fear of loss. Feeling of jealousy, of beliefs and/or followers turning against you.
Realize that during and after periods of stress you can be a source of reassurance to others.	Feeling of inertia and uneasiness. Fear of change. Others get bored and impatient with you.
Know that the value of Earthly things is simply that they serve to keep bodies happy and healthy.	Feelings of self-disgust and dissatisfaction, of life lacking any meaning. Addicted to sensations.
SOLUTION	PROBLEM

If you find yourself on the receiving end of negative traits, it is because you are not expressing the opposing positive traits.

THE SUN IN GEMINI

ESSENCE

LIVING THROUGH COMMUNICATING

THE CONTACT-MAKER   **FOREVER YOUNG**

Gemini may be likened to blossom and to the playful spring breezes that spread its petals hither and thither. Your touch is light but effective, broadcasting and collecting wit and knowledge over a wide area – although it can be shortlasting and superficial.

Gemini is famous for its dualistic or even contrary nature. This can be hugely fascinating because word and mind play is an endless source of amusement to you as synchronous events and paradoxical paradigms abound. On the other hand, it can only amount to a sort of psychological doodling which achieves nothing more than pushing air and nerve cells around. What your talent is really intended for is getting the message and putting it across.

You are aiming to avoid the logic trap of "this" as opposed to "that", and are potentially able to bridge the gap between two extremes, be they people, philosophies, beliefs, character traits or whatever. This you do by zipping back and forth between them with such speed and alacrity that the differences become like the two sides of a spinning coin. Intuitively, you see no difference between any one thing and another – everything is equally interesting (a favourite word!). Because of this, Gemini is probably the least prejudiced of all the Signs – and one of the friendliest.

Mythologically, the Heavenly Twins Castor and Pollux each divided their time between living in Heaven and on Earth. This means that as a Geminian, you can mentally dwell in pure abstraction, and at the same time be able to turn your hand to the most mundane of tasks. You are nothing if not versatile.

Other important dualities of Gemini are those of the Magician/Mimic and the Rogue/Villain: the former uses the quickness of hand, eye and tongue to create wondrous effects and illusions; the latter merely employs nimble fingers and the gift of the gab to make a relatively small profit. You are also the Juggler. You can keep a tricky issue up in the air, postponing coming down to Earth almost indefinitely. Just when it seems that you are going to crash, you sud denly appear on the other side of the street – still juggling. However, you are not infallible, even though you could talk your way out of a document shredder!

The last word is that as a Geminian you have a very lively imagination, and you are therefore one of the most artistically creative Signs. Conversely true to form though, you can lack the imagination to see that using the imagination draws you into a closer intimacy with life itself – and getting deeply involved is the Twins' weakest suit. After all, they themselves got separated between Heaven and Earth. Yet the answer to your eternal Geminian question still lies in the imagination, not the brain.

LIKES
Reading and talking · Being on the move
More than one interest · The quirky
and the unusual · Novelty and variety

DISLIKES
Mental stagnation · Being tied down
Lack of interest / education · Ruts that
turn into graves · Yesterday's papers

If you are a woman, this could be the kind of man to whom you are attracted – but it is really you, so realize it and express it.

THE SUN IN GEMINI

TRANSFORMER

POSITIVE	NEGATIVE
Amusing Perceptive Witty Eloquent	Cheap Glib Sarcastic Chatterbox
Swift Ingenious Quick on uptake Mobile	Fly Devious Shifty Evasive
Versatile Flexible Adaptable Imaginative	Dabbler Two-faced Fickle Chases rainbows
Non-dogmatic Sees both sides Light touch Objective	Non-committal Indecisive Superficial Aloof
Acquisitive mind Clever Informative Resourceful	Blind to whole picture Inane Gossip Bluffer
There is a need out there for what you know and how you express it – so meet it!	Becoming a mine of useless information with conflicting views that amount to little.
Appreciate how refreshing your stereoscopic vision of life is to others.	Identity crises. Beset by feelings of insubstantiality. Troubled conscience.
Respect your own dreams, and avoid cutting corners in the pursuit of them.	Jack of all trades, master of none. Plans that come to nothing.
Others aren't as speedy as you and don't jump to the same unlikely conclusions.	Constantly looking over your shoulder. Feeling the world's designed to catch you out.
Pay attention to the value of what you say; how you say it looks after itself – admirably.	Feelings of being ignored or not being taken seriously.
SOLUTION	PROBLEM

If you find yourself on the receiving end of negative traits, it is because you are not expressing the opposing positive traits.

THE SUN IN CANCER

ESSENCE

LIVING THROUGH NURTURING

HOLD ON WITH LOVE   MY FAMILY IS HUMANITY

Everything about the Sign of Cancer may be tracked down to the experience of birth: the instinct for survival; the attachment to the mother; the baby's soft sensitivity to the world into which it is being born, and the utter dependence upon the mercy of that world; the mother's sensitivity to that dependency and the fear born of it; the innate enthusiasm to succeed gloriously in this world, or, sheer resentment at ever having being born into the harsh reality of this world at all.

Behind all these feelings lie the most fundamental urges of your curious and dreamy Sign – those to protect, nourish and nurture. As a child, you, like everyone else, needed to receive protection, nourishment and nurturing, but a denial or shortage of them would be more damaging to Cancer in later life than to any other Sign. This is because you would continue, vainly, to look for a "mother" in your adult life, or would overdo being a mother – smothering – by way of compensation. In either case an unhealthy fear of revealing your inner self to the outside world is produced, along with a need to blame others.

Esoterically, it is written that all Souls are first born on to Planet Earth in the Sign of Cancer, simply because they know intuitively that the Cancerian Will is the one most likely to find a way of being looked after in their new home. Cancer has been called the "Lighthouse of Welcome", which is something the individual Cancerian would do well to become. When you seek to protect rather than just seek protection, your essential qualities of neediness, sympathy and emotional receptivity then become a recognition of where nourishment and care are needed, along with the motivation and method required to give and sustain them, rather than an aching dependency in itself. What were clinging claws, that would clam up at the slightest sign of emotional intrusion, then become a pair of open arms that holds firmly and cradles gently. The acute awareness of another's feelings, which can be used negatively to exert emotional blackmail, becomes a ray of healing. Vulnerable side-stepping becomes sensitive approach.

Being such a maternal, home-making Sign, you probably find this easier to express if you are female. Male Cancerians can have a problem with laying themselves open emotionally, and can seek to protect themselves under a hard macho shell. Ironically, though, it is the soft sensitive meat within that is so attractive in both men and women. But, most importantly, and whatever your sex, you need to avoid being an apology for yourself as a result of feeling neglected or neglectful. The ultimate discovery for the Cancerian is that one is cared for all along by the greatest mother of them all – Mother Nature. As a Cancerian you need roots, and so you must go digging for your Sign's essential truth, which is that your Family is the Human Race itself. Mother Nature looks after her own.

LIKES
Kindness and tenderness · To belong
Warmth and reassurance · Solitude and
reminiscing · Being around strong people

DISLIKES
Bluntness and direct confrontation · Uncertainty
Discomfort · Soul-baring and bad
memories · Feeling weak and neglected

28

If you are a woman, this could be the kind of man to whom you are attracted — but it is really you, so realize it and express it.

THE SUN IN CANCER

TRANSFORMER

POSITIVE	NEGATIVE
Tenacious Dependable Abiding Thrifty	Clinging Dependent Apathetic Hoarding
Protective Caring Home-maker Hospitable	Smothering Possessively doting Stay-at-home Anti-social
Tender and responsive Sympathetic Psychically aware Self-sacrificing	Oversensitive Self-pitying Touchy Self-deluding
Subtly supportive Kind and consoling Emotionally encouraging	Devious and indirect Argumentative Emotionally blackmailing
Adaptable Childlike Watchful Enchanting	Moody Childish Over-cautious Sickly sentimental
Trust the Universe. Remember that all things must pass and that every day is new.	Feeling threatened by the future. Feeling both haunted by and a yearning for the past.
Remember that your emotional awareness is more acute than that of most others – so use it, constructively.	Feeling avoided and victimized, resented and resentful.
Objective sensitivity to others rewards you. Exclusive sensitivity to yourself hurts you.	Feelings of melancholy and martyrdom. Irritable but out of touch.
Withdraw and contemplate exactly in what way and to what extent others need you. Affirm to yourself "I belong".	Feeling guilty and resentful, agoraphobic and unappreciated.
Establish and execute your responsibilities generously.	Feeling insecure and helpless. Sluggish. Alternately grudging and apologetic.
SOLUTION	PROBLEM

29

If you find yourself on the receiving end of negative traits, it is because you are not expressing the opposing positive traits.

THE SUN IN LEO

ESSENCE

LIVING THROUGH CREATING

CHILD OF THE SUN   I AM MY OWN ROLE MODEL

As the Sun is Dignified in Leo, your main qualities are best expressed and understood in terms of the Sun. You want to shine and be the centre of attention. No matter how shy or how lacking in confidence you might feel inwardly, you will want to be noticed in some way. For this reason, it is necessary for you to feel happy in the spotlight, which means that respect is vitally important, both for yourself and from others. In fact, respect from others is dependent upon self-respect, so for Leo honour really does have to be bright.

In effect, Leo shines in any event. How warm and bright, how noble and creative that light that radiates from you happens to be is the crucial point. You can bring warmth and illumination to situations where they are needed like no other Sign. And this radiant glow is often quite physically noticeable. In this way, you create a focal point and a generator for anything that is happening. As you do so, you imply Leo's well-known royal presence. Leo creates an "Air of Certainty" that makes possible so many things – as if by royal decree. And you need to be aware of your royal presence. The apparent confidence that streams forth from your Heart gives the lie to the fact that you are highly dependent upon being appreciated. A king or queen without subjects or with no audience is not much of a monarch, just as the Sun cannot function without the sky around it.

This great Leonine possession – your natural ability to generate light, warmth and centrality in the form of creative, healing or commanding expressions – needs to be controlled. The Sun is, after all, an enormous nuclear reactor, and if it is not constantly checked, the Leonine ego can lead to a "meltdown" (wild destructive passions) or to "sunspots" (losing face or facial blemishes). This means that you need to pay as much attention to your critics as to your admirers, if you are to avoid the danger of being blinded by your own light, and destroying the very thing you originally sought to vitalize and maintain, be it a relationship, your home, health, profession, or even your own children. Again, like the Sun, Leo cannot see the shadows that it casts.

Your brightness can also blind others to your vulnerability. And when Leo is wounded, it is like the Sun disappearing behind a cloud; the world is a colder and duller place for it. Such sensitivity could, of course, be seen merely as vanity, which is your most dangerous negative quality as others are unlikely to praise and appreciate what appears as immodesty, and so a vicious circle can begin. At a certain critical stage, Leo has to realize that its power and influence shine through it, and not from it. Thus your undeniable brightness shows others their path to the glory of good, and so, ultimately, your own. Like Leo, the Sun as it is seen – as that shimmering disc called the photosphere – is not really the Sun itself, but just how it is seen by mortal eyes.

LIKES
A good time
To rule well · To affect others
Gaining respect · Style

DISLIKES
Bad timing or repetition
Ruin or drudgery · Being ignored
Losing face · Drabness

If you are a woman, this could be the kind of man to whom you are attracted – but it is really you, so realize it and express it.

THE SUN IN LEO

TRANSFORMER

POSITIVE	NEGATIVE
Noble Confident Generous Gracious	Pretentious Self-righteous Flamboyant Supercilious
Encouraging Commanding Ambitious Enterprising	Domineering Demanding Intolerant Overestimating
Proud Cultivated Dramatic sense Impressive	Vain Snobbish/Stuck-up Melodramatic Show-off
Self-expressive Wealth of ideas Fun to be with Warm	Self-centred Overbearing Overblown Scorching
Affectionate Loyal Irrepressible Romantic	Affected Fierce Impossible Unrealistic
Those who love you, love your inner glow more than your outer show.	Getting away with murder, and still feeling unwanted.
The Sun never tries to shine or set conditions – it just shines. So should you.	Crestfallen as a result of expecting too much both of self and of others. Loss of dignity.
False pride comes before a fall – true pride comes after one.	Falling from grace. Excesses have invited a decrease in lifestyle.
Leo controls others as much as it controls itself. Rank imposes obligations.	Banishment. Close associates withdraw support or investment. Secret feelings of insecurity.
Recognize, appreciate, respect and pardon both yourself and others – they will then follow suit.	Fearful of humiliation and of not being recognized, appreciated or respected.
SOLUTION	PROBLEM

31

If you find yourself on the receiving end of negative traits, it is because you are not expressing the opposing positive traits.

THE SUN IN VIRGO

ESSENCE

LIVING THROUGH ANALYSING

THE FAITHFUL SERVANT   THE PERFECTIONIST

Virgo has its roots in the Vestal Virgin principle which stresses the importance of maintaining the purity of the individual – or anything else – and ensuring that it remains unsullied by society's polluting and corrupting ways.

As the Sign of the harvest, your task is to separate the wheat from the chaff, the useful from the useless. Through such constant analysis you strive to reach a state of purity, of being a clear channel of expression.

There are two types of Virgoan: the Purist and the Puritan. The Puritan attempts to avoid anything regarded as physically unwholesome, emotionally threatening or mentally indigestible. This is the picky squeaky-clean type, who is not really pure in the sense of being "you and only you". The Purist, on the other hand, trusts his or her innate purity to not only withstand involve ment with potentially corrupting elements, but actually attempts to influence them with that purity. It should be noted that as a Virgoan, you may have elements of both the Puritan and the Purist distributed through your personality. For example, the Purist could get involved on a mental and a physical level, but the Puritan could be uninvolved on an emotional level. There are, of course, other permutations here, but this is probably the most common one, which can lead to being abandoned by your mate—or to not having one at all. And although you can appear to be self-sufficient, you in fact need mutual caring and sharing – albeit of a very particular kind!

As a Virgoan, you must have a "work" or be of some kind of service in order to make sense of life. You are constantly preparing for something, and unless you know or feel quite what that something is, you can become frustrated with an all-work-and-no-play-makes-for-a-dull-life type of situation. The task of Virgo is a difficult one, and so you need to perfect some form of technique, through study and training. This will minimize wear and tear (especially of the nervous system and the intestines) and will also equip you for an efficient work role, without which you are unhappy.

Virgo is the Sign of health which, in addition to technique, means giving yourself the time and the space to assimilate things properly through regular rest and retreat, and correct diet. More esoterically, Virgo's concern is where and how the psyche meets the soma, the Soul interacts with the body. So your body is very much the barometer of your psychological condition. However, you should endeavour not to allow your physical state to rule your life, but rather to understand that your body will serve you well if you observe carefully and inwardly what it is telling you.

Discover precisely what you are devoted to, and you will then realize that you need not be so hard on yourself. Blessed be.

LIKES
Natural methods · Orderliness
Making lists · Being helpful
Earthiness

DISLIKES
Being a "Puritan" · Sloppiness
Making mistakes · Being a martyr
Crudity or violation

If you are a woman, this could be the kind of man to whom you are attracted – but it is really you, so realize it and express it.

THE SUN IN VIRGO

TRANSFORMER

POSITIVE	NEGATIVE
Thoughtful Analytical Lively mind Observant	Thinks too much Sceptical Worrier Critical
Scholarly Precise Pure intentions Discriminating	Dry Pedantic Too earnest Fault-finding
Helpful Problem-solving Wholesome Health-conscious	Interfering Problem-making Fusspot Hypochondriacal
Industrious Methodical Efficient Reliable	Workaholic Inflexible Mechanistic Spoilsport
Dispassionate Modest Considerate Pure	Clinical Unsure Stand-offish Sterile
There must be passion there in order for you to purify it – so quietly express it.	The "wallflower". Left on the shelf. Intact but lonely.
Conceive of a more wonderful reason for striving. Put some "madness" into your method.	Life becomes a meaningless drudge. Your efforts are taken for granted.
If it works don't try to fix it. Help where it isn't needed doesn't help.	Irritable and worried all the time. Unaware that a bit of chaos is "in" order.
True perfection consists of being able to accept life's imperfections.	Life feels increasingly uncomfortable with every flaw you detect.
Regard your mind as a lens – not as a light, a film or a screen.	Living in your head – and the skull is one very cramped space.
SOLUTION	PROBLEM

33

* If you find yourself on the receiving end of negative traits, it is because you are not expressing the opposing positive traits.

THE SUN IN LIBRA

ESSENCE

LIVING THROUGH RELATING

A QUESTION OF BALANCE   MY LAW IS MY WILL

As a Libran, your life is concerned with creating and maintaining a set of values that will guide you as you constantly endeavour to relate to one and all in a just and pleasant fashion. The Sun here, being in the Sign of its Fall, means that to a certain extent the expression of your individual Will is determined by others. However, the irony is that to be truly balanced you have to offset such an obliging manner with an edge as hard as the fulcrum upon which an actual set of scales balances. This means that when it comes to the common Libran problem of indecisiveness, making a hard and fast decision for its own sake – and keeping to it – is far better than no decision at all. Being unable to make up your mind can be more annoying and anti-social than most things! And on the subject of the Scales themselves, Libra is the only Sign whose symbol is an inanimate object rather than an animal or a human being. You can, therefore, be inclined to live life as an immaculate concept rather than as a living, breathing, fallible creature. You need to remember that it is all right to make mistakes. After all, it is only when you "tip" the scales (put a definite measure of weight on one side) that the point of balance is determined and the desired result reached.

But for you as a Libran, the balancing act goes on and on, as the proverbial pendulum of life swings back and forth. And it is your ongoing relationships that give you the measure of your success here. Again, you must establish yourself as having a definite value or personality in the first place, in the knowledge that through relating you will change and grow. You can rely on your natural charm and your sense of harmony to attract relationships and to conduct them skilfully. But you should base these relationships on and maintain them according to your innate sense of balance – that is, your awareness of what is pleasing or fair both to yourself and to the other party. And "relationships" mean interchanges with one person or between many, on a professional or on a private level – between your inner world and the outer world, or between one stage of life and another.

Like a bee, a Libran likes to taste many different flowers in order to arrive at the perfect "honey", or way of relating and expressing him/herself. The danger is that this can become such a sweet lifestyle that you gloss over the nasty bits, or actually indulge in them, too. And so, to avoid or to get off such a not-so-merry-go-round of increasingly meaningless social dalliance, remember that pleasures got from sex and money are the means through which you seek to find the joy of union, the true balance that lies beyond what is merely pleasant. Libra is a "cardinal" Sign, which means that you are supposed to be an initiator of social activities and values – not merely a response to them. Libra is also the Sign of the Peacemaker, which points to the fact that rather than ignoring areas of conflict, disharmony or injustice, these are where your art is most needed and appreciated.

LIKES
Pleasing surroundings · Peace and justice
A partner / Companions · Gentleness
Following fashion

DISLIKES
Discordant atmospheres · Violence and
injustice · Zero social feedback
Brutishness · Being a slave to fashion

If you are a woman, this could be the kind of man to whom you are attracted – but it is really you, so realize it and express it.

THE SUN IN LIBRA

TRANSFORMER

POSITIVE	NEGATIVE
Aesthetic Graceful Peaceful Calm	Affected Superficial Non-committal Lazy
Socially orientated Popular Co-operative Amenable	Lacks self-reliance Indulgent / Indulged Yes-person Insincere
Attractive Refined Subtle manner In tune with the times	Vain Easily upset Lacking confidence Style victim
High principles Idealistic Socially aspiring and aware	Compromising Peace at any price Elitist and class-conscious
Diplomatic Harmless Friendly Good counsellor	Indecisive Insipid Smarmy Ingratiating
Other people are not God. God is your awareness that life is manifestly both hard and soft.	Feeling like a nonentity; merely a human counterweight to other humans. Frustrating others.
Libra's role is to initiate social activities that blend the rough with the smooth.	Feeling taken advantage of. Feeling awkward in certain types of company.
To be both attractive and secure, sensitivity requires spiritual strength and awareness.	Uncomfortably delicate. Made to feel ill (at ease) by what to others is merely disagreeable.
Truly please yourself and you will truly please others.	If only you liked yourself as much as others appear to like you.
Your outward poise will remain as long as it subordinates itself to your inner values.	Finding yourself in social situations that have no depth and little real value. Divorce.
SOLUTION	PROBLEM

35

If you find yourself on the receiving end of negative traits, it is because you are not expressing the opposing positive traits.

THE SUN IN SCORPIO

ESSENCE

LIVING THROUGH DESIRING

THE PHOENIX	THE URGE TO MERGE

Scorpio is the most powerful Sign of the Zodiac. This is because you can sense what is going on beneath the surface in most situations, but especially where intimate relating or business dealing is concerned. So with such an emotional awareness of what is motivating someone or something, you have a certain "inside knowledge" with which you are able to influence or to manipulate, to corrupt or to purge, to harm or to heal.

Once you have realized that you have this power, then two burning questions arise: How may such power be used, and is there anyone out to disempower you? This poses a moral dilemma, because if you use your inside knowledge to further low or mean intentions, you then fall into a downward spiral of defending yourself against something that you yourself started. On the other hand, when you get on top of your main weakness, which is simply a fear of admitting to having a chink in your armour, then, by using your penetrating insight you are capable, like no other Sign, of bringing to the surface what is causing trouble, be it a heartache, a disease, a financial problem, or anything else. The former or negative type of Scorpion is called the "Serpent of Evil"; the latter or positive type is called the "Serpent of Wisdom" or the "Eagle".

Your have an awareness of what sex is for and what it is about. Again this is connected with your ability to penetrate beneath the surface. You can really get under people's skin, to the roots of feeling and desire. This can lead to a great intimacy with life itself – even brushing with death. The extent to which you are conscious of this sexual awareness can make the difference between deliverance and disaster. In any case, though, you thrive in a crisis; you achieve more when the going gets rough. Just think of the difficulty a Scorpion would have progressing across a smooth surface.

Your Scorpionic power can appear as a magnetic charm that can be totally disarming, or as downright cruelty, trampling others and striking unexpectedly. You can raise others from the depths – or hurl them down there! Behind this power is a kind of nuclear energy that can drive on through the night, literally or metaphorically. You also like to test such grit by indulging in the lowest levels of life experience, and then coming up not only intact but positively regenerated. Some don't come back, though.

You can be relied upon to possess deep and genuine emotions, and will unerringly test out the emotions of others, while hiding behind a "smokescreen" that conceals your own depth. A probing and secretive person, you are emotionally frightening (or frightful) when invasion threatens. However, when you let go and allow someone or something in, a magical effect, an alchemical release occurs as your "sting" is transformed from a defensive or self-destructive weapon into a healing lance.

LIKES
Total involvement · Rooting out hidden causes · Being persuasive · Meaningful work · The untarnished truth

DISLIKES
Superficial relationships · Scratching the surface · Being got one over on Demeaning tasks · Flattering and flattery

If you are a woman, this could be the kind of man to whom you are attracted – but it is really you, so realize it and express it.

THE SUN IN SCORPIO

TRANSFORMER

POSITIVE	NEGATIVE
Intense Loyal Passionate Faith-inspiring	Obsessive Possessive Fanatical Emotionally sapping
Dynamic Regenerating Compelling Magnetic	Coercive Degrading Enforces allegiance Seductive
Penetrating insight Scrutinizing Shrewd Resourceful	Black looks Suspicious Cunning Revengeful
Compassionate Strong and deep Brave Firm views	Self-punishing Scornful of weakness Cruel Rigid outlook
Powerful Healing touch Self-sacrificing Intimate	Corrupt Manipulative Jealous Resentful
Power is not in you, but comes through you. If you hate, power kills. If you love, power heals.	Overstretched but not admitting it. Supplanted but not accepting it. Close but not seeing it.
Your greatest weakness is denying weakness; your greatest strength is forgiving weakness.	Descending down a dark spiral of self-disgust. Disdainful of help and of others.
Look deeply into anything or anyone and you will find only yourself and the power therein.	Attracting enemies who waste your energies. Feeling persecuted. Struggling with powers that be.
When you know how not to, you can show others how to – which they find irresistible.	You've got everyone where you want them but you still don't like it.
When you reach a point where you are no longer after anything, you begin to realize what you are after.	Obsessed and possessed to the point of acute anxiety. Driven blindly from bad to worse.
SOLUTION	PROBLEM

If you find yourself on the receiving end of negative traits, it is because you are not expressing the opposing positive traits.

THE SUN IN SAGITTARIUS

ESSENCE

LIVING THROUGH SEEKING

THE ADVENTURER   THE OPENER OF WAYS

Sagittarius is probably the most positive Sign of the Zodiac, for the simple reason that you see life as an opportunity. So it never matters just how hard the road ahead might look, for it is still a road, and roads go places! Sagittarius rules and loves the highways – literal and symbolic.

Your sense of "going places" also gives you a strong sense of history and culture, and of where things are bound. This sense of trend can keep you abreast or ahead of the times, or locked into some sub-culture that's had its day. You can be embarked upon some genuinely spiritual quest, or merely be "trendy". In any event, you are adept at furthering anything and anyone that you believe in, but be careful not to take over everything and everyone in the process, or others will ultimately find your enthusiasm tiresome rather than awesome.

"Belief" is a keyword for Sagittarius, and you are as believable as what you believe in . . .!? The dualistic nature of your Sign (the Centaur: animal and human) can make you appear hypocritical, as one moment you aspire to the Divine, with high-flown theories and philosophies, and the next, you get down with the beastly best of them in order to keep earthed. You are thus seeking to marry the Spirit with the Flesh, and reveal the one in the other, which is what your adventurous nature is really about. You have the power to proliferate, so attaching too much importance to the material side of life can either cause the physical rapidly to go out of control, such as in your becoming grossly overweight, or mean that you are denied something money cannot buy.

In whatever sphere or at whatever level you are functioning, you have a marvellously intuitive grasp of how life works. You are the "manager" of the Zodiac. And, being half-horse, you cover a lot of ground and get to know the lie of the land. You also require the freedom and possess the energy to do this. It is your libidinous drive that also creates your main trouble, for such galloping get-up-and-go can find you overstretched, overbearing and over-confident. Sagittarius has the peculiar problem of the superiority complex, and you will resort to equally peculiar tactics to give yourself a more "human" stature. In other words, because you are so aware of how society as a whole is shaping up, you have a comparatively weak sense of how you feel personally. So you resort to rubbing others up the wrong way in the hope of getting some kind of personal reaction. You also do this in order to get to the underlying truth of a given situation. This can be very effective for it clears the air and opens up the way ahead.

Like an Archer-Charioteer with a team of four spirited horses, you have great power at your disposal. If you let the horses run wildly, you have a great ride followed by a great crash, as a result of which you are torn apart. With reins held lightly, in touch with your animal drive, and with a high target to aim at, for Sagittarius, anything is possible!

LIKES
Freedom and space · Travelling (fast and far) · Getting on with it
The general feel · Laws and meanings

DISLIKES
Being constrained · Being domestically tied · Kicking your heels
Details · Glib theories

If you are a woman, this could be the kind of man to whom you are attracted – but it is really you, so realize it and express it.

THE SUN IN SAGITTARIUS

TRANSFORMER

POSITIVE	NEGATIVE
Benevolent Generous Enthusiastic Jovial	Promises too much Excessive Over-zealous Overbearing
Optimistic Lucky Far-sighted Positive thinker	Blind to details Jammy Jumps to conclusions Cocksure
Stimulating Outspoken Colourful Open and honest	Contentious Inconsiderate Exaggerative Embarrassing
Able Good judgement Honourable Mobile	Boastful Moralizing Pompous Volatile
Expansive Adventurous Carefree Vitalistic	Scattered Irresponsible Careless Lascivious
Focus upon one thing that will satisfy you. Be true to it, and it'll be true to you.	Exhausted and exhausting. Exasperated and exasperating. Frustrated and frustrating.
Look down and you go down; look up and you go up. You know that ruts make poor runways.	You can't move: your feet are set in the concrete of dogma, or are not touching the ground at all.
Your target area is way beyond the boring, but just short of the unbelievable (or unbearable).	Others cease to confide in you or to take you seriously. What was warm now burns – there's the rub.
There's always a direction in which to head, and a 1,000-mile journey begins with the first step.	Feeling lost and disillusioned. Out of gas. No map. No compass.
Be sure you have a product to match your advertisement. Is it for a fact or for effect?	Too many irons in the fire. Others look askance at you and have no time for you.
SOLUTION	PROBLEM

If you find yourself on the receiving end of negative traits, it is because you are not expressing the opposing positive traits.

39

THE SUN IN CAPRICORN

ESSENCE

LIVING THROUGH BUILDING

THE SEA-GOAT   THE PRAGMATIST

Capricorn is concerned with making a success of life. This could be said of any Sign, but you aim to do this by getting the hang of how things actually "work" down here on Planet Earth. You are, therefore, a decidedly down-to-earth person who won't cling to abstract concepts and lofty ideals in order to justify being here. What satisfies this urge in you is a sense of purpose and of responsibility. You feel a part of this world when you can feel its weight upon your shoulders and its ground beneath your feet.

Traditionally, you are interested in external, socially established values of life rather than inner ones. To be honest, you assess anything or anyone in terms of how useful they are. As your Sign's symbol, the Mountain Goat, implies, you make your way to the summit of material success by taking one sure-footed step after another. You fix your attention on a vantage point and secure it. Sometimes a foothold can be someone else's head! And as you build your pile, you want solid value and solid values. With regard to what you consume, you like the right brand-names and to have a sense of belonging to the upper echelons of society – at least in terms of how your particular section of society currently sees itself.

However, you are far more complex than this, and have more subtlety than to be concerned solely with the outside world and what can be got out of it, an attitude that runs the danger of acquiring a blind spot. This can be seen by looking at the original symbol of Capricorn, the Sea-goat. This creature is half-goat and half-fish. The upper, or goat, half represents what has been described above – the earthy and persistent climber. But when the climber stumbles or falls, or just begins to realize that there is more to life than can be physically sensed, you begin to acquaint yourself with that other world of the fish – the mystical, irrational, unconscious inner realm. And when Capricorn gets spiritual, it does so with the same pragmatic efficiency with which it dealt with the material world. In fact, at an evolved level, you do not see any difference.

And so you come to realize how truly useful an awareness of the reality of invisible forces (such as thoughts, feelings and, most importantly, the imagination) is, and that roots and foundations – upon which everything is actually built – are usually out of sight.

The Capricorn who does not tune into his/her fish-half and the watery realm in which it dwells, can slip up on it and smell decidedly fishy, like Richard Nixon, who was undone by something called Watergate! But when and if you are practically attuned to the underlying mystical realities of life on Earth, rather than just being superstitious, then you are truly able to reach the pinnacle of Earthly success, the highest point, from which the next step up is Heaven, a little bit of which you can then bring down to Earth, with which to guide and govern.

LIKES
Being worldly · Knowing your limits
Order and control · Being busy
Traditions

DISLIKES
Feeling groundless · Feeling boundless
Feeling helpless · Feeling useless
The untried

If you are a woman, this could be the kind of man to whom you are attracted – but it is really you, so realize it and express it.

THE SUN IN CAPRICORN

TRANSFORMER

POSITIVE	NEGATIVE
Materially aware Responsible Efficient Orderly	Status slave Unscrupulous Ingratiating Wet blanket
Ambitious Organizer Industrious Takes the reins	Cold Calculating Slave to self Dictatorial
Reserved Patient Thoughtful Deep understanding	Inhibited Intolerant Worrisome Inscrutable
Resourceful Canny Persevering Disciplined	Tight Suspicious Rigid Austere
Earthy Senses others needs Employs others Solid	Philistine Opportunist Uses others Hard
Flood the market and you drown the demand. Elevate people's needs rather than increase them.	What started out as a good living has turned into a monster that cannot be satisfied.
Capricorn can get by on the smell of an oily rag – but only when it has to!	Life becomes existence. Work becomes drudge. Body becomes stiff. Friend becomes foe.
When you begin to appreciate fully your invisible qualities, so will others.	Nobody knows you – and they've almost given up trying to.
Indeed "Ambition is the devil's own sin", unless you strive in a spirit of redemption.	The warm smell of success becomes an icy blast. Alone in your ivory tower with a white elephant.
Apply your talents to what is inferior and you go down, do so to what is superior and you go up.	Backed the wrong horse. Made your bed and having to lie in it. Only cold comfort available.
SOLUTION	PROBLEM

If you find yourself on the receiving end of negative traits, it is because you are not expressing the opposing positive traits.

THE SUN IN AQUARIUS

ESSENCE

LIVING THROUGH LIBERATING

BEFRIEND THE TRUTH   HIGH MIND–LOW PROFILE

Aquarius is the Water-bearer, and Water symbolizes emotion. This means that your goal is to experience and to express your feelings without getting "wet", i.e., emotionally biased, overly attached or upset. In order to accomplish this you strive to be free of whoever or whatever has an emotionally cramping influence over you. However, in your effort to liberate yourself, you run the danger of throwing the baby out with the bath water, by pretending not to have feelings for anything other than the reasonably manageable. Furthermore, your convoluted mind is able to detach itself from the very fact that you have detached yourself in the first place! This is why the Sun is in its Detriment in Aquarius, for your Will can lose itself in the "sky" of your urge to be free.

This would not matter if it were not for the fact that more than any other Sign, you hold the key to what being a human being is. This has to do with the "Truth" that originally there was nothing to fear, like a clear sky. But along with being born came the apparently unchosen situation of being emotionally involved with someone, like your father or your mother. As an Aquarian, you have chosen to free yourself (and others) from the family, class, racial and religious conditioning that holds the Truth in bondage. So you have to discover a way of loosening these bonds, which requires first having had a good look at them.

Aquarius is said to put everything in the shop window, and to keep nothing back in the shop. This means that in the attempt to present your ideal and most evolved but uninvolved self, you actually overlook much of your all too human goodness, a goodness that you keep out of sight, regarding it as too emotional or autocratic. This is one way, but not the right way, of "bearing Water", or of containing and expressing emotion.

The positive, and most obvious, meaning of the Water-bearer symbol is that of refreshing the masses. With the Dawning of the Age of Aquarius, this is one of the main tasks on humanity's agenda for the next two thousand years. In order to accomplish this, the Aquarian qualities of teamwork and group effort have to be employed. So if you find that your life is a pointless struggle, it is probably because you are not enlisting yourself as part of a group, a flight of Souls aiming for the same goal. It appears necessary for you to place more importance on the sky than on the Sun, to put the requirement of the masses above your own individual desires. Yet paradoxically, it is equally necessary for you to maintain a firm sense of individuality in order to uphold and express the Aquarian democratic ideal, and not just be an ego-less space. Above all, you are seeking freedom for yourself and others through developing a greater sense of what life on this Planet is about.

LIKES
Good companions · Rebellious causes
Good times past · Future dreams
Equality and originality

DISLIKES
Excessive loneliness · Causeless rebels
Mawkishness · Pie in the sky
The ordinary and imitation

If you are a woman, this could be the kind of man to whom you are attracted – but it is really you, so realize it and express it.

THE SUN IN AQUARIUS

TRANSFORMER

POSITIVE	NEGATIVE
Impartial Cool Broad-minded Fair judge	Avoids intimacy Aloof Non-committal Emotionally inept
Friendly Gregarious Humanitarian Democratic	Impersonal Antisocial Lacks sympathy Hypocritical
Reformist Idealistic Inventive Original	Reactionary Impractical Cranky Elitist
Unaffected Convincing Intuitive Outwardly calm	Mocking Imposes ideas Cutting Secretly anxious
Clownish Free-thinking Free-loving Open-ended	Sarcastic Scatty Flighty Pointless

Life is a masquerade. Removing one mask merely reveals another. Enjoy the masquerade – live life.	Being afraid of presenting an emotional persona, you miss your role in the human drama.
To err is human, and your sense of the truth is all the more appreciated for being so.	As you observe and deride others' weaknesses, they leave you uncomfortably alone with your own.
Everyone is unique, and has the right to be so. Others' quirks are reminders of your own.	It annoys you when someone or something is either too odd or not odd enough.
The evolving personality turns fear into love; so first you have to acknowledge your fears.	You love humanity, but are not so keen on people. Such aversions are fears that bind you.
Treat yourself with as much understanding as you are afraid to expect of others.	Difficulty in relating to the opposite sex. Your mental guard becomes a mindless watchdog.
SOLUTION	PROBLEM

43

If you find yourself on the receiving end of negative traits, it is because you are not expressing the opposing positive traits.

THE SUN IN PISCES

ESSENCE

LIVING THROUGH ACCEPTING

LIFE IS A MYSTERY   I AM A MYSTERY

There are two fishes: the upstream one and the downstream one. As the upstream fish, you make an effort, you fight against the current, looking for inspiration in order that you may give it. As the downstream fish, you foster the notion that everything and everyone will wind up where they're going to get to sooner or later, so what's the point in trying.

The upstream fish has a point, the downstream fish doesn't. However, the upstream fish can push so hard that it misses the point, which is that sensitivity and acceptance are essential to Pisces, whereas the downstream fish can go with the flow and wind up in the swim. The addictive personality that you can be (fishes get hooked!) is the escapist looking for a way out that in time may prove to be a way in. For example, ex-alcoholics founded Alcoholics Anonymous. Faith comes with acceptance, and vice versa.

Ideally, you are plotting a course while letting things take their course. Such a way of handling life can give many impressions of who you are, ranging from the genuine altruist to the subtle manipulator, from the mystic to the misfit. This all stems from your sense that all is one and one is all. You can be anything – or virtually nothing. But the inescapable fact is that you are definitely here as a feeling being, and so you devise many a disguise to camouflage your immense sensitivity, which is your greatest possession. And although your need to camouflage yourself is behind much of your incomprehensibility, it is also what enables you to present one thing as another, for example horror as beauty, or curse as blessing, and so you can enlighten or relieve those who look or listen. You might not be able to fathom yourself, but you are adept at understanding others and their failings. You have to contend with a greater emotional input than any other Sign, and to channel it or evade it.

You may also unconsciously protect such emotional sensitivity and universal awareness with fierce analysis and scientific rationalization. Although this is often highly necessary to offset the frequently indiscriminate "anything goes" attitude of Pisces, it can also be an evasiveness of the most subtle kind, for it appears to be the opposite.

You are innately aware and appreciative of all walks of life. You may periodically protest and complain about the ways of certain others, but you eventually flip back into your more usual mode of ongoing acceptance. This makes you identify and side with the underdog. Fundamentally this is because you recognize that the Soul of anything or of anyone is synonymous with sensitivity, which is synonymous with suffering, which is something of which you are exquisitely aware. Joy and sorrow are one.

LIKES
Dreamy solitude · Mystery
The discarded · Getting lost
The absurd

DISLIKES
Criticism · Pedantry
The obvious · Feeling lost
Know-alls

If you are a woman, this could be the kind of man to whom you are attracted – but it is really you, so realize it and express it.

THE SUN IN PISCES

TRANSFORMER

POSITIVE	NEGATIVE
Compassionate Self-sacrificing Suffers artistically	Self-pitying The human doormat Suffers needlessly
Unassuming Self-effacing Gentle Still but stirring	Indecisive Self-limiting Wimpish Inwardly storm-tossed
Wise Accepting Adaptable Confided in	Inner doubts Oblivious Vague Unforthcoming
Sensitive Fascinating Mysterious Imaginative	Escapist Deceptive Self-mystifying Impressionable
Multi-talented Selfless Devoted Easygoing	Unenterprising Pointless Slaving Lazy
Give yourself a starting point and an end that endures; then trust in life's creative process.	Many possibilities dissolve into many improbabilities. Life becomes a thankless task. Weary.
Your mystical allure, your ancient understanding – solidly express and appreciate them.	Adrift. At sea. Confusion reigns. Like a bucket of water without the bucket.
Learn to face the music, then you'll know the score – how you and others fit in.	Caught in the net of the fear of being caught. Every move you make gets you more entangled.
You inspire others, so don't forget to take some credit for it – then forget it.	Drowning in a sea of your own despair – and no one knows.
Be a part of what you feel for. Give yourself to yourself before anybody else. Illuminate.	Being walked all over leaves you flat. Are you cut out for crucifixion?
SOLUTION	PROBLEM

45

If you find yourself on the receiving end of negative traits, it is because you are not expressing the opposing positive traits.

THE MOON

Keyword: SECURITY

The Moon, as it reflects the light of the Sun, your will, symbolizes your FEELING RESPONSES to life in general, and being SUBJECTIVE to the will of others. In CHILDHOOD, while your will was still UNCONSCIOUS, having your SECURITY NEEDS met made you totally DEPENDENT upon others, especially your MOTHER.

Consequently, much of your PERSONALITY became conditioned by the HABITS and BIASES of your MOTHER, your FAMILY, CLASS, RACE etc., for good or ill. Positively this gives you a sense of BELONGING and INNER SUPPORT, whereas negatively it can amount to CLANNISHNESS, a FEAR OF THE UNKNOWN and CLINGING TO THE PAST, which can effectively eclipse your individual sense of being – the Sun.

Your Moon-Sign position therefore shows how you experience life subjectively, how you REACT to it as a result of maternal and other conditioning. It also shows how you INSTINCTUALLY seek to satisfy your own needs and SYMPATHIZE with those of others.

The Lunar sense comes more naturally to females, so if you are male you may be attracted to females who embody your Moon-Sign qualities. Sooner or later, through life's experiences and relationships, you come to realize and to express the qualities of your EMOTIONS.

THE MOON IN ARIES

ESSENCE

SECURITY THROUGH DOING

THE ETERNAL YOUTH   BE HERE NOW

You experience life as something that never stands still, which in the strictest sense it is. However, if you are feeling insecure about any part of your life, then this can prod you into attempting to resolve things more quickly than is is naturally possible. So you are predisposed to racing around as if there is some ghastly time limit set upon you. And since Aries Moon makes for a strong personality, you can either precipitate predicaments where hurrying seems unavoidable, or use such forcefulness quickly to begin to slow down, decide what you are after, and then establish your own more comfortable pace.

However, what actually motivates you into doing anything in the first place is a sense of insecurity, which was very likely inherited from your mother. To feel peaceful can therefore be rather meaningless, even boring, to you. So you also have difficulty in being calm, and can wear yourself out before you know it. All the same, you have the marvellous ability to recover quickly from traumas, be they physical, mental or emotional. You have a large helping of that human capacity to recharge yourself in times of need, when alone in the wilderness. You could be regarded as the warrior or scout type of personality. Equally, your resilience is marked by being subject to emotional surges rather than lingering moods. You experience life as a thing of the moment, and should train and trust yourself to respond to the needs of that moment. Travel light. You have a temper that can frighten and amaze, but this too flares up and dies down suddenly, and this is born of frustration – again from/with your mother – rather than maliciousness.

The "battle stations" mode is one that seems to prevail, and you actually thrive on conflict, even though other dimensions of your personality may suffer because of it, and refuse to accept it. You feel that there are only two alternatives – either breaking through or breaking down. This has a decidedly see-saw effect on your intimate involvements in particular, and on all relationships in general. Even so, everyone depends upon you to provide excitement and unpredictability. However, somewhere along the line you need to cultivate a steadier emotional rhythm, and remember that you are not under continual threat of hostile forces. Even though you like to regard life as a battle, bear in mind that "like" should be the operative word.

Above all, you are after something that will last, which is quite a quest in itself, maybe *the* quest. As you view your probably rapid social or romantic turnover so far, you may leap to the conclusion that sustaining anything is just not part of your game-plan. But look again and you will see that what persists is persistence itself and, most of all, your childlike sense which inspires both you and others with the primary assumption that life is a thrilling and unique experience.

LIKES
The chase · New experiences
Leading · Honesty
Outdoor adventures

DISLIKES
Anti-climaxes · Inactivity
Being told what to do · Soppiness
Emotional confinement

If you are a man, this could be the kind of woman to whom you are attracted – but it is really you, so realize it and express it.

THE MOON IN ARIES

TRANSFORMER

POSITIVE	NEGATIVE
Spontaneous Direct Straightforward Sharp	Impetuous Brusque Unsubtle Blunt
Energetic Stimulating Quick responses Lively	Frenzied Too excitable Jumpy / Irritable Impatient
Open Daring Self-assertive Independent	Tactless Reckless Pushy Unco-operative
Trail-blazing Original Future sense Spirited	Ahead of self Inaccessible Tense Restless
Ever-ready Arousing Unstoppable Unbeatable	Fit to burst Precipitous Bad finisher Sore loser
Know that whatever is required of you – but no more, and no less – is always possible.	Meteor-like, you spend yourself too soon, and create situations where you cannot win.
A fire must have fuel to burn on. To continue, recognize your needs as well as your wants.	Lonely and ill at ease with yourself.
Ensure that what you are after is consciously constructive, not unconsciously defensive.	People and things either get in your way or don't go along with you.
It's driving you. And it won't let you down, so there's no need to hurry unnecessarily.	Although your fiery energy can be fun, are you driving it, or is it driving you?
Between your refreshing outbursts, be mindful of others' finer feelings – and express your own.	Unaware of others' sensibilities, they cannot be aware of yours. Are you aware of this?!
SOLUTION	PROBLEM

49

If you find yourself on the receiving end of negative traits, it is because you are not expressing the opposing positive traits.

THE MOON IN TAURUS

ESSENCE

SECURITY THROUGH STABILIZING

CHILD OF NATURE   BOUNTY OR BURDEN

Security is sought through stability, which sounds straightforward enough, and indeed with Moon in Taurus you are usually known for your practical and materially dependable nature. A minimum of change is seen as equalling a maximum of security. This emotional stability is the reason for the Moon being Exalted in Taurus, but unless you are quite happy with a predictable, down-home sort of life, or have made the ultimate realization that the only totally consistent factor is change itself, then such a need for stability is not going to be so simply met. Complications are then likely to become manifest in a number of ways: someone else upon whom you are dependent creating a change; changes in your body state – especially diseases of the throat and the reproductive system; feelings of boredom and inertia; deadlock situations as you try to fulfil needs of security in one camp and of pleasure in another; becoming a beast of burden through failing to appreciate the value of your own broad back; staying too long in an unfruitful relationship.

Behind all of this is an issue of self-worth. If you are not sure what you are or what you are worth, then a never-ending search for some form of external value (material security being mistaken for emotional security) is going to try your decidedly persistent nature in a rather unrewarding fashion. In other words, peace with yourself has to be found before you can really expect it to occur on the outside. And even if it does, it comes at a very high price. As a child you possibly felt threatened by some kind of ominous disruption – or were actually a victim of it. Or perhaps your mother had such an anxiety which was transmitted to you and developed into a blind fear of change or a blind need for material security. Another cause of self-doubt could be that your mother had similar doubts about herself and therefore was not able to notice and affirm your worth.

So what is having Taurean Moon worth? Most essentially it is a feeling about you of physical substance and sensuousness that is very reassuring and attractive to others. Instinctively, you know how to identify and satisfy those needs. The personal applications of this talent are obvious; the professional ones include any activities that cater for physical needs, such as food and drink, comfort, property, management and production generally – also areas of healthcare that connect directly with the physical body, like massage, osteopathy etc. Artistic senses are pronounced, too – especially singing or country crafts. You also have a way with animals that could serve a useful purpose.

As Nature's child, you have deep, rich emotions as a result of being so close to the Earth. But there is no need to bury yourself in it through seeking too much material security. The gift of a Taurean Moon is that material supply will always be forthcoming – unless you doubt it.

LIKES
Material security · Bargain-hunting
Quality · Predictability
Ownership

DISLIKES
Change · Waste and extravagance
Letting go · The unknown
Borrowing

If you are a man, this could be the kind of woman to whom you are attracted – but it is really you, so realize it and express it.

THE MOON IN TAURUS

TRANSFORMER

POSITIVE	NEGATIVE
Dependable Consistent Pragmatic Robust	Stick-in-the-mud Habit-ruled Tunnel-visioned Dense
Methodical Painstaking Patient Persistent	Wooden Overloaded Slow-reacting Bulldozing
Affectionate Sensuous Generous Good-natured	Demanding Carnal Self-indulgent Hedonistic
Materially aware Organizer Good taste Thrifty	Money-minded Bossy Consumer snob Mean
Steady Placid Self-reliant Attuned to nature	Brooding Listless Insecure Melancholic
When you hit the bottom you'll know which way is up. Relax into your inner beauty.	Feeling very uncomfortable with yourself and the world. Feeling let down and hung up.
As you measure what things are worth, be mindful of what actually constitutes the quality of life.	Knowing the price of everything and the value of nothing, you are in charge but not in clover.
The rarer the gift, the more valuable it is. Your body is your most valuable physical possession.	Beset by demands that are physically impossible to meet – and they're consuming you.
Appreciate others' values and they will appreciate yours. Lend some weight and lose some.	Others seem to be either constantly resisting you and avoiding you, or forgetting you.
Look beyond your fears of loss and identify what you need and what you have right now.	Waiting in vain and unable to see your way ahead.
SOLUTION	PROBLEM

51

If you find yourself on the receiving end of negative traits, it is because you are not expressing the opposing positive traits.

THE MOON IN GEMINI

ESSENCE

SECURITY THROUGH COMMUNICATING

THINKING IS FEELING   **FEELING IS THINKING**

Security is found through communicating your feelings not only to others but also to yourself. You have a knack of keeping difficult emotions on mental hooks, and thereby create an illusion of emotional lightness. This is just fine until you run out of hooks; you then have to start clearing the closet of all those unlooked-at doubts and fears – or hang-ups.

The bane and the boon of Gemini Moon are the constant flow of emotion through your mind. In a positive sense this means that your feelings can be readily and cleverly expressed through the written or spoken word. On the other hand, without a serious sense of purpose, what you are thinking or saying will be experienced like a television that is continually having its channels changed. However, you certainly have the gift of the gab. No one can compete with you when it comes to spontaneously holding forth. Your ability to verbalize a stream of consciousness is remarkable, and should prove itself in such fields as literature, journalism, counselling or public speaking.

You also have a talent for putting your finger on it when it comes to assessing the emotional state of a person or an occasion. However, accurate as such appraisals are, take care not to overlook deeper and more powerful emotional drives that are present. Similarly, a lack of commitment from another suggests that there is an area of your own feelings that is being skimmed over. Others (without Gemini Moon) do not find it so easy to take things at face value. Until you begin to discover and reveal deeper layers of your own personality, a partner is going to be equally evasive or hard to find.

Geminian duality is very marked here. For example, on the one hand you have a flair for making light of heavy emotions that can be quite relieving, but on the other, such a sticking-plaster approach can deceive both you yourself and others into thinking that everything is fine when really it is not. Also, your natural ability to intellectualize emotions may enable you to keep a cool head – but a cold heart, too, if you are not too careful. Others find a cool head good to have around, but with a cold heart there won't be anyone around!

Underlying your breezy emotional nature is a deep need to keep everyone informed of the fact that life is but a passing show, and that the world of opposites always prevails, in that there can be found joy in sadness, amusement in boredom, absurdity in profundity – and, of course, vice versa. What is important is the interplay between the main poles of thinking and feeling. This can often be just a case of your not knowing when to stop talking as you juggle and shunt your notions and emotions back and forth. But when you are aware that you are doing this, sparks of genius begin to fly.

LIKES
Variety · Mental stimulation
Being in the know · Keeping on the move
Grooves

DISLIKES
Predictability · Clods
Being lost for words · Being pinned down
Ruts

If you are a man, this could be the kind of woman to whom you are attracted – but it is really you, so realize it and express it.

THE MOON IN GEMINI

TRANSFORMER

POSITIVE	NEGATIVE
Easygoing Light touch Uncomplicated Lively	Heavy weather Superficial Simplistic Manic depressive
Mobile Witty Quick Live wire	Restless Worrisome Impatient Anxious
Versatile Multi-faceted Fast responses Fast learner	Spread too thin Two-faced Flip Sketchy
Good conversationalist Friendly Charming Delightful	Gossip Nosy Insincere Deceitful
Intelligent Broad-minded Interesting Perceptive	Too rational Shallow Dissatisfying Trivial
Trust your mind to express and understand feelings, not replace them.	Others can't feel for you – neither can you! Mistaking your reactions for reasons.
Think big as you talk small. Feed the grapevine with your sparkling mind.	Caught in the web of your own words and thoughts. The victim of your own curiosity.
Having too many irons in the fire slows you down. The ultimate string to your bow is thoroughness.	Projects take off but then disappear altogether. Feeling hard-pressed to maintain position.
Being habitually speedy is no joke. To be smart, avoid outrunning yourself.	Nervous exhaustion. Insomniacal. Strung out.
Admitting to your contradictory nature is refreshing. Let others enjoy it, too.	Others cannot see where you're coming from or going to, so they don't wish to accompany you.
SOLUTION	PROBLEM

53

If you find yourself on the receiving end of negative traits, it is because you are not expressing the opposing positive traits.

THE MOON IN CANCER

ESSENCE

SECURITY THROUGH NURTURING

EBB AND FLOW · THE WORLD IS MY HOME

Security is gained through classic security-producing traditions such as home and family – and the activities that are associated with them: cooking, gardening, domestic skills and supplies etc., so there is a homely, familiar feel about you that others are drawn towards. You should not underestimate or lose sight of such an attractiveness, for Cancer Moon's greatest weakness is being so subjective that you fail to notice your hearth-like warmth and focus – and then so do others.

As you exude this aura of strength and dependability, which is the hallmark of the Moon being Dignified in the Sign of the Crab, guard against its preventing you from showing your own hurts and doubts. Apart from causing such feelings to fester, this would actually inhibit rather than create the secure relationships that are so important to you. Partners and family can become habituated all too easily to your doing all the caring. This is more likely to be the case if you are female, whereas males are often inclined to doing the leaning. With both males and females, the ties to your mother are strong – for better or for worse. You may need to put some space between you and her.

Your feeling nature is well-developed, which can mean, on the one hand, a great ability to tune into the moods of others, and, on the other, being rather wrapped up in your own emotions. With a natural ability to nurture and protect, you make a good parent or a supportive friend. However, you have to watch overdoing this, for it can lead to being smothering or patronizing, which in turn can lead to others' growing too dependent or feeling resentful. Your natural nurturing ability also extends to animal and plant life.

You have a sentimental nature, and a good memory – of both favours granted and wounds inflicted. Learning to forgive and forget is necessary in order to forestall spells of brooding, which can devolve into rank depression. In any event, you are prone to much emotional fluctuation, but this blesses you with a great ability to adapt to changing situations, and others depend on this. Recognizing and going with the ebb and flow pattern of your life is absolutely central to governing your emotions rather than allowing them to govern you. You can be melancholy, touchy and bemoaning your fate in the morning, and then a tower of strength in the afternoon. You also need to withdraw periodically to recharge your batteries in order to avoid exhausting your own – and others' – emotions. In some respects you tend to have a limited scope or viewpoint, but your rich emotional expression, which warms and reassures all within your sphere of influence, more than compensates. However, it would still be well to cultivate open-mindedness and a measure of detachment without any trace of rancour. Such nurturing as this truly creates a feeling of belonging in this world.

LIKES
Your own patch · Secure home and home-life · Peace and quiet
A family feel · The natural world

DISLIKES
Feeling rootless · Being uprooted
Carelessness · Unkindness
A plastic world

If you are a man, this could be the kind of woman to whom you are attracted – but it is really you, so realize it and express it.

THE MOON IN CANCER

TRANSFORMER

POSITIVE	NEGATIVE
Sympathetic Caring Devoted Accommodating	Oversensitive Clinging Fawning Harbours wounds
Tenacious Dependable Regular Self-reliant	Flogs dead horses One-sided Habit-prone Self-absorbed
Home-loving Home-making Family-conscious Firmly rooted	Agoraphobic Limited Clannish Entrenched
Enchanting Introspective Receptive Meditative	Lost Withdrawn Defensive Brooding
Emotionally attuned Deep feelings Responsive Nurturing	Manipulative Deeply needy Despondent Swamping

Identify the needs you feel cannot be met, then realize they represent others' needs for you.	Eventually others find it impossible to relate to your bottomless pit of neediness.
Retreat and regenerate with a strong, creative and deliberate purpose in mind.	Feeling controlled by your feelings, and a victim of circumstance.
Seek professional help to cut the ties that bind you to your negative past. Re-root yourself.	Tied to the home. Your horizons appear to get narrower and narrower.
Check that "love" is not need in disguise. Be conscious of what you are holding on to, and why.	Apparently you have given your all, only to be taken for granted and even abandoned.
Let someone into your space, but leave the door open in case they want to go – then they'll stay.	Feeling desperately alone and unloved. Emotionally exhausting both to yourself and to others.

SOLUTION	PROBLEM

69

55

If you find yourself on the receiving end of negative traits, it is because you are not expressing the opposing positive traits.

THE MOON IN LEO

ESSENCE

SECURITY THROUGH CREATING

THE NATURAL THESPIAN   THE CLOSET SHOW-OFF

Security is sought through creating a definite impression and gaining some kind of acclaim. Often, however, when you eventually get caught in the spotlight you can feel uncomfortably self-conscious. Why should this be so? It is important that you feel good about this need for recognition for you have it in you to draw the limelight, and to hold it naturally and gracefully. Conversely, seeking attention and not really knowing what for can lead to all sorts of complications. Your liking for money and status is also strong – as is your ability to attain them. But again, if you are the "closet" type of Moon in Leo, you may play down these matters, almost to the point of perversity.

If you suffer from any of the negative cases above, then look for the possibility of not wishing to repeat overt or negative expressions of ego as practised in the past – by your mother or by yourself. For example, as a child, insistent demands for attention may have been either always indulged or unavoidably ignored. Behind everything lies a fear of criticism and, consequently, an inability to take it. As the Moon is indicative of unconscious behaviour patterns, and since both negative and positive patterns are dramatized so grandly in Leo, it is necessary for feedback to be received, acknowledged and acted upon. Otherwise, such precious and self-justifying egocentricity can lead to others' expressing their discomfort at it in a far more dramatically upsetting fashion than merely telling you what they think of you.

With such fiery and lively emotions you have a natural sense of drama and creativity. You are also a wow with children – being childlike yourself. You can overreact to relatively insignificant situations, but you can also make a dull situation into an exciting one. With this childlike sense of fun and games, you can find the absurd and ridiculous in everything – except yourself, perhaps. It is difficult for you to create a sense of detachment; everything is taken as personal praise or insult. So when it is essential to let go of something or of someone, it is best achieved in a spirit of grace rather than favour. In this way your all-important dignity may be kept intact, and your feathers remain unruffled.

On one level you are not quite sure if you have any right to have an ego at all. But on another, you can be highly perturbed and upset by the thought of being taken in vain. One way of expressing this is by your appearing to be easygoing and flexible, when really you are not. On the other hand, too rarely do you show your sincerity, emotional warmth and generosity. No doubt someone or something made you feel small and insignificant in the past – or else you gained a false sense of pride. In any event, you'd best come out to play and meet both the embarrassment and the glory that go with having a human ego.

LIKES
Being centre of attraction · Children and parties · Romantic involvements · Privilege and grandeur · An influential position

DISLIKES
Feeling self-conscious · Stuffy social occasions · Lack-lustre relationships · Going second class · Being answerable to others

If you are a man, this could be the kind of woman to whom you are attracted – but it is really you, so realize it and express it.

THE MOON IN LEO

TRANSFORMER

POSITIVE	NEGATIVE
Impressive Self-confident Majestic Noble	Demanding Praise-seeking Subtly domineering Snobbish
Popular Lively Sunny Dignified	Easily flattered Easily hurt Self-centred Vain
Dramatic Leader Creative Persevering	Overbearing Power-tripper Self-important Stubborn
Cheerful Charming Magnetic Proud	Hedonistic Conceited Attention-seeking Arrogant
Loyal Sincere Warm Good-hearted	Possessive Inflexible Overreacts Prima donna

Find solace in your principles, and comfort in magnanimity.	Feeling threatened and about to be taken advantage of. Sulky. Wounded pride.
Even the bright Sun has spots! As you radiate show your doubts, too.	Feeling dissipated, unappreciated and misunderstood.
Try expressing yourself honestly rather than trying painfully to prove yourself.	Frightened that your insecurity will be found out and that you'll be shot down in flames.
Be aware of that light within; it can never be extinguished, so set no limits on it.	Feeling cheated and crestfallen, and being self-righteous only makes matters worse.
Recognize your obvious pride, then master it – and what it is in.	Feeling indignant. Rejected and avoided by others, but not openly.

SOLUTION	PROBLEM

If you find yourself on the receiving end of negative traits, it is because you are not expressing the opposing positive traits.

THE MOON IN VIRGO

ESSENCE

SECURITY THROUGH ANALYSING

SECURITY IN PURITY   TRUST YOUR DARKER SIDE

Security is sought through analysing, which can lead either to a pure and well-ordered emotional lifestyle, whereby you consistently weed out influences that are detrimental to your well-being, or to one that is prudish and fastidious, whereby you try to govern feelings as if they were things to be tidied away. In either case you would need to cultivate some open-ended tolerance and acceptance of life's imperfections.

Behind such exacting emotional requirements as you feel subject to, there lies your mother's influence, which, on the positive side, was likely to have been clear and wholesome or, on the negative, may have been critical and narrow. In either case this could have led to your being afraid of your dark side showing – "dark side" meaning anything that your mother or any other influential childhood figure found unacceptable. For example, your more Earthy or raw emotions possibly got branded as vulgar or crude, with the result that the healthy but sticky passions that keep relationships glued together became repressed, and devolved, instead, into a lurking urge. Apart from weakening bonds in this fundamental way, there is the added strain of constantly trying to maintain a goody-two-shoes image. Because such emotional fastidiousness can leave you on the shelf, or at least left alone too often, it is advisable for you to trust life to unfold according to itself, rather than how you think it ought to. Sanity is not always sanitary, and what is wholesome obviously includes everything.

A feeling of security can also be attained through being of service in some way, in particular with regard to health. You can go to great lengths to help others, as if you thrive on it – and you do. This sense of service can also satisfy your need for Purity, in that you are able, with great thoroughness, to clean up anything that is messy or polluted. Or else you can go around as if you have a bad smell under your nose – what could that be? Virgo is a Sign that can polarize; this strong need to be so orderly and clean can turn into the opposite: your being untidy or loose – either voluntarily or otherwise.

As a rule you have a liking for animals, especially small ones or pets. This is because they have a certain purity of being that humans seem to lack. But then observe how "natural" animals are with their Earthy habits. This is an example of one of those grey areas that you can fail to see, or avoid seeing, as you are predisposed to seeing life in black and white. But it is to these grey, misty areas that your unconscious will always draw you, as it urges you to understand that there is as much purity in darkness as there is in light, and that you can trust the mysterious more than the logical. What you don't know is always greater than what you do.

LIKES
Order and plans · Hygiene
Making lists · Wholesomeness
Health aids

DISLIKES
Uncertainty · Squalour
Sloppiness · Sordidness
Health hazards

If you are a man, this could be the kind of woman to whom you are attracted – but it is really you, so realize it and express it.

THE MOON IN VIRGO

TRANSFORMER

POSITIVE	NEGATIVE
Conscientious Dutiful Straight Upright	Worrier Austere Prudish Rigid
Shrewd Methodical Precise Discriminating	Cold Exacting Pedantic Carping
Neat Clean Health-conscious Helpful	Neurotic Clinical Health freak Interfering
Modest Unassuming Gentle Light touch	Falsely modest Undemonstrative Timid Creepy
Finely tuned Keen instincts Analytical Concerned	Hypersensitive Prejudiced Labelling Anxious
Life ahead of you is a multi-coloured experience, so why switch to black and white?	Reducing life to a set of theories and pigeon-holes results in your being fearfully restricted.
It takes time to be aware of your true worth, but when you are, others will be so automatically.	Feeling underestimated and rejected. Afraid or unable to express your deepest feelings.
Healthy body = healthy mind? Not necessarily; but a pure heart emanates a healing aura.	Your well-intentioned pre-occupation with health makes others avoid you like the plague.
Realize that the idea behind any method is to reduce wear and tear.	You no longer enjoy your full-time job maintaining the illusion of control.
Who or what are you serving? Are you devoted or enslaved?	Feeling that life is all uphill, and that everything will fall apart if you relax.
SOLUTION	PROBLEM

59

If you find yourself on the receiving end of negative traits, it is because you are not expressing the opposing positive traits.

THE MOON IN LIBRA

ESSENCE

SECURITY THROUGH RELATING

THE NEED FOR BALANCE　　　**THE EMOTIONAL MIRROR**

Security is sought through feeling socially involved – having a partner; having a definite social position. Your refined instincts are readily able to achieve this, but you can run the risk of finding yourself attempting to be all things to all people. Your undeniable social graces, like metaphorical clothing, need to be worn lightly in order to prevent this predisposition to please becoming unpleasantly restricting for you. Such a need to please – which can be very enjoyable to others – may merely have its roots in your having felt that you had to please your mother, father or whoever brought you up. However, sooner or later, what pleases you has to emerge and take priority – and that might not please anyone else at all!

Until then, all this makes you very difficult to dislike, which is both your boon and your bane, because although popularity has its obvious advantages, people can find it hard to confront you with what they don't like about you. You are then made to feel socially excluded or emotionally rejected for no apparent reason. When you realize that a Libran Moon attracts the kind of people and social situations that eventually force your individually held principles into conscious awareness, the instinctive sense of beauty and harmony that you most surely have will become a creative and dynamic expression of you, rather than a passive and insecure reflection of others that makes it hard for you to accept the consequences of your actions.

The need for balance and harmony is essential to your Moon position. This need can manifest itself negatively, in the form of abortive relationships and fickleness – in either yourself or your partner – that have resulted from your attempting to keep things "nice" rather than getting down to the nitty gritty. This reluctance to look at and to express your darker and more powerful urges and feelings again probably stems from your sensing that your mother or father would not have liked it; or there could have been an incident in your childhood in which this darker side to your nature was thrust upon you in the form of a traumatic experience. The simplest, clearest, most rewarding and most relieving thing that you can do is to share both your good and your bad feelings with your partner. If this cannot be done, then seek counsel or therapy in order to disperse your fear of just being yourself as you are, as opposed to what you feel others expect you to be. Learning to trust your natural talent for making things appealing is all-important. This can take the form of a flair for cooking, décor, fashion, entertaining, or be expressed as the basic ability to make others feel they are a part of something. Perversely, not trusting this social sense can make you rather anti-social. Your soothing presence, which may even have the voice or musical ability to go with it, should be recognized as a powerful tool with which you can influence the social and emotional climate around you.

LIKES
Fine people and fine things
Sharing · Knowing social pitch
Conviviality · Being agreeable

DISLIKES
Coarseness and vulgarity · Emotional
tight-fistedness · Feeling outcast
Inhospitality · Being misjudged

If you are a man, this could be the kind of woman to whom you are attracted – but it is really you, so realize it and express it.

THE MOON IN LIBRA

TRANSFORMER

POSITIVE	NEGATIVE
Romantic Charming Graceful Affectionate	Silly Insincere Superficial Unfaithful
Refined Aesthetic Gentle Kind	Shallow Glossy façade Limp Vague
Pleasing Richly expressive Attractive Friendly	Self-indulgent Affected Seductive Flirt
Tolerant Tactful Reasonable Gracious	Yes-person Indecisive Insipid Disappointing
Socially aware Hospitable Dependable Relaxing	Anti-social Neglectful Unreliable Lazy
Do not resist your basic need to feel liked, and put both others and yourself at ease.	Your need to please has exhausted itself rather than matured into a social skill.
Do not accept peace at any price; after all, you know what it takes to keep it.	Your fear of being thought badly of has created that very thing.
People who matter are attracted to all your qualities, not just to the ones you like.	No one seems able or available to please you because they cannot get to the real you.
You have a need to make nice what's nasty, so acknowledge what's nasty!	Feeling empty and unfulfilled. Reluctant to face life's deeper or harsher realities.
Know that your lightness attracts heaviness, thereby challenging your charms.	Failed relationships – either you become fickle or you invite fickleness. In love with love.
SOLUTION	PROBLEM

61

If you find yourself on the receiving end of negative traits, it is because you are not expressing the opposing positive traits.

THE MOON IN SCORPIO

ESSENCE

SECURITY THROUGH DESIRING

A SOUL NEEDS A SOUL   TRUST OR PERISH

Security is found in strong, deep feelings, which necessarily poses the acknowledgement of your equally deep need for a profound and gut-wrenching relationship. This is because the Moon is said to be in its Fall in Scorpio, which means that some kind of emotional death has to be experienced before you can begin to feel able to manage the intimate bond that is so important to you. Light-hearted affairs are, therefore, doomed to failure because they fail to purge you in this way. However, paradoxically, a failure to purge can be experienced as a purging in itself!

As your emotional experiences strike right to your heart and soul with great intensity, understandably you make great attempts to control your emotional environment. Such control is made possible by an intuition that is as profound as your feelings. Unfortunately, this need for control can lead to your using underhand means, such as hitting another person where it hurts before they hit you. The fact that they probably have no intention of striking you at all is a point worth considering.

Behind this lie experiences from childhood that made you feel at the mercy of traditions and attitudes that had no conception of your emotional sensitivity and of the nature of your desires. Consequently, you felt betrayed and abandoned, and may still continue to guard against such threats. You should grasp the fact that your emotional intensity and insight can put anyone where you want them. You need to let go of that fear of betrayal, because holding on to it will simply attract it—such is your power. Abandon your fears or be abandoned because of them.

You see yourself as a survivor. While it is true that you have great emotional stamina, be careful that it does not merely take the form of resisting involvement of an intimate kind. Being proud of your inscrutability is rather like being Houdini on a bad night – the audience can't see in, and you can't get out.

Not surprisingly you have an unerring ability to detect the emotional state of others, even when it is well hidden. Although this talent can sometimes be misused to drag them down into the hole that you are in yourself, at your best you cannot fail to see what has to be done in order to rectify or to quicken a given situation – even if it might result in your losing something or someone. Until you reach such a level of emotional awareness and expression, you are in danger of being driven by a self-destructive pressure to hedge your bets or to sublimate such strong emotions through overwork, alcohol, drugs or simply talking incessantly. More than any other Moon-Sign you are capable of seeing beyond the trivial, the cheap and the immediately attainable. "It is a far, far better thing that I do, than I have ever done."

LIKES
Intimacy · Soul mates
Moving experiences · Profound feelings
A sense of finality

DISLIKES
Superficiality · Meaningless ties
Being controlled · Insipidness
Dragging things out

If you are a man, this could be the kind of woman to whom you are attracted – but it is really you, so realize it and express it.

THE MOON IN SCORPIO

TRANSFORMER

POSITIVE	NEGATIVE
Magnetic	Unyielding
Genuine feelings	Apparently unfeeling
Intuitive	Suspicious
Compassionate	Scornful
Energetic	Maniacal
Passionate	Jealous
Powerful	Gloating
Determined	Obsessive
Self-sacrificing	Grudging
Just	Revengeful
Persevering	Unforgiving
Stoical	Emotionally denying
Inscrutable	Unreachable
Self-reliant	Lonely
Deep	Brooding
Self-possessed	Self-destructive
Complex	Subtly dominating
Influential	Manipulative
Shrewd	Underhand
Firm	Obstinate

Others fall easily under your spell, so bless and be blessed – or curse and be cursed.	Your security feels threatened by the very things you vainly use to gain it.
The true test and validation of your secret world is to let a chosen few into it.	Feeling abandoned, betrayed and misunderstood.
The price of getting what you want is exactly equal to what you give up.	Poisoned by your own bitterness. Gutted by your own emptiness.
Taking hold only in order to let go will continually absorb you.	After you have got what you want, you are quickly, if not immediately, dissatisfied.
Trust the depth of your feelings and insight to attract people to your level.	Fearful of submitting. Unable to trust others and to show your love.

SOLUTION	PROBLEM

If you find yourself on the receiving end of negative traits, it is because you are not expressing the opposing positive traits.

THE MOON IN SAGITTARIUS

ESSENCE

SECURITY THROUGH SEEKING

A NEED TO ROAM   THE GYPSY SOUL

This is the Lunar position of the Soul that has sought for a long time. You are the natural philosopher – the habitual seeker. However, it is actually through habit that you may have forgotten that seeking is your greatest need, that you must find a system of belief, or a mission, that will guide and give meaning to your life. In the process of seeking you may well have to learn to make the distinction between your own beliefs and those that you were taught or that were bred into you as a child. Because you naturally prefer your spiritual or religious beliefs to be kept fluid and free, any dogmatic indoctrination in the past can be reacted against later, when you may completely reject any kind of spiritual or ethical code – or can result in your becoming even more dogmatic. But, for your security's sake, some kind of faith or philosophy is required. Insisting on being without any – a dogma in itself – is tantamount to cutting off your nose to spite your face.

You are also a gambler, looking for the big chance, the unique, the ideal, which ultimately could only be yourself. Without risk-taking, nothing is discovered or gained – a phrase that could be your personal motto. On the other hand, you can get into the habit of taking risks for the hell of it, as a kind of compensation for not taking more calculated risks in aid of furthering your quest – or, initially, of just discovering the nature of the quest itself.

You are basically a positive person, and you maintain that positivity most easily in a changing environment; no matter what darkness falls across your path, you will magically find a new direction to take, and will come up smelling of roses. As you believe in Providence, so she looks after you. Equally refreshing is your natural inclination to be spontaneous and outspoken – you clear the air, and the way, whenever confusion or despondency reigns. However, cheerful and optimistic as you are in company, unless you discover where such feelings are coming from, you can sometimes feel hollow and empty when on your own.

At root, you have an almost mystical sense of life's "story" – that it is all going somewhere, and coming from somewhere. It is this innate and primitive faith that allows you to see the light at the end of the tunnel, when others are stumbling and crestfallen. This sense also gives you the desire to embrace more and more of life's meanings and experiences. To inhibit such a natural urge can give rise to blind indulgences and listlessness. So at all costs, if your feet feel itchy, hitch your caravan to the brightest star, your most inspiring thought-feeling, and embark upon another chapter in your life's history.

LIKES
Freedom and adventure ·
Drama and story-telling · Honesty
Extremes · Travel and the outdoor life

DISLIKES
Restrictions and small thinking · Humdrum
normality · Pretentiousness · Prejudice and
pedantry · Morbid soul-searching

If you are a man, this could be the kind of woman to whom you are attracted – but it is really you, so realize it and express it.

THE MOON IN SAGITTARIUS

TRANSFORMER

POSITIVE	NEGATIVE
Philosophical	Unrealistic
Enthusiastic	Restless
Cheerful	Hysterical
Sense of fun	Irresponsible
Sincere seeker	Offhand
Sense of mission	Non-committal
Devout	Amoral
Concerned	Careless
Wise and understanding	Pompous and narrow-minded
Humanitarian	Holier-than-thou
Frank	Blunt
Outspoken	Arrogant
Innocent	Gullible
Naturally trusting	Naïve
Open-minded	Dizzy
Optimistic	Unreliable
Alert	Idle
Lively	Listless
Playful	Silly
Generous	Self-indulgent

Stir yourself and give of yourself – and be the exception that proves the rule.	Feeling sluggish and tired, and that life is just an unfair game. Overweight
Others learn to trust in life more by your example – as long as you get your facts right.	Feeling taken advantage of. Overstretched and out to lunch.
Learn to be receptive to others' feelings and viewpoints as you express your own.	Others feel unable to approach you. You feel lonely.
The only point that life has is the one you make or discover for yourself.	Feeling neglected and pointless. Others are indifferent to your predicament.
Treat life more adventurously, others more seriously, and yourself less seriously.	Feeling humiliated and anxious about your credibility. Distress and confusion reign.

SOLUTION	PROBLEM

65

If you find yourself on the receiving end of negative traits, it is because you are not expressing the opposing positive traits.

THE MOON IN CAPRICORN

ESSENCE

SECURITY THROUGH BUILDING

THE NEED TO BE NEEDED   THE END JUSTIFIES THE MEANS

Security is built upon a base of being useful to society and seeking just-ification in its eyes – for better or for worse. Such a need can incline you to undervalue what you want from and for yourself. This in turn can lead to feeling unloved, unwanted or inferior in some way. This is why the Moon is said to be in its Detriment in Capricorn, for seeking external approval to allay inner doubts proves detrimental to your personality as a whole.

Whether it shows or not, you have a great need to be needed. So others come to rely on you to keep things together materially in some way. This can make you indispensable, but if having this need met means losing sight of your inner worth, you can wind up feeling a bit of a slave. In other words, by not trusting the importance of your own inner values and subscribing to those that outside pressures seem to dictate, you are in danger of feeling let down, by both yourself and the state of affairs around you.

However, it is important to recognize how and why this distrust of your inner self occurred in the first place, and subsequently created a distrust of others. The Moon symbolizes the Child – both literally and in the sense of the "Child within". Capricorn is the Sign that governs the "big, bad world out there" – concrete or man-made reality. So the Moon is not happy in Capricorn, for the Child is thrust harshly into the material world. This can mean that you literally had a hard or deprived childhood. Burdens were piled upon your small shoulders; austere and oppressive surroundings were your lot. There may have been something lacking in your father, or a lack of him altogether, and this could have cast a shadow over your mother that was passed on to you in some way. Whatever your childhood circumstances, you learnt, through their material or emotional difficulties, to become a survivor.

The most likely expression of this "survivorship" is being able to function well in the material world, as a way of compensating for that inner emotional blight. Such a shrewd and businesslike streak can take you far up the socio-economic ladder. But at some stage the outer trappings that you have built up around you can no longer seal you off from that feeling that something is missing, and it is this very feeling that makes you reluctant to be the outright materialist go-getter that you have or could become. As this new type of "survivor" you can turn into quite a special sort of human being, because you manage to combine your childlike charm with strong instincts of how the material world works. And just how it works, you discover, is built upon that real "real world" within you. Ultimately, and usually after the age of thirty, you stand to become an influence over others, because you are an example of the no-nonsense human being who has survived against the odds.

LIKES
The tried and the true
Strong people · Organization
Steadiness of purpose · Firm foundations

DISLIKES
Pie-in-the-sky · Spinelessness
Feeling out of control
Having no purpose · Shaky set-ups

If you are a man, this could be the kind of woman to whom you are attracted – but it is really you, so realize it and express it.

THE MOON IN CAPRICORN

TRANSFORMER

POSITIVE	NEGATIVE
Self-controlled Cautious Modest Reserved	Repressed Distrustful Self-doubting Inhibited
Serious Disciplined Pragmatic Prudent	Depressive Austere Unimaginative Boring
Achiever Hardworking Determined Shrewd	Status-conscious Slave to system Cold-hearted Crafty
Loyal Influential Steadfast Respected	Sycophantic Name-dropper Unctuous Insincere
Sensitive Self-sacrificing Efficient helper Dignified	Insensitive Uses others Self-serving Conceited
To rule truly is to serve. Improving the lot of others improves your self-image.	For all your selfish attention to your ambitions, you are still dissatisfied.
Relate to others in the knowledge that they are after what you are after: respect.	Licking others' boots only gets you a kick in the face. Loss of self-respect.
When you realize that what you are after cannot be found in the outer world, look within.	Feeling that life is just a meaningless struggle. Disillusioned.
Seriously consider not taking yourself so seriously; humour is a necessity, not a luxury.	Feeling grey and downcast. Unable to see beyond your deeply furrowed brow.
What you need to keep under control is that voice from the past that says "Not good enough".	Feeling inadequate and unappreciated. Lonely and alienated.
SOLUTION	PROBLEM

67

If you find yourself on the receiving end of negative traits, it is because you are not expressing the opposing positive traits.

THE MOON IN AQUARIUS

ESSENCE

SECURITY THROUGH LIBERATING

INVENT YOURSELF   LONG-DISTANCE LOVE

Security is gained through liberation, which means that idealistically you aspire to be free of negative emotions such as greed, fear, anger, jealousy etc. But you should be careful not simply to pretend that you are so, for this can lead to others' expecting you to be impossibly tolerant of their negative emotions. As Aquarius is the Sign of Humanity, with the Moon placed in it you should remember to be merely human, and not more than human. Being unaware of your feelings and natural instincts can mean that you will attract quite drastic upheavals and confrontations, as your unconscious mind makes a bid to get you in touch with who you truly are, as opposed to who you like to think you are.

Emotional experiences of your mother and your childhood have often been disruptive, alienating or out of the ordinary. Although these also helped to get you in touch with your individual feelings, they also probably initially distanced you from so-called normal social interplay. Thus you began to become an observer of rather than a participant in life, which gave you an awareness of human nature. Now, as the natural psychologist or counsellor, you are sought after, professionally or personally, for your fitting and impartial advice.

Another type of emotional response peculiar to Moon in Aquarius is usually experienced in adolescence, but leaves its mark for years to come. This is the inclination to think of yourself as more emotional than you in fact are, with the result that you become romantically attracted to others who are indifferent or unavailable in some way. This pattern persists until you realize that you are trying too hard, and that it is your own air of unavailability that is so attractive. However, this can be carried to the extreme where you are emotionally unreachable, and thus remain attracted to the unattainable or far-distant.

An important need of yours is to have a lover as a friend. It is vital for you to be able to share and to discuss views and feelings on an intellectual level. Until this kind of relationship is attained, you tend to be happier in a group situation, rather than an intimate one. In this way you are able to disguise or to forget your emotional fears, as things can be kept light and breezy. For this reason, a group situation is best for getting you in touch with your feelings. You can then get back into the one-to-one scene with a renewed sense that it is all right to be an emotional being.

Your need for freedom of expression is ever-present, and will consistently jolt others, as well as yourself, out of any complacency that has built up through mere illusions of freedom. This can produce much mood-swinging and unpredictability, but with an Aquarian Moon you know that in order to be moved to liberation, one first has to be stirred, if not shaken.

LIKES
Being unique · Openness
The unusual · Clear minds
Keeping cool

DISLIKES
Being ordinary · Emotional
confinement · Stick-in-the-muds
Over-emotionalism · Show-offs

If you are a man, this could be the kind of woman to whom you are attracted – but it is really you, so realize it and express it.

THE MOON IN AQUARIUS

TRANSFORMER

POSITIVE	NEGATIVE
Impartial Dispassionate Broad-minded Candid	Impersonal Not earthed Indiscriminate Insubstantial
Courteous Friendly Human Good listener	Artificial Superficial Unreal Unresponsive
Reformist Progressive Intuitive Individualistic	Rebellious Unpredictable Insensitive Misfit
Own person Paradoxical Knowing Open	Stubborn Perverse Know-all Closed
Observant Cool Unbiased Detached	Aloof Icy Non-committal Remote
Look and you will see that there are others just as far out as you think you are. Befriend them.	It begins to bother you that you only seem to enjoy your "freedom" on your own.
Knowing and accepting that feelings are irrational is your ticket to freedom.	Having both fixed ideas and a liberal attitude gives both you and others a tense time.
Your personal view of the world is both your cue and your clue to bettering it, not beating it.	At odds with yourself, you secretly dwell on the chances of getting even.
Remember: what you really like about people is that they belong to the same species as you.	Feeling very unsure of what you are feeling. Unable to show yourself.
Choose a standpoint that allows you to be fair and comfortable with yourself.	The unbearable lightness of being. Feeling that you are not quite here.
SOLUTION	PROBLEM

69

If you find yourself on the receiving end of negative traits, it is because you are not expressing the opposing positive traits.

THE MOON IN PISCES

ESSENCE

SECURITY THROUGH ACCEPTING

GOT TO HAVE A DREAM   THE SOUL OF SENSITIVITY

Of all the Moon-Sign positions, this one has the acutest emotional sensitivity – and, consequently, the most complex responses to life situations. You find a million and one ways to enhance or to evade whatever might present itself to your super-receptive nature.

Most positively, you have the qualities of the healer, poet or mystic. Most negatively, you are inclined to experience the refined senses that make this possible as a distaste for mundane existence and thus you seek to escape it. The notion of "what you could be" is endlessly used as a means of keeping you in a fascinated state of being neither special nor ordinary. Owing to childhood feelings of being "a fish out of water", you wind up "at sea". But when you truly embark upon a creative or spiritual quest, your fertile imagination is capable of transporting you (and others) to rare heights, and depths, of human experience. Fantasizing about such things as high hopes or morbid fears involves the illusion of not getting hurt. However, this is, in fact, a delusion, for you still feel pain even – or most of all – in your imagination. So eventually you pursue, or through some real crisis are forced to pursue, the lofty role that you originally envisaged falling into your lap. In effect, with a Piscean Moon you need a vision of a better life for one and all that not only will act as a focus for all your compassion, imagination and sensitivity, but also is practically attainable. Otherwise your fantasy overdrive will continue to get you nowhere.

You are malleable, seductive and seductable, and looking for a "dreamboat" to take you away on the morning tide. Your imagination is, in fact, so vivid that this dreamboat actually appears to arrive. However, after a few months or years at sea, the dream evaporates and by contrast you seem to be living off hard-tack biscuits and brackish water – that is, your partner seems boring and emotionally tainted. In fact, of course, neither extreme was real; the ordinary, but sad and beautiful human being is what is real – which, naturally, includes yourself.

Not surprisingly you can have an addictive personality, be it to drink, drugs, cream cakes, seafood, men with beards or girls in turquoise rubber. An addiction is essentially a distraction; you are pulled towards something that your Soul desires, but because this poses a real sacrifice, you opt for the phoney sacrifice of throwing yourself away on something self-destructive, dissipating, fetishistic or insidiously inconsequential. However, sooner or later, you will have to go for the Soul's desire – no other drug will do. Poetically enough, that desire will eventually entail the relief or guidance of those mortals who, similarly, have lost sight of their Soul's desire. So rather than looking for a dreamboat, you become a lifeboat.

LIKES
Highs and lows
Music and poetry · The fascinating
Romantic quests · Taking off

DISLIKES
The commonplace
Aesthetic starvation · The obvious
Confronting reality · Coming down

If you are a man, this could be the kind of woman to whom you are attracted – but it is really you, so realize it and express it.

THE MOON IN PISCES

TRANSFORMER

POSITIVE	NEGATIVE
Imaginative	Escapist
Inspiring	Deceptive
Mystical	Spaced out
Creative	Wool-gathering
Empathetic	Impressionable
Psychic	Too open
Compassionate	Hypersensitive
Mediumistic	Easily drained
Devoted	Idolatrous
Highly adaptable	Self-doubting
Amiable	Seductable
Romantic	Unfaithful
Selfless	Weak-willed
Kind	Indiscriminate
Healer	Victim
Yielding	Leaf-in-the-wind
Tolerant	Too easygoing
Gentle	Weak
Relaxed	Lazy
Understanding	Excuse-making

Making fewer allowances for shortcomings increases the value of your virtues.	Life has lost its shape and direction. Procrastination is stealing all your time.
Offer your services to an institution/ movement that works quietly to relieve others.	Easily exploited and forced to carry the can for others, because you do not carry your own.
Look for the highest quality that you can find in yourself and develop it.	A slave to your senses and fantasies. Resentment grows as does your dependency.
Learn to locate – protect – use – your chakras or energy centres and they will serve, not sap you.	Prone to infection and invasion by lower astral phenomena. Easily irritated or upset.
Use your imagination or it will use you. Build castles in the air, but don't move in.	Confusion, self-pity and bitterness reign. Drug and alcohol abuse. Discontented.

SOLUTION	PROBLEM

If you find yourself on the receiving end of negative traits, it is because you are not expressing the opposing positive traits.

MERCURY

Keyword: THINKING

Mercury, the Messenger of the Gods, symbolizes your ability to CONNECT one thing to or with another – most particularly in your head, as RATIONAL THINKING, in your body, as your NERVOUS SYSTEM, and, externally, via COMMUNICATION, PERCEPTION and DEXTERITY.

So your Mercury-Sign tells you how well and in what manner you think and communicate, what your nervous disposition is, how well "WIRED" you are, and your capacity to LEARN on an INTELLECTUAL level.

Negatively, Mercury can be expressed as OVER-RATIONALIZATION, which leads to DRYNESS and a LACK OF FEELING, which in turn can give rise to NERVOUSNESS.

Your Mercury-Sign can also give some indication of the kind of work that suits your MENTALITY, thereby providing clues to fruitful areas of EMPLOYMENT for both your MIND and your HANDS.

MERCURY IN ARIES

ESSENCE

THINKING THROUGH DOING

THE WRANGLER	ACTION SPEAKS LOUDER THAN WORDS

Yours is a mind that has to be active, and wants thoughts and words to become deeds rather than be left merely in the realm of ideas. So firstly, it is important for you to receive not only mental stimulation but also challenges, and secondly, it will probably be necessary to remain mindful of the fact that it takes time for an idea or an aim to be realized.

You have a terrier-like mentality that gets hold of a thought, word, idea or piece of information, and wants to push it forward as if it is the most important thing in the world. Positively, this signifies an ability to learn, communicate or teach quickly and effectively; it also confers on you a flair for selling. However, negatively, you can have a one-sided point of view and a tendency to make decisions and form opinions before all the facts available have been considered. For this reason, it should be no surprise that there can be a lack of follow-through with certain projects.

Your brisk and headstrong mentality is just as disinclined to dwell on old grievances as on outworn interests. This gives an impression of broad-mindedness, when it is actually more a case of not having the time or room for stuffy thoughts or feelings.

Without enough mental input or assertion of your intellectual outlook, there is a danger of nervous or physical restlessness that can develop into more serious mental or emotional conditions, with circumstances to match. You should never be afraid to argue a point, but you should also be aware that although arguing for its own sake will release tensions of the moment, it might simultaneously provoke in others antagonism that creates further tension. Your bellicose brain runs according to the formula that there is no stimulation without some aggravation, which is fine as long as you learn that the secret is to be good-hearted and to respect your opponent for being your opponent.

Needless to say, you often speak before thinking, which leads to your making *faux pas* at times, and coming refreshingly right to the point at others. At some stage it is more than likely that you will have to "make the running", in the sense of taking the initiative workwise, setting a precedent, going out on a limb, or rattling a few cages in your neighbourhood. This is unavoidable in order for you to make some progress – or merely to get out from under.

LIKES
Hot debate · Intellectual competition
Immediate reactions · Brain-teasers
Straight talking

DISLIKES
Delays · Lack of opposition
Slowcoaches · Mind-games
Pussy-footing

Mercury is your tool for making connections and getting leads.

MERCURY IN ARIES

TRANSFORMER

POSITIVE	NEGATIVE
Quick-thinking Spontaneous Quick-acting Decisive	Impatient Irritable Quick-tempered Premature
Mentally forceful Stimulating Fighting spirit Fiery	Headstrong Hectoring Quarrelsome Spitting
Frank Witty To the point Observant	Thoughtless Sarcastic Terse Precocious
Initiates ideas Thinks on feet Mentally active and agile	Snap opinions Snap decisions Verbally/mentally restless
Eloquent Verbally assertive Intellectually confident	Strident One-sided viewpoint Intellectually arrogant
Your tongue is a sensitive muscle; hold it and appreciate what it's attached to.	Carried away by your own verbal powers, you're now overworked and your concentration is flagging.
You'd enjoy your mental muscles more if you flexed them less often. Where's the fire?	On a moving mental pavement and you can't get off. Nervy and bordering on the hysterical.
Add a dash of humility to your candour and others will more readily take your point.	Later regretting what you have said. Failing to cover this up with more blustering.
Make sure you have a cause to match your force. Be aware of your contentiousness.	You probably don't spot it, but others get out of your way when they see you coming.
Slow down enough to clarify your objectives, then trust that you'll rise to the occasion.	Out of step with yourself. Competing with yourself. Strife at work.
SOLUTION	PROBLEM

75

If you find yourself on the receiving end of negative traits, it is because you are not expressing the opposing positive traits.

MERCURY IN TAURUS

ESSENCE

THINKING THROUGH STABILIZING

THE CONCRETE MIND   SEEING IS BELIEVING

Yours is a mind that likes to chew things over, and so you acquire depth of knowledge as a result of thoroughly enjoying the process of learning – rather as you would a good meal. A taste for the traditional rather than the newfangled is also in evidence. Once you have learnt and assimilated something, you will probably never forget it. However, should an idea come along that challenges an already existing concept, you are very reluctant to accept it. You are slow to form opinions, and equally slow to change them.

You are materially-minded, which means that you are a practical thinker and are not too happy with total abstractions. If it is really necessary mentally to digest complex theories, they are more easily understood when expressed or taught in a visual or a practical way.

In money matters you are either efficient, sometimes to the point of being a bit miserly, or lazy, at the price of someone else holding the purse-strings. This depends on the particular set of values that you are used to, and at some time or other these may be the very values that have to be changed.

As your mind works at a natural pace, you develop steady working habits, and are therefore thorough and produce solid results. Tasks are performed evenly from start to finish. From a more philosophical or spiritual point of view, your intellectual role in life is to keep matters of the mind running on an even keel, and to prevent the waste of resources through unwise investments and impractical ideas. For this reason, you can also make a good manager.

Dependable and reassuring as your conservative way of thinking is, if it is carried to extremes in resisting change, others might have to resort to more emotional methods of making their point. If you, in turn, regard this as unreasonable or even underhand, you are really asking to get buried in the very rut in which you insist on staying. With Mercury in Taurus it is supremely sensible to guard against your firm grip on concrete reality's setting into mental obstinacy.

Above all you have the gift of being able to see how any plan will work out – if at all – in physical terms. And so you have a natural bent towards arts and crafts, and also towards construction skills such as carpentry and building. Quite simply, yours is the kind of mind that gives value for money – or for any other kind of energy.

LIKES
Common sense · Good workmanship
Peace of mind · Time to ponder
Concrete evidence

DISLIKES
Airy-theory · Practical ineptitude
Being badgered · Deadlines
Blind faith

Mercury is your tool for making connections and getting leads.

MERCURY IN TAURUS

TRANSFORMER

POSITIVE	NEGATIVE
Sound mind Thorough Patient Cautious	Slow mind Plodding Tardy Guarded
Shrewd Resourceful Sensible Realistic	Mean-minded Money-grubbing Boneheaded Purblind
Good concentration Mentally sure Deliberating	Blinkered One-track-minded Overburdened
Practical thinker Sense of form Steady mind Enduring	Limited thinker Mechanistic Stubborn mind Stodgy
Mentally laid-back Docile Ruminating Undemanding	Lazy-minded Dumb Misses point Couch potato
Give your wholesome mind something wholesome – and worthwhile – to chew on.	Feeling uncomfortably stuck in one of life's intellectual lay-bys.
Regard your strong concrete thinking as a foil or foundation to others' wilder ideas.	You find it hard to understand or accept abstract concepts and so reject them.
Take definite steps to add another string to your bow. Retrain.	Dissatisfied with your working life. Overworked and underemployed.
You have the ability to master money – by conquering your fear or love of it.	The material world gives you, or those with whom you are financially involved, a headache.
Take your time, and use visual aids to brush up on those areas of knowledge that you are unsure of.	Difficulty in grasping subjects that threaten to ridicule you.
SOLUTION	PROBLEM

If you find yourself on the receiving end of negative traits, it is because you are not expressing the opposing positive traits.

MERCURY IN GEMINI

ESSENCE

THINKING THROUGH COMMUNICATING

WIZARD OR SMART ALEC   THE ECLECTIC

Your mind is fed and furthered through making contact with as many people and as many subjects as possible. Your intellect is all wired up and raring to go; it more or less constantly needs to be occupied, otherwise nervous irritability or feeling restlessly at a loose end can result. Your brain, hands and nervous system can be likened to a highly sophisticated piece of electrical equipment. If there is not enough "output" the whole thing gets too hot and a circuit blows. Your mind is efficient in that it is quick and acquisitive, but the quality of it is only as good as what is being fed into it via social, business and educational pursuits. Mercury in Gemini can be an eloquent speaker or a gossip, clever or facile, fluent or flippant. What you read and who you mix with have everything to do with this, so "input" is just as important as output. Because you are quick-witted and articulate – no matter what anyone says – and because you possess a natural sense of curiosity, you should have no trouble in finding suitable friends and employment – once you put your mind to it!

You are capable of thinking on two or more levels at once, which can make you a whiz at work or at play. However, if there is not some serious direction or intention given to such mental acrobatics, there is a danger of your mind becoming confused in a sort of mental traffic jam. You require an absorbing and ongoing interest that has some emotional content that will keep your agile mind from revolving on its own spot and prevent your suffering from scattered energies, divided attention, or a lack of continuity of purpose.

You usually have a friendly attitude, for you are naturally interested in all walks of life. Such a light and unbiased touch is welcome in almost every place, and you would be wise to capitalize on this. This typically Mercurial talent for being able to talk about anything at any time anywhere stands you in good stead for activities that require this contact-making ability, such as journalism, publicity, buying and selling, transport, courier work etc. You are also proficient in the use of all basic mental functions, like communications and mathematics, and are naturally logical and dextrous – only some serious pathological affliction would contradict this.

Above all is that need to have a motivation or goal that organizes your undeniable dexterity and mental versatility. Then, rather than learning parrot-fashion and acquiring knowledge merely for its own sake, your mind becomes your servant and not a tyrannical master or rogue who blinds you to the fact that it is not so much a product or an end in itself, but rather a shining multi-purpose tool which you hold, so to speak, in your hands, to use as you see fit.

LIKES
Mental stimulation · Facts and figures
A quick turnover · Getting around
Intellectual style

DISLIKES
Intellectual deserts · Biased opinions
Slow thinking · Being tied down
Dead-heads

Mercury is your tool for making connections and getting leads.

MERCURY IN GEMINI

TRANSFORMER

POSITIVE	NEGATIVE
Articulate Curious Well-informed Widely read	Chatterbox Nosy Gossip Superficial knowledge
Quick-witted Lively mind Fast learner Dextrous	Highly strung Unruly mind Unpersevering Fidgety
Clever Humorous Sharp Fluent	Crafty Mischievous Flippant Facile
Inventive Versatile Original Handy	Makeshift Slipshod Imitative Simplistic
Interesting Agreeable Unbiased Logical	Trite Scatters energies Unfocused Misses point
Obviously you can only go in one direction – your own. This is what influences others.	Apparently going along with everyone while obviously no one goes along with you.
Do one thing at a time, well; then do another, better – as only you can.	Much that you do either falls apart or never comes together.
Learn to put and keep levity and gravity in their appropriate places.	Others either distrust you or fail to take you seriously.
Make your undeniably keen mind your servant, not your master. Learn correct breathing.	Irritable, irritated and irritating. Nervy. Working agitatedly. Unfinished tasks.
Respect the value and efficiency of your own mind: watch what goes into it and what comes out of it.	Triviaphilia: knowing a little about everything and a lot about nothing.

If you find yourself on the receiving end of negative traits, it is because you are not expressing the opposing positive traits.

MERCURY IN CANCER

ESSENCE

THINKING THROUGH NURTURING

THE CARING MIND   KNOW YOUR FEELERS

It is said that the eyes are actually an extension of the brain, but with Mercury in Cancer it is rather as if you have a set of feelers, like a moth ...or a crab...that pick up the thoughts and feelings around you in a super-sensitive fashion. Because of this you need to take great care how you receive such information, and not to take everything personally; you also need to remind yourself to look at the facts rather than the opinions of the people concerned. These precautions would also help guard against being conditioned by having taken on board the erroneous ideas of others, which, left unchecked, can give rise to problems whose roots are hard to detect at a later date. In fact you are quite adept at sensing whether someone is genuine or not by the sound of their voice.

Positively speaking, such a sympathetic mind as yours can make you an effective speaker, as you can tune in to the listener's emotional and mental state. The way you speak and what you say have a "stroking" quality that is persuasive and therapeutic. All of this mental sensitivity, your feelers, is due to your conscious mind being very close to the unconscious. You draw upon your awareness of what makes anything or anyone feel looked after and are able to express it – or deny it. It is, therefore, very important that such a talent is guided by a strong set of ethics, and is used with a constructive purpose in mind. Without this kind of deliberate intention to employ your feelers in some positive way, you are merely suggestible and prey to being or to feeling manipulated – consequently you yourself feel tempted to manipulate. The vicious circle of suspicion that this hatches is the polar opposite of the reassuring atmosphere that you are capable of creating, be it in a home environment, with your sheer physical presence, or whatever. Put another way, if you are aware of your own source of light and warmth, you are less likely to be drawn, like a moth, into someone else's flame.

Not surprisingly, you have a good memory – that serves and disserves. Conversations can be remembered almost word for word, and you can yank to the surface long "forgotten" information in times of need. As long as you learn to let go of painful feelings and not to nurse them like a sore tooth, your memory will serve you well.

Fundamentally, you are concerned with creating good memories, which is a thought worth remembering in itself! Whereas bad memories create bad feelings which in turn lead to narrow and defensive thinking, collecting good memories through the caring use of your sensitive mind gives rise to good feelings, and to clear, positive thinking.

LIKES
Gentle interactions · Sentimental surroundings · Collecting (old things) · Reminiscing · Local interests

DISLIKES
Verbal violence · Unfamiliar territory
Breaks in continuity · Changing attitudes
Language barriers

Mercury is your tool for making connections and getting leads.

MERCURY IN CANCER

TRANSFORMER

POSITIVE	NEGATIVE
Mentally tenacious Good memory Reliable	Mentally habit-ridden Distracted Inflexible
Sensitive mind Poetic Intuitive Agreeable	Impressionable Impractical Irrational Yes-person
Absorbs information Attuned to public opinion Profound	Too open Taking things too personally Depressive
Polite Softly-spoken Discreet Diplomatic	Self-conscious Unclear Incomprehensible Diffuse
Arouses sympathies Emotionally appealing Persuasive speaker	Prejudiced Capricious Untruthful
Your natural ability to influence others is worthy of only the highest motives.	A failure to look at the truth is followed by a failure to recognize it.
Reassure others of your doubts and intentions and they will be happy to reassure you.	Insecurity owing to difficulty in getting to the root of a problem. Foggy-brained.
A mind like yours is sensitive to bigger issues, so it must address itself to same.	Mentally confused and easily upset. Distraught and not quite knowing why.
Tuning in to your finer feelings and expressing them is bound to be rewarding.	So susceptible to the opinions of others, you rarely know your own mind.
Remember what you are after, who you are with and why – and stick with it.	Frustration as a result of clinging to outworn ideas and attitudes.
SOLUTION	PROBLEM

69

If you find yourself on the receiving end of negative traits, it is because you are not expressing the opposing positive traits.

MERCURY IN LEO

ESSENCE

THINKING THROUGH CREATING

| THE IDEAS PERSON | HONOUR YOUR CRITICS |

With Mercury in Leo you are, or should be, proud of your intellectual talents and capabilities. Because your mind is, so to speak, close to your heart, you show great passion and strength, as well as originality, in the manner in which you think and communicate. But Leo, like all the Fire Signs, is actually quite often as insecure as it appears to be the opposite, that is, confident. This can lead to either your coming on too strong when expressing your ideas and opinions, or, conversely, your underestimating the power of your mind, and not making it clear either to yourself or to others what is going on in your head. In the first case you would be inclined to ignore any negative feedback, and in the latter, you would be paralysingly oversensitive to criticism.

Mercury, which symbolizes the logical ability to see things merely as they are, functions best when it is cool and detached from the ego, whose bias is towards getting what it thinks it wants. But this is difficult in self-conscious Leo, where your personal aims and intentions seem to be all-important, and other factors of far less importance. The danger here is that such egocentricity wants to bat and bowl at the same time, and so you cannot win because you are also busily but unconsciously trying to defeat yourself. The answer lies in finding a balance between the two extremes described above. Firstly, you can use your pronounced talent for mental concentration to focus upon the enthusiasm and vitality that is roaring away inside you, and which can so easily radiate warmth and wit in much of what you say and do. And secondly, like a wise king or queen – for you have a regal mind – you can take heed of the advice or comments given by trusted friends and associates. If they won't speak their minds to your face for fear of having their heads bitten off – or simply being ignored – they could well turn into your enemies, creep up behind you, and pinch your ideas! You would then have good reason to feel unappreciated. People soon give up trying to help someone who always thinks he/she knows better. On the other hand, combining your obviously creative and enterprising mind with an awareness of the ideas and attitudes of the other people involved in your drama will benefit everyone – and not least of all your own projects.

After all, you tackle problems imaginatively and energetically. You are also able to teach effectively because you encourage interest in a subject through your creative and dramatic treatment of it. The way you speak has authority built into it, and so others will automatically take you seriously. You have so many good ideas that giving them away and allowing them to be mixed with and slightly altered by the input of others will strengthen and enrich them. Rather than being a frustrated one-person show, your mind will thus become the vital spark that ignites a greater group endeavour.

LIKES
Artistic pursuits · Being your own boss
Combining work with pleasure · A positive
reaction · A creative purpose

DISLIKES
Lack of recreation · Being answerable
to others · Not having your own work-space
Dull people · A meaningless production line

Mercury is your tool for making connections and getting leads.

MERCURY IN LEO

TRANSFORMER

POSITIVE	NEGATIVE
Mentally creative Distinctive verbal style Warmly articulate	Mentally conceited Likes sound of own voice Voluble
Identifies with popular ideas Grasps whole issue Intellectually confident	Only interested in own ideas Overlooks details Mentally arrogant
Focused concentration Fixed intentions Continuity of purpose Enthusiastic worker	Inflexible mind Stubborn and one-track mind Self-centred Feels superior at work
Convincing speaker Outspoken and optimistic Knows own mind	Craves appreciation Verbally overbearing Self-conscious
Teaching and planning ability Foresight Executive mind	Talks at others Wrapped up in pet projects and theories
Remember you teach what you wish to learn. Do your plans include others' plans?	Losing your place in midstream – falling from grace in midscheme.
You owe it to yourself to stand or fall by what you say and how you say it.	Compensating for fear of humiliation by saying too much or too little.
With your strong and creative mind, you could and should diversify your interests.	Trapped by putting all your eggs in one basket, especially at work.
Never ignore that "still small voice" that plays such a vital part in the greater whole.	Projects falling apart at the seams, stitch by stitch. Lack of cohesiveness.
What springs from your lips is only as good as what dwells in your heart.	Turning around one day, you find that no one is listening to you.
SOLUTION	PROBLEM

83

If you find yourself on the receiving end of negative traits, it is because you are not expressing the opposing positive traits.

MERCURY IN VIRGO

ESSENCE

THINKING THROUGH ANALYSING

THE WORDSMITH   THE PURE MIND

It is very unlikely that you lack intelligence, with Mercury placed in Virgo. The ability to reason functions well and easily in this precise and analytical Sign. Its failing is simply due to the fact that you find it easier to think than anything else — and than most other people, too. And so you can come to live in your head and not realize it, forgetting that there is a big difference between knowledge and experience. You can also be critical of others' lesser mental powers (how could they be otherwise?!), but this overlooks the fact that what they may be lacking intellectually is more than made up for by their emotional qualities.

Your amazing analytical ability tells you that everything has its place — hopefully including your amazing analytical ability! In other words, you have the mind of the specialist and are able to excel in your chosen field of work because you make it your business to know precisely how a given thing operates. But at the same time it would be a mistake to apply your specialist knowledge to all other spheres of life. Brilliant as it is, the way you think is just the way you think, not the way of the world. This point is worth pondering, for your preoccupation with thinking life is only as you see it can give you much cause for anxiety, especially with regard to being more critical of yourself than of anyone else. In truth, what you are seeking is as clear a mental viewpoint as possible, with an absolute minimum of prejudice and misinformation. For this reason, you are particularly good at helping others to see more clearly. This can, of course, take many forms: writing, editing, counselling, teaching, drawing, translating, to name just a few.

Very little avoids your perceptive gaze, and your computer-like memory is very valuable. You are able to assimilate vast amounts of complex information and then represent it in a far more digestible form, with all repetitions and non-essentials removed. But, curiously, when it comes to expressing something close to your heart, you can obscure the very point that you are attempting to make with all manner of irrelevant references and dead-end data. At the top of each of your many lists there should be a reminder of exactly what you wish to express.

Having such a marvellous mental potential as yours, it is rather important that initially you gain a thorough grasp of a specific subject. Without training or education you are liable to suffer far more than others from being unemployed, underemployed or unemployable. However, paradoxically, the ultimate objective of your tidy mind is to tidy itself away, which means that eventually you appreciate that what gets in the way of understanding life is thinking about it too much. A totally clear mind is no mind at all.

LIKES
Reading · Knowledge
Mental clarity · Mental freedom
Being occasionally crazy

DISLIKES
Idle conversation · Wasting time
Woolly thinking · Intellectual regimentation
Being constantly reasonable

Mercury is your tool for making connections and getting leads.

MERCURY IN VIRGO

TRANSFORMER

POSITIVE	NEGATIVE
Analytical Objective Systematic Logical	Unfeeling Remote Clinical Cold and dry
Discerning Precise Meticulous Clever	Hypercritical Pedantic Trivial Worrisome
Eloquent Well-read Well-informed Accurate	Wordy Bookish Intellectual snob Misses point
Retentive memory Fast learner Highly efficient Good worker	Greedy mind Impatient Highly strung Workaholic
Modest Matter-of-fact Helpful Practical	Self-critical Sceptical Slave (to reason) Pointless
Mysterious axiom: the justification for just being what you are is just being what you are.	Trapped on the treadmill of trying to prove what cannot be proven. Nothing rhymes.
Remember the old formula for health: work, rest (give others some, too) and play.	Mentally overloaded. Irritated by your intolerance of your own and others' fallibility.
The point you wish to make: remember it, research it, rehearse it – then express it.	With all your hard work, others still do not appreciate what you say or do. Scorned even.
Make the best of what you know, and trust what you do not know to look after itself.	Not seeing the wood for the trees, you spend some lonely nights in the forest.
It's easy for you to work out that you are not just a mind, albeit a fine one.	Knowing everything and feeling nothing; others know what you think but not what you feel.
SOLUTION	PROBLEM

If you find yourself on the receiving end of negative traits, it is because you are not expressing the opposing positive traits.

MERCURY IN LIBRA

ESSENCE

THINKING THROUGH RELATING

| THE SPOKESPERSON | AGREE TO DIFFER |

It is said that if Moses had formed a committee, the Children of Israel would still be in Egypt! So he probably did not have Mercury in Libra – but, then again, maybe he did, because when expressed positively this Planetary placement results in the ability to consider all the facts, and then to make a decision or lay down a law that is just and equitable. However, its weakness is to get stuck at the stage of forming that consensus of opinion, which gives rise to interminable stalemate situations in which no one feels satisfied or justified.

As the way you think is based largely on how you feel in relating to others, you are inclined, naturally enough, to agree at the expense of failing to contact how you yourself actually feel about a given issue. This results in the person to whom you relate most intimately becoming frustrated through not knowing which side of the fence you're on. What they don't see is that you are striving to keep the peace amongst a wide variety of people and opinions. However, the point that any close associate is trying to make is that you have to have a yardstick of your own, otherwise no one will get your measure, and consequently will find you hard to take seriously. And this would be a shame, considering that your decision – when finally made – is the one most likely to be the fairest.

You have the style to make another see things your way – and to get them to see things from a third party's point of view. But in your bid to gain approval, do not forget that it is your actual sense of justice that carries the weight, rather than having someone agree with you. Others are aware of your fair mind, and either they will seek to take advantage of it and to get you on their side, or they will respect it – therefore, so must you. The kind of work that suits a mind such as yours includes anything that requires an awareness of how people tick – something that fascinates you: public relations, politics, psychology, law, sociology, to name but a few. A guideline for you could be "anything that appeals to the masses" – a phrase worth pondering.

What underlies much of your thinking is a desire for agreement. As you like to be honest – or like to be seen to be honest – reflecting upon what exactly it is that you want others to agree to is vitally important in order to maintain the integrity that you hold so dear. If this is vague, then others will also feel vague about what you are proposing. On the other hand, because you are so keen on mental balance and order, you can overlook the fact that others are not as disciplined in this respect as you. As others look to you for wise counsel, what or who you look to yourself hinges on something holy.

LIKES
An honest reputation · Refined minds
Good manners · Moral justice
Learning through others

DISLIKES
Being underestimated · Mob rule
Uncouthness · Rough justice
No one to talk with

Mercury is your tool for making connections and getting leads.

MERCURY IN LIBRA

TRANSFORMER

POSITIVE	NEGATIVE
Agreeable Flexible Diplomatic Prudent	Yes-person Weak-minded Non-committal Turncoat
Persuasive Charming Well-spoken Communicative	Smooth-talking Insincere Affected Prattling
Hardworking Disciplined Scholarly Orderly	Rat-racer Blindly obedient Doctrinaire Officious
Eclectic Fair judge Good arbitrator Reasonable	Unoriginal Insipid Indecisive Banal
Team-spirited Principled Honourable Open-minded	Sheep-like Cowardly Phoney Vacuous

Mentally striving to uphold your heartfelt principles inspires others.	The people who matter to you are wondering whether you matter to them.
Remember that your talent for deliberating is wholly in aid of making a fair decision.	To be honest, you often bore yourself. To be even more honest, others are bored by you.
There is! As long as the spirit of the law supersedes the letter of the law.	Secretly a voice in your head echoes: "There has to be more to life than this!"
Make sure that your brilliant patter is matched by what you are promoting.	The more convincing you pretend to be, the emptier you feel inside.
Meeting others halfway is a good starting point for negotiations.	Torn between toeing the line and putting your best foot forward.

SOLUTION	PROBLEM

If you find yourself on the receiving end of negative traits, it is because you are not expressing the opposing positive traits.

MERCURY IN SCORPIO

ESSENCE

THINKING THROUGH DESIRING

X-RAY EYES   THE SLEUTH

What you want and what you fear are heavily entwined in your mind. This is because such a profound and probing intellect as yours is quite likely to have attracted attacks from others who have seen it as a threat. Such antagonists in your past may very well have been those who should have known better, like teachers or anyone else who had authority over you – even older brothers or sisters.

The essential point here is that yours is a mind that sees through people and situations, and as such can be satisfyingly employed digging out anything of trouble or of interest. This can include many occupations, but particularly favours psychological, political, research or detective work. However, if you are ruled by a hidden agenda of emotional vulnerability caused by the above-described intellectual disempowerment, you can misuse your own powers by stabbing at others' tender spots in order to pre-empt their having a poke at you first. This ensures that you are never insipid and that you have a mind of your own, but such cunning defensiveness can turn your mental state into a police state.

Your delving mind does not miss many tricks – hopefully including your own. This failing of Mercury in Scorpio to suspect malice of intent where there is none, can give rise to mental convolutions that are almost impossible to work out – except, maybe, for Mercury in Scorpio! Perhaps you create intrigue in order to keep your mind on its stealthy toes, which is fine just as long as you do not get foiled by your own mental swordplay. Looked at another way, yours is a fundamentally sharp and efficient mind as there is always something that needs looking into – and you cannot resist – so your mental muscle is constantly exercised.

However, learning to leave well enough alone is a talent that you also have, or that you should develop. This is a sign of real mental power and superiority. Equally, you are able to wait and watch silently which can be quite unnerving for others. In this way your insight is sharpened and confidential information is mysteriously absorbed.

Providing that they do not have the emotional truth unceremoniously thrust upon them (as a kind of indirect revenge on your part), other people benefit greatly from your penetrating insight. However, this is only one hundred per cent effective when you are not involved personally – keenness is therefore dependent upon detachment. This means that you are happiest when not ruled by personal fears and phobias, because they cloud your judgement. So with Mercury in Scorpio your powers of perception are ultimately proven by eliminating your own mental twists and ruses.

LIKES
Brain-teasers · Mental control
Intrigues · Smoke-screens
Cut and thrust

DISLIKES
Mental inactivity · Weak-mindedness
Lack of subtlety · Fudged issues
Mincing words

Mercury is your tool for making connections and getting leads.

MERCURY IN SCORPIO

TRANSFORMER

POSITIVE	NEGATIVE
Sharp Incisive Subtle Satirical	Cutting Acidic Sneaky Sarcastic
Perceptive Penetrating mind Stealthy Audacious	Suspicious Paranoid Intrusive Abusive
Accurate Investigative Punchy Emphatic	Uncharitable Grilling Scathing Overstated
Determined Good concentration Quick-minded Dextrous	Argumentative Mentally tense Presumptuous Meddlesome
Profound Confidant(e) Insightful Strategic	Incomprehensible Secretive Devious Scheming

Secrecy is an art – not a game.	Your intrigues have become tangled webs that mystify you more than anyone else.
Use your ability to leave no stone unturned in order to find what you're really after – yourself.	Living on your nerves, you start at shadows – your own. Anxiety creates itself.
Pick a target worth your beady eyes. Push an idea worth your mental weight.	Deflating others' ideas and inflating your own is distrust that breeds distrust.
Your mental powers can transform your fear of being found out into a desire to find out.	It is no fun being on a 24-hour alert, and keeping on the outside what's already on the inside.
Just because you're able to get to the bottom of things, there's no need to be a creep.	All that acid is giving you indigestion, and your wit has sunk out of sight.

SOLUTION	PROBLEM

89

If you find yourself on the receiving end of negative traits, it is because you are not expressing the opposing positive traits.

MERCURY IN SAGITTARIUS

ESSENCE

THINKING THROUGH SEEKING

THE ETERNAL STUDENT   EYES OF WONDER

You have a broad and active mind that is capable of cultivating itself and being aware of many different aspects of life. Work could or should involve travelling around or mixing with a wide assortment of people; and you should avoid being stuffed away in some corner. If there is no focus to the knowledge and experience that you readily gather, so that it becomes a personal philosophy of life, you are likely to have merely a scattered collection of disconnected thoughts and ideas.

Yours is a seeking mind; it is looking for a meaning to life – with and without the joky connotation of such a pursuit. In fact, your sense of humour is second to none, for you appreciate that anything worth seeking had better be fun, too. For the same reason you make a wonderful travelling companion along the road of life. In the process of seeking, your mind can get involved with many different schools of thought, yet avoids settling for a "ready-made" philosophy or belief system.

This mental or physical roaming gives you a feel for how society and human thought are developing. On the one hand, this bestows on you a prophetic insight and a sense of history; on the other, it can pose merely as being fashionable. So your mind has the makings of anything from a creator of religious, social or political opinion, to just being hip to the latest craze.

You speak your mind, and this is refreshing for it clears the air and allows you to see where you stand with others, and where they stand both with you and with themselves. At first such candour as you possess can give rise to embarrassing situations, but the essential fact is that you have lifted a matter out of the fog that obscures the truth, and have thereby created the opportunity to see things more clearly and to breathe more freely. Getting things off your chest is very important to you, otherwise you can have difficulties with breathing or with communication. However, equally, you are inclined to say too much. This is due mainly just to enthusiasm on your part, but others could read it as being gushing and mentally undisciplined – and they may have a point. Nevertheless, you have a lofty line of reasoning that can be an inspiration to others. At the same time you should be aware that to many people your far-sighted ideas border on the barmy, at least, or are just plain hypocritical, if you are committing your cardinal sin of being all mouth and no action.

Fundamentally, yours is a "native intelligence" which is instinctively filled with wonder at all the world has to offer. To you, everything is there for the finding. With just the right amount of schooling, your natural mind has the world to offer – and to teach, in return.

LIKES
Mental freedom · Hot debate
A laugh and a joke · Great thoughts
Life's promise

DISLIKES
Too many ideas · Tepid talk
Long faces · Small minds
Wet blankets

Mercury is your tool for making connections and getting leads.

MERCURY IN SAGITTARIUS

TRANSFORMER

POSITIVE	NEGATIVE
Frank Sincere Open-minded Speaks mind	Indiscreet Gauche Irreverent Garrulous
Versatile mind Speculative Intuitive Noble-thinking	Scattered mind Irrelevant Illogical Poor concentration
Thinks big Learned Clever Far-sighted	Grandiose ideas Academic Impractical Short-sighted
Philosophical Fair judge Sees truth Enthusiastic	Sermonizing Opinionated States obvious High-handed
Cultured Eclectic Informed Well-connected	Trendy Fanciful Pedantic Pompous
A mind of its own knows that fashions are not facts but opinions.	You know the right faces and places, but secretly you still lack identity.
Ponder on what you feel most strongly about, then make a case for what opposes it.	For all your apparent confidence, you are not at all sure where you stand.
Complement your native intelligence with formal training, or vice versa. Look and listen.	Occupational difficulties: all experience and no knowledge, or vice versa. Missing the obvious.
Cleave your thoughts to an end that endures or a cause that inspires.	Disconnected thoughts rattle round your head, frustrating both you and others.
Your honesty is not in question, but the way you express it is. Think before speaking.	Social ineptitude finds you socially alienated and/or emotionally compromised.
SOLUTION	PROBLEM

If you find yourself on the receiving end of negative traits, it is because you are not expressing the opposing positive traits.

MERCURY IN CAPRICORN

ESSENCE

THINKING THROUGH BUILDING

THE MIND RULES MATTER   **THE ORGANIZER**

"Thinking through Building" means two things mainly. Firstly, when building, you have to have a plan, which means that some sort of goal is is essential. Your mind has to have something worthwhile to chew on, otherwise solving petty problems or dealing with endless paperwork could be your mental lot. Yours is either a dull or a constructive mind, depending on what you are directing it towards.

Secondly, building is always done in definite stages. On the one hand, this means that you have a decidedly methodical mind, the kind that can produce a good organizer and successful business person. But on the other, you can be inclined to get stuck on one level of thinking, which can lead to mental or professional stagnation. So keep building, but add a definite dash of idealism to your natural pragmatism.

As the motto reads, "The Mind Rules Matter", not the other way around. In other words, if you let material considerations defeat or rule over you, you have missed the point of having the kind of mind that is designed to overcome just such difficulties.

You have most likely been conditioned to regard knowledge and your ability to think as the main assurances that you are on the right track and will get on in the world. If, however, you found formal or book learning painfully difficult, you could have lurched the other way and become quite scornful of intellectuality. On finding that this puts you at a social or professional disadvantage you might then strive to become a master of one particular subject – the more definite and structured, the better. For, in fact, when you put your mind to learning something, you do so with admirable thoroughness.

However, it is not the facts that your mind contains that determine its quality – and this is possibly why you were wary of filling it with them in the first place – any more than it is the architectural plans of a building that appeal to its occupants. It is how you use your mind and what you use it for that count. Being unaware of this can make you feel stiff and wooden at times, as you become afraid of using the wrong word, or obsessed with using the right one. Your essential lesson is to learn to use concrete facts and not to be weighed down by them.

When you have surmounted these inherent snags of Mercury in Capricorn, you will find that you'll be able to see the ultimate absurdity of being a slave to material status and belongings, and to the demands that they make. As a result of this, you are known for a wry humour that is based on a firm awareness of the vagaries and subtleties of physical existence. And through your sense of irony not a little wisdom shines.

LIKES
Time-tested values · Mental order and feasibility · Skill and efficiency · Economy and industriousness · Knowing your standpoint

DISLIKES
One-hit wonders and false ideals · Sloppy thinking · Poor workmanship and laziness Wasting time and materials · Being taken for a ride

Mercury is your tool for making connections and getting leads.

MERCURY IN CAPRICORN

TRANSFORMER

POSITIVE	NEGATIVE
Good timing Mentally cautious Not easily fooled Retentive mind	Procrastinating Slow learner Sceptical Mentally overloaded
Methodical mind Orderly mind Serious when necessary Level-headed	Lacking originality and imagination Given to melancholy Boring and pedestrian
Canny Discriminating Shrewd Profits from least	Suspicious Censorious Cunning Avaricious
Employs others Sober Clear and deliberating mind	Uses others Stern Dry and pigeon-holing mind
Strong concentration Painstaking Patient	Blinkered or narrow-minded Too exacting Intolerant
Inspire others with the goal that you should be able to see more clearly than they can.	Feeling frustrated and angry with others – especially co-workers.
You have the mind of the boss, so use it without doubt or rancour.	Dissatisfaction, even though everything and everyone are in their right place.
You will never lose what really counts – your resourcefulness.	Feeling that others are out to undo you, get the better of you and take advantage of you.
Give your mind a break – or it will! Loosen what's too tight. Tighten what's too loose.	You are constantly "at work" and feel like a wet blanket.
It is better to appear a fool than it is to be one. You won't forget what's worth knowing.	Stuck in a rut. Afraid of losing your mental grip. Intellectually constipated.
SOLUTION	PROBLEM

93

If you find yourself on the receiving end of negative traits, it is because you are not expressing the opposing positive traits.

MERCURY IN AQUARIUS

ESSENCE

THINKING THROUGH LIBERATING

THE EXALTED MIND   **THE FREE THINKER**

"A paradox is the truth standing on its head to attract attention." The bright spark who said this may or may not have had Mercury in Aquarius, but it expresses perfectly both the way in which you see the world and how you think. This is because your mind goes through the kind of processes that are "plugged in" to what has been called the Universal Mind, and so you perceive things in a manner that to others can seem highly unlikely – even odd – because it often goes against the emotional bias or moral attitudes of your family, peer group, colleagues etc.

So often you have to stand and work alone with your original, but sometimes quirky, ideas. It is very important that you express them at the same time, for in this way you will attract people of like mind, who interpret reality from the same elevated viewpoint as you, and who occasionally experience exactly the same flashes of insight as you.

There is a definite streak of stubbornness running through your mind, which is part and parcel of having a sense of the Truth, of understanding how things really are. After all, this is how the Truth eventually gets through. You could be regarded as part of a team that aspires to making known the kind of thinking that is coming in with the New Age – the Age of Aquarius. The type of work that suits you includes anything that aims to reveal the Truth, or to see the bigger picture; a few examples would be: psychology, astrology, astronomy, the sciences, the mass media and anything that aims to make known a humanitarian viewpoint.

Your blind spot is where such detached objectivity as yours is inclined to miss the emotional "count" in a given situation. You can overlook even your own feelings until they become an issue that challenges your airy vision of how things ought to be.

When you're as quick at understanding people's feelings as you are things of the mind, you are able to express your revolutionary ideas in a clear and appealing fashion. Yours can be the common touch that gets through to friends and co-workers – or even to the masses – because you are attuned to that Universal Mind and what it thinks. You are aware today of how others will think tomorrow. The challenge for you is to communicate that vision, to help others to see life from a point beyond their personal hopes and fears – or to see that those hopes and fears are not as personal as they think they are!

Your enthusiastic interest in all things new and full of Truth means that living a lie will sit very uncomfortably in your mind. The slightest shade of hypocrisy, whether in yourself or in others, is something that you'll root out vigorously. And, either consciously or unconsciously, you are attracted to people and to pursuits that force you to do just this.

LIKES
New Age thinking · Mental stimulation
Team or group work · Open-mindedness
Emotional honesty

DISLIKES
Chauvinism · Mental stagnation
No one to share ideas with · Closed minds
Emotional reactions

Mercury is your tool for making connections and getting leads.

MERCURY IN AQUARIUS

TRANSFORMER

POSITIVE	NEGATIVE
Original thinker Inventive Unorthodox Comprehensive	Way-out thinker Cranky Eccentric Disjointed
Scientific Objective Concise Well-informed	Clinical Lacks warmth Abrupt Unfeeling
Unshockable Open-minded Truth-loving Perceptive	Indifferent Fixed opinions Contrary Emotionally blind
Progressive thinker Utopian Reformist Socially aware	Out of time Unrealistic Reactionary Anti-social
Intuitive Cosmically aware Telepathic and inspiring mind	Scatterbrained Spaced out Overactive mind
Tune out the "static" by tuning in to what others need to hear.	Mentally distressed. Contradiction reigns. Everything is nothing is everything.
In other words, having the courage of your convictions depends on your convictions.	Either you are a rebel without a cause or a cause without a rebel.
The truth awakens like a flash of lightning. Are you ready to be struck by it?	As life tries to move or influence you, you toss between caring and not caring.
Knowing that knowing is but one side of the spinning coin of life is knowing indeed.	You can see it all so clearly but cannot get anyone else to.
As an independent mind you've chosen a lonely road and a high goal. Stick with it.	No one seems to understand or appreciate your ideas.
SOLUTION	PROBLEM

95

If you find yourself on the receiving end of negative traits, it is because you are not expressing the opposing positive traits.

MERCURY IN PISCES

ESSENCE

THINKING THROUGH ACCEPTING

THE POETIC MIND   DREAMER OF DREAMS

Yours is a sensitive mind that absorbs as much information as, if not more than, it learns. Ideas and solutions seem to surface, as opposed to actually being worked out. Because of this mental osmosis you are sometimes not quite sure whether it is your own mind that is doing the thinking. How this kind of receptive mentality is likely to be handled or experienced depends greatly on what kind of person you are generally, and whether you are left-brained/rational or right-brained/intuitive.

If your ego is the type that likes to maintain the illusion of being in command of everything that passes through the mind, you will put together a firm intellectual framework of facts and figures. Armed with this mental battery you present a formidable opponent to anyone whom you regard as a woolly thinker. However, you are in effect opposing the sensitivity of your own mind. Because certain thoughts and notions seem to come from "somewhere else", you doubt their veracity. Eventually this leads to a form of mental exhaustion as a result of resisting your cerebral sensitivity.

If, however, you are not so concerned about whether the thoughts coming through your head have your ego's stamp of approval, then you let the ideas stream forth, and give them some kind of creative and inspiring form. Although yours is the mind of the poet rather than of the technician, you are able to "dream up" both scientific and artistic visions. You think in pictures, and can profit much through drawing from your dream life.

However, the chances are that you waver somewhere between these two extremes of how Mercury in Pisces operates. But the fact remains that you are fortunate or unfortunate enough, depending on your attitude, to be in touch mentally with the Collective Unconscious, which is like a vast sea of all the thoughts and feelings that ever were or ever will be. Your mind, like a boat, can either trust and explore this ocean of notions and ancient wisdom, or distrust it and attempt to keep it out with a mental sea-wall of concrete knowledge, or with a sea-mist of fantasy, evasiveness, alcohol or drug abuse.

One way or the other, it is wise to accept and to understand the channel-like quality of your mind, and always to give expression to what is coming through it. Giving form to your thoughts is the correct means of maintaining mental security. Keeping them to yourself because some appear to be quite weird, will eventually make you feel quite weird yourself. ("Weird" literally means "what must be".)

As a sign of your fluid-like mentality, you are ill-disposed to being pinned down to facts – other than those of your "own" making, that is. Such "facts" may even include this definition of Mercury in Pisces!

LIKES
Dreaming · The mysterious
Nostalgia · Feeling inspired
Soft spots

DISLIKES
Rude awakenings · Lack of imagination
Bad memories · Feeling invaded
Hard facts

Mercury is your tool for making connections and getting leads.

MERCURY IN PISCES

TRANSFORMER

POSITIVE	NEGATIVE
Imaginative	Suspicious
Sensitive mind	Evasive
Visually aware	Easily freaked out
Artistic	Lazy
Obliging	Easily swayed
Psychic	Irrational
Good instincts	Fearful
Receptive	Gullible
Humorous	Obscure
Versatile	Vague
Good mimic	Parrots others
Highly perceptive	Uncommunicative
Philosophical	Absent-minded
Dreamer	Wool-gathering
Good long-term memory	Bad short-term memory
Accepting	Elusive
Refined mind	Weak-minded
Contemplative	Slow
Gentle	Wimpish
Sympathetic	Sycophantic

What you lack in knowledge you make up for in understanding. Take your time.	Others' apparently superior mental powers making you feel at a disadvantage.
Seeing to the boring details of life will allow you to reflect on greater issues in peace.	Caught out or feeling threatened by what you have "accidentally" forgotten.
Others are only too pleased to know your inspired version of the human condition.	Uncomfortably at a loss for words. Afraid of being pinned down or giving yourself away.
You have the power to choose what you take on board. Discover how to use it.	Feeling like a leaf in the wind. Invaded by the thoughts and opinions of others.
Use your imagination creatively rather than being a victim of it.	Disturbed by what others might be saying or thinking. Seeing things.

SOLUTION	PROBLEM

97

If you find yourself on the receiving end of negative traits, it is because you are not expressing the opposing positive traits.

VENUS

Keyword: LOVING

Looked at more intuitively, Venus symbolizes ATTRACTION, in that your Venus-Sign shows what you are drawn towards so that you may give or receive by way of LOVE and AFFECTION, BEAUTY and HAPPINESS. Negatively it poses INDULGENCE and SUPERFICIALITY.

Venus also represents the way you RELATE, and create and appreciate HARMONY through SOCIAL or ARTISTIC expression. If you are an artist of any kind, your style will resemble your Venus-Sign manner of loving and relating. Venus is what you LIKE.

If you are a male, your Venus-Sign will intimate the kind of female to whom you are attracted – although it is actually a part of you. If you are a female, you express and embody the qualities of your Venus-Sign quite directly. With either sex, if you find that you are on the receiving end of negative Venus-Sign traits, it is because you are not expressing the positive ones.

VENUS IN ARIES

ESSENCE

LOVING THROUGH DOING

LOVE AT FIRST SIGHT   LOVE ELEMENTAL

You love as a child loves, seeing human relationships as natural and uncomplicated – at least at first. You are generous, guileless and direct, and expect others to be the same. You are crestfallen when you find that they are not, but not, as a rule, heartbroken. You get back up again as quickly as you fell in love in the first place.

This impetuosity of yours certainly possesses a quality that is immediately attractive to others. They sense this innate notion of yours that love is a quest and deed for the doing. Essentially, you are absolutely right, but, unlike children, adults have a backlog of unmet needs and unresolved fears from their own childhood. So, although you have a talent for appealing to the child in others in a way that reminds them of an almost Eden-like simplicity, you also stimulate their more immature traits.

But the truth is that their immaturity is merely reflecting your own. If you fail or refuse to see this, you are headed for a precipitous life of loving and leaving, or of being left. But, then again, this could all be included in your feeling that love is a quest, and that your lovers are co-adventurers. Indeed, a companion-in-arms-like quality is very desirable to you – as long as you make sure that your partner sees it that way, too. Then you are on your way back to Eden – together – before the Fall.

In fact your love nature can be condensed into one small and simple word – imp. You are impish in that you are naughty and that you delight in getting others to misbehave. You are impudent in your manner of boldly and shamelessly pursuing the object of your desires. You are also impulsive and impatient in all matters of love and relating. An imp is, essentially, an elemental, or something that was there at the beginning. In other words, you have a rather primitive approach that can be either enchanting or disenchanting. More refined parts of your personality may try to suppress this, but there is something wild and gleeful in your manner of loving that should never be altogether eclipsed by so-called civilized behaviour – as long as you maintain some sensitivity to the sensibilities of others, while you tease their own impishness to the surface.

In affairs of the heart, not only are you trying to "get back to the Garden", but also you sense that way back. The hunger that is born of this sense may well make you mistake sex for love more than once. Your greatest lesson is probably learning that sex is a flower that blooms in love far more often than the other way around. Know that as a romantic idealist you are looking for someone who can strike a blend of loyalty and elusiveness, vibrancy and veracity. Know also that this blend must first be found in yourself.

LIKES
Independence in partner · The chase
A social whirl · Spontaneous affection
Bold romance

DISLIKES
Clinging vines · Being too cosy
Social inactivity · Undemonstrativeness
Feeble advances

If you are a man, this could be the kind of woman to whom you are attracted – but it is really a part of you, so realize it.

VENUS IN ARIES

TRANSFORMER

POSITIVE	NEGATIVE
Erotic Winning style Passionate Playful	Licentious Flirtatious Lustful Irresponsible
Demonstrative Outgoing Basic Straightforward	Blunt Inconsiderate Coarse Unsubtle
Popular Sparkling Generous Appealing	Unenduring Fanciful Wanton Teasing
Childlike charm Romantic idealist Easily roused Ingenuous	Naïve in love Fool in paradise Easily hurt Clueless
Persuasive Ardent Warm-hearted Quick off the mark	Pushy Forces affections Self-centred Impatient in love
What keeps you in love is the chase. Go for it, but don't (imagine you can) catch it.	After you get what you want you don't want it, or you don't know what you've got till it's gone.
Falling in love with love – what else can you do?! Keep falling. Keep questing.	Feeling let down, disillusioned, trodden on, abused and confused.
Give your best to get the best.	The delightful has a habit of turning into the detestable.
It becomes you to come right out and say or ask what is and what isn't agreeable.	Either you feel the victim of a turn-off or a bore, or you're being one.
As you are so attractive, check out what you're actually attracting.	You may have a lot of fun – but a merry-go-round just goes round in circles.
SOLUTION	PROBLEM

If you find yourself on the receiving end of negative traits, it is because you are not expressing the opposing positive traits.

VENUS IN TAURUS

ESSENCE

LOVING THROUGH STABILIZING

NATURE'S CONNOISSEUR   HEART OF OAK

You possess the best qualities of Venus as expressed in the physical or material sense, which means that in you the five senses are well-developed.

So you have a strong sensuousness that others find attractive, although if this is allowed to become excessive, subsequent grossness can have the opposite effect. Such awareness as yours of what satisfies the physical senses can, of course, make you successful in a number of areas: art – you may be especially good at singing, or at least have a pleasant-sounding speaking voice; cooking, and other means of offering others comfort and enjoyment; consumerism – you may have a good market sense; healing – your sense of touch can be highly evolved.

Your wonderful feel for bodily and Earthly things also makes you dependent on physical evidence of your worth and desirability. You greatly need shows of physical affection in order to feel loved – mere words or implications will not suffice. However, the more aware you are of your physical charm, which is a kind of emanation rather than solely good looks, the more likely you are magnetically to satisfy your needs. Additionally, you must bear in mind that most others are not as naturally skilled in expressing affection, so you should take the lead here, ever teaching how to enjoy the body more.

Fundamentally, you have a sense of how Nature enjoys her own existence, her own poetic and seasonal interplay. This sense is reflected to a great extent in your emotional needs and sexual inclinations. You have such love for certain physical aspects of Nature, like another human being or a work of art, that you just have to have them. But you cannot really possess them, for Nature's gifts, like rain, come and go in their own time. The secret to obtaining the object of your desires and maintaining the kind of stable relationship that is so important to you, is to recognize that anything or anyone outside yourself will only become truly a part of your life when your value and values are a reflection of, and in harmony with, Nature herself. Until then, you will always be involved, either unconsciously or deliberately, in some sort of "deal" whereby you foster the illusion that you're getting, or not getting, value for your "investment".

Venus in Taurus is one of the strongest Planet-Sign indications of a love of Nature. Apart from the above-described implications of what this means, you are also quite likely to be concerned with ecology and conservation. But the same Natural Truth persists here, namely that what you love and care about is only as sound and secure as you feel inside. After all, Nature is here to provide for our development. You are particularly trusting of, and entrusted with, Nature's gifts, which includes a true appreciation of Nature.

LIKES
Physical contact · Creature comforts
Beautiful surroundings · Being depended on
Natural products

DISLIKES
The physically distasteful · Scarcity
Spartan conditions · Gold-diggers
Synthetics

If you are a man, this could be the kind of woman to whom you are attracted – but it is really a part of you, so realize it.

VENUS IN TAURUS

TRANSFORMER

POSITIVE	NEGATIVE
Attractive	Avaricious
Earthy	Materialistic
Affectionate	Cupboard love
Artistic	Self-indulgent
Aesthetic	Hedonistic
Peaceful	Indolent
Sensuous	Sensual
Satisfying	Self-satisfied
Steadfast	Stubborn
Loyal	Possessive
Wholesome	Smug
Constant	Too abiding
Sympathetic	Sybaritic
Encouraging	Misguiding
Comforting	Dissipating
Pleasure-giving	Insatiable
Nature-loving	Limited viewpoint
Deeply trusting	Gullible
Sound values	Precious
Conservational	Green green

Deep down you know that Nature's needs reflect your own, therefore look to and after them.	Your concern for what you think matters is a cause for concern in itself.
Your undeniable awareness of what feels good should lead to what feels even better.	Believing you can't have too much of a good thing is becoming harmful both to you and to others.
What makes you feel loved is your persistent faith in your own love nature.	Your need to be loved posing as fidelity makes you feel threatened.
Follow your nose to what smells sweeter, whatever the cost.	Rotting in the rut of your own sense of what pleases – and it doesn't.
Yours are a natural wealth and beauty, giving and receiving in their own time, like the seasons.	You're being greedy for something but not realizing it is creating an empty feeling.

SOLUTION	PROBLEM

103

If you find yourself on the receiving end of negative traits, it is because you are not expressing the opposing positive traits.

VENUS IN GEMINI

ESSENCE

LOVING THROUGH COMMUNICATING

LOVE IN BUD   **THE SPARKLING PERSONALITY**

As Venus is the Planet of Love, and Gemini is the Sign of the Lovers, you would imagine this to make for rewarding relationships. However, if you are blindly expecting security and predictability in your love life, then you are in for a disappointment. This is because Gemini is the Sign of Youth, and as such you have a strong urge to prevent stagnation and maintain fluidity in your relationships. A partnership that is not allowed change and freedom is doomed to failure, whereas being true to your desire to pursue youthful dreams and ideas will literally rejuvenate flagging relationships.

Venus in Gemini is Love in Bud rather than in full bloom, so you have to give it a chance to develop, be more steadfast, and not abandon it or leave it to the winds of fate. You like variety, but it is better to seek diversity within a relationship than outside it, for obvious reasons. Similarly, do not allow your easygoing nature to be interpreted as a lack of commitment. Loving through Communicating means that if you feel love for someone, you should let it be known to them rather than sitting on the fence. You have a natural sparkle that is there to highlight your love and your loved one as you discover more and more bright facets of the Jewel of Love.

It is natural for you to make social contact in an easy and undemanding fashion. You like to get around – or to do the rounds. If you were to cut yourself off from a variety of friends and acquaintances this would exert pressure on you that would eventually cause you and your more intimate relationship to suffer. Sexual or family ties are your "heart", but it is your diverse social relationships that are your "lungs", that breathe life into your being. It is these ongoing communications that breathe fresh air into the lives of others as well.

Your love of communication can also bestow upon you a literary talent, or at least a love of the written and the spoken word. Having a wide range of knowledge should be something on which you can draw, for in this way you are able to discover and to express the ultimately important mental and spiritual aspects of love, as opposed to seeking superficial gratification, which can be a weakness of Venus in Gemini, as you attempt to keep things too breezy for your own good.

Gemini is the Sign of Duality, so you will experience not only the above-described opposition of security versus freedom, but also that of what you want versus what you think you want. In fact, you will only attract what you truly desire, and that is to meet your own shadow or alter ego, with which, like Narcissus, you are in love.

LIKES
Poise · Keen minds
A lively partner · Social variety
The romantically unexpected

DISLIKES
Gracelessness · Dullards
"Settling down" · Tired relationships
Routine romance

If you are a man, this could be the kind of woman to whom you are attracted – but it is really a part of you, so realize it.

VENUS IN GEMINI

TRANSFORMER

POSITIVE	NEGATIVE
Amusing and friendly Coolly affectionate Light-hearted Emotionally objective	Flirtatious Flippant and flighty Makes light of others' feelings
Socially at ease Emotionally buoyant Stimulating company	Social butterfly Superficial values Lack of commitment
Lively conversationalist Ear to the ground Good-humoured Expressive	Meaningless banter Shallow gossip Empty gestures Verbose
Agile and witty Socially adaptable Emotionally flexible Well-connected	Restless and fickle Double standards Inconsistent partner Social opportunist
Charming Courteous Tactful Co-operative	Ingratiating Insincere Insipid Easy come – easy go
Others will truly appreciate you, if you truly appreciate them.	Feeling avoided and not taken seriously. Empty and dissatisfied.
Expressing your feelings verbally will break new ground both emotionally and socially.	Divided interests creating unstable personal relationships. Jilted – two-timed / two-timing.
Try listening to your heart rather than to your own and other peoples' voices.	Nil response from those who matter to you. Left out in the cold.
Show your dark side – and your light side will be brighter!	Afraid of intimacy. Uncomfortable with feelings or silences in company.
Trust your natural wit and appeal, and be the wiser for the asking.	Unsure of how others are "reading" you, and of social or sexual direction.
SOLUTION	PROBLEM

105

If you find yourself on the receiving end of negative traits, it is because you are not expressing the opposing positive traits.

VENUS IN CANCER

ESSENCE

LOVING THROUGH NURTURING

HOME IS WHERE THE HEART IS   ON THE SENTIMENTAL SIDE

Your expressions of love are intricately tied up with your need to give or to receive comfort and security. The love, or the lack of love, forthcoming from your mother (or mother-figure) greatly affects both how you show and how you need affection. Being unsure of mother-love will make you cling blindly to partners, and possibly indulge your own children – or pretend to be indifferent towards them. Conversely, feeling sure of mother-love will give rise to a well-balanced fondness for and care of loved ones. Any kind of deprived family background is likely to have a serious influence on your love-life as an adult. Feelings of being misunderstood and unloved can be, well, Cancerous, for maudlin sentiments and sulky behaviour will be triggered off by normal emotional confrontations as a reaction to past hurts.

As with most Planets placed in Cancer, there is a strong subjectivity, which with Venus means that in being unconsciously so concerned with receiving love, you forget the quality and quantity of love you are actually giving. In a way your love is of the most instinctual kind, for it is characterized by an automatic nurturing of whatever needs it, be it the young, the sick, the weak or the needy. Feelings of insecurity on your part are in aid of furthering your awareness of the same in others, rather than laying you open to exploitation. Your value, like the home and hearth and Mother Nature herself, is all too easily taken for granted. So, occasionally, you may have to go on strike, make the earth quake, let them know which side their bread is buttered, then they'll come running!

Romantically you lean towards the sentimental. An intimate dinner for two at home is more likely to set your heart-strings playing than a night out on the tiles. You are also a bit old-fashioned, and like women to be ladylike and men to be chivalrous.

You have a changeable nature with regard to showing or accepting affection owing to inner feelings of doubt about your attractiveness. If this is a problem for you, then try to make the distinction between security needs and your innate lovability. In other words you should be loved for what you are, not for what you need.

The home and family are central to your happiness. You are, therefore, very sensitive to the needs and hurts of loved ones, and to the home or house atmosphere as a whole. It is also very likely that you possess cooking, decorating and other domestic skills. Naturally enough, a fear of change and disruption in the home and family scene can give rise to worry, which can be expressed physically, in the form of stomach problems. Remind yourself that such worry has to do with the past rather than the future, and that Venus, as the Planet of Attraction, will always eventually favour you with the nest in which to nurture those you feel to be in need of your nurturing love.

LIKES
Hearth and home harmony · The domestic scene · Familiar faces and places
Security before romance · Praise for caring

DISLIKES
Domestic strife · Inhospitality
Alien territory · Emotional threats
Being taken for granted

If you are a man, this could be the kind of woman to whom you are attracted – but it is really a part of you, so realize it.

VENUS IN CANCER

TRANSFORMER

POSITIVE	NEGATIVE
Gentle	Timid
Kind	Soppy
Tender	Fawning
Romantic	Gooey
Sentimental	Maudlin
Sensitive	Easily hurt
Compassionate	Moody
Dreamy	Muddle-headed
Devoted	Clingy
Loyal	Too attached
Unselfish	Weak-willed
Dependable	Dependent
Caring	Doting
Protective	Parsimonious
Motherly	Old-womanish
Sympathetic	Fuss-pot
Home-making	Shy
Reassuring	Insecure
Familiar feel	Fears unfamiliar
Comforting	Gluttonous

Knowing what it's like to be without, you cater well to the same plight in others.	The "waif" in you is taking over – running and hiding, and gobbling down scraps.
Use Mother Nature as your role model for how to nurture and nourish.	Acting like Old Mother Hubbard gets you a bare cupboard! What's called "poverty consciousness".
Gladly allowing others to lean on you will help stop you leaning on someone else.	Difficulty letting go of negative feelings and relationships.
Admitting to your hopes and hurts encourages others to do so – everyone then benefits.	Not looking at your emotional vulnerability gives rise to mental and emotional confusion.
Your softness is one of your most attractive features, so don't overstate or undersell it.	Others are either repelled by your ingratiating behaviour, or take advantage of it.

SOLUTION	PROBLEM

If you find yourself on the receiving end of negative traits, it is because you are not expressing the opposing positive traits.

VENUS IN LEO

ESSENCE

LOVING THROUGH CREATING

COURTLY LOVE   LOVE COMES SHINING

Venus in Leo makes for such a romantic nature that your love feelings would in some ways be better expressed in poem, picture or song than in real life. At least, to give some form of creative expression to your ardour would give personal relationships more chance of surviving. Otherwise, the expectations that you have of any mere mortal are very unlikely to be met.

At first your paramour cannot believe his or her luck at having found such an enthusiastic lover, then they realize that you have (unconsciously) written them into your own particular romantic script. You can also be fiercely loyal on the one hand – and expect the same from your mate – yet still feel entitled to flirt, and even to have an affair if such a passion seizes you. However, if there is the slightest sign of infidelity from your partner, then there is hell to pay. Rather than on love's terms, you very much want things on your own terms, alongside which a healthy emotional interplay cannot exist.

At the root of this dilemma is the same old Leo problem: a deep-seated doubt of your own lovability that is totally undetectable from the outside, as you come across as passion posing as confidence, or as aloof and dignified. Either you are desperately trying to prove your desirability by playing at being Romeo or Cleopatra, or you are pretending not to care. If, before it's too late, you get your pride into the proper perspective and give the object of your desires just a glimpse of the human being who is playing these roles, then they will be not only impressed, but relieved at not having to live up to such a figure as the one you're projecting. They will also be more able to meet your needs. You are certainly generous and warm-hearted – unless you have limped off to some lonely lair as a melodramatic consequence of playing one of the above roles. In a sense you are paying homage to romantic love, with your lover as the altar. As long as your partner is aware of and alive to this acting out of a myth, and you do not lose sight of each other as individuals, you can create a very noble and rewarding relationship. Put another way, Venus in Leo needs to combine its sense of "royal privilege" with a sense of equal rights; the "queen" should regard her mate as the "king" (and vice versa), with all the courtly respect and honour that this understanding entails.

Artistic sense is strong in you. Life is seen as an ongoing creative experience, which, of course, it is. This is what can be so sunny and wonderful and attractive about Venus in Leo. Pride in physical appearance and sexual prowess is also strong, which is fine provided it does not become neurotic. At a certain stage you must go looking for your inner beauty, which is beautiful indeed. "I see Love shining in the shining Sun."

LIKES
Admiration · Mutual respect
Lavish parties · Showing off your partner
Classic courtship

DISLIKES
Slightest rejection · Insulting behaviour
Second-rate dos · Being shown up
Lack-lustre love

If you are a man, this could be the kind of woman to whom you are attracted – but it is really a part of you, so realize it.

VENUS IN LEO

TRANSFORMER

POSITIVE	NEGATIVE
Romantic Ardent Passionate Loyal	Unrealistic Sexually obsessed Consuming Too loyal
Artistic Dramatic Entertaining Fun-loving	Prima donna Overbearing Demanding Inappropriate
Radiant Outgoing Warm Openly affectionate	Self-centred Showy Brassy Flirtatious
Charming Attractive Benevolent Gives a lot	Seducing Flaunting Patronizing Expects too much
Social pride Personal pride Number one Fun to be with	Snobbish Vain Competitive Game-playing
The only thing that you can be compared with is your own self-respect.	Preoccupied with physical appearance or social position. Jealousy.
What you have to give is priceless – so why put a price on it!	Doubting your charms and overstating them as you swing from too little to too much confidence.
Love – and be loved in return. Send out the waves, pause, and feel them come back.	Everyone can see what you've got going for you – except you.
Channel your larger-than-life energy into larger-than-life pursuits or pastimes.	Creating scenes that upset you more than they please you.
For better results, bestow your affections judiciously rather than squander them blindly.	Never getting back what you are putting in. Feeling let down and unappreciated.
SOLUTION	PROBLEM

109

If you find yourself on the receiving end of negative traits, it is because you are not expressing the opposing positive traits.

VENUS IN VIRGO

ESSENCE

LOVING THROUGH ANALYSING

BEHOLD THE BEAUTY	LOVE LOVE'S PARADOX

Venus is said to be in its Fall in Virgo, because Love and Beauty do not really bear analysis, and so one or the other has to go. The choice is, as ever, up to you, but here we assume that a world of Love and Beauty is preferable to one of analysis.

The ultimate result of analysing love and art, or objects thereof, is that eventually you come to realize that you must surrender to their mystery and analyse no more. However, in the meantime, during your constant routine of spotting and removing the fly from the ointment, you acquire a finely tuned sense of social, emotional and artistic values. As far as love and relating are concerned, it could be said that you are going through a kind of cleansing process as you rid yourself of impure thoughts, feelings and values. However, the tendency is to see these impurities in others, and in sexual partners in particular. As a consequence of this you can place yourself either temporarily or permanently in bachelor- or spinsterhood. This may of course be entirely to your liking, but the critical question is, are you keeping yourself to yourself in order to have an unadulterated look at yourself, or are you just misguidedly condemning everything but yourself as being "unclean". If such self-denial is not to your liking, then you are prone to doing something apparently out of character, such as being promiscuous or unkempt. This is because the moral strait-jacket that you have fashioned for yourself becomes so horribly restricting that you streak from one end of the ethical spectrum to the other. As a result of being as loose as previously you were tight, you unconsciously think that you are getting what you desire. This reversal can occur the other way round, too, from being loose to being tight.

When you realize and admit to this perversity with regard to your sense of what pleases, you could then ask yourself: Who am I to judge or be critical of anyone else? However, the poles swing around swiftly here, for the fact is that you have a fine and valuable sense of discrimination. But ultimately one has to be discriminating about being discriminating. In learning this, as you analyse and sensitively balance your moral values with your emotional desires, you become closer to distilling the perfection that you originally envisioned, warts and all! Realizing the Paradox of Love, that perfection is the acceptance of imperfection, is the goal and the gold of Venus in Virgo.

All of the above can also apply to how you view or create art or craftwork. Be aware that you cannot prove that a rose is beautiful by pulling it apart petal by petal – on the contrary, this destroys it. When you can resist this temptation to tamper with what is already simply attractive, and let the technical take second place to the inspirational, you can be second to none in appreciating, expressing and upholding the exquisite fragility of Love and Beauty.

LIKES
A spotless reputation
A working relationship · Good manners
Sexual hygiene · Pure or natural art

DISLIKES
Mud being thrown at you
A non-mental relationship · Feeling stiff
Sordid affairs · Art hypes

If you are a man, this could be the kind of woman to whom you are attracted – but it is really a part of you, so realize it.

VENUS IN VIRGO

TRANSFORMER

POSITIVE	NEGATIVE
Knowing what you like Discriminating Fine aesthetic and design sense	Critical of partners Fussy and nagging Easily dissatisfied Neurotically artistic
Sincerely affectionate Subtle love signs Simple and clear	Inhibits affection Undemonstrative Dry and clinical
Quietly charming Strong character Impartially kind Coolly helpful	Socially stiff Hides sensitivity Emotionally absent Cold exterior
Precision worker Refreshing at work Specialist worker Painstaking	Too exacting Retreats into work Indecisive of work Restrained
Pure and modest lover High moral sense Socially discerning Privately sensuous	Feels sexually inferior Puritanical Social misfit Self-effacing
Be mindful that amidst today's murky moral quagmires, you are a refreshing spring.	Loneliness and frustration. Over-reacting to this with loose thought or loose living.
Recognize that yours is a labour of love, so employ both feelings and judgement.	Frustrations as a result of divorcing personal feelings from working life – or vice versa.
It can be your quiet attention to social details that makes things go with a swing.	Lack of spontaneity means that others cannot relax in your presence. Party pooper.
Any emotional expression of how you feel is better than no expression at all.	(Fear of) being supplanted or spurned. Disappointment in love.
Concentrate on what pleases – not what displeases.	Eternal bachelor or spinster. Feeling that nothing and nobody is good enough.
SOLUTION	PROBLEM

If you find yourself on the receiving end of negative traits, it is because you are not expressing the opposing positive traits.

VENUS IN LIBRA

ESSENCE

LOVING THROUGH RELATING

THE AESTHETE   THE SOCIAL TOUCHSTONE

You appreciate and understand art and society on their own levels. This means that you have an inner sense of harmony which, quite naturally, sees life in terms of Beauty and Justice. But this sensibility is essentially born of your mind, rather than of your emotions, so the nature of your feelings, security needs and cultural conditioning is possibly going to intrude on how you would like to express your artistic skills and social charms.

As you recognize that beauty is important, the question arises as to whether it is more than or merely skin-deep. The answer is both, as you are bound to find out sooner or later. If you are looking for a partner who is glamorous and blemish-free, and has all the social graces, then with your charms you are quite likely to attract such a person. In time and after getting to know them – and them you – something quite other than that vision of loveliness or handsomeness could emerge. At this point you either go looking elsewhere or start criticizing the contents of the product and forget the wrapping. Alternatively you could be attracted to someone's inner beauty, then find their outer appearance to be not up to magazine-myth standard.

The answer to this is to remember that "Beauty is in the Eye of the Beholder" – and should not be misted up by some notion of beauty that has been devised and promulgated by the mass media. Be that as it may, it is very difficult to separate what you find truly attractive and lovable from what you have been led to believe to be so. This is precisely where Venus in Libra's sense of harmony and beauty must come into its own. At some point you become a leader rather than a follower of fashion. Unless you are faithful to your truest and deepest inner vision of grace, beauty and fair play, you will paradoxically find yourself either being guilty of boorishness, infidelity or indifference, or being the victim thereof. Ultimately others will look to you as being a social or artistic success – or disaster! As you are in touch spiritually with what the Ancient Greeks called "The Golden Mean", the perfect balance, others will measure themselves by you or against you.

As a result of this natural charm, you are likely to attract either popularity or wealth, or both. And .because you enjoy the pleasures of art and society, you like to make sure that this wherewithal – in the form of money and looks – is ever-present. This can, of course, result in your being neurotic about money and extremely vain. In any event, what you are most probably afraid of is conflict and disharmony. But the ultimate proof of your undeniable Venusian sense is your ability to lend grace where there is awkwardness, and understanding where there is strife.

LIKES
Social harmony · Tastefulness
Being in love · Beautiful surroundings
True marriage

DISLIKES
Ugly scenes · Philistines
Feeling unattractive · Uncouth behaviour
Pretended love

If you are a man, this could be the kind of woman to whom you are attracted – but it is really a part of you, so realize it.

VENUS IN LIBRA

TRANSFORMER

POSITIVE	NEGATIVE
Eye for beauty	Hung up on appearances
Strong colour sense	Oversensitive
Good ear	Music
Artistic	Art snob
Affectionate	Takes liberties
Likable	Frivolous
Magnetic	Seducing
Fair-looking	Vain
Refined	Foppish
Graceful	Affected
Pleasant	Phoney
Socially correct	Etiquette freak
Romantically steadfast	Conventionally superficial
Relates well	Insincere
Harmonious	Avoids conflict
Just	Indifferent
Empathetic	Cold
Broad-minded	Cynical
Social touchstone	Social outcast
Such a fine social sense as yours, at some stage, just has to be tempered by tolerance.	Your innate understanding of human society finds you at a loss. Familiarity has bred contempt.
Relationships prosper on love – of the best *and* the worst.	Not showing how you really feel leads to your not knowing how you really feel.
Manners maketh not man. Others can benefit from your style – but only if they want to.	Limited, compromised and agitated by others who are apparently not up to your standard.
You need not indulge in your obvious charms, unless you doubt them – and doubt breeds itself.	Strife in personal relationships through your arousing insecurity in your partner.
Your ideal is something to strive towards not insist on. It may even lie beyond the human.	There is always something out of place or not quite right.
SOLUTION	PROBLEM

113

If you find yourself on the receiving end of negative traits, it is because you are not expressing the opposing positive traits.

VENUS IN SCORPIO

ESSENCE

LOVING THROUGH DESIRING

ALL OR NOTHING   HARMONY THROUGH CONFLICT

As the song said, "You've got what it takes – but it takes a lot to give it away". With Venus in Scorpio it is as necessary for you to control your strong emotional awareness of what turns people on – or off – as it is hard for others to resist it. With a sexual bag of tricks such as this you might think that, like Svengali or Mata Hari, you could get anyone to do your bidding. But the catch with Venus in Scorpio is that it has you in its trap more than you have anyone in yours. In other words, the Power of Love is what Venus in Scorpio is about, and it will ultimately have its way with you, rather than the other way round.

Your feelings of love always have an undeniable streak of desire running through them, which means that there is something desperate or fated about your love life. You exude a strongly attractive sexual emanation, matched by that deep sense of another's emotional nature and sexuality. The danger arises either when you use this power blindly to build a feeling of security, or when you resist this power because you know it will attract relationships that will force you to change your lifestyle.

In the first case it can lead to a Faustian situation in which the source of your emotional security or the object of your affections exerts a definite but invisible power over you, because they know that the deal is "Don't prod me and I won't prod you – at least, not so you'd notice it" (other than a vague sense of being trapped). In the second case your avoidance of emotional transformation can lead you down a sleazy trail of desire trying to get the better of love.

Fundamentally you have a deep desire to find love – true, genuine love, the love that purges you of petty values, that transforms your life from travesty to destiny, via tragedy and ecstasy. Such a deep and fulfilling love could already be with you. However, the surge of Venus in Scorpio does not ever really rest for it is seeking out your depths, and, more particularly, what can and must be given from those depths. As a result of this emotional delving, you may feel that you have to be quite guarded about your intimate life, throwing up a smokescreen to maintain secrecy. That smokescreen could even be an apparent openness, for you are nothing if not subtle. You may withhold love in order to control your partner, because you are unsure of how to handle your own depths of emotion and the vulnerability that goes with them. All you need to remember is that the trust comes with the depth!

Yet, in the end, all these expressions of Venus in Scorpio lead to the same thing, an inescapable intimacy with yourself, where all taboos must be broken, and you become the purged and faithful exponent of the Power of Love.

LIKES
Heartfelt emotions · Gutsy experiences
Sexual revelation · Depth of aliveness
Plenty of soul

DISLIKES
Insipidness · A banal lifestyle
Exposure to ridicule · Superficial beings
Lack of soul

If you are a man, this could be the kind of woman to whom you are attracted – but it is really a part of you, so realize it.

VENUS IN SCORPIO

TRANSFORMER

POSITIVE	NEGATIVE
Sexually aware Sensuous Colourful Rapturous	Sexually obsessed Licentious Blue Depraved
Stimulating Fruity Magnetic Influential	Hurtful Bitter Hateful Poisonous
Sultry Subtle Self-controlled Self-sacrificing	Immoral Underhand Manipulative Self-destructive
Dignified Confidant(e) Sense of secrecy Intimate	Tight-lipped Unforthcoming Conspiratorial Close
Faithful Passionate Gives all Intense	Possessive Jealous Expects all Fanatical
When you find you cannot get enough, start giving all you can.	Your appetite for love is a bottomless pit – with you at the bottom of it.
For every secret you keep, respectfully reveal one of your own. Break a taboo today.	Keeping doubts and desires to yourself and a few other moles is creating emotional claustrophobia.
Your invasive charms ultimately have to be used for more than just sating your desires.	Misusing your subtle powers finds you subtly disadvantaged; on the road to dereliction.
You see your own unrealized potential in others. Bring it to life – don't beat it to death.	Attracting figures who reflect your self-disdain in order to scorn them is doing you in.
Sex without love goes nowhere – except down. What price carnal knowledge and experience?	Finding yourself in degrading relationships or scenes. Sexual diseases.
SOLUTION	PROBLEM

115

If you find yourself on the receiving end of negative traits, it is because you are not expressing the opposing positive traits.

VENUS IN SAGITTARIUS

ESSENCE

LOVING THROUGH SEEKING

THE JOY OF LOVE   THE BON VIVANT

Above all you are aware of Love's bounty and inexhaustibility. As such this can mean either that you have an enthusiastic appetite for love – or lust – that never actually seems to amount to much, or that through thick and thin you never lose faith that love is always bound for glory. Philosophically you know that you cannot have good times without bad, and that good times here mean better times down the road. As you look back down your life track, you will appreciate your heart's experience more when you consider it in terms of quality rather than quantity, of love gained rather than love lost.

You see love as an adventure, a true romance, and seeking it can – and should – lead you far afield. Fortune or the one you crave could well be found some way beyond your original and possibly limited horizon. A homey and predictable love life or partner is not really to your taste, until you have spread your wings and sown enough wild oats to appreciate that love is an adventure wherever you are and whoever you are with. Indeed, it is your expansive and unbounded sense of love and pleasure that can inspire and warm another's heart when it has become a little cold and damp along the way. In your natural awareness of Love's infinite supply, it is important that you really give something of value to others. Promising and not delivering can be your most common and infuriating fault. When you express your sense of Love's bounty in a focused and discriminating fashion, you truly teach and convey Love's majesty and wonder, and this is what truly satisfies you. This also applies to any artistic expression, in that you can and must put across something of lasting and eternal value.

Venus in Sagittarius is basically concerned with the bonding, or rather the inseparability, of physical love and spiritual love. However, as you prefer to learn from experience rather than from a book, it is quite likely that initially you will try to keep the two apart; if not, you will find it hard to keep them together. In other words, either your physical need for love can somehow divorce itself from a moral sense of social behaviour, which could lead to separation and divorce itself; or your need for sanctity in intimacy can be unmet by your partner, or forced by yourself, with the same unhappy result. Another alternative could be to find a philosophy to justify your sexual escapades or emotional shortcomings.

However, eventually a set of beliefs and principles that dictate your manner of loving and relating is essential to your happiness. So in a relationship you should discover and establish an agreed moral / spiritual basis of understanding – and keep to it – otherwise love will fly out of the same window through which it flew in.

LIKES
Quick emotional responses · Honest, upfront relating · "Religious" art
Horsing around · Gallantry and philanthropy

DISLIKES
Hanging back · Leaving things unsaid
Meaningless fashions · Restraint and inactivity
Flattery and empty façades

If you are a man, this could be the kind of woman to whom you are attracted – but it is really a part of you, so realize it.

VENUS IN SAGITTARIUS

TRANSFORMER

POSITIVE	NEGATIVE
Romantic imagination Light-hearted Warmly affectionate Generous	Easily attracted Impressionable Flirtatious Unkept promises
Guided by definite standards Benevolent and loyal	Forces beliefs on to partner Cannot face emotional truth
Idealistic Ardent feelings Demonstrative Non-possessive	Hard to please Escapist Scatters emotions Fickle
Emotionally frank Honest with lover Broad-minded	Brutally and offensively tactless Impersonally affectionate Licentious and amoral
Socially active Vivacious Popular Friendly	Name-dropper Promiscuous "Groupie" Squanders affections
Set a higher value on yourself and you'll be that much more appreciated by others.	You feel "The more I give the less I get". Feeling unloved and unlovable.
You will be truly loved for expressing how you truly feel about yourself.	Feeling secretly disliked, you tease and taunt as a vain compensation.
Identify your ideals and your needs and seek to express them, then you will find love.	Feeling that there is no one in the world who can love and understand you.
Recognize that love grows through its trials. Don't expect too much too soon.	Love never lives up to your expectations; something always seems to spoil it.
Giving should be its own reward – and you have a lot to give.	Feeling taken for granted. Good-time girl/guy reputation.
SOLUTION	PROBLEM

117

If you find yourself on the receiving end of negative traits, it is because you are not expressing the opposing positive traits.

VENUS IN CAPRICORN

ESSENCE

LOVING THROUGH BUILDING

THE TEST OF TIME   LOVE IS NO BUSINESS

You have an apparently restrained love nature, and, as a rule, are not given to being openly affectionate – at least, not when you really mean it. You can be formally fond, in the sense of being tactile and gracious in the current socially accepted manner, but where your true amorous intentions are concerned, only one person will know about them for quite a while. This is because basically you are not inclined to committing yourself to a relationship until some form of commitment has been shown by the other party. This points to the likelihood of your being attracted preferably to someone who is more demonstrative and more direct than yourself, otherwise a mutual attraction might never lead to anything, despite itself.

You look for the traditional values in a relationship, like fidelity and constancy, and until a partnership has stood the test of time, distrustfulness can be in evidence. To prevent this in itself becoming a blight on the survival of the relationship, you may need to get to the root of why you can be so lacking in trust. Once these formalities have been observed, you then reveal a rather passionate, if somewhat sculptured, kind of love nature, with an enduring relationship (probably marriage) to match.

As there is a measure of unreachability about you emotionally, you are perennially attracted to those who also exude a certain mystique. It is as if you find pleasure in seeking a balance between total reliability and eternal elusiveness. This can mean that you stray from the very path that you originally insisted everyone keep to – and this would be in direct proportion to how much you were keeping certain feelings too close to your chest. In other words, not giving expression to your wilder and less conventional desires would, at some stage, attract you to someone wild and unconventional. The secret to all this is that the partner you already have probably has similar urges just waiting to be identified and unearthed – by you! However, if not, then making off into the romantic undergrowth will be both necessary and unavoidable.

On those other Venusian subjects of art and values, you are someone who can either carefully blend them through expressing yourself artistically in a valid and substantial fashion, or appreciate art and perhaps even deal in it. However, on the negative side, you could either fail to place the right value on your social or artistic merits, or, conversely, attempt to use your charms to gain money and status. But, fundamentally, you know that neither love nor art is a business. The paradox with Venus in Capricorn is seen in the fact that really you want a deeply spiritual kind of love relationship – with a person or with your creations – but unless you open up and surrender your heart, all you will feel is short-changed.

LIKES
Mature relationships · Knowing social pitch
Working spouse · Traditional/classical art
Testing the water

DISLIKES
Romantic illusions · Embarrassments
Bimbos / Toy-boys · So-called "Art"
Love at first sight

If you are a man, this could be the kind of woman to whom you are attracted – but it is really a part of you, so realize it.

VENUS IN CAPRICORN

TRANSFORMER

POSITIVE	NEGATIVE
Committed Serious lover Steadfast Constant	Possessive Jealous Inflexible Self-righteous
Cautious Trustworthy Disciplined Objective	Inhibited Distrustful Stern Indifferent
Genuine affections Modest Cool exterior Reserved	Undemonstrative Mean Cold manner Unfeeling
Dignified Sense of composure Self-controlled Upright	Snobbish Too formal Self-contained Stiff
Practical Resourceful Affluent Self-made	Materialistic Money-grubbing Penny-pinching Selfish
Establish what you are worth and feel good about it, then you are bound to obtain it.	Money problems as a result of attaching too much or too little importance to it.
Your strength of character need not be forced, for it will show itself in the course of time.	Trying to conceal your social shortcomings only serves to perpetuate them.
When you let someone know how you feel, they really know how you feel.	Feeling cut-off and unappreciated. Others' ignorance of your plight only exacerbates this.
Temper your self-restraint with the knowledge that the better things are worth waiting for.	Life feels a joyless and lack-lustre affair. Everything seems flat and pointless.
You can only be true to love, as you see it – not to the loved one.	Fretting over what – or rather who – you think is "yours". Uncomfortably justified.
SOLUTION	PROBLEM

If you find yourself on the receiving end of negative traits, it is because you are not expressing the opposing positive traits.

VENUS IN AQUARIUS

ESSENCE

LOVING THROUGH LIBERATING

SET YOUR LOVE FREE   BEAUTY AWAKENS

With the Planet of Love and Beauty in Aquarius, you have an open and experimental approach to relating and to artistic expression. On the one hand this can be both relaxing and stimulating, as it allows others to loosen up and be more themselves, but then again it can make it rather difficult for others to know where you're coming from emotionally, as your style can be disconcerting, even shocking, or just plain odd.

You have a liberal attitude that aspires to accommodating all types of people, but unless you actually devise some kind of individual moral code, relationships can float away on the breeze as your free-and-easiness turns out to be a case of hedging your bets. Your coolly and impersonally affectionate nature goes down very well with friends and at social gatherings, but it can also make it quite easy for someone closer than a friend to up and leave.

With such a blithe and deceptively undemanding air about you, it may be difficult for you to comprehend why you experience so much heat and hassle in emotional relationships. The key to understanding how your personal magnetism and manner of relating attract such dilemmas hinges on the meaning of the word "freedom". Your problem is that you want to allow a partner the freedom and the space to do as they please, but if you give them too much then they think you don't care. Alternatively, you will put it the other way round and pretend that it is you who doesn't care, which makes your opposite number feel so insecure that he/she begins to impinge upon your freedom.

The secret is to reveal, in a heartfelt way, your opinions and questions concerning freedom of love for the person or persons to whom you feel the closest. They will then feel included in your quest for freedom. If they should hotly disagree with or reject your views then you can grant them the freedom to do and to think as they please – but tell them to remember that it is you who wanted to find freedom with them. Furthermore, you can help to awaken them to the nature of their own love and values by enquiring, in your charming manner, what exactly it is that they think freedom means. But, above all, show your love, otherwise anything done in the name of freedom will just be a sham, that is, the freedom not to love.

You can be socially inventive and creatively innovative, and you are naturally drawn towards the forefront of artistic styles and cultural values. If your partner does not share similar views or does not feel able to express such differences in a friendly way, then sudden disaster could strike. Conversely, sharing a "contemporary" lifestyle should not be a substitute for a genuine emotional rapport. With Venus in Aquarius, love and friendship must coexist; and freedom loves to be found by two people at once in the midst of the beauty of both their joy and their sorrow.

LIKES
Lover to be a friend · Personal code of ethics · Freedom in marriage Social experimentation · Openness

DISLIKES
Not sharing everything · Being tied down Being clung to · Outworn social values Jealousy

If you are a man, this could be the kind of woman to whom you are attracted – but it is really a part of you, so realize it.

VENUS IN AQUARIUS

TRANSFORMER

POSITIVE	NEGATIVE
Free-loving Idealistic Easygoing Liberal	Lacks feeling Naïve Indiscriminate Erratic
Original lover Non-possessive Unique Mild	Odd lover Non-existent Peculiar Touchy
Cultured Experimental Progressive Eclectic	Insincere Kinky Superficial Promiscuous
Sparkling Popular Friendly Tongue-in-cheek	Scatty Impersonal Flattering Sarcastic
Convincing Refined Quietly persevering Humane	Stubborn Manipulative Uncompromising Reactionary
The values that you espouse are only as effective as they are gentle and considerate.	Mania posing as morality is totally immoral and leaves others no choice but to leave – suddenly.
A sense of self-ridicule is the critical ingredient that makes you utterly attractive.	To make you to their liking, others have to take you with a pinch of salt.
Through it all, you discover ultimately that healthy sexuality blooms most of all in love.	Your attempts to be sexually enlightened/enlightening founder on reefs of sexual self-doubt.
Letting it be known that only one side of you is that cool will make others warm towards you.	Relating to you is like hugging thin air that occasionally and unaccountably crackles.
True liberalism is about telling the difference between your fears and your principles.	Your ideas on how to relate seem to create more misunderstanding than understanding.
SOLUTION	PROBLEM

If you find yourself on the receiving end of negative traits, it is because you are not expressing the opposing positive traits.

VENUS IN PISCES

ESSENCE

LOVING THROUGH ACCEPTING

LOVE OF ALL   LOVE IS ALL

Venus is said to be Exalted in Pisces because Love and Beauty can find their fullest expression in this sensitive, imaginative and compassionate Sign. But, as ever, to reach great highs you may first have to encounter great lows – lows that are the result of your expression of love being too full, your expectations of love too naïve. At heart you know and feel that love is everything, but the world as it currently is still puts things like money and self-preservation at the top of the list. So you have to learn some discrimination and awareness of how best to express such a universal love sense as yours, otherwise you are prone to being too vulnerable and impressionable, and to having your fundamentally caring nature taken advantage of.

You regard everything as being alive and sacred, from a minute insect to a human being, from a fluffy toy to an angel. As a result of this lover-of-the-universe quality that you have about you, one-to-one relationships can run into trouble through your trying either to give or to get all this sense of love to or from one person. This is the gallon-in-a-pint-pot syndrome, whereby either your partner can be drowned by your love and affection, feel unable to live up to it, and possibly then go off with someone else who they feel is not so demanding; or, you yourself can become so frustrated that your partner does not meet all your needs and longings that you are then unfaithful (which is rather ironic) – or promiscuous, which is a rather wonky way of loving the world!

Venus in Pisces makes for a complex love nature. This is mainly because, on the one hand, you have a highly evolved sense of love as unconditional and of beauty as a healing property; and, on the other, your fears and doubts as an ordinary, fallible human being are inclined to make you see love as something you need and beauty as something to get or to own. The truth is that you are already a thing of love and beauty, but if you doubt this because of emotional and social conditioning, you then lay yourself open to being used and abused.

So, in order to channel and express appropriately such a love nature as yours, some form of art or service should be practised, in such forms as painting, music, nursing, animal welfare or any other that enlightens or relieves. This in turn gives you an increased sense of self-worth, a lack of which is what lies behind the pain, confusion and hopeless longings that arise from your looking for something in someone else which you have inside you. This yearning can also be experienced as a religious fervour in which you worship someone or something as a substitute for loving your Self, which you doubt. Venus is Exalted in Pisces because you are intuitively aware that God and Love are within you, even though the path to such Exaltation can be strewn with false gods and goddesses – of your own making.

LIKES
All living things · Relieving suffering
Romance and exotica · Poetry of the soul
A peaceful touch

DISLIKES
Insensitivity · Witnessing suffering
Pedestrian love life · Commercial hypes
Rough handling

If you are a man, this could be the kind of woman to whom you are attracted – but it is really a part of you, so realize it.

VENUS IN PISCES

TRANSFORMER

POSITIVE	NEGATIVE
Compassionate Sympathetic Appreciates unity of all life	Martyristic Too sentimental Fanciful choice of lover
Congenial Evocative Sensitive lover Easygoing	Too passive Seducing Idealizes lover Lazy lover
Artistically inspired Natural healer Self-sacrificing	Romantically deluding Hypersensitive Self-pitying
Selfless Highly affectionate Altruistic Very generous	Weak-willed Wanton No self-value Undiscerning
Loves unconditionally Gentle Philanthropic Peaceful	Fears rejection Soppy Indulging Evasive

SOLUTION	PROBLEM
Yours is a case of learning to turn the other cheek, and accepting pain as a way to, not of, love.	Fear of involvement. Enforced isolation. Subjected to emotional cruelty.
When you love for love's sake rather than your own there are no bounds to your love.	Pretending to fall or be in love in the vain hope of feeling loved and worth something.
Redirect your sensitivity and imagination towards pursuits that relieve or enlighten.	Feeling disillusioned. Unrequited love. Suffering for love. Lovesick.
Remember that, in truth, you associate love less with the body and more with the Soul.	Unsure of love aims and your lovability. Confusing love with sex or need. Lovelorn.
You can only love the world as much as you love yourself as a part of the world.	Feeling taken advantage of, and that others are too dependent on your selflessness.

123

If you find yourself on the receiving end of negative traits, it is because you are not expressing the opposing positive traits.

MARS

Keyword: GETTING

Mars symbolizes the urge to GET what you WANT. This takes DRIVE, which includes SEXUAL DRIVE, INITIATIVE and COURAGE. But Mars is RAW ENERGY, and as such needs Direction and Consideration. Without these, Mars is merely SELFISHNESS, ABUSE and, at its most extreme, VIOLENCE.

Your Mars-Sign shows how you best express your DESIRES, without being PUSHY or feeling PUSHED.

If you are female, your Mars-Sign will point to the kind of male to whom you are attracted – although it is actually a part of you. If you are male, you express and embody quite directly the qualities of your Mars-Sign. With either sex, if you find that you are on the receiving end of negative Mars-Sign traits, then it is because you are not expressing the positive ones.

MARS IN ARIES

ESSENCE

GETTING THROUGH DOING

THE DOER   THE RAMROD

The best and the worst expressions of Mars's self-assertion burst forth in Aries. You have a reliable but uncontainable supply of raw energy which must have an outlet and, more importantly, a direction. Unless you have some more introverted personality traits, you are unlikely to see the complications to life that seem to beset so many others. This enables you to get on with things without being side-tracked by the pros and cons.

Simple and straightforward as this no-nonsense approach and unfettered style of yours is, it can cause you to miss more subtle points and undercurrents. If you are as thick-skinned as you are hard-nosed, then this probably doesn't bother you. However, if you feel that in not grasping some vitally important element you are failing to get what you want out of life, then it would be wise to stop and ask yourself "What am I actually after?" But this simple question is unlikely to be asked until quite a few spills and collisions have occurred with both animate and inanimate objects. You certainly have plenty of get-up-and-go, and hard knocks are taken in your stride – or charge, more like.

Courage and initiative are firmly on your list of virtues, but love and patience are not, and may need to be learned. And the combative or even soldier-like quality of Mars in Aries can have a get-sex-while-I-can kind of attitude. Sexual stamina is in abundance, as a rule, and if you are female you may well be attracted to military-, macho- or even violent-type males.

You can spark enthusiasm in others, and your confidence and daring set an effective example. However, unless there are more steady and persevering qualities present, such as indicated by Planets in Taurus or Capricorn, you could be poor on follow-through. You can and should learn to finish tasks through recognizing what it is about yourself that you are unsure of, and doing something about it. Many of your troubles are the result of using your undeniable energy to go forward in pursuit of some external challenge in order to evade an internal conflict. What you then end up with is an external conflict. Your obvious courage will be needed at a certain stage to penetrate your psychological jungle – rather than a green, fleshy or concrete one. This stage is very noticeable when you – or your partner – begin to react more and more hotly to anything that points to any feelings of inferiority.

You are very much the "warrior" or "Amazon" – or supersalesperson. The worst expression of this is a coarse or bullying nature that interferes and dominates with sheer physical force, and is insensitive to the feelings of others. The best expression is as the untiring champion of the underdog, when you use both word and deed to promote your cause, cutting through obstacles and red tape like a machete through hollow green stems.

LIKES
Fast satisfaction · Quick returns
Competition · Action
Getting your own way

DISLIKES
Watching and waiting · Complicated conditions
Opposition · Kicking your heels
Interference

If you are a woman, this could be the kind of man to whom you are attracted – but it is really a part of you, so realize it.

MARS IN ARIES

TRANSFORMER

POSITIVE	NEGATIVE
Self-assured Self-willed Independent Survivor	Inner doubt Egocentric Unco-operative Selfish
Bold Energetic Fighter Fearless	Aggressive Pushy Militant Violent
Direct Brisk Championing Outspoken	Unsubtle Intolerant Irascible Quarrelsome
Daring Dashing Exhilarating Spirited	Foolhardy Bumptious Exhausting Ostentatious
Leader-type Strong stamina Enthusiastic Self-starting	Bullying Insensitive Insatiable Self-defeating
Showing people what you can do – rather than what they should do – sets an inspiring example.	Dissatisfaction with others as a result of seeing them as objects of your unsatisfied desires.
When you've discovered what you're driving at you'll have no trouble getting there.	In your hurry to get "it" and give the impression you've got "it", you've forgotten what "it" is!
It benefits you to direct your energies into a worthwhile cause rather than badgering others.	Feeling raw and uncomfortable with yourself. Others are as short with you as you are on patience.
Take up a pursuit that suits your martial nature, but that isn't unnecessarily harmful.	You are making some part of your life or being into a horrific battlefield.
Knowing who and what you are dependent on both emancipates and supports you.	Being left to your own devices but not getting very far. Lack of staying power.
SOLUTION	PROBLEM

If you find yourself on the receiving end of negative traits, it is because you are not expressing the opposing positive traits.

MARS IN TAURUS

ESSENCE

GETTING THROUGH STABILIZING

SHARE YOUR WEALTH	LIGHTEN YOUR LOAD

Getting what you want means laying your hands on conventionally recognizable assets, such as money and property. With Mars in Taurus you are able to progress easily and steadily in the material sphere of life, and use your patience and worldliness (or someone else's) to make your pile, or at least to secure a quiet corner somewhere.

However, as is often the case with seemingly uncomplicated Taurus, there is a snag. In the case of Mars the snag is that whatever you initially set in motion in order to achieve these material ends – and this you may have done quite unconsciously, through marriage or inheritance, for example – cannot easily change direction. It just keeps chugging along, churning out what eventually can be meaningless and frustrating. Where you were once close to the Earth, you could, at a later date, find your feet stuck in clay. What was obtained in the name of stability becomes a millstone around your neck. Alternatively, the money-making-machine could just grind to a halt.

As you are basically intent on achieving stability, the secret lies in your establishing what truly constitutes stability, rather than blindly conforming to an overly materialistic society's idea of it. This strongly implies a need for the change in direction that you hitherto found so difficult to negotiate. In making the change, two points should be borne in mind.

Firstly, the nature of the change in how you view material stability could be said to hinge on the Law of Infinite Supply, which states that in order to keep supply flowing in, you must keep it flowing out. In other words, continually investing whatever you possess in people or in causes in which you believe, without just thinking of gain for yourself, will ensure that your incoming supply line is maintained. Secondly, you cannot be expected to make such changes overnight, because you are rather like a very low-geared vehicle – you have great pulling and pushing power, but are a devil to stop or to steer. Nevertheless you have the strength to hold steady as you turn, so to speak. For this reason, whenever you make a change, be it personal or professional, there is no going back.

Your sexual drive could also be likened to this "low-geared vehicle", in that it is slow to start but hard to stop – and has great pulling and pushing power! Yet, like a bull, you can sometimes be led by the nose. Your decidedly sensuous nature should also find appealing the notion that ploughing back into the Earth what you have gained from it, in the form of possessions, pleasures or experience, will naturally yield forth fresh fruits.

LIKES
Wealth and comfort · Concrete results
Being dominant or dominated
Taking your time · Planning and foresight

DISLIKES
Scarcity or just making do · Abstract objectives
Wishy-washy relationships
Being pushed · Sudden changes

If you are a woman, this could be the kind of man to whom you are attracted – but it is really a part of you, so realize it.

MARS IN TAURUS

TRANSFORMER

POSITIVE	NEGATIVE
Capacity for work Earning power Productive / Industrious	Materialistic Avaricious Wealth for wealth's sake
Methodical Practical Persistent Patient	Plodding Boring Slow to change Slow to act
Close to nature Craftsperson Mechanically skilled and able	Cloddish/Brutish Philistine Mechanical and thick-headed
Dependable Sexually attractive Sensuous Passionate	Jealous and possessive Smouldering Carnal Intense
Executive ability Formidable Powerful reserves of strength	Vindictive Bullying Violent when pushed
Identify your "beast" and re-channel its energy; transform its nature. Be strong with yourself.	Getting into violent and distressing situations. Trouble with the Law.
Your Earthy appeal is at its best when you enjoy it for what it is yet observe its limitations.	Sexual frustration. Acute and persistent emotional pain.
Search for, recognize and express your sense of beauty and physical order.	A dull and unrewarding time. No ray of hope or sign of meaning.
You know that you must make a change. You know that in time it will work out for the better.	Lack of direction. The agony of indecision born of inertia and boredom.
Focus on how your material awareness or position could benefit others.	Successful but not satisfied. Meaningless material pursuits. Financial dilemmas.
SOLUTION	PROBLEM

If you find yourself on the receiving end of negative traits, it is because you are not expressing the opposing positive traits.

MARS IN GEMINI

ESSENCE

GETTING THROUGH COMMUNICATING

THE LIVE WIRE   TOUCH AND GO

"Those who don't ask, don't get" is a saying that could apply to Mars in Gemini, for a couple of reasons. If you want or want to know something, it won't be too long before you go and ask. If you find yourself hanging back, then possibly it's for the other reason, that unless you've asked yourself what you want in the first place, you're unlikely to ask anybody else. However, since your desire nature, your tongue and your nervous system seem to be wired up to each other, you can find yourself quite impulsively getting something – or someone – and then wondering what to do with it – or with him/her. So it won't be long before your restless mind and mobile body start looking for something else, getting it, and, again, not quite knowing why – and so on.

Your sexual drive has almost as much to do with nervous energy as with anything else. Attaining the object of your desires and satisfying them can be achieved quickly, and often in the same deft stroke. The relief at having made some kind of definite contact is very important to you, because it both eases your nervous tension and makes you feel desirable – until you next need topping up. However, what you are in fact experiencing is that initially described urge to find out what it is you really want, for if you don't, you're likely to get trapped in a round of tasting the "goods", not feeling too sure and sitting on the fence as you try to have your cake and eat it, then coming back on second thoughts and finding the goods gone. Ideally you need to slow things down in order to see what is happening so that you might discover what your heart desires. This does not mean slowing down to the point where you are always at the talking/thinking stage, because that can leave you very tense or testy – and still with no answer.

As is ever the case with Planets in Gemini, the contact you are truly trying to make is with yourself. You can talk the hind leg off a donkey, dazzle any sexual target with your personal light-show, and sell something that nobody wants to anyone. Yet until you concentrate your attention and distinguish between what you want, what you have, and what you can't have, you will be at the mercy of your nervous system's running the show, which is like setting a chimpanzee loose in a telephone exchange.

Your highly-strung energies need an almost constant outlet, examples of which may be ferreting out information, or intense mental or physical activity. Alcohol abuse would be a sign that you were trying to suppress these energies, but then so would too much self-denial, especially sexual, for you can cerebralize your urges only too well. Whoever you have made contact with who absorbs, pre-occupies or frustrates your energies, you must follow the "current" back to the "generator" – ask what it is about them that is really driving you – be it upwards, downwards, forwards, backwards, wild or just plain crazy, for it'll really be something inside you.

LIKES
Intellectual contests · Thrills and spills
Variety · Being kept guessing
Keeping them guessing

DISLIKES
Dull company · Nothing happening
Routine · The predictable
Being pinned down

If you are a woman, this could be the kind of man to whom you are attracted – but it is really a part of you, so realize it.

MARS IN GEMINI

TRANSFORMER

POSITIVE	NEGATIVE
Sharp-witted Humorous Droll Stimulating	Sharp-tongued Sarcastic Irreverent Argumentative
Ingenious Dextrous Resourceful Adaptable	Mischievous Light-fingered Meddlesome Unreliable
Quick Agile Lively Mobile	Hasty Jumpy Unrelaxing Restless
Eloquent Inquisitive Communicative Contact-maker	Verbose Nosy Rambling Gets wires crossed
Versatile mind Flexible Full of ideas Multi-talented	Scatters thoughts Changeable Lacks perseverance Motley
Focus your attention on developing one talent; the rest will progressively cleave to this.	Strung out, spread too thinly, nothing hanging together. Getting nowhere fast.
When you've made it clear to yourself what's going on, make it crystal-clear to others.	Your nervous desire to be in the know disguises your fear of being known. Misunderstandings.
Find a pursuit that involves both danger and discipline, speed and judgement.	The thrills you seek are not worth the havoc they wreak. Irritation breeds irritation.
The devil need only make work for idle hands (and minds) – not ones as capable as yours.	Getting involved in dubious schemes and affairs. Hairy, touch-and-go situations.
You're the most amusing person to be with – when you see your own joke.	Mocking what you cannot understand gets plenty of reaction, but no respect.
SOLUTION	PROBLEM

131

If you find yourself on the receiving end of negative traits, it is because you are not expressing the opposing positive traits.

MARS IN CANCER

ESSENCE

GETTING THROUGH NURTURING

FIGHT OR FLIGHT   **BURY THE HATCHET**

Direct, forceful and uncomplicated Mars is not too happy in Cancer, with its deep and convoluted emotions. You want to make your desires known but not at the expense of laying yourself open to insecurity or embarrassment. Consequently, those desires – or fears – are all too often not clearly expressed and not recognized by others, with the end result exactly as you feared – neither party knowing where the other stands. For this reason the Red Planet is said to be in its Fall in the Sign of the Crab, meaning that your old way of getting what you want out of life has to "die", and a new way be devised.

Quite simply, when you really care about something you want, you can get it. On the one hand this means taking the trouble to separate carefully your desires from your fears, and to discover how your desires unerringly put you in touch with your fears. In this case you may have to seek help in tracking down what it is from your past that drives you both towards and away from the object of your desires. On the other hand, you need to get in touch tenderly with the fears and needs of the ones who matter to you, which is why you already have the ability to seep into another's most private and hidden areas – an ability that should only be trusted as long as it has honourable intent behind it. In effect, you are able to heal other people of their doubts and fears, and, in so doing, achieve the same for yourself. This is where the indirectness of Mars in Cancer becomes a positive quality, because you can get alongside a sensitive area without its running away and hiding. Having the courage to push on into the emotional heartland, in the face of pain and vulnerability, is the essential challenge here.

You are fiercely protective, particularly of your family. However, unconscious motivations are strong in Cancer, which means that in protecting others close to you, you may also be attempting to conceal what you're unsure of within yourself. For this reason you will attract relationships that force such fears into the open. What these fears most often contain is a certain amount of unconscious anger, which in turn can draw bad temper, strife or even fire or violence down on you, especially in the family/domestic sphere, for this is where such anger probably originated, in your own childhood. For a more peaceful life you have to bury the hatchet – but in order to do so you have first to dig it up.

Your sex drive is strong, largely because it has emotional need behind it, which is both a good and a bad thing. Bad, because when your insecurities overshadow your desires, there occur a sexual indolence and doubt, which can be very frustrating, and can lead to insecurity for both you and your partner. Positively, though, you are able to tune keenly in to the needs of your mate, making him/her feel both excited and secure at the same time, which is very special.

LIKES
Close involvements · Secure sex life
Striving for your kin · Active home life
Rooting around

DISLIKES
Lukewarm emotions · "Unsafe" sex
Distressing the family · Domestic conflagrations
Inner doubts

If you are a woman, this could be the kind of man to whom you are attracted – but it is really a part of you, so realize it.

MARS IN CANCER

TRANSFORMER

POSITIVE	NEGATIVE
Sensuous Provocative Passionate Sexually subtle	Irritable Evasive Too intense Sexually unsure
Tenacious Protective Bold Hardworking	Possessive Defensive Surreptitious Compulsive
Complex Adaptable Sensitive Healing	Neurotic Moody Quarrelsome Confusing
Instinctual Intuitive Original Occultly aware	Unaware of urges Fatalistic Weird Spooky / Spooked
Binds family Strongly sympathetic Fights for security	Splits family Blind allegiance Domestically domineering

A happy person makes a happy family, so go for what makes you happy, but not guilty.	Domestic strife through not distinguishing between emotional priorities and passing desires.
Deliberately going upstream to seek the source of your desires will reveal hidden depths.	Allowing yourself just to float downstream has found you at sea.
Find out what's really making you angry. Recognizing your own quirks helps others to do so, too.	Suppressed anger wells up, and causes temper tantrums that blow things just at the wrong moment.
Ascertain what or who you really care about, and make it known in a direct and energetic fashion.	Your hidden fear of losing someone or something is causing exactly that.
Learn to recognize the fine line between stimulation and aggravation.	Sexual involvement puts you in touch with problems by exploding them in your face.
SOLUTION	PROBLEM

69

If you find yourself on the receiving end of negative traits, it is because you are not expressing the opposing positive traits.

MARS IN LEO

ESSENCE

GETTING THROUGH CREATING

ALL THE WORLD'S A STAGE   THE WARRIOR KING OR QUEEN

There is nothing tepid about Mars in Leo. Whatever else is present in your personality, this makes for a hot and fiery streak that should find some form of dramatic, creative or romantic expression.

Mars in Leo lends a very "masculine" influence, which means that if you are a male you lean towards the macho and chauvinistic. If you are a female you find this kind of man irresistible, often despite yourself. If this expression of such rank masculinity invites trouble, then it needs to be taken to a higher, more sophisticated, level. Perhaps Carl Jung's definition of the masculine principle, which is present in both men and women, will be of help here: masculinity is the desire to get what you want and the ability to do so.

You are determined and confident – at least, outwardly. But the impression you give is what's important to you – and you don't get a second chance to make a good first impression! It is crucial, therefore, to know your pitch and to be able to call the shots. And, as you wish to soar to the heights, you need a head for them, which includes being prepared to be shot down.

You love to be seen to shine and excel. Although this can lead to a neurotic need for admiration, it also demands that you have the honour, dignity and ability that command respect. You can be tempted to enforce respect and obedience in others, which is "creating" in the wrong sense, and this leads to extreme humiliation, which is something that you dislike, nay fear, more than anything else. You can definitely be an inspiring figure, for you have a strong sense of personal power, which you should maintain through being loved rather than feared. You may well occupy a position of authority, for such vitality and will-power as yours cannot, or should not, go unnoticed.

You are a gallant or gracious lover. To you the opposite sex is the most attractive thing in the world, which keeps the "royal blood" coursing through your veins until the end. Your desire nature is very reliable, and, although it inclines you to possessiveness, makes sure that you get your man or your maid.

You have a feeling of invincibility within you and without you. If you interpret this in a selfish or small way, you then overact and overreact to everything, which can lead to heart trouble, be it of the medical or the romantic kind. When you recognize this triumphant feeling as an expression of the Eternal Spirit (symbolized by the Sun, the Planetary ruler of Leo) your sense of glory goes beyond petty ego drives, and the way in which you set about getting is truly creative, for it becomes a gift.

LIKES
Centre stage · Pride in partner
Respect · Excitement
Honesty

DISLIKES
Feeling insignificant · A dowdy partner
Humiliation · Losing control
Small-mindedness

If you are a woman, this could be the kind of man to whom you are attracted – but it is really a part of you, so realize it.

MARS IN LEO

TRANSFORMER

POSITIVE	NEGATIVE
High-spirited Passionate Ardent lover Energetic	Melodramatic Possessive Jealous lover Coercive
Dignified Zealous Proud Heroic	Pompous Self-righteous Vain Tyrannical
Enthusiastic Vital Speculative Exciting	Offensive Brutal Wild gambler Over-excited
Self-assured Determined Strong-willed Leader-type	Feels infallible Quarrelsome Domineering Egoistic
Consistent desire Ambitious Magnetic Fearless	Overbearing Ruthless Conceited Arrogant
"When the going gets tough, the tough get going" is all.	A force greater than you has got you in its sights – or has already opened fire.
Your way out is your way forward is what you are absolutely sure you do best.	As long as you don't admit that you're cornered, you'll stay cornered.
Staking your life on following your life and harming no other, is your best – your only – bet.	Feeling threatened or humiliated – or just hoping against hope. Accused and accursed.
As you hold your head high and take over, make sure there's no egg on your face.	Embarrassing or intimidating others so that they either ignore or oppose you.
If you're as magnificent and unique as you make out – and you do have style – then fear no rivals.	Haunted by a monster, a green-eyed monster – a monster that is you!
SOLUTION	PROBLEM

135

If you find yourself on the receiving end of negative traits, it is because you are not expressing the opposing positive traits.

MARS IN VIRGO

ESSENCE

GETTING THROUGH ANALYSING

SLAVE-DRIVER OR SLAVE-DRIVEN   HEALTH IS EFFICIENCY

Mars in Virgo can make for such an exacting nature, both in yourself and in others, that there comes a time when it is necessary to give it a break and to begin to let life live itself, according to its own rules. Although your accuracy at work and at play is something to be marvelled at, you tend to forget that you are only supposed to be doing your best, not the impossible!

As is often the case with Planets placed in Virgo, a lesson needs to be learnt from the opposite Sign of Pisces. This means giving in to the mystery of life, the world, sex etc., and putting everything on automatic pilot for a while. This will mean asking yourself the question: What exactly am I striving for? When analysing what it is that you wish to get, you will be surprised to discover either that it is very simple or that you haven't got a clue. Next question: So why all the hassle?

If you do not get this Piscean message written in Virgoan script, then it is more than likely that you will find yourself involved in some sort of reversal of the usual expression of your desires. For example, where you are normally so in charge of your physical well-being, you could be subject to ill-health (relating to nerves, stomach, guts, muscle cramps or to some more mysterious complaint). Or, you could be making a hash of things at work, when you pride yourself on taking pains to be efficient. In either case, this reversal is mainly due to loss of energy and concentration, as a result of thinking you have to keep tabs on every little issue, or to unsatisfied desire mixed with consequent irritation. You may even end up being work-shy, as opposed to workaholic. In general, where work is concerned you are very reliable, but prefer not to be responsible for the whole show: you are happier serving than ruling. However, you can be so utterly efficient that it can go painfully unnoticed, as there is no sign that the work had to be done in the first place. If this should ever be the case, then go "on strike" for a bit.

Probably the most interesting area of this character reversal is your sexuality. A Virgoan Mars can zip (!) between chastity and promiscuity like no other. For a start, if there is any sexual repression lurking in the past, you won't miss it. You can sit on it, but it's better to have an experimental attitude and sort it out. Taboos won't get laid until they are so! There is quite likely to be more sexual guilt in you than in most, but you are very good at disguising it in some way, through promiscuity, for instance. Desire (Mars) and Purity (Virgo) have always been uneasy bedfellows, and given rise to extremes as they react to each other. One way of being sexually involved but "untouched" at the same time would be voyeurism, or seeing yourself doing it as if in a film, while you take notes. But sex is essentially a trip into the unknown, so you need to keep a wary eye on it, but avoid judging or keeping score, for this smacks of repressed desires.

LIKES
Fine precision work · The professional touch
Getting it right · Sexual hygiene
Technique

DISLIKES
Inaccuracies · Bodging
Those who do not try · Tacky sex
Ham-fistedness

If you are a woman, this could be the kind of man to whom you are attracted — but it is really a part of you, so realize it.

MARS IN VIRGO

TRANSFORMER

POSITIVE	NEGATIVE
Fine sexuality Hits the spot Watchful Even-tempered	Frustrating Sexually exacting Voyeuristic Repressed
Helpful Healing ability Attentive Subtle touch	Interfering Hypochondriacal Neurotic Precious
Industrious Methodical Energy-saving Thorough	Workaholic Inflexible Energy-wasting Never finishes
Shrewd Correct in procedure Clever Ingenious	Exploitative Sanctimonious Wheedling Cantankerous
Precise Accurate Clean Economical	Critical Fussy Clinical Niggardly
Allowing room for human error will actually create less of it. Take it easy.	Difficult or even impossible to work with or to be with.
The first step towards getting something is learning how to get it – but don't try too hard.	Feeling lonely and isolated, and uncomfortable with your ways of trying to resolve this.
For best results, apply your fine awareness of efficiency to your own mind and body.	Feeling exhausted and run-down. Overworked but under-productive.
"Physician heal thyself" – and then anyone else who asks.	Being a pain in the neck, butt etc., both to yourself and to others.
Allow yourself the time, grace and opportunity to explore your sexual mystery.	Frustration from being sexually inhibited and inhibiting. Feeling undesirable.
SOLUTION	PROBLEM

If you find yourself on the receiving end of negative traits, it is because you are not expressing the opposing positive traits.

MARS IN LIBRA

ESSENCE

GETTING THROUGH RELATING

THE SOCIAL MOVER   **BALANCE YOUR IMPULSES**

As Mars symbolizes the urge to be independent and assertive, it has its wings clipped in socially-conscious Libra. If you are wanting to make a decisive move or statement, you find it cannot easily be done without some prior sanction or approval from others in general, or from one person in particular. So the challenge is to get what you want but to fit it in with social values and emotional requirements. This is challenging indeed, and the dynamics of Mars in Libra seem to force you into finding this balance one way or the other ...

Until you are able to adjust your needs and values to your desires, and vice versa, you are liable to be controlled by whoever you are sexually involved with, or want to be sexually involved with. In effect, you are attracting a conflict of wills in order that your desires be tested and realized. Additionally, and for the same reason, you are likely to attract an aggressive, energetic or quick-tempered partner. One difficulty here might be that of confusing your own desires with those of the other party, which is one reason why they will appear to have you dangling on a string, like a set of scales!

Libra also has the effect on Mars of softening its hard-cutting edge. This is particularly hard-going on the male ego, but, of all the planetary influences, selfish and hard-headed Mars has probably been most responsible for the harm and strife in the world. So it can be very worthwhile (indeed manly) to use such force and drive sensitively, rather then selfishly.

This is a subtle placement because you could be seeking approval of a kind that has nothing to do with your own values. For example, feeling that you have to live up to some social or sexual role that is being created by your peers, when in truth such a standard is not your style at all. So ...

Essentially, you are an initiator of social activities and new social values. Your desires spring from a feeling of wanting everyone to be in harmony and to pull together. So your forceful and impatient qualities really have to be expressed in a graceful or aesthetic fashion in order for you to make your point. However, what can happen is that your own wishes and opinions do not get put across at all for fear of social ridicule or sexual rejection. The anger and resentment that can mount up as a result of this may then come out in an anything but graceful way. You can see both sides of an argument, but this should not be regarded as a reason for not acting at all. In fact, at an evolved level, Mars in Libra often finds itself with the casting vote, which is when you have to be aware of your own moral convictions, and have the courage of them, which is what Mars in Libra is truly all about.

LIKES
Togetherness · Doing it with style
The social whirl · Knowing your desires
Equal partnerships

DISLIKES
Injustice · Being blunt
Social vacuums · Indecisiveness
Being dominant or dominated

If you are a woman, this could be the kind of man to whom you are attracted – but it is really a part of you, so realize it.

MARS IN LIBRA

TRANSFORMER

POSITIVE	NEGATIVE
Attentive lover	Fawning
Enthusiastic	Idolizing
Skilful lover	Impersonal
Gentle	Tentative
Fair	Bland
Easygoing	Indecisive
Diplomatic	Insincere
Co-operative	Misleading
Persuasive	Devious
Binding	Separative
Discreet	Awkward
Perceptive	Judgemental
Idealistic	Unreal
Intuitive	Unfeeling
Principled	Self-limiting
Measured	Inhibited
Polite	Vulgar
Considerate	Selfish
Agreeable	Disputatious
Sedate	Impulsive

SOLUTION	PROBLEM
True good manners naturally follow when you consider the ways of others and yourself equally.	As a reaction to your forced good behaviour, you now see yourself as behaving badly.
Your concept of a better life and society has to be based on a vision – not a need.	Narrowing your social horizons for the sake of maintaining your security needs proves unrewarding.
Quietly achieve your objectives through being sure of yourself – not of others.	Juggling people and situations towards your idea of harmony is having the opposite effect.
You are learning the art of diplomacy – but hardly at the expense of being ill at ease.	Caught in a netherworld of not knowing your social values from your individual desires.
To gain the object of your desires, focus on what they really are, not what you presume they are.	Whatever you try in order to gain the object of your desires still finds you at a disadvantage.

139

If you find yourself on the receiving end of negative traits, it is because you are not expressing the opposing positive traits.

MARS IN SCORPIO

ESSENCE

GETTING THROUGH DESIRING

DO OR DIE   **THE FRONT-LINER**

This indicates a primal nature of the highest – or lowest – order. In other words, you have a powerful sense of survival and sexuality, as well as how these two drives become intertwined. This amounts to a kind of magnetic intensity about you that has such an effect on your surroundings that you never elicit a bland response from others – you always get to them in some way, whether you mean to or not. This underlying "poke" that you have was just as apparent when you were a child, in fact it was probably more so for you may since have tried to conceal it, and so it is likely that you invited extreme friendship or extreme hostility from quite early on. It was, and still is, as if you strongly and automatically challenge or champion other people's most basic hopes and fears.

The psychological effect that this has had on you is important to consider, for it will have similarly coloured all your subsequent relationships, especially those of an intimate nature. It is vital for you to admit to possessing this provocative energy that continually hums around and about you, and to understand its qualities and conditions. You are not about to get or to go for anything unless you really desire it: merely liking, needing or, least of all, going along with something is not sufficient for you. Your defiant aura, be it active or passive, will always attract great loyalty or great enmity, and not much in between. For you it is a case of either get or be got, or have or be had. Metaphorically speaking, your safety-catch is permanently in the "off" position.

You are thus capable of creating quite a stir, and gaining the object of your desires in the process. However, what can queer your pitch is a reluctance to assert yourself in this powerful way as a result of having been abused in some way yourself, or having a strong urge to get your own back for this reason. In either case you are likely to be filled with a degree of self-disgust, or at least self-criticism. In turn, you will express or disguise this with an air of politeness, or the complete opposite.

Ultimately, therefore, the inherent strength and power of Mars in Scorpio are best used to heal or to transform your environment in some way, beginning with your own self-image. Merely trying to keep yourself to yourself, often in a smugly unassailable way, is a result of that previously-felt threat of destruction. However, a fear of being destroyed can lead to self-destruction – witness a cornered Scorpion! In ancient times, astrologers would instruct army generals to put troops with Mars in Scorpio in the front-line of battle. Even today you have no equal when it comes to pushing for changes and improvements where they are most needed, be they for your personal evolution or for society in general.

LIKES
Intimate involvement · Emotional intensity
Being influential · Firing from the hip
Winning against the odds

DISLIKES
Indifference · Compromising
Being manipulated
Going down on your knees · Giving up

If you are a woman, this could be the kind of man to whom you are attracted – but it is really a part of you, so realize it.

MARS IN SCORPIO

TRANSFORMER

POSITIVE	NEGATIVE
Charismatic Highly sexed Irresistible Emotionally rich	Megalomaniac Degrading Dissipated Resentful
Strong-willed Indestructible Forceful Courageous	Stubborn Self-destructive Brutal Seething
Thorough Exhaustive Determined Ambitious	Cruel Exhausting Unrelenting Ruthless
Probing Healing Discreet Perceptive	Prying Manipulative Devious Caustic
Passionate Deep Red-blooded Powerful	Jealous Dark Cold-blooded Revengeful

The life-force is omnipotent, omniscient and omnipresent – it has you, go with it.	Feeling very depressed, meaning that you are fighting against the life-force.
Discovering that you are able to get the best out of others allows you to do the same for yourself.	Not being prepared to find your own better nature, you look for the damnable in others.
Tempering your taking to task with a measure of affection is what successfully completes it.	Taxing, scorning or denying others is a sign that you have no love for yourself.
You also know there is a power in life that is for the good, and you feel it at the core of you.	Stuck in the pit of your own bloody-mindedness – and you know it.
There is something about you that others look to or are drawn to – you can and must live up to it.	Dissatisfaction with yourself, which is reflected in perverting yourself or others.

SOLUTION	PROBLEM

If you find yourself on the receiving end of negative traits, it is because you are not expressing the opposing positive traits.

MARS IN SAGITTARIUS

ESSENCE

GETTING THROUGH SEEKING

DEFENDER OF THE FAITH   IS MIGHT RIGHT?

Mars in Sagittarius gives you a built-in sense that freedom of movement is your birthright, that you should be able to make off over some distant horizon in any direction whenever you feel the urge to do so. Furthermore, you usually possess the energy and enthusiasm to take you there. However, the operative phrase is "in any direction", or, more precisely, it's a burning question of "in what direction?". For Mars in the Sign of the Centaur is essentially a very raw and untamed kind of energy, and, as such, needs directing and controlling, rather like a team of spirited horses, otherwise you are liable to feel torn apart by conflicting urges, or, even worse, to bottle them up, in which case the very least you can do is to get plenty of physical exercise.

For you to get what you want in life has to be through seeking a definite goal. What should guide your "team of horses" is a strong sense of crusading for some ideal, be it religious, artistic, scientific or whatever you believe to be worthy of your considerable energy, for it is really only something "big" that satisfies Mars in Sagittarius. Without this cause to consume your exuberance, you could be driven to merely raging around, both physically and emotionally, or to being the armchair philosopher, forever holding forth about this and that opinion, but never acting upon any.

Not surprisingly, your sex life has a lot to do with how you are channelling your vibrant libido. When you want sex you want a lot of it, right there and then. But, at other times, you can be curiously matter of fact, take it or leave it. It all depends what is currently calling you onward, a sense of mission or a sense of frustration, an absorbing relationship or a habitual one.

When you avoid getting carried away on your own fanatical wave of beliefs, or being stuck in the mud of not having any beliefs at all, you excel at rallying others (and yourself) out of apathy, and exhorting them to act out their sense of adventure or to reveal what is inhibiting it. This could be in the living room or in the world at large. You enjoy the splendour and majesty of being on the march towards some lofty goal, or, at least, the idea of it.

Yes, without a dream on which to focus your energies, you can be a very wild Centaur indeed, and might well wind up "hobbled" by something that Saturn cooked up that forces you to find a new direction – or indeed, any direction. In other words, if you feel constricted by any of life's situations, is it because you have not considered what you actually want freedom for? There is something mighty about you, but might without just cause can never be right. Imagine that you have a personal banner – and what is emblazoned upon it!

LIKES
Firm and fiery principles
Honesty and hot debate · Outdoor activities
Sports and games · Pageantry

DISLIKES
Lukewarm beliefs · Lying and small-talk
Being cooped up · Physical inactivity
The humdrum

If you are a woman, this could be the kind of man to whom you are attracted – but it is really a part of you, so realize it.

MARS IN SAGITTARIUS

TRANSFORMER

POSITIVE	NEGATIVE
Independent Far-sighted Espouses and grants freedom	Opinionated Overlooks obvious Demands unlimited freedom
Explorative Daring and bold Adventurous Optimistic	Tangential Impetuous Scatters energies Wildly hopeful
Forcefully convincing Crusading Effective teacher Active idealist	Self-righteous Fanatical Ear-bashing Preaching
Frank and open To the point Clears the air Enthusiastic	Tactless and rude Harsh Argumentative Extremist
Lusty and vigorous Mobile Spirited Very friendly	Lustful and carnal Restless Boisterous Lecherous

SOLUTION	PROBLEM
Your concerted energies are as uplifting as your rampant energies are disturbing.	Feverishly frustrated by your desires' not being met or when you feel baulked.
Allowing others to come out with what's bothering them will release what's bothering you.	Confusion and resentment resulting from others' feeling reluctant to confront your hotheadedness.
Your visions and ideals are as good as others' understanding of them.	Out of touch with prevailing trends. Blinded by your own beliefs.
The ultimate adventure: getting lost in order to discover where, who and what you are.	Biting off more than you can chew. Lost for direction. Constantly shifting objectives.
Are your beliefs allowing you the freedom you desire in order to further yourself?	Missing the point, and frustrated by your inappropriate convictions.

If you find yourself on the receiving end of negative traits, it is because you are not expressing the opposing positive traits.

MARS IN CAPRICORN

ESSENCE

GETTING THROUGH BUILDING

THE MASTER-BUILDER   THE EXECUTIVE

Mars is said to be Exalted in Capricorn, which means that, ideally, you go about getting what you want in such a deliberate, pragmatic and sure-footed fashion that what you get stays got. In effect, you are basing your achievements on firm foundations, and are not, as a rule, inclined to taking short cuts, for you know that they end up being the long way round. However, it is highly possible that you do not fully realize just how broad and deep are those foundations on which you are building your endeavours, especially if there is an impatient streak somewhere in your personality. The key to appreciating that you are getting somewhere is to trust that "building work" is going on, even though it could be taking place unconsciously, beneath the surface, where foundations are based.

You are also aware of the facilities and structures society and business have to offer, and should make use of them in order to further your ambitions. However, although one secret of your success is an evolved sense of how various systems work, this can also be your downfall if you allow them to eclipse your own, independent, methods and values. Alternatively, your Exalted sense of what achieving really means could well necessitate your having to go it alone, without even being able to subscribe to the standard procedures that others follow. Mars in Capricorn is a great indication of the self-made person, sooner or later.

Sexually you are quite passionate, but only someone whom you have allowed yourself to become intimately involved with would or need be aware of this. Essentially, your Earthiness ensures that you understand both the gross and the subtle nature of the human body. Again, the Exalted status of Mars in Capricorn more or less demands that you do this, and not just indulge in a body for its own sake, without appreciating that it houses a Soul.

Conversely, or even perversely, you can suppress your passion and curb your drive with your basically disciplined nature. But, potentially, you are more capable than most of determining the fine line between being sexually aware and being just plain sexy, between sexual restraint and sexual inhibition.

The ability to delegate and regulate is an essential quality of Mars in Capricorn. This applies both to the professional and to the personal spheres of your life. This ability rests mainly on having a purpose and a plan, and a sense of timing. You know, or learn, that everything can be accomplished, using time as your instrument. So, whether they concern a business deal or a sexual relationship, your ends can be achieved as long as you pace yourself and do not allow yourself to be hypnotized and pressured into meeting a deadline or target that is a convention of others, born of their fear of failure, as opposed to your certainty of ultimate success.

LIKES
Knowing your pitch · Professionalism and status · Direction and purpose · Sexual reliability · Firm foundations

DISLIKES
Vagueness · Ridicule and ignominy Dead-end jobs · Being fantasy-ruled Hare-brained schemes

144

If you are a woman, this could be the kind of man to whom you are attracted – but it is really a part of you, so realize it.

MARS IN CAPRICORN

TRANSFORMER

POSITIVE	NEGATIVE
Persistent Single-minded Nobody's fool Industrious	Pig-headed Disagreeable Dog-eat-dog attitude Workaholic
Works according to plan Earthy and practical	Cold and calculating Insists on material results
Authoritative Respects order Disciplined Commands respect	Uses others Lust for control Disregards others' rights Slave-driving
Sexually disciplined Capable of celibacy Strong sex drive Self-reliant	Sexually controlling/Controlled Suppresses libido Lacking affection Lonely
Energetic worker Decisive Cuts red tape Inscrutable	Restless at work Agonizing Bucks system Self-mystifying
Avoid wasting time and energy seeking external approval – and realize your ability to organize yourself.	Feeling thwarted and down-trodden, underemployed and directionless.
Your fears create an austere love life, whereas prudence would create a well-regulated one.	Feeling unapproachable and emotionally dried-up. Impotent or frigid. Lonely.
Balance your sense of order with that of others. Self-discipline comes before order.	Feeling that others are not being efficient or co-operative. Rejected advances.
Base your plans or ideas on what is practical and expedient – and then stick to them.	Getting bogged down in your own system – or your lack of one. Progress slow or halted.
Rather than fighting the way of the world, you are able to tailor your ambitions to suit it.	Feeling all alone in the world. Working very hard merely to keep the wheels going round.
SOLUTION	PROBLEM

145

If you find yourself on the receiving end of negative traits, it is because you are not expressing the opposing positive traits.

MARS IN AQUARIUS

ESSENCE

GETTING THROUGH LIBERATING

THE FREEDOM FIGHTER　　　**LEADER OF THE PACK**

"If you wish to get the fruit – you have to go out on a limb" is a suitable maxim for Mars in Aquarius. In other words, for you to be moved to get what you want, your actions have to involve an element of the unusual, something that sets you apart from the crowd. If they suggest doing what everyone else is doing then you become quite inactive, even withdrawn. Whatever the case, what truly motivates you is having some kind of system to buck, and "system" can mean family, state, partner, friends or anything that appears to be limiting your freedom. In fact, as you can also be rather disinclined to stick your neck out without good reason, it may have to be the sudden realization that you have got yourself hemmed in that forces you to act for yourself. For without sufficient freedom you are the first person to suffer, as your vital energies get dammed up inside you.

At a more evolved level, getting what you want entails doing something that helps beings with less freedom of thought and movement. You can be a social activist on a small or great, an individual or collective scale. You are motivated by goals for the common good, which can include benefiting all forms of life, not just the human. It is also highly likely that, at some stage, you will begin to appreciate that certain goals cannot be attained other than through teamwork. You may even be unconsciously aware of this, and be a compulsive joiner of groups and clubs – and an unpredictable leaver of them, because you have yet to discover your own act. However, ultimately, your interest in yourself has be to aligned with the interest of others. Owing to this desire both to do your own thing and to be a part of a team, you are quite difficult to understand. But mucking in with others is your true métier, whereas being selfish is justifiable only when you are developing yourself in order to find your social niche, rather than being reluctant to have one at all, owing to a fear of getting lost in the grey mass of human society.

This complex reserve that you possess is very marked in your manner of relating sexually. You are more capable than most of enjoying sex, free of guilt and other negative conditions, and will demand the freedom to do so. However, you are also capable of keeping your desires locked up in your head, as a result of being afraid to bring your emotional needs into the sphere of sexual intimacy. But, then again, you may enjoy sex entirely as an expression of freedom rather than of love or of the senses.

All in all, you just don't want to do things the way others do. Although you are prone to throwing the baby out with the bath water when a given situation becomes stale, your inventiveness, especially in emergencies, and the quickness with which you learn from your mistakes, are a strong example to others of how a human being can best get along in this world.

LIKES
New methods · Teamwork
Just causes · Freedom
Unusual activities

DISLIKES
Outworn methods · Blind dependence
Blind authority · Rigid conservatism
Predictability

If you are a woman, this could be the kind of man to whom you are attracted – but it is really a part of you, so realize it.

MARS IN AQUARIUS

TRANSFORMER

POSITIVE	NEGATIVE
Independent Unconventional Complex Original	Cantankerous Perverse Contrary Peculiar
Progressive Reformist Humanitarian Idealistic	Impatient Rebellious Superficial Escapist
Resolute Resourceful Group leader Co-operative	Inconstant Insular Loner Unco-operative
Surprising High-spirited Very active Stimulating	Erratic Disruptive Indolent Shocking
Sexually free Sexually experimental Non-possessive Cool	Sexually loose Sexually irresponsible Unfeeling Cold

You are after knowing what strings are attached – not having no strings attached at all.	You put no human or emotional value on what you want, so what you get seems valueless.
As you jolt others out of their complacency, point to a more attractive alternative.	You make your point, but your way of making it appeals to nobody. Being in a majority of one.
The purpose of being alone (all-one) is to discover that one is for all and all is for one.	On your own but not liking it. Maybe you've not noticed this, but then neither have many others.
Make it known both to yourself and to others what you want freedom for, not from.	Surrounded by people who are irritatingly unaware of your way of acting and being.
When and where there is no precedent – make one. Don't expect immediate understanding.	Getting yourself into situations that have no apparent meaning or way out or way through.
SOLUTION	**PROBLEM**

If you find yourself on the receiving end of negative traits, it is because you are not expressing the opposing positive traits.

MARS IN PISCES

ESSENCE

GETTING THROUGH ACCEPTING

TEASE OR TONIC   THE SOFT TOUCH

You get what you want through subtle or indirect means. This can be likened to the angler who baits and casts his line, and then sits and waits, ready to accept what Life's current will bring. Yet strong emotional undercurrents are influencing your actions, so you need to discover what these are if you are to avoid being tugged this way and that, which in turn can compromise your asserting yourself. The resentments or regrets that build up as a result of this can lead to unconscious ways of expressing your anger or desire, such as sarcasm or secret liaisons. This kind of underhandedness ultimately meets with equally obscure reactions from others, and confusion then begins to reign.

What's really going on with Mars in Pisces is that you have an uncanny ability to drift and seep into the feelings of others. But what it is that enables you to do this is something that is invisible, rather as moods are infectious. It is as if you emanate a subtle aura that others respond to hypnotically. However, unless you tune in to this subtle aspect of your being, and endeavour to refine your coarser or more material desires, you are likely to be seduced by your own seductiveness.

As much as your moods are infectious, so too are you easily infected, both clinically and psychologically. Being aware of this is half the battle won; making sure you are not over-exposed to people and situations with whom or in which you feel uncomfortable. So much here depends on your being sure of what you actually want, and not giving in to your vagueness, which you use as a kind of get-out clause in case you fail to achieve your objective. The activities that galvanize you are ones that employ imagination or compassion. Occupations that do not cater to your finer feelings will tend to find you listless and easily fatigued. Yoga, Tai Chi and other subtle forms of exercise are most suited to keeping your body and energy supply healthy. Dancing is also something that you thrive on and can also be particularly good at. Work that involves mental or physical healing is something else to which you are well-suited; and working behind the scenes will also appeal to your somewhat shy and self-effacing nature. This could also include activities that require you to be present but not too noticeable, like photography.

Where your sexuality is concerned, either these finer feelings can lend a delicate and delicious quality to your style of love-making, or they can cause you to be quite confused or misled. It is best to remember that your sexual drive is highly dependent on your emotional state, which means that you can resort to pretence, fantasy or artificial stimulants in an effort to simulate excitement. But what is so exciting about Mars in Pisces is something you possess that is more emotional than physical, of the Soul rather than of the body. Tune in to that, and so will others.

LIKES
Quiet surroundings · Sexual mysteriousness
Subtle stimulation · Exotica
Creating illusions

DISLIKES
Being pressured · Banal sex
Coarseness · Mundanities
Direct confrontation

If you are a woman, this could be the kind of man to whom you are attracted – but it is really a part of you, so realize it.

MARS IN PISCES

TRANSFORMER

POSITIVE	NEGATIVE
Fascinating Charismatic Subtle Diffuse	Neurotic Volatile Evasive Unfocused
Charitable Congenial Self-sacrificing Tender	Seductable Malleable Self-deluding Weak / Lazy
Inspiring Imaginative Generous Psychic	Gushing Fanciful Indiscriminate Temperamental
Stealthy Sensuous Healing Intuitive	Furtive Treacherous Confusing Invasive
Compassionate Diplomatic Humorous Fluid	Resentful Frustrating Absurd Inconsistent
When you have admitted to your anger, lust or whatever, you will make room for your finer points.	Frustrated by others who are frustrated by your not being honest about negative feelings.
Employ your talent for gently asserting yourself and subtly revealing the soul of the matter.	Involved in or the victim of secret affairs, leading to social scandal or emotional confusion.
Something sublime and wonderful is calling from your imagination – not from someone else's personality.	Not knowing where you're coming from or going to. Tossed upon your own wave of imagined desire.
Check your motives before giving yourself away – but give yourself you must, eventually.	Feeling listless or dominated, impotent or frigid. Throwing yourself away gets you dumped on.
Identify that part of you to which others are drawn and which you, too, must follow. Surrender.	Psychosomatic complaints – usually as a result of misdirected energy, for example work versus play.
SOLUTION	PROBLEM

If you find yourself on the receiving end of negative traits, it is because you are not expressing the opposing positive traits.

JUPITER

Keyword: GROWING

Jupiter symbolizes GROWTH and the LAWS, BELIEFS and ETHICS that govern it and make it possible.
Jupiter is also a sense of EXPANSION and FURTHERANCE that leads to OPPORTUNITY, WEALTH and FAITH.

So your Jupiter-Sign will show the way in which you seek to BROADEN your knowledge, horizons and
UNDERSTANDING, through such pursuits as HIGHER EDUCATION, TRAVEL, RELIGION, PHILOSOPHY etc.
Negatively, Jupiter's Sign will point to ways in which you can be EXCESSIVE and OVER-something
(over-indulgent, overweight, over-optimistic, over-careful, over-zealous, over-the-top etc.). At its
highest level, Jupiter and thus your Jupiter-Sign indicate how you actually, or how you may, express
and experience JOY and GOODWILL, and what you hold to be your "Image of God".

Note: Jupiter takes twelve years to orbit the Sun and to go through the twelve Signs of the Zodiac,
therefore it takes a year to pass through one Sign. Because of this, everyone born in the same
twelve-month period will share the same Jupiter-Sign. This in itself indicates the fact that Jupiterian
qualities such as Beliefs and Moral Values depend to quite a degree on the social climate into which
you were born. However, the more you study and understand all your Planet-Sign qualities, the more
able you will be to make your Jupiter-Sign qualities very much your own.

JUPITER IN ARIES

ESSENCE

GROWING THROUGH DOING

FOOLS RUSH IN . . .   . . . WHERE ANGELS FEAR TO TREAD

You have the enthusiasm and faith of a child, whatever age you actually are, and because of this you can go far in life. However, you need to be careful that your natural eagerness does not become arrogance, or that your magnanimity does not get swallowed up by extravagance.

Your faith rests on the principle that Life looks after those who live it; trusting spontaneously is your most positive mode of being. When things go wrong this philosophy tells you that there is always more to come, that Life's supply of opportunity and experience is inexhaustible.

Not surprisingly, Jupiter in Aries invites quite a few knocks and falls, mainly because you are inclined to bite off more than you can chew as a result of a surfeit of enthusiasm but a lack of know-how, plus a failure to appreciate or to enlist the abilities of others. Nevertheless, high hopes and high spirits invariably carry you through, and, most importantly, it is your readiness to plunge into an experience that leads to your learning what you need to know. Your Soul ever precipitates challenges that demand growth on all levels, and, by the same token, major developments usually occur on the spur of the moment.

Your Image of God is a force that is always up and at it, abandoning or renewing what is outmoded and unworkable, forever marching on to the next step forward, and to the next, and the next . . . So you strongly and continually need to feel that your life is going somewhere, and will invest great amounts of time, money and energy to ensure this. Such an attitude will attract followers, especially if there are other leadership traits in your personality (indicated by your other Planet-Sign positions).

This can, of course, also attract lame ducks and sheep, with the result that you appear to have to do almost everything. But really it is for you to get things going and to make sure that certain others will keep them going, while you lead on – and on – following your youthful star. Joy for you is found in experiencing Life as a procession with you at, or somewhere near, the head of it. Your goodwill is expressed as you pass back and down the vision you behold that lies forever ahead.

LIKES
Active occupations · Travel
Forward-looking people · Optimism
The Pageant of Life

DISLIKES
Sitting around · Being housebound
Dead-ends and dead-wood · Pessimism
Faint-heartedness

Jupiter is your clue to making more of life.

JUPITER IN ARIES

TRANSFORMER

POSITIVE	NEGATIVE
Crusading	Self-righteous
Exhorting	Bullying
Adventurous	Overbearing
Aspiring	High-handed
Enthusiastic	Over-optimistic
Quick grasp of whole	Ill-prepared
Zestful	Rash
Honourable	Naïve
Generous	Gives to impress
Thinks big	Extravagant
Enterprising	Boastful
Unshakable	Over-confident
Innovative	Precocious
Self-sufficient	Pig-headed
Carefree	Careless
Noble	Stupid

In all matters relating to Jupiter, a critical point of development occurs every twelve years when it returns to the Sign in which it was placed at the time of your birth. In effect, this marks the beginning of a new cycle of growth and understanding.

Your ability to overcome even the direst dilemmas gives rise to new ideas and strengths.	Finding yourself in seemingly impossible situations – often alone.
Keeping something back is proof that you have even more to offer and to rely on.	Self-importance – apparent or real – arouses resentment in others that leads to harsh treatment.
Any high-flier checks his/her instruments before taking off – then the sky's the limit.	Dubious speculations. Overspending. Losses in business and in friendship.
What inspires you is where you're going. What inspires others is how you get there.	Getting others' backs up when you want them to back you up.

SOLUTION	PROBLEM

If you feel subjected to the negative traits or values, you will overcome this by accentuating the positive ones.

JUPITER IN TAURUS

ESSENCE

GROWING THROUGH STABILIZING

THE TRUSTEE   **THE FUND-RAISER**

Material possessions and development, together with the position and comfort that they give, is what you believe in. And, to a greater or lesser degree, you are also quite able to attract wealth in some way or other. However, as our society currently bases its beliefs on material values, it is important for you to understand the Cosmic Law that governs the accumulation of material things. Failure to do so would mean that you were possibly going to amass wealth, wallow in it, and then lose it or lose control of it, or be dogged by a fear of losing it or by a need for something that money cannot buy. Alternatively, you could find it excessively difficult to make much at all in material terms.

In the first case, there is a lack of understanding of the Law of Infinite Supply, which states that in order to maintain wealth you must invest what you have in furthering others, and not just hang on to it for its own sake. In the second case, you are not aware that, if you need and use it for something worthwhile, material wherewithal will always be forthcoming. Jupiter in Taurus poses the issue of what you do with money. Growing through Stabilizing means that the improvement in your material circumstances has everything to do with understanding that stability is a natural state that everyone is entitled to, and that it is maintained by keeping resources flowing in through keeping them flowing out. Meanness just does not suit you.

When you have begun to appreciate this wisdom that Jupiter in Taurus offers, you are likely to find yourself in a position of management or trust, or one in which you are actually responsible for fund-raising. Yet "all that glistens is not gold", and sooner or later you become aware that it is a sense of wealth, rather than wealth itself, that really matters.

For this reason your expression of Jupiter's joy is quite obvious and tangible as you are usually merry and generous. However, this feeling of bounty can be abused through various forms of physical indulgence, or by frittering away funds that have come your way too easily. When you have got through or around this area of prodigality, you are capable of embodying your Image of God, which could be said to resemble Father Christmas, Old King Cole or Mother Nature's Horn of Plenty.

LIKES
Good things of life · Being the provider
Material wealth · Traditional values
Warmth and comfort

DISLIKES
Bare existence · Wastefulness
Being in debt · New-fangled ideas
Sparseness and scarcity

Jupiter is your clue to making more of life.

JUPITER IN TAURUS

TRANSFORMER

POSITIVE	NEGATIVE
Sound judgement Contemplative Practical philosopher	Self-opinionated Too cautious Blinkered philosopher
Comfortable Gives stability Steady progress Trusting	Smug Expects ease Stick-in-the-mud Cynical
Jovial Good-humoured Generous Good appetite	Hedonistic Irresponsible Wasteful Gluttonous
Affluent Moneywise Furthers economy Charitable	Greedy Penny-pinching Exploitative Status-conscious

In all matters relating to Jupiter, a critical point of development occurs every twelve years when it returns to the Sign in which it was placed at the time of your birth. In effect, this marks the beginning of a new cycle of growth and understanding.

The wiser your use of material resources, the more available those resources become.	The more material position means to you, the more you feel threatened by material collapse.
You have a sense of life being infinitely abundant – but your lack of faith tries to prove it otherwise.	Physical or material degeneration – or both – through misunderstanding the meaning of abundance.
Believing that there is more to life than you know would find you – and others – so much better off.	Resisting or failing to see changes in the world around you finds you at a dead-end.
When you've weighed all the odds in your inimitable style, you realize that life is good.	Obsessed with your own viewpoint, you fail to see how others can figure positively in your life.
SOLUTION	PROBLEM

155

If you feel subjected to the negative traits or values, you will overcome this by accentuating the positive ones.

JUPITER IN GEMINI

ESSENCE

GROWING THROUGH COMMUNICATING

THE FURTHER ONE TRAVELS ...	...THE LESS ONE KNOWS

Your natural enthusiasm for encountering as many facets of life as possible is in aid of getting to know the one who's getting to know – that is, yourself. The trouble with Jupiter in Gemini is that it can get so caught up with the endless attractions and distractions that life has to offer that it can forget this vital point. Who is being attracted? Why are you seeking distraction?

In effect, you are gathering information in order to weave it into a comprehensive whole, gathering knowledge to attain understanding, and drawing a circle to find its centre. In the process of doing this you naturally acquire many contacts which would serve you well as any kind of agent (for travel, employment, services etc., or for something more unusual). At a more intellectual level your "gathering" can enable you to see the general trends of society, as well as its individual points of interest; this has the qualities of the social commentator or historian. At any rate, being a mine of information in one or more areas is central to your capabilities.

You are rather like a tree with many broad, shallow roots rather than one narrow, deep root. In addition to the possibility of being the intellectual dilettante described above, you can also subscribe to two or more philosophies or sets of morals simultaneously. On the surface this may seem quite convenient, but it could also mean having to lead a double life, which, in turn, could mean falling between two stools, but then again this might suit you nicely. You are mobile and adaptable, but also easily uprooted.

So your widespread roots should be employed to give you a broad grasp of life, through which your faith in life will be established. This is preferable to merely skimming the surface of a subject or a culture, as if life were some kind of package tour. Your Image of God resembles an infinitely large library in which everything that needs to be known can be found, as long as you are prepared to open the book, and to see yourself reflected in what you find. Your joy is the joy of making things known and available to others, which at some point necessarily involves your becoming known and available to yourself, and to others, too. Gemini's paradox here is that there is always more to know, but only ever you to know it.

LIKES
Travel and literature · Human networks
Being in the know · Food for thought
Analogies and mental models

DISLIKES
Lack of variety and interest · Lack of
communication · Being out of circulation
Idle chatter · Disconnected thoughts

Jupiter is your clue to making more of life.

JUPITER IN GEMINI

TRANSFORMER

POSITIVE	NEGATIVE
Well-travelled Well-connected Popular Sociable	Scattered interests Disconnected Not known Restless
Knowledge-seeker Broad-minded Grasps general outline	Mere dabbler Shallow interest Sketchy knowledge
Knowledgeable Scholarly Mentally alert Many-sided	Academic Intellectual snob Verbose Tangential
Obliging Well-mannered Witty Cheerful	Hypocritical Crafty Indiscreet Empty

In all matters relating to Jupiter, a critical point of development occurs every twelve years when it returns to the Sign in which it was placed at the time of your birth. In effect, this marks the beginning of a new cycle of growth and understanding.

Amusingly let it be known that you are only prepared to be light and breezy up to a point.	Your semblance of acceptability is not acceptable to yourself. Too many twists to your turn.
You are after something that is worth knowing – that would be worth saying.	Saying a lot but communicating little, or saying nothing and communicating even less.
Travel broadens the mind – knowing where you are deepens it. You're the centre of your own circle.	Curiosity killed the cat. Your intelligence is severely limited by a fear of discovering yourself.
Realize that you are as interesting and as appealing as any place or face you come across.	After all the faces and places you've got to know, both you and others still have no idea who you are.
SOLUTION	PROBLEM

If you feel subjected to the negative traits or values, you will overcome this by accentuating the positive ones.

JUPITER IN CANCER

ESSENCE

GROWING THROUGH NURTURING

THE PHILANTHROPIST	ROOT AND BRANCH

As the key phrase "Growing through Nurturing" implies, you possess the highest standards when it comes to developing anything or anyone, for you understand the most basic of Nature's laws, that what is cared for usually prospers. For this reason, Jupiter is described as being Exalted in the Sign of Cancer.

Your feeling nature is both broad and deep, and you try to accommodate everyone. But wherever Jupiter is there lies the possibility of excess. So you can be overly emotional and sentimental and, literally, too kind. People are inclined either to run away from you or to walk all over you. This "over-care" is often a compensation for the emotional understanding and nurturing that you did not receive from your own mother and family. If this is the case you need to be as kind and considerate towards yourself as you are towards others. If you are often a "port in a storm" for others, believe in always having a safe haven for yourself, and you shall.

The wisdom that Jupiter in Cancer represents, as implied by Nature, can be expressed in a number of ways. Perhaps most importantly, because of the tendency to "over-care", you should be aware that at a certain stage a being needs to be "hardened off", in the same way as a gardener will put young plants outside, in order that they might gain the strength they need to survive in the outside world. This is Nurturing in the highest sense because the concern is for the ultimate welfare, rather than just the seemingly unselfish satisfaction of taking care of someone or something.

In truth, your undeniable sense of goodwill rests upon a belief, conscious or otherwise, that we all spring from the same root, that the Family of Man has one family tree. At one level you could experience this as a great sense of closeness to your immediate family or to your country, but this could lead to your feeling rather limited by it. At a more evolved level you begin to realize that all living things are related and need the same care and consideration. You greatly enjoy the family scene or your sense of nationality, but you can, and maybe must, find a greater joy in this sense of our common ancestry. Your Image of God is of the World Mother, of the Planet Earth, as a living, caring being, Gaia, and is most profoundly felt and expressed by you as the Milk of Human Kindness.

LIKES
A caring society · Quiet, homely pleasures
A home to be proud of · Domestic skills
A home from home

DISLIKES
A dog-eat-dog world · Nowhere to go
Bad accommodation · Inhospitality
Feeling rootless

Jupiter is your clue to making more of life.

JUPITER IN CANCER

TRANSFORMER

POSITIVE	NEGATIVE
Hospitable	Too accommodating
Protective	Spoiling
Caring	Doting
Becoming	Indulging
Charitable	Conscience-stricken
Sympathetic	Soppy
Super-receptive	Touchy
Friendly	Gushing
Loyal to family	Biased
Patriotic	Prejudiced
Abundant feelings	Sickly sentimental
Exuberant	Overdone
Good-natured	Affected
Kind	Too kind
Sharing	Self-effacing
Generous	Mean with self

In all matters relating to Jupiter, a critical point of development occurs every twelve years when it returns to the Sign in which it was placed at the time of your birth. In effect, this marks the beginning of a new cycle of growth and understanding.

Having a good impression of Nature's fullness, you can give a good impression of it.	Not trusting what you actually believe in, you give too much to others and not enough to yourself.
Your deep love of your heritage must lead you ultimately to a realization of our common ancestry.	Being overly attached to what you are familiar with drives the familiar away.
Charity begins at home: when you feel at home with yourself you'll feel at home with others.	Continually bothered by what you have to do – or avoid doing – in order to be appreciated.
Caring for everyone has to include yourself – and "hardening off the young ones".	Others expecting too much of you – or you of yourself. Weight problems for self or others.

SOLUTION	PROBLEM

159

If you feel subjected to the negative traits or values, you will overcome this by accentuating the positive ones.

JUPITER IN LEO

ESSENCE

GROWING THROUGH CREATING

THINE IS THE KINGDOM . . .   . . . THE POWER AND THE GLORY

There is something very self-evident about Jupiter in Leo, for you believe that your sheer existence is a testament to your worth. So it could be said that growth and development are achieved simply through an enthusiasm for yourself. There is a danger here of egotism and self-importance, but in some ways this is better than being falsely modest or shrewish.

However, although your sense of grandeur can lead to great displays of confidence and wealth, it can also lead to a fall from grace. But, then again, thinking or acting small could find you equally pressured to pull something extra out of the bag. So with Jupiter in Leo there comes a time when the nature of greatness has to be properly understood.

As with other placements in Leo, looking at it in terms of the Sun can be very illuminating. The Sun just pours out energy all day and every day, but it can also scorch and cause things to wilt. Likewise, your enthusiasm can miss the point that energy supply is one thing, but the nature of what it is feeding is another. In other words the people and the things in which you invest your time, money and feelings have certain qualities, requirements and limitations that can be easily overlooked by you, with consequent disappointment either on your part or on theirs, or on both. When you stop for long or often enough to note what real effect you are having on others, you will get a far better idea of just how powerful you are, and will then avoid your most common mistake, which is to overplay your hand. For the same reason, not being aware of your potential can cause you to underplay your hand.

"The more you make, the more you get" could be a reliable golden rule for you, as long as you appreciate that what you get is in aid of serving others, rather than merely so that you can bask in its glory. Joy for you is similar to the satisfaction that a king or queen would take from being the benevolent monarch who appreciates his or her subjects – friends, partners, subordinates etc. – as being what make him/her feel great. Your Image of God is therefore of the Sun-King or the Sun-Queen who is the Earthly expression of Divine Will, who bestows with wisdom, governs with compassion, and pledges his/her all to the glory of something greater than his/her ego. For you, God is like the Sun who shines for all.

LIKES
Gambling and speculation
Pageantry and ceremony · Drama
and grandeur · Children · Lavishness

DISLIKES
Playing it safe · The dull and the ordinary
Mean-heartedness / Small-mindedness
Having no dependants · Penny-pinching

Jupiter is your clue to making more of life.

JUPITER IN LEO

TRANSFORMER

POSITIVE	NEGATIVE
Big-hearted Benevolent Altruistic Inspiring	Bigheaded Pretentious Self-serving Misleading
Sense of glory Prestigious Honourable Noble	Vainglorious Self-aggrandizing Unkept promises Hollow
Self-confident Radiates warmth Energetic Strong stamina	Egomaniac Ostentatious Overbearing Intolerant
Self-assured Generous Entrepreneurial Thinks big	Over-confident Spendthrift Overblown Unrealistic

In all matters relating to Jupiter, a critical point of development occurs every twelve years when it returns to the Sign in which it was placed at the time of your birth. In effect, this marks the beginning of a new cycle of growth and understanding.

SOLUTION	PROBLEM
Basing your expectations on what you can give rather than get has the desired effect.	Unwise speculations, possibly leading to financial ruin. Losses in love / children.
Once you've stopped trying to gain attention you'll find yourself doing so – but in the right way.	Others find you impossible to get through to – so neither can you get through to them.
What ultimately impresses others is what initially impresses you. What is that?	The impression you have given is an act you are finding hard to live up to.
What you really have is a sense of greatness. Walk tall by looking up to what is greater than you.	Others are demanding that you deliver more than you really have.

If you feel subjected to the negative traits or values, you will overcome this by accentuating the positive ones.

JUPITER IN VIRGO

ESSENCE

GROWING THROUGH ANALYSING

SLOW BUT SURE   **THE NOBLE HELPER**

This is not the easiest Sign in which to have Jupiter placed, as the analytical and perfectionist nature of Virgo can, at times, make the Jupiterian growth and expansion almost imperceptible. The resolution of your frustration here rests on making a choice between either scaling down whatever your projects might be so that some sort of readily noticeable and therefore encouraging advances are made possible, or, philosophically accepting the notion that you have got a large and complex exercise in operation and that the "tale will grow in the telling". Additionally, analysing what it is that is growing through your efforts will help you become aware of the vital but relatively small role that you are playing in some greater operation that possibly involves many other people. On this score, a part of your work could very likely involve the enlisting of men and women to take part in that "greater operation" that serves the common welfare.

However, because the first and lesser choice of scaling down could lead to your becoming a big fish in a small pond, the increasing confidence but diminishing satisfaction that would arise from this would inevitably urge you to launch into being a part of that greater endeavour, which is the latter alternative. It helps you to understand that the next step up from being, so to speak, at the top of the second division is being at the bottom of the first. Indeed, perceiving the pattern and manner of (your) growth and development leads to a greater sense of understanding, which is growth in itself, but on a mental rather than a material level, and that is what Jupiter in Virgo is largely about.

In this respect you are also peculiarly able to make an orderly whole out of a sea of apparently unrelated details. In fact you experience joy in doing this for your Image of God is of some gigantic but precise Plan to which life and evolution are keeping. So your religious persuasions can amount to being puritanical, but they can also be profoundly practical and relevant. However, as a reaction to this possible over-concern for physical correctness, you can swing towards being quite the opposite by way of relief, so your hedonistic behaviour and pie-in-the-sky beliefs can surprise others. Yet as a result of this pendulum-like process of development, you arrive at an increasingly workable philosophy of life.

LIKES
Encouraging others · Cleanliness and order
A practical philosophy · Sense of long-term
purpose · A philosophy of health

DISLIKES
Bad working atmosphere · Being
over-organized · Armchair philosophy
Meaningless labour · Superficial healthcare

Jupiter is your clue to making more of life.

JUPITER IN VIRGO

TRANSFORMER

POSITIVE	NEGATIVE
Urge to learn Organized progress Persevering Professional	Too studious Self-limiting Brain-bashing Materialistic
Pragmatic Realistic Judicious Methodical	Cynical Pedantic Petulant Too analytical
Ethical Philosophical Virtuous Honest	Prudish Moralizing Narrow-minded Glib
Practical helper Conscientious Upstanding Thorough	Solicitous Sanctimonious Priggish Mean

In all matters relating to Jupiter, a critical point of development occurs every twelve years when it returns to the Sign in which it was placed at the time of your birth. In effect, this marks the beginning of a new cycle of growth and understanding.

Use your fine awareness to ascertain precisely where, when and how you are needed.	Rejected offers of your help and your opinion find you feeling offended and unappreciated.
In truth, something is only right and good if it both looks and feels right and good.	You think you are right but you are not enjoying it one bit. Bottled-up emotions.
Know that trying to work things out both in detail and way into the future is counter-productive.	You make mountains out of molehills, and cannot see the wood for the trees. Overworked.
Be aware that you are moving ahead – but on a broad front, and for a far-reaching purpose.	Working very hard but apparently getting nowhere.

SOLUTION	PROBLEM

163

If you feel subjected to the negative traits or values, you will overcome this by accentuating the positive ones.

JUPITER IN LIBRA

ESSENCE

GROWING THROUGH RELATING

THE SOCIAL ANIMAL   THE PEACEMAKER

As the key phrase suggests, you take your greatest strides forward in life through learning to relate in a manner that is wise and fair. As ever with Jupiter, your moral values, which are the basic guideline to relationships, are not so much your own as you might think; and this is particularly the case with socially-conscious Libra. The ethical / religious influences in your life have a direct bearing on the success of your personal relationships. Furthermore, you are inclined initially to take on board the more conventional moral attitude. If you are comfortable with this then well and good, and you probably have or will have a stable marriage, forever guided by the yardstick provided by your cultural background.

If, on the other hand, you find that this is not suitable to your needs and desires, then you will probably encounter at least one emotional upheaval that involves a major shift in your moral philosophy and sense of fair play, and possibly even includes some kind of litigation. For with Jupiter in Libra you are effectively standing in judgement – either consciously or unconsciously – both of yourself and of others. If your own "inner" judge is not being objective enough, then your "case" comes before a "real" judge.

And so you are constantly weighing your needs and desires against your beliefs and values. Sometimes the former is the heavier influence, and you are the regular socialite, being very much the person on everyone's guest list, and sometimes being quite intemperate. At other times you become immersed in trying to justify what you are and how you behave. You make the effort to be mild and temperate, but if your blood is on the red side you soon swing back into being taken up with the highs and lows of socializing and interpersonal relationships. This pendulum-like lifestyle can continue for some time, swinging between the intemperate, fun-loving but somewhat superficial you that craves social position and adulation, and the well-behaved, temperate you that places both you and others in the dock to be judged.

Eventually, joy comes your way when you realize that you are actually your own lawmaker and lawgiver, and that the God that judges you has the Image of the Peacemaker, which you yourself can become, when you realize that peace is simply an end to conflict, inner conflict, created by an imbalance between pleasures and moral values.

LIKES
Feeling socially "in" · Art and culture
Good companions · Romantic journeys
An attractive belief system

DISLIKES
Being alone · Cultural deserts
Feeling unwanted · No sense of occasion
Harsh self-denial

Jupiter is your clue to making more of life.

JUPITER IN LIBRA

TRANSFORMER

POSITIVE	NEGATIVE
Cultured Cultivates others Encouraging Shares riches	Snobbish Patronizing Flattering Toadying
Well-meaning Benign Conciliatory Grandly sympathetic	Superficial Too nice Ingratiating Expects too much
Sense of justice Sound morality Obliging and considerate	Too conceptual Misguided standards Double standards
Honourable partner Idealistic Enduring lover Sociable	Fanciful Promises too much Too abiding Juggles options

In all matters relating to Jupiter, a critical point of development occurs every twelve years when it returns to the Sign in which it was placed at the time of your birth. In effect, this marks the beginning of a new cycle of growth and understanding.

SOLUTION	PROBLEM
Either stick to your principles or change them – then you'll live up to them admirably.	Suddenly finding yourself being disloyal – or suspected of being so. Too many close ties.
When you've gained a truly impartial viewpoint, you're just as you'd like to think you are.	Legal or moral difficulties arise as a result of what you think being different from what you do.
Base your good intentions on what you believe, not what you need, and good you'll feel.	Your excessive need for praise makes you untrue to yourself, and thus others are untrue to you.
When you know a culture is something you grow in, not jump in or stay in, you set a fine example.	Being out of touch with your own values causes you blindly to subscribe to those of others.

If you feel subjected to the negative traits or values, you will overcome this by accentuating the positive ones.

JUPITER IN SCORPIO

ESSENCE

GROWING THROUGH DESIRING

AS ONE DOOR CLOSES . . .   . . . ANOTHER ONE OPENS

Who or what you find irresistible will push you to your limits. Whether you know it or not, your philosophy is of the "no gain without pain" variety, and that gain can apply to either your material or your emotional life. In fact, the two have a natural inclination to become heavily intertwined. However, to be more precise, it is really a case of "no gain without loss – of what you no longer need".

The desire that springs from this philosophy is powerful indeed, for it makes you hunger after the deep, the dark and the mysterious, and eventually leads you to find it. Alternatively, you are the one who is deep, dark and mysterious, and someone will find you out! So Jupiter in Scorpio does not gladly suffer superficial displays from other people, or from yourself, either. The dark side of your nature is where the gold lies, and one way or another you will go through hell and high water to knock off the soppy or wobbly bits that inhibit or compromise the discovery of that "gold".

The sexual dimensions of experience offer you the most opportunity in your search for the profound and cathartic. In the process you are likely to over-emphasize sex in some way, in order that it get your bigger wheels going round. Unusual sensations and reckless experimentation are also likely to be on your erotic menu, which could lead to "indigestion" in the form of degradation, complaints of the sexual organs and emotional destabilization. However, this is all par for the course for you, grist to the mill. The darker it gets, the brighter one has to be.

Another – although probably less conscious – way of living dangerously is through financial involvements that stand to make or to ruin you. This also gives you this sense of being close to the edge, of dicing with death. The belief that you gain through some kind of loss can be expressed more simply as making money through inheritance or settlement. At its "tamest" level, Jupiter in Scorpio can manifest itself as a lack of enterprise, owing to a fear of the transformation that growth would bring.

A more direct, and more dangerous, method of delving to satisfy your intense feeling, to confirm your deep convictions, is through involvement with the Occult – black, white or off-white. It will be found that your Image of God is like Isis Unveiled, which is life as it truly is at the core, not as we have fearfully and superficially disguised it. The joy that issues from this ongoing search is being able to help others through deep and dark places and periods. But, most importantly, you yourself should learn to transcend life's difficulties in a disciplined, informed and organized fashion.

LIKES
Fateful challenges · The occult and the mysterious · Sexual adventures · A philosophy of the soul · Deep joy through deep sorrow

DISLIKES
An uneventful life · Superficiality Automatic sex · Passionless philosophies Lukewarm lifestyles

Jupiter is your clue to making more of life.

JUPITER IN SCORPIO

TRANSFORMER

POSITIVE	NEGATIVE
Full-bodied	Heavy-going
Provocative	Dangerous
Intriguing	Scheming
Subtle strengths	Subtle weaknesses
Ambitious	Materialistic
Shrewd	Uses others
Flair for business	Power gamester
Resourceful	Devious
Inner strength	Obsessive and fanatical
Sees things through	Unrelenting
Healing	Exacerbating
Occultistic	Dabbler
Efficient	Intolerant
Confident	Dogmatic
Keen judgement	Judgemental
Utterly truthful	Fanatically blind

In all matters relating to Jupiter, a critical point of development occurs every twelve years when it returns to the Sign in which it was placed at the time of your birth. In effect, this marks the beginning of a new cycle of growth and understanding.

SOLUTION	PROBLEM
Being as convinced as you are, you can afford to show your doubts, and be even more convincing.	Your anger at yourself for trying to be too strong is reflected in others' weaknesses.
Remember the harder you push the harder you pull. You know that a rebirth means a death of some kind.	Unwise involvements that are hard to get out of. Attracting what you cannot cope with drains you.
You know that being feeble doesn't suit you – so get down to developing the muscles you need.	Emotional or money troubles through over- or under-estimating the powers you're dealing with.
Discover and accept hidden weaknesses, and you will find and use hidden strengths.	Getting out of your depth, or someone else out of theirs – or both. Degradation.

167

If you feel subjected to the negative traits or values, you will overcome this by accentuating the positive ones.

JUPITER IN SAGITTARIUS

ESSENCE

GROWING THROUGH SEEKING

LUCKY?   YOU'D BETTER BELIEVE IT!

To one degree or another, you subscribe to the ultimate philosophy that "life is what you make it". Accordingly you have a natural yearning to broaden your horizons, be it through travel, academic experience or just living itself, for you know that one thing leads to another, and that one lap of your journey will furnish you with what you need for the next, and so on. Consciously or otherwise, you believe in Providence, and your Image of God is the Golden-haired Goddess of Opportunity.

The real question that arises is how aware you are of this good relationship with Providence. At one level you could regard it merely as something that never leaves you wanting for too much, and often seems to provide you with the right thing at the right time. At a lower level you may just rely on it to get you out of a scrape, knowing that "something will always turn up". However, in a more evolved sense you are aware that Providence is much more than merely some sort of cosmic nanny who is forever making sure that you don't fall over and hurt yourself. You recognize that the Golden-haired Goddess of Opportunity is someone who can see around the curve of Time, and prepare you and others for the future by providing you with whatever is necessary. And so you believe, or at least feel the urge to believe, that there is some form of overall Intelligence System governing and furthering existence.

However, depending on other components of your personality, this System could be seen in somewhat narrower terms than those described above, as a dogmatic religious belief, for example, or as an inflexible set of morals, which at the same time professes to be the opposite. Alternatively, you may have no system of belief at all, for this is one way of keeping your options open, as open as the arms of Providence herself, maybe. You could also go overboard for some philosophy that says there is no plan, no limits, no nothing, just never-ending expansion.

What is common to all these views, irrespective of whatever your own might be, is that there is "something", some "rule" that binds everything together, that there is something common to everything. You therefore have some measure of interest in history, law, publishing, religion or any subject that concerns the search for a common and meaningful thread. And you find your joy in discovering this thread, in experiencing what it can show you and give you, and in revealing its truth, as you see it, to others.

LIKES
Big questions · Philosophizing
To believe in luck · Travel
Anything that furthers

DISLIKES
Small talk · Pointlessness
Negative thinking · Being confined
Stasis

Jupiter is your clue to making more of life.

JUPITER IN SAGITTARIUS

TRANSFORMER

POSITIVE	NEGATIVE
Philosophical Aspiring Explorative Strong beliefs	Opinionated Self-justifying Irresponsible Irreverent
Liberal-minded Tolerant Ethical Just	Cavalier Wasteful Self-righteous Narrow
Far-reaching mind Prophetic Speculative Optimistic	Wool-gathering Superstitious Fanciful Unrealistic
Jovial Enthusiastic Noble-hearted Kindly	Preposterous Extravagant Pretentious Indulgent

In all matters relating to Jupiter, a critical point of development occurs every twelve years when it returns to the Sign in which it was placed at the time of your birth. In effect, this marks the beginning of a new cycle of growth and understanding.

SOLUTION	PROBLEM
The secret of freedom lies in limitations, the secret of joy in sorrow. Rejoice in these and others.	Your limited sense of the unlimited finds you disappearing into infinitely confusing scenarios.
To come down from the mountain you first have to climb it.	Excessive expectations have given rise to excessive fears. False prophecy.
Believing the Universe to be just, you confess your doubts, are pardoned – then become an example of it.	Making vaguely generous gestures to conceal your doubts proves both restrictive and unprofitable.
Understanding that one set of beliefs eventually takes you to the next makes you quite believable.	Others keep trying to knock you off your high horse – or find it hard to take you seriously.

169

If you feel subjected to the negative traits or values, you will overcome this by accentuating the positive ones.

JUPITER IN CAPRICORN

ESSENCE

GROWING THROUGH BUILDING

STEP BY STEP . . .   . . . AND THE OCCASIONAL LEAP

You inherited a traditional set of beliefs and values that serve you well in the ordinary day-to-day sense. However, when change, even in the form of opportunity, comes your way, what normally holds you in good stead holds you back. The key phrase "Growing through Building" suggests that you have a reliable way of progressing in life, but your life is like a building of more than one storey, and so, occasionally, you have to put aside one set of plans or beliefs, and look for another that will serve and guide you appropriately for the next storey or the next chapter in your life.

The foundation upon which you are building your life – your cultural background – was most likely quite well-established, in its own way. This solid base is therefore something that you can probably always fall back on, be it a certain type of education, a religious, communal or professional tradition, material wealth, or something quite unusual, but nevertheless long-standing. However, this background, although it provides the backbone of society, is something that can keep you chained to its limitations as well as reassured by its traditions.

Any radical or highly individualistic streak in your personality will force you to free yourself from the negative tradition that is a part of your background. However, "the town may change but the well doesn't", which means that you may have shaken off that drab set of beliefs and morals, but you are still going to need some kind of belief system, or a rebuilding programme. An ongoing danger with Jupiter in Capricorn is the tendency, as a reaction to your cultural conditioning, to believe in nothing that cannot be proved. In the process, you'll settle for whatever the "system" says is so, and blindly mould yourself to fit in with it, while at the same time jealously preserving a few personal quirks to foster the illusion that you are your own person.

These difficulties are due to Jupiter being in its Fall in the Sign of Capricorn, which means that unless you drop your inclination to subscribe to the letter of the law rather than the spirit of it, your sense of joy in life will be as meagre as your ethics are narrow and confining, reliable though they may be. Your Image of God is all too likely to be non-existent, or of the most conventional and bigoted kind, or of Mammon. To get your rebuilding under way, and to put a spring in your step, a blend of Earth Magic and Common Sense would serve you well.

LIKES
A position in life · A practical philosophy
Physical evidence of beliefs
The traditional · A sound plan

DISLIKES
Lack of direction · Pie in the sky
Fanciful cults
The newfangled · No plan

Jupiter is your clue to making more of life.

JUPITER IN CAPRICORN

TRANSFORMER

POSITIVE	NEGATIVE
Conscientious Loyal Conservative Correctly behaved	Austere Bigoted Hide-bound Stiff
Productive Industrious Disciplined Capable	Pointless Slogging Self-restricting Dull
Highly esteemed Authoritative Successful Delegating	Sycophantic Brow-beaten/beating Status slave Buck-passing
Attracts wealth Prudent Philanthropic Economical	Avaricious Miserly Indian giver Penny-pinching

In all matters relating to Jupiter, a critical point of development occurs every twelve years when it returns to the Sign in which it was placed at the time of your birth. In effect, this marks the beginning of a new cycle of growth and understanding.

SOLUTION	PROBLEM
You only get out what you put in. And man does not live by bread alone.	Always on the breadline, or feeling threatened by the prospect of it.
Use the system to further yourself – but don't let it use you or take you over.	Either you've fallen from grace, or you never seem able to rise at all.
Developing your talent for meeting a collective need for growth satisfies your earnest beliefs.	Working merely to keep body and Soul together – but not recognizing the Soul's real needs.
You are honourable and responsible – but to what? Make sure it is worth your while.	Feeling you're wasting your life and time. Your mean idea of life is self-perpetuating.

171

If you feel subjected to the negative traits or values, you will overcome this by accentuating the positive ones.

JUPITER IN AQUARIUS

ESSENCE

GROWING THROUGH LIBERATING

SHARE AND SHARE ALIKE   THE CALL OF THE NEW

With Jupiter in Aquarius the question arises of how the World ought to be. This makes you want to view life in as open and democratic a way as possible. In effect, you feel that in order to plot a course into the future, some form of consensus of opinion is necessary, that everyone should agree with everyone else, or at least agree to differ. This idealistic and humanitarian philosophy of yours therefore has to develop and make itself real through your sharing your individual views with others, through friendships, teams, groups or any form of association.

But the paradoxical and vitally important point is that you have to start out with a belief of your own before you can offer it up to others. And then, by getting it mixed in with their beliefs, a "new" set of beliefs is arrived at that suits the aims and intentions of the group. The idea is that, taking this a number of steps further, all of humanity will eventually subscribe to a common ideology. So your Image of God is of a World Religion. Your philosophy is very much that of the New Age – the Age of Aquarius. So this is a long-term plan.

The catch to the wonderful idea that humanity can be together as One is that you have to have the "one" first, that is, one's own only too human and imperfect self. In other words, in order to further this aim, as you initially put forward your own beliefs, you should do so in the knowledge that there is bound to be some dogmatic and unrealistic content in them. This involves applying to yourself the same high standards of tolerance and openness to debate that your principles themselves engender. The weakness that arises here is the common Aquarian one of using an ideal with which all your friends or associates agree, in order that your personal shortcomings may be ignored in the fervid pursuit of the "cause". Such associations inevitably become unreliable and fall apart because they are built on a desire to escape rather than to liberate.

Joy for you is arrived at by recognizing that we all have something in common, and that through sharing both our hopes and our fears we will reach that common consciousness, an agreement based on the knowledge that love and acceptance are the beginning and end of human existence. It will be reached in no other way, and will take a long time. Your joy is also in knowing that we and you are on our way.

LIKES
Brotherhood/Sisterhood
Democracy · Sharing all
Universal morality · Feelings of togetherness

DISLIKES
Inhumanity
Fascism · Fear and greed
Dogmatism · Factionalism

Jupiter is your clue to making more of life.

JUPITER IN AQUARIUS

TRANSFORMER

POSITIVE	NEGATIVE
Broad-minded	Amoral
Impartial	Offhand
Unprejudiced	Undisciplined
Intuitive	Tactless
Idealistic	Spaced out
High principles	Aims too high
Reformist	Rebellious
Innovative	Upstart
Liberal	Woolly
Tolerant	Wimpish
Congenial	Impersonal
Friendly	Too casual
Philanthropic	Patronizing
Humanitarian	Self-righteous
Non-dogmatic	Dogmatic
Diplomatic	Insincere

In all matters relating to Jupiter, a critical point of development occurs every twelve years when it returns to the Sign in which it was placed at the time of your birth. In effect, this marks the beginning of a new cycle of growth and understanding.

SOLUTION	PROBLEM
Allow yourself the same rights and understanding that you are insisting everyone should have.	Your good intentions have become a mask for bad feelings, and the mask is slipping.
The naturally soft standards to which you subscribe gain effectiveness with a hard edge.	Others find it hard to relate to a human marshmallow – so you feel easily squashed. Ignored.
Return to first principles; first know yourself – then you and everything else will change.	Blindly following some lofty revolutionary concept has left you hanging in mid-air.
Be open to the possibility that something will happen – not just that anything *can* happen.	Anything goes – but nothing new comes along. You relieve pointlessness with pointed remarks.

If you feel subjected to the negative traits or values, you will overcome this by accentuating the positive ones.

JUPITER IN PISCES

ESSENCE

GROWING THROUGH ACCEPTING

BLESSED ARE THE MEEK ...   THE METAPHYSICIAN

The word "meek" is very appropriate for you because, like you, it is commonly misinterpreted as feeble or wimpish. What it really means is soft, mild and gentle, and this truly describes your philosophy of life and the beliefs to which you subscribe. It does not mean that you have to be a self-effacing push-over, which is possibly an uncomfortable image you have of yourself, and it is very likely that in the past you have been too obliging and consequently had too much expected of you. As a result, you may have become self-indulgent, suspicious of religious doctrines and others' intentions, and prone to exaggerating your own difficulties in a rather crooked attempt to reveal your misunderstood sensitivity.

Yet in typically Piscean fashion, this can all be flipped over to reveal that your growth and development in life hinge on trusting in the power of your sensitivity and goodwill. For the positive qualities of Jupiter in Pisces are essentially of the spiritual kind. The joy that can be yours rests on an unshakable belief in the beauty and goodness of the Universe. Your tragedy is the waste, indolence and frustration that can result from not maintaining this belief. The danger of this happening is due to your confusing your natural acceptance of things with a reluctance to take a stand until you feel cornered. Passive resistance can be both your best and your worst policy.

Inclined as you are to be the visionary artist or teacher, and someone who is often moved to help the underdog, it is important that you retreat regularly from society, especially into Nature, in order to recharge your spiritual batteries. However, this retreat should not take the form of wrapping yourself up in a security blanket that seals you off from past misunderstandings, for you are thus liable to find yourself sealed off from almost everything.

Likewise, some form of structured spiritual search is advisable, as opposed to free-wheeling in a self-comforting but meaningless fashion. However, on the other hand, you can easily be drawn to "follow" someone or something that you elevate to god- or goddess-like status, only to be ultimately disillusioned. Wrapping yourself up in your own pet beliefs is a very likely reaction to this possiblity.

Your true Image of God is of the "Master", the Christ or Messiah. God in human form, in fact. And the winding road of life leads you to the realization that this human form is your own.

LIKES
Beauty in simple things · Feeling great feelings · Mystical adventures Sensitive friends · Peace and quiet

DISLIKES
Lack of subtlety · Lack of inspiration Workaday existence · Being misunderstood · Oppressive noise

Jupiter is your clue to making more of life.

JUPITER IN PISCES

TRANSFORMER

POSITIVE	NEGATIVE
Mystical Visionary Imaginative Subtle humour	Peculiar Self-deceiving Paranoid Too obscure
Altruistic Compassionate Selfless Understanding	Parasitical Indiscriminate Self-indulgent Evasive
Mysterious Reclusive Sagacious Inner contentment	Unsociable Inaccessible Incomprehensible Self-contained
Unmercenary Flexible Good value Fair	Undervalues self Wishy-washy Self-effacing Weak

In all matters relating to Jupiter, a critical point of development occurs every twelve years when it returns to the Sign in which it was placed at the time of your birth. In effect, this marks the beginning of a new cycle of growth and understanding.

Money is merely a symbol of worth. What anything is actually worth is entirely up to you.	Not putting a price on anything to avoid putting a price on yourself finds you hard-up.
Remember you originally retreated to re-evaluate, then to re-emerge and reveal what you'd remembered.	The living human fossil – disguising your longing to be discovered as quite the opposite.
Sooner or later you find that living for others is the perfect complement to furthering yourself.	Either you look to others for the world, or you wallow in your own. Spinning in your own pond.
Your great sense of the wonder of the Universe should take you closer to it – not away from it.	Submerged in your own safe little backwater, which is self-comforting but self-defeating.

SOLUTION	PROBLEM

If you feel subjected to the negative traits or values, you will overcome this by accentuating the positive ones.

SATURN

Keyword: TESTED

Saturn symbolizes the LESSONS we have to LEARN in life. So, naturally enough, it also represents what we are least sure of, or, more simply, what we FEAR. Through FORCE OF CIRCUMSTANCES we are driven to find the DISCIPLINE, EFFORT and SENSE OF ORDER to overcome LIMITATIONS and OBSTACLES, and to pass the TESTS that Saturn sets us.

So your Saturn-Sign will show how you encounter the above through your experience of CONCRETE REALITY, the STATUS QUO and AUTHORITY FIGURES (especially your FATHER). It also suggests a way in which you cope with and pass these tests, with the result that in TIME you become an authority in your own fashion, and become the author of your own destiny. Saturn also describes in what way you are AMBITIOUS, and what you regard as valid MATERIAL STATUS. It shows what your TASK is, and what you have to WORK at and how.

As Saturn is symbolic of your SHADOW – the part of yourself about which you have doubts – there is a tendency to conceal your doubt, even to the point of giving the impression of doing quite the opposite, in the form of a polished VENEER. Your Saturn-Sign will also indicate the way in which you might become RIGID through being held back by such a SUPERFICIAL DEFENCE SYSTEM, and how you may overcome this.

Saturn symbolizes the metal LEAD, and through passing its heavy tests (major ones every twenty-nine and a half years, lesser ones every seven years or so) we reach the Gold that is the radiance and confidence represented by your Sun-Sign.

SATURN IN ARIES

ESSENCE

TESTED IN DOING

THE SPARTAN   THAT LONESOME ROAD

This is basically a case of learning to be self-assertive and sure of your standpoint, whatever that might be, as indicated by your Sun-, Moon- and other Planet-Sign positions. In order that this lesson be learnt, you will often find yourself left to your own devices. It could be said that the first lesson here is one of learning to enjoy and make use of the freedom of movement and expression that this offers – or rather imposes.

Saturn is said to be in its Fall in Aries, which means that any form of order other than that which you have won through your own efforts will not stand up. You are having to drive in the first post and blaze the first trail. "Beaten paths are for beaten people," as a leader once said.

One of the main problems that can result from this kind of test is a lack of feedback, which can make it difficult for you to ascertain how well you're doing in your own right. This can, in turn, lead to bad timing and pushing too hard. Furthermore, provocation and defensiveness may be present in your effort to elicit any sort of response. But this is self-defeating, because the very sense of inadequacy that you are trying to appease is what others then take a poke at.

So being a bit hard-nosed – but not hard-bitten – will, at times, be the only way in which progress can be made. There is no need to feel bad about this as long as there is some justification, some point down that lonesome road of self-discovery or self-expression on which you have fixed your gaze. Gaining and not losing sight of this point is of paramount importance as otherwise such a need for self-justification becomes habitual and neurotic. The noble but lonesome traveller should not be allowed to become a mumbling, shambling vagabond – at least, not for too long a stretch of the road.

Not surprisingly you are hard to please, because you know deep down that this can only be done by you. On the other hand, the simplest of things can delight you for hours. But ultimately, the only thing that satisfies you is the development of your own will, like a polished sword of tempered steel glinting in the first light of your day.

LIKES
Physical activity · Arguments
Overcoming the odds · Having a goal
Self-discipline

DISLIKES
Being out of condition · Losing
Push-overs · Lack of direction
Imposed discipline

Saturn says: "Time is your instrument – not your enemy. So take your time."

SATURN IN ARIES

TRANSFORMER

POSITIVE	NEGATIVE
Self-reliant Singular Independent One-pointed	Self-justifying Egocentric Hard to please Headstrong
Enduring Determined Persistent Strong	Austere Hard-hearted Unsubtle Cruel
Bold Assertive Strategic Self-assured	Defiant Reactionary Impatient Defensive
Disciplined Self-denying Resourceful Reserved	Restrained Mean with self Unsympathetic Unapproachable

With all matters relating to Saturn, a critical point is reached every twenty-nine and a half years, when it returns to the Sign position in which it was placed at the time of your birth. This is a life-progress report, when inner and outer pressures serve to demolish what is weak in you, and to consolidate what is strong.

Learn to trust the value of limitations, but avoid making a hair shirt out of them.	Expecting the worst allows very little room for the best. Tightness squeezes.
The more you learn the secret of timing, the more confident your actions will be.	Your intense expectation of opposition actually invites it, thereby frustrating your plans.
Surviving should not be an end in itself, but a means to an end that endures.	Feeling raw and uncomfortable, more grim than determined.
Once you've convinced yourself of yourself, others will follow, as a flight does an arrowhead.	Lonely. Insisting that others recognize your standpoint merely drives them away.

SOLUTION	PROBLEM

179

If you seem oppressed by any of the negative traits in others, it is because you are not taking responsibility for them in yourself, and transforming them into the positive.

SATURN IN TAURUS

ESSENCE

TESTED IN STABILIZING

THE BANKER   **FOR WHAT IT'S WORTH**

You are learning to set the correct value on things. Initially, this usually means that you have a particularly good sense of material values, but tend to undervalue intangibles or "invisible assets": qualities in life, yourself and others that are not immediately obvious.

Naturally enough, money can be a critical source of worry or concern, either because you are frightened of losing what you already possess, or because you are in debt, or funds seems hard to come by. In the first case you are probably attaching too much importance to material possessions; in the second you have probably not taken them seriously enough; and in the third you need to understand that cash flow has not so much to do with external circumstances as with how well-off you feel inside that you ought to be. At the root of this preoccupation with material worth is a fear resulting from an impecunious situation in early life, most likely due to your father. And so you feel that this area of life needs to be sorted out above all others. But, as ever with Saturn, an essential part of the test is gaining a sense of balance, and not overcompensating by evaluating life in purely material terms, or by being cavalier about it.

You are, or are seriously seeking to be, physically reliable and financially stable. Even if you appear to be laid-back about money matters, you quietly keep a wary eye on finances and subscribe to the usual investments like deposit accounts, stocks and shares, insurance etc.

If ever you find yourself counting the cost of things to such an extent that there ceases to be any real enjoyment of life – or that you feel tied to whoever or whatever it might be that is determining your material stability – then the time has come to review just what is worth what. Left unattended to, such a need for major re-evaluation could quite possibly involve the very loss you feared.

In order to pass Saturn's test in Taurus, it must never be forgotten that what is on trial is your sense of material and physical values, and not so much what you possess of material and physical value. Underlying the failure or success in this test is really only one of two issues: either a fear of (being without) money, or a sound understanding of its proper place in the scheme of things.

LIKES
Material stability · Practical methods
Dependable people · Physical proof
Business and bargaining

DISLIKES
Material limitations · Abstract reasoning
Wishy-washy people · Emotional doubt
Being unproductive

Saturn says: "Time is your instrument – not your enemy. So take your time."

SATURN IN TAURUS

TRANSFORMER

POSITIVE	NEGATIVE
Economical Wise buyer Frugal Realistic	Miserly Penny-pinching Grudging Dour
Financially stable and aware Acquisitive Affluent	Mercenary Grasping Avaricious Materialistic
Patient Persevering Imperturbable Concentrated	Inhibited Plodding Unobservant Limited
Constructive Purposeful Methodical Conservative	Stubborn Restricted Leaden Dull

With all matters relating to Saturn, a critical point is reached every twenty-nine and a half years, when it returns to the Sign position in which it was placed at the time of your birth. This is a life-progress report, when inner and outer pressures serve to demolish what is weak in you, and to consolidate what is strong.

With a purpose in mind nothing can stop you. Without one nothing can start you.	Stalemate and inertia. Consistently resisting change leaves you feeling like a lump.
Your discipline and hard work can be a pleasure in themselves, but should also be justly rewarded.	Head down and yoked to the task, you find that life is passing you by.
In reality you are making the choice between trusting and not trusting yourself.	Weighed down by your material considerations, you're making the simplest decision a heavy one.
The worth of what you give and get is exactly equivalent to what you think to be your own worth.	So afraid of being short-changed that your desire to get your money's worth just isn't worth it!
SOLUTION	PROBLEM

If you seem oppressed by any of the negative traits in others, it is because you are not taking responsibility for them in yourself, and transforming them into the positive.

SATURN IN GEMINI

ESSENCE

TESTED IN COMMUNICATING

RIDDLE MY RIDDLE   A MATTER OF MIND

Saturn indicates what one is least sure of, and therefore needs to become more versed in. When this Planet is placed in Gemini the issue becomes one of learning to use your mind efficiently and correctly. However, as rational thought has dominated our society for several hundred years, you must be careful to ascribe the right value to Reason – to use it, not to be ruled by it.

As is typical with the Sign of Gemini, it can go to one of two extremes: either you are the type who virtually worships the intellect, and for whom everything has to have a logical explanation, or you are hampered by not being able to reason things through.

If you belong to the first, and more common, type then you have the obvious advantage of being able to fit in fairly comfortably with the status quo. The conventional job market with its clearly defined roles that involve the use of minds and hands offers opportunities and few complications. This is especially so because you probably got fed through the educational system in the way that was intended: to produce citizens to fill the jobs available.

If you fall into the second category, you probably have an intuitive type of personality, and therefore your idiosyncratic mentality can encounter many difficulties and set-backs at school and in securing a stable job. However, this dilemma breeds in you a very resourceful and versatile mind that can rise to many different occasions.

Nevertheless, Geminian duality persists, and either type can split yet again, or turn into the other. The intellectual type can become too rigid and specialized, and suddenly find him/herself out of a job or feeling uncomfortable in our fast-changing world. This would lead to his/her having to become more flexible and intuitive. Alternatively, the intuitive type can become so suspicious of clever-clever intellectualism and so stuck with lots of opinions but no practical or broader knowledge, that he/she is forced to knuckle down to gaining just that.

The riddle of Saturn in Gemini becomes clearer upon pondering the key phrase "Tested in Communicating". The mark of an efficient mind is that it communicates, both to others and within itself. This entails having one side of the brain complementing and in contact with the other, the intuitive with the logical. If you cannot work it out, then let it work itself out, and, as ever, vice versa.

LIKES
Brain-teasers · Well-defined thoughts
Things in black and white · Facts and
figures · Recognition of mental ability

DISLIKES
Mental quandaries · Keeping your options
open · Grey areas · Being mentally
pinned down · Feeling awkward or ridiculed

Saturn says: "Time is your instrument – not your enemy. So take your time."

SATURN IN GEMINI

TRANSFORMER

POSITIVE	NEGATIVE
Good intellect	Doubts intuition
Literary	Bookish
Learned	Unoriginal
Clever	Boring
Scientific	Sceptical
Systematic	Rigid attitude
Disciplined thinker	Pedantic
Practical mind	Cynical
Problem-solver	Problem-maker
Mentally resourceful	Mentally inundated
Painstaking	Painful
Serious	Pessimistic
Steady nerves	Tense
Cool	Cold
Observant	Critical
Versatile	Devious

With all matters relating to Saturn, a critical point is reached every twenty-nine and a half years, when it returns to the Sign position in which it was placed at the time of your birth. This is a life-progress report, when inner and outer pressures serve to demolish what is weak in you, and to consolidate what is strong.

Like the riddle of the Sphinx, the answer is not to attempt to find an answer. Wait and watch.	Awkwardly stretched between thinking you should have the answer and not knowing the question.
In addition to your mental deliberations, trusting what time will bring will attract a resolution.	Seemingly insoluble dilemmas. Damned if you do and damned if you don't.
Knowing the limitations of the logical mind lends a power to your mind as a whole.	Being suspicious of anything that cannot be proved is proving to be a serious limitation.
Trusting your wits gives them a lightness that lends weight to what you say and how you think.	For all your knowledge you still fear being caught out and ridiculed.

SOLUTION	PROBLEM

183

If you seem oppressed by any of the negative traits in others, it is because you are not taking responsibility for them in yourself, and transforming them into the positive.

SATURN IN CANCER

ESSENCE

TESTED IN NURTURING

COOL BUT CARING   I RISE ABOVE MYSELF

As a rule, feeling responses do not come easily to Saturn in Cancer. It is as if you have to take a step back from emotional involvement, be it with family, partners, friends or the world in general. Cancer represents an uninhibited emotional flow/response that is instinctual and naturally caring. However, with Saturn in this Sign, this would be denied you unless you had learnt what you truly feel and feel for. In other words, you have to become very sure of what your emotional values are, what or who you consciously care about in life, and what actually gives you a sense of belonging.

None of this comes easily, a fact that could possibly stem from and account for your early life's having lacked a certain kind of emotional support, which in turn has led to your withdrawing your feelings in a certain way. Such deep insecurity can also make it hard to muster the discipline and perseverance necessary to make or to maintain progress in the professional world outside. So, in order that you be made aware of your feelings, you are at times made to feel again unsupported and cut off from sympathies and sentiments. The trick here is not to react too emotionally, yet at the same time to avoid not reacting at all. Show that you care, and need caring for, for a denial of both underlies your withdrawn and inhibited feelings.

Obviously this truly is a test, which is why Saturn is in its Detriment in Cancer, for expressing nurturing is very difficult when you have little or only a distorted idea of what it means. It is therefore important that you frequently make the attempt, even though it might prove abortive, to re-enter the emotional fray, and do not feel morbidly self-justified in self-imposed isolation, when your mawkishly or awkwardly expressed feelings are met with misunderstanding, or even scorn.

You are looking for a very real sense of belonging. When found, others come to rely on this greatly, and you become known for a matter-of-fact type of caring attitude that more than makes up for what could be interpreted as a lack of empathy. Ultimately Saturn in Cancer demands a sincere and selfless response to life and to the needs of the world around you. When you are successful in this expression of care, which is what confers true status upon you, there are usually no fanfares, just a quiet but sure sense of your being in the right place at the right time.

LIKES
Genuine sentiments · Being highly motivated · Material security · Domestic order Knowing the emotional score

DISLIKES
False emotions · Meaningless commitments · The rat race · Feelings of rootlessness · Being compromised by feelings

Saturn says: "Time is your instrument — not your enemy. So take your time."

SATURN IN CANCER

TRANSFORMER

POSITIVE	NEGATIVE
Emotional self-control Dignified Strength of character	Emotionally inhibited Hides feelings Lack of warmth
Subtly kind Practically protective Unsensationally supportive	Self-pitying Preoccupied with self Mistrusts feelings
Concern for public welfare Aids humanity Paternal / Maternal	Avoids own feelings Blind to others' feelings Self-serving
Quietly persevering Shrewd Ambitious Economical	Lack of discipline Lack of empathy Self-centred Miserly

With all matters relating to Saturn, a critical point is reached every twenty-nine and a half years, when it returns to the Sign position in which it was placed at the time of your birth. This is a life-progress report, when inner and outer pressures serve to demolish what is weak in you, and to consolidate what is strong.

SOLUTION	PROBLEM
Forget yourself and direct your attention and talents outwards to the needs of the world.	Feeling unable to make your way in life. Feeling unprovided for.
Instead of being stricken by your conscience, listen to it and act upon it.	Feeling guilty and paranoid. Merely worrying about loved ones or the world.
You must discover what and who you truly care about, and how you may express that care.	Feeling inadequate (as partner or parent). Difficult family life.
Eventually such trials will have earned you a true and deep sense of inner security.	Feeling cut-off, lonely and misunderstood. Emotionally crippled.

185

If you seem oppressed by any of the negative traits in others, it is because you are not taking responsibility for them in yourself, and transforming them into the positive.

SATURN IN LEO

ESSENCE

TESTED IN CREATING

RULE THYSELF . . .   . . .OR BE RULED OVER

The task here is one of expressing Saturn's limiting and conservative nature through bright and expansive Leo. The test is to establish self-esteem without getting too big for your boots, and to command respect without being dictatorial. Self-importance when carried too far attracts a fall from grace.

However, since Saturn frequently represents doubt, fear and what we're not sure of, there is a strong likelihood of your being so anxious about that possible fall from grace that you hide your light under a bushel. But this is hardly putting yourself to the test, so Saturn makes sure that something else comes into your life, in some form of authority, such as parent, partner, school, church or government, or a certain imposed responsibility, that forces you either to develop your creative potentials or merely to bemoan your fate.

However, whatever the case, as Leo is such a powerful Sign you are bound to attempt to attain some form of respect. The arch-enemy here is self-doubt, probably caused by early suppression or lack of a positive example of self-expression. Apart from the down-trodden feeling that this creates, it would also cause you to be defensively puffed-up. Self-assuredness needs to be flexible, not brittle, and pretending to be confident shows like skin disease, but because of your vanity no one would tell you.

You need to take command of all that you have at your disposal as an individual human being, and to express it creatively, heart and Soul. Don't be afraid to be proud, but avoid feeling stiff. Enjoying having an ego is the antidote to Saturn's stern presence. However, carrying it too far the other way, and being autocratic and too full of yourself, would bring Saturn's rod down on your back in the form of some kind of loss or affliction. Saturn in Leo states that what is important is the act of creation, not so much the creator or the creations themselves, by they of an artistic or business nature, or children.

Saturn in Leo demands true strength of will and nobility of character. Living in the knowledge that this is what you are working towards is the guarantee of its attainment.

LIKES
Lasting respect · Recognition of efforts
Feeling truly entitled · Being in command
Responsibility

DISLIKES
False praise · Living in someone's shadow
Snatched pleasures · Being ruled by pride
Lack of dependants

Saturn says: "Time is your instrument — not your enemy. So take your time."

SATURN IN LEO

TRANSFORMER

POSITIVE	NEGATIVE
Controlled self-expression Brilliant, warts and all Commanding	Inhibited self-expression Dogmatic and demanding Hypocritical
Self-assured Strong-willed Composed Dignified	Self-contained Stubborn Defensive Stands apart
Authoritative Organizer Impressive Centred	Autocratic Dictatorial Imperious Egotistical
Responsible Efficient Contented Good-hearted	Anxious Workaholic Self-conscious Strained

With all matters relating to Saturn, a critical point is reached every twenty-nine and a half years, when it returns to the Sign position in which it was placed at the time of your birth. This is a life-progress report, when inner and outer pressures serve to demolish what is weak in you, and to consolidate what is strong.

Taking pride in your self-development will attract and maintain all that you desire.	Being ruled by your fear of losing someone or something is taking the pleasure out of life.
Getting rid of your self-importance reveals your true self and vanquishes your doubts and foes.	One dictator deserves another. The tyrant in your life is a reflection of your own inner tyrant.
Involvement with others on their own level reveals the true measure of your self-esteem.	Isolation. Locked inside yourself with only your pride for company.
You are your own power station. Take responsibility for it and turn on the lights.	Dissatisfied with your life. One person or another seems to be responsible for this.
SOLUTION	PROBLEM

If you seem oppressed by any of the negative traits in others, it is because you are not taking responsibility for them in yourself, and transforming them into the positive.

SATURN IN VIRGO

ESSENCE

TESTED IN ANALYSING

THE HERMIT   THE SCHOLAR

You are learning to distinguish between essentials and non-essentials, between what is "good" and what is "bad" for you. Such tests as this implies can drive you to extremes of self-denial, and of self-indulgence, by way of compensation. At times your conscience is like an altar at which all desires for Earthly pleasures are sacrificed; at other times you busily set about desecrating it.

The task before you is therefore one of establishing a certain purity of being without it becoming so exacting as to be almost masochistic, of living simply without stripping yourself down to less than the bare essentials. However, the "bare essentials" may well be the circumstances you find yourself in with regard to a particular area of your life, most likely an emotional area, that is possibly reflected in a certain sparseness domestically. In your industrious efforts to separate the wheat from the chaff, at some point you find yourself with only a "husk". This is a critical stage because you are now able to see what you are, stripped of the trappings and influences of society. But unless you grasp that this was your objective in the first place, the self-denial can become so obsessive as to find you branding more and more things and people as impure, not good enough, stupid, improper, unhealthy etc.

Saturn is about control. When it is placed in Virgo you are controlling the impulse to purify through keeping a weather-eye upon that very impulse. So allowing yourself consciously to take a break from your "duties", introducing playtime into your work schedule, and hanging loose occasionally, will prevent you from descending into a dark and self-justifying spiral of withdrawal and misanthropy. "Laugh and the world laughs with you; weep, and you weep alone."

If you really feel that a cloistered life of study and self-abnegation is the one for you, then pursue it gladly as a necessary path, rather than allowing it to be suffered by yourself (and others) as an imposed punishment. But before doing either, check back on your experience of authority figures in your life, in order to ascertain who was too strict or not strict enough, for this will be a clue to your own inclination to austerity, or your rakish reaction to it. The real objective of Saturn in Virgo is for you to be an example of living simply yet enjoyably.

LIKES
Rites and rituals · Orderliness
Purity of intent · Knowing the odds
A clear conscience

DISLIKES
Meaningless formalities · Feeling constrained
Waywardness · Taking risks
False impressions

Saturn says: "Time is your instrument – not your enemy. So take your time."

SATURN IN VIRGO

TRANSFORMER

POSITIVE	NEGATIVE
Ascetic	Austere
Morally upright	Too strict
Prudent	Priggish
Cautious	Misanthropic
Meticulous	Punctilious
Attentive	Hypercritical
Precise	Pedantic
Efficient	Workaholic
Serious	Humourless
Concerned	Worrier
Health-conscious	Valetudenarian
Wise	Aloof
Discreet	Tight-lipped
Orderly	Stiff
Conscientious	Guilt-ridden
Well-measured	Restrained

With all matters relating to Saturn, a critical point is reached every twenty-nine and a half years, when it returns to the Sign position in which it was placed at the time of your birth. This is a life-progress report, when inner and outer pressures serve to demolish what is weak in you, and to consolidate what is strong.

The controlled and occasional bite from "forbidden fruit" forestalls your choking on it.	Keeping your wilder instincts and ideas bottled up mounts to collapse or explosion.
Seriously consider not being so serious. A true panacea includes something of its opposite.	Depression or ill-health. Inner conflict created by suppression of physical desires.
Your exacting nature eventually discovers that being less exacting is exactly what's required.	Keeping busy seems to be an answer to everything – except overwork.
Not merely self-denying, the true ascetic works upon what underlies the need for self-denial.	Feeling lonely and misunderstood.

SOLUTION	PROBLEM

189

If you seem oppressed by any of the negative traits in others, it is because you are not taking responsibility for them in yourself, and transforming them into the positive.

SATURN IN LIBRA

ESSENCE

TESTED IN RELATING

DUTY TO LOVE   LOVE OF DUTY

It could be stated that Saturn in Libra represents that point where all other Planet-Sign positions converge, or, put another way, where a focus or point of balance has to be found between the needs and urges of the individual on the one hand, and the demands and conditions of life and society on the other. The most essential test of all is that of Relating, of establishing right relations between oneself and anything or anyone outside of oneself. For this reason Saturn is said to be Exalted in Libra; Order and Authority are best expressed through the qualities of Balance and Justice.

You are thus learning the most important lesson of life: Balance, such a simple word that can be skipped over with hardly a thought. But if you apply a sense of Balance to any situation with some imagination and objectivity, then a solution or guiding principle will begin to take shape. For example, if someone appears not to be giving you enough of their time, then it is probably because you are giving them too much of yours. The remedy is, therefore, to give more time to yourself, and then others will begin to have more time for you. Conversely, if another is paying too much attention to you, increase your attention to them through getting to know what they're really after, and then their attentions will eventually decrease or become more appropriate and manageable. There are, of course, many degrees and combinations possible with such "balancing acts", and the ability to make fine adjustments is an art that you can develop and profit from.

How well you do this will determine and establish your place in the professional and personal scheme of things. With time well-spent and tests dutifully submitted to, you can become quite a paragon of human grace and social skill. On whatever level you are having to make an effort, you can be sure the external reality is reflecting exactly your inner reality. As love and marriage are the main testing grounds for Saturn in Libra, it should be noted that you are unerringly attracted to people who display those qualities that are over- or under-emphasized in your own personality. In effect, your duty to love is to tune in to what the relationship itself is telling you, rather than to force another into being some conventionally romantic ideal, which would only make them want to escape such a pressuresome expectation. Saturn in Libra teaches that "another" is simply a reference point to which you are drawn, by love, and that enables you to establish your own identity and exalt your place in the world.

LIKES
Feeling committed · A "worthy opponent"
A serious partner · Learning through love
Establishing right relations

DISLIKES
Being without relationship · Being unevenly
matched · Flippant relationships · Unresolved
relationships · Leaving relationships to chance

Saturn says: "Time is your instrument — not your enemy. So take your time."

SATURN IN LIBRA

TRANSFORMER

POSITIVE	NEGATIVE
Sense of moral obligation Loyal Honourable and co-operative	Over-committed Blind trust Weak sense of self
Just Impartial Diplomatic Tactful	Unforgiving Indecisive Insincere Stiff
Socially aware Good timing Well-mannered Composed	Socially unsure Bad timing Unrelaxed Rigid
Abiding partner Esteemed Idealistic Responsible	Insecure partner Resented Unrealistic Too particular

With all matters relating to Saturn, a critical point is reached every twenty-nine and a half years, when it returns to the Sign position in which it was placed at the time of your birth. This is a life-progress report, when inner and outer pressures serve to demolish what is weak in you, and to consolidate what is strong.

SOLUTION	PROBLEM
As the perfect partner you recognize that a perfect partnership is only as perfect as you are.	Sorrow in love owing to your stubbornly insisting that some impossible standard be maintained.
Know that where you are and who you are with is your reality. Harmonize with that and no other.	Confusion over where you fit in. Being with the wrong person at the right time, or vice versa.
Being fair to yourself and others is a balance created between your views and theirs.	Arousing enmity, frustration or awkwardness in others.
Assessing the exact nature of a relationship determines your exact role in it – and out of it.	Loss of marital or social status as a result of being unmindful of your own needs.

191

If you seem oppressed by any of the negative traits in others, it is because you are not taking responsibility for them in yourself, and transforming them into the positive.

SATURN IN SCORPIO

ESSENCE

TESTED IN DESIRING

TO USE OR ABUSE   THE MASTERSTROKE

This is really about learning effectively to express any kind of power, be it sexual, political, financial or whatever. You have a sense of power, but whether you experience it as oppressive or creative is another matter. In any case, there is an intensity about the way you pursue your aims and the objects of your desire, and it is very hard to stop you once you have decided on a particular course of action. Equally, and maybe because of this, you can agonize over what course of action to take; this is understandable considering the damage that could be wrought if your energies were misdirected.

You could not – or should not – ever be described as insipid. Attempting to hedge your bets or pull your punches would have an almost retrogressive effect, and you'd gain the reputation of a shrew or a weasel into the bargain. However, at the other extreme you can be quite fanatical about your individually-held principles.

This is an ambitious position for Saturn because both this Planet and the Sign of Scorpio like to have a sense of control. Here lies a killer instinct which can be expressed in a ruthless and scheming way. You may be the victim rather than the perpetrator of such, but it still points to the necessity of looking at your own repressed desires, for, as it is said, "If you don't do it, someone else will do it for you – and to you." Saturn always points to what we are learning about in life, and therefore what we are least sure of – but potentially may become masters of. Scorpio is about Power and Influence, Sex and Death. You therefore draw your authority from decidedly deep levels; superficial motivations and so-called civilized attitudes come to naught. Yet you are also aware of the value of cultivating and maintaining secret bonds that enable the execution of your plans. Additionally, you know the value of keeping others guessing while at the same time acquiring inside information. Saturn in Scorpio means business.

The fervour with which you hold to what you believe in can give rise to rigidity, in the form of arthritis and stones. But such physical complaints can also result from not letting some deep conviction be known, in which case skin problems could be in evidence. The insight and ability that belong to Saturn in Scorpio should not be allowed to go to seed or be used up in mere posturing. You are capable of achieving a great deal when your convictions are identified and acted upon.

LIKES
Organized power · Intense commitment
Knowing secrets · Sanctioned intimacy
Strong characters

DISLIKES
Losing control · Half-heartedness
Not being in the know · Philandering
Weak characters

Saturn says: "Time is your instrument – not your enemy. So take your time."

SATURN IN SCORPIO

TRANSFORMER

POSITIVE	NEGATIVE
Purposeful	Ruthlessly ambitious
Eye for main chance	Opportunist
Persistent	Obstinate
Disciplined	Rigid
Sexually disciplined	Sexually controlling
Sexually self-assured	Sexually controlled
Intriguing	Jealous
Sexually aware	Twisted
Uses system to advantage	Slave-driver
Improves status quo	Impatient of weakness in others
Iron-willed	Megalomaniac
Serious	Morose
Capable	Burdens self
Resourceful	Constipated
Insightful	Sceptical

With all matters relating to Saturn, a critical point is reached every twenty-nine and a half years, when it returns to the Sign position in which it was placed at the time of your birth. This is a life-progress report, when inner and outer pressures serve to demolish what is weak in you, and to consolidate what is strong.

Look for a power to your life that goes beyond a mere secret yen for superiority.	Losing sight of a deep sense of purpose makes you feels as if destiny has abandoned you.
A brave awareness of your and others' failings enables you positively to transform a situation.	Frightened of putting a foot wrong you continually tread on everyone else's feet.
Regarding sexual activity as a friendly bout of psychological wrestling is mutually empowering.	Regarding sex as some kind of lever or emotional trade-off is progressively more dissatisfying.
Be mindful that your particular kind of forward push depends on who you have behind you.	The enemies you make on the way up, you meet up with on the way down. Stalemates.

SOLUTION	PROBLEM

If you seem oppressed by any of the negative traits in others, it is because you are not taking responsibility for them in yourself, and transforming them into the positive.

SATURN IN SAGITTARIUS

ESSENCE

TESTED IN SEEKING

THE SERIOUS SEEKER   DEVIL'S ADVOCATE

The task of Saturn in Sagittarius is to build a sound set of religious and moral principles that will guide and give meaning to your life, and thereby to the lives of others. As if to force this issue, it is quite likely that you have a background of religious dogma which to one degree or another has had the effect of limiting your sense of scope in life. Or, in your past you may have been dealt with unjustly, giving rise on the one hand to resentment, but on the other to a sense of how not to go about the business of living. Or, yet again, it may be merely that social and cultural influences have kept you to the straight and narrow at the expense of experiencing something that might have broadened your concept of Self and Life. Although you may have done many exciting things and been to many faraway places, the lack of a feeling that you solidly believe in something, or something in you, persists.

This lack can amount to a great need for social and educational sanction, qualifications etc. You feel that this will "put you on the map", and, indeed, because of this need such honours are very likely to be won. However, without an understanding of what "Tested in Seeking" really means, the fear of moral or social censure lingers on. Having a handle to your name does not necessarily give you something to hold on to when the chips are down emotionally.

Tested in Seeking means exploring thoroughly as many avenues of furtherance as possible – mentally, emotionally, physically and spiritually – so that you progressively formulate and reformulate what is "right" for you. You are more than likely to believe you've arrived at such a conclusion whenever someone or something offers a more comprehensive and impressive philosophy or lifestyle, and you will energetically propound such newly discovered beliefs. Alternatively, and in some ways more significantly, you will play Devil's Advocate to the spoutings of ardently emotional "believers". This kind of testing of other people's beliefs and opinions, providing it is not merely masking a lack of your own, plays a particularly valid role in making sure that feet are kept firmly on the ground when minds are seeking higher meaning.

LIKES
Searching for truth · Further education
Purposeful adventures · A good reputation
Physical and metaphysical exercise

DISLIKES
Blocks to discovery · Being a non-runner
Aimlessness · Being dishonoured
Vegetating

Saturn says: "Time is your instrument – not your enemy. So take your time."

SATURN IN SAGITTARIUS

TRANSFORMER

POSITIVE	NEGATIVE
High moral fibre	High-minded
Honourable	Self-righteous
Prudent	Priggish
Superior	Superior
Philosophical	Intellectual pride
Reflects on life's meaning	Tritely theoretical
Ascetic	Hypocritical
Devoted	Too easily hurt
Fearless	Tactless
Earnest	Insincere
Trustworthy	Fears disapproval
Good teacher	Lays down law
Well-informed	Merely academic
Focused attention	Brow-beating
Deft	Smug

With all matters relating to Saturn, a critical point is reached every twenty-nine and a half years, when it returns to the Sign position in which it was placed at the time of your birth. This is a life-progress report, when inner and outer pressures serve to demolish what is weak in you, and to consolidate what is strong.

SOLUTION	PROBLEM
You know that the most valid knowledge comes from within. Contemplate. Meditate. Be sure.	You don't feel as satisfied as you sound. An open-and-shut case you and life ain't.
Putting beliefs to the test with a view to accepting what is valid creates guidance and support.	Defensively shaking up others' beliefs to protect the shakiness of your own serves no one.
Knowing that one has to take both the high road and the low road leads to where it's at.	Religious problems. Conflicts of belief. Not being taken seriously.
Bearing your doubts gives you a dignified bearing. Respecting others' means they respect yours.	Insisting that others subscribe to your beliefs is having the opposite effect.

195

If you seem oppressed by any of the negative traits in others, it is because you are not taking responsibility for them in yourself, and transforming them into the positive.

SATURN IN CAPRICORN

ESSENCE

TESTED IN BUILDING

| TRUE OR FALSE INTEGRITY | BUILD YOUR OWN |

Being placed in the Sign that it rules, and therefore said to be Dignified, Saturn in Capricorn poses a task which is simply that of Saturn itself: to know your place. However, this can be interpreted in two ways.

Negatively expressed, "knowing your place" can mean anything but. In other words, you can be inclined to succumb to what society expects from your particular class, creed, race, material standing etc. However, there could be a compensatory reaction to this whereby you avoid and resist what these things demand of you, or brand you as, but without actually doing your own thing, either. So both of these interpretations would find you subjected to restrictions – self-imposed or otherwise.

Alternatively, you realize that the place you find in the world is what you establish through your own efforts. And with Saturn in Capricorn there is definitely a strong streak of self-determination at some level of your being, together with an inherent sense of discipline and structure.

First of all you have to establish a starting point, a foundation. This would mean building on whatever you have at hand, as opposed to getting bogged down in it. You instinctively make use of the materials that exist about you, in the form of business or governmental agencies, for example. This can take time, and you could get sucked back into anonymity. So not only is patience an essential part of Saturn in Capricorn's test, but so too is diligence. In effect, you are able – and are rather supposed – to make more order out of the existing order; and this also employs your liking for helping those who help themselves.

You go to meet reality with a healthy sense of ambition, of making your mark and amounting to something, or you are plagued with a sense of inadequacy. Saturn demands here that you be objective in the face of life's adversities, for feeling overcome by them is liable to invite creeping and self-perpetuating pessimism. With Saturn in Capricorn, its positive and negative qualities can therefore become sharply divided. It is very much up to you, and the image you have of the material world, which way it goes.

LIKES
Professionalism · Successful people
Making a social contribution
Prestige · Firm objectives

DISLIKES
Amateurishness · Dead-heads
Going to waste
Loss of status · Impractical advice

Saturn says: "Time is your instrument – not your enemy. So take your time."

SATURN IN CAPRICORN

TRANSFORMER

POSITIVE	NEGATIVE
Disciplined Hardworking Serious-minded Dutiful	Programmed Slave to system Depressed Repressed
Businesslike Career-minded Ambitious Industrious	Hard and cold Status freak Ruthless Unscrupulous
Self-sufficient Economical Capable Dignified	Lonely Austere Under-employed Stuck-up
Self-controlled Canny Helps others Patient	Controlling Suspicious Uses others Restrained

With all matters relating to Saturn, a critical point is reached every twenty-nine and a half years, when it returns to the Sign position in which it was placed at the time of your birth. This is a life-progress report, when inner and outer pressures serve to demolish what is weak in you, and to consolidate what is strong.

SOLUTION	PROBLEM
You notice that your and society's progress are inextricably linked, so you aid both.	Seeing the world as a hostile place finds you constantly on the offensive or defensive.
Know that your respectful place in the scheme of things is based on meeting mutual needs.	Fear-induced ignorance of the nature of society is preventing you from utilizing what it has to offer.
Trust that your time and effort will bring you to your rightful place.	The more you (try to) attain, the more dissatisfied and uncomfortable you feel.
Use the status quo to further yourself – with a view to being true to something greater.	Stuck with the lowest common denominator of what the state dishes out.

If you seem oppressed by any of the negative traits in others, it is because you are not taking responsibility for them in yourself, and transforming them into the positive.

SATURN IN AQUARIUS

ESSENCE

TESTED IN LIBERATING

THE PRACTICAL IDEALIST	REDEMPTION IS

This position of Saturn makes for a complex set of rules in life, because somehow you want Freedom and Order rolled up together. You can get into a bind when you find yourself, or others, struggling against the very principles that you devised in order to attain your liberation. You then make adjustments that will accommodate your actions or those of others. This pattern continues until another adjustment has to be made, and then another, until you are seemingly surrounded by ideals and circumstances that are painfully at odds with one another.

Truly to free yourself from whatever is inhibiting you, which is the task of Saturn in Aquarius, you need first and foremost to identify what it is from your past conditioning that is preventing you from contacting or maintaining a consistent flow of emotion, for this is what lies at the root of your difficulty in finding freedom, and not some external factor in your present life. A very likely source of this dilemma would be a father – or father-figure – who did not give you a clear sense of authority or affection because he did not recognize you as an individual in your own right.

So you now create certain principles, be they moral, political, psychological or whatever, as a substitute for that lack of a strong feeling about yourself, your rights and your place in the world. Indeed these intellectual concepts can develop into real ideologies and a scientific and impartial view of life, which in turn can serve you and society well in the professional, but non-emotional, areas of life.

However, the freedom that you are striving to make a reality will not become so until you tear down all those social concepts and rationalizations about yourself and life, and get right down to the wood, which is the real, unique you that was originally seen as just plain odd. The challenge is to transform the odd into the ordinary, but not at the expense of your natural peculiarities, which are the hallmark of individuality. What follows on from this transformation is your becoming a very solid example not only of the supreme power of individuality, but also of the fact that one is redeemed simply through being what one essentially is.

LIKES
The impartial truth · Human nature
Freedom · The common touch
Living ideals

DISLIKES
Misrepresentation · Distortion of nature
Suppression · Elitism
Compromise

Saturn says: "Time is your instrument – not your enemy. So take your time."

SATURN IN AQUARIUS

TRANSFORMER

POSITIVE	NEGATIVE
Scientific Observant Level-headed Open-minded	Pseudo-scientific Clinical Cunning Bends rules
Individualistic Cool but friendly Genuine Deliberate	Elitist Apparently friendly Hollow Too formal
Humane Unresentful Impartial Thoughtful	Intolerant Belligerent Indifferent Insensitive
Visionary Idealistic Just Sincere	Airy-theory Unrealistic Dogmatic Glib

With all matters relating to Saturn, a critical point is reached every twenty-nine and a half years, when it returns to the Sign position in which it was placed at the time of your birth. This is a life-progress report, when inner and outer pressures serve to demolish what is weak in you, and to consolidate what is strong.

SOLUTION	PROBLEM
When your thoughts are matched by how you feel and what you do, you are utterly convincing.	Your suppositions know no limits – except that your suppositions are limitations in themselves.
If you cannot forget yourself, forgive yourself. Your blessing is your appreciation of the absurd.	Your crankiness is bordering on craziness is bordering on your being impossible to know or be with.
Make friends with yourself as if you were the most socially desirable person in the world.	Feeling alienated. Friendships built on false hopes or rigid expectations prove unreliable.
You have a talent for spotting what obscures the truth. If the mote's in your own eye, remove it.	Having devised your own but suspect version of reality, you are hard-put to maintain it.

If you seem oppressed by any of the negative traits in others, it is because you are not taking responsibility for them in yourself, and transforming them into the positive.

SATURN IN PISCES

ESSENCE

TESTED IN ACCEPTING

THE ANCIENT SOUL   MYSTIC OR MISFIT

There is a deep understanding and inner seriousness with Saturn in Pisces. You could be described as an Ancient Soul, with all its woes and wisdom. You have suffered at the hands of others, and are therefore sympathetic to others' suffering; you emanate a gentle and somewhat solemn light that guides and comforts in a very subtle way.

Indeed, there is a subtlety to your character that is connected in some way with the necessity simultaneously to dissolve inhibitions and stabilize your sensitive spots. This can be expressed in a number of ways, from camouflaging them as some oddity that has barely anything to do with you at all, to being able to rise above doubts and fears and see them for the illusions that they are. In addition to this there can be indiscriminate limiting of your potentials, as a kind of mock humility, while on the positive side, you express your talents and shortcomings, your joys and sorrows, as being of equal value.

"Tested in Accepting" therefore sets you the task of striking a balance between being oblivious of life's demands and being far too ready to take on unconditionally the problems of other people, between turning a blind eye and turning the other cheek, in fact. To plot this middle course sooner or later you (have to) find a way of drawing on the wisdom of that Ancient Soul of yours. To accomplish this, and to avoid getting caught in a sort of pyschological whirlpool of despair, you need first to allow yourself regular quiet and solitude, and then to plumb your indigo depths through meditation, creative inspiration, psychoanalysis, or some other form of inner guided tour. The results of such disciplined introversion bring forth much relief and enlightenment, both to you and to others. It is also equally important that you offer up your discoveries in a certain way, and turn your attention to the outer world as well as the inner one, for even when you are enjoying your private spaces, that "psychological whirlpool" can suck you under. In any case, you are a natural in helping others discover, investigate and escape from their own whirlpools. You have to go down there in order to discover what's been lost (treasures such as wisdom, vision and insight), or to release what may be trapped, like a tail in a long-forgotten net (a nagging pain from the past). The Ancient Soul longs for that Ancient Peace.

LIKES
Peace and quiet · Grotto-like places
Deliberate diffusion
Composure · A clean sheet

DISLIKES
Constant uproar · Feeling trapped
Being pigeon-holed
Being discountenanced · A murky past

Saturn says: "Time is your instrument — not your enemy. So take your time."

SATURN IN PISCES

TRANSFORMER

POSITIVE	NEGATIVE
Humble Modest Self-sacrificing Retiring	Self-negating Falsely modest Self-defeating Withdrawn
Enlightening Philanthropic Easygoing Accepting	Indecisive Undervalues self Lacks discipline Fears failure
Gentle Sensitive to suffering Understanding Concerned	Timid Suffers needlessly Too abiding Fretful
Meditative Imaginative Receptive Thoughtful	Morose Paranoid Disorderly Wool-gathering

With all matters relating to Saturn, a critical point is reached every twenty-nine and a half years, when it returns to the Sign position in which it was placed at the time of your birth. This is a life-progress report, when inner and outer pressures serve to demolish what is weak in you, and to consolidate what is strong.

Peace of mind is always here now – somewhere inside you. Look for it – it's looking for you.	Trapped in the past between the memories that haunt you and the times you pine for.
When you've quietly patched up your own boat, you can and do go quietly rescuing others.	Drowning in a sea of (others') troubles. Feeling hopelessly weak in the face of adversity.
Gradually you learn how to keep life's treadmill turning with one toe, and teach others how to, as well.	Struggling in vain, leading to regret. Dogged by regrets, you struggle in vain.
When you've eliminated a false sense of yourself, the real thing emerges, quietly and naturally.	Feeling joyless, hopeless and useless. Undoing yourself and feeling a perverse sense of achievement.

SOLUTION	PROBLEM

If you seem oppressed by any of the negative traits in others, it is because you are not taking responsibility for them in yourself, and transforming them into the positive.

TABLES FOR
PLANET-SIGN POSITIONS

HOW TO READ THE TABLES

SIGN-NAME ABBREVIATIONS

Aries	– ARI	Cancer	– CAN	Libra	– LIB	Capricorn	– CAP
Taurus	– TAU	Leo	– LEO	Scorpio	– SCO	Aquarius	– AQU
Gemini	– GEM	Virgo	– VIR	Sagittarius	– SAG	Pisces	– PIS

EXAMPLE BIRTH TIME AND DATE: 22 JULY 1945 at 4.10 p.m. British Summer Time

1) All the tables are in Greenwich Mean Time (GMT), so convert Birth Time to that, if necessary. In our example, then, we subtract one hour to give 3.10 p.m. (BST is one hour ahead of GMT.)

2) All times given in the tables are in 24-hour clock time, so our example becomes 15.10 GMT.

3) Turn to the page of the year in question. Example 1945 (page 221).

4) First of all we find the Sign positions for SUN, MERCURY, VENUS, MARS, JUPITER and SATURN, which are given in the panels on the top half of the page. Each of the tables for these planets gives the MONTH (mth), DAY (dy) and TIME (time) when the relevant planet changed or entered a Sign. Using our example of 22 JULY 1945 at 15.10 GMT, we look at the SUN table and see that this time and day fell between 21 JUNE 18.52 when the SUN entered the Sign of CANcer, and 23 JULY 05.45 when the SUN left CANcer and entered LEO. At our example time and day, then, the SUN was in CANcer. If, however, our example was for the same time but a day later (i.e. 15.10 on 23 JULY), then the SUN would have been in LEO. Note: If you were born at the exact time that a planet entered a new Sign, then that would be that planet's Sign position.

   Using the tables for MERCURY, VENUS, MARS, JUPITER and SATURN in the same way as for the SUN will give for our example (22 JULY 15.10) the following Sign positions: MERCURY in LEO, VENUS in GEMini, MARS in TAUrus, JUPITER in VIRgo, and SATURN in CANcer.

5) Now we will find the Sign position for the MOON which is given in the panel on the bottom half of the page. This is set out differently because, compared with the other planets, the Moon moves so quickly through the Signs.

   First go to the MONTH column. Example: JULY (jul). Then go to the DAY (dy) of the month in question (example: 22nd) and there will be given the Moon's Sign position, OR, when it is a day that the Moon entered a new Sign, a time is given in GMT / 24-hour clock for when that Sign change occurred (in the case of our example, 16.29). If you were born BEFORE that changeover time, then the Sign Position of the Moon will be given immediately ABOVE that changeover time (i.e. the previous day) or at the bottom of the previous column. If you were born AFTER or EXACTLY ON that changeover time, then the position of the MOON will be given immediately BELOW that changeover time (i.e. the following day) or at the top of the next column.

   In our example, then, the MOON was placed in SAGittarius.

   NOTE: In a few cases, when the MOON has changed Signs twice within 48 hours, because of the space available, both the time of the changeover and the new Sign that the MOON has just entered are given on the same line. An example of this is 13 February 1957, where it is written: 00.19 > LEO – meaning that the MOON moved from CANcer to LEO at 00.19 GMT. On the following day the time given for the Sign change is read in the usual way, i.e. looking to the Sign name above or below the line. In this example of 13 Feb 1957, then, on the following day of 14 Feb the time given is 23.17, meaning that the MOON moved from LEO to VIRgo at 23.17 GMT.

6) With all the above concerning Moon Sign positions, for 1 January birthdays, you may have to refer to 31 December of the previous year for the Sign position. Likewise, for 31 December birthdays, you may have to refer to 1 January of the following year.

7) Now turn to the index on page 272 to find the relevant pages for your seven Planet-Sign positions.

1930

SUN
mth dy time –> sign

JAN 1	00.00 –> CAP
JAN 20	18.33 –> AQU
FEB 19	09.00 –> PIS
MAR 21	08.30 –> ARI
APR 20	20.06 –> TAU
MAY 21	19.42 –> GEM
JUN 22	03.53 –> CAN
JUL 23	14.42 –> LEO
AUG 23	21.26 –> VIR
SEP 23	18.36 –> LIB
OCT 24	03.26 –> SCO
NOV 23	00.35 –> SAG
DEC 22	13.39 –> CAP

MERCURY
mth dy time –> sign

JAN 1	00.00 –> CAP
JAN 2	10.25 –> AQU
JAN 23	00.31 –> CAP
FEB 15	15.09 –> AQU
MAR 9	22.39 –> PIS
MAR 26	23.36 –> ARI
APR 10	17.05 –> TAU
MAY 1	05.30 –> GEM
MAY 17	11.06 –> TAU
JUN 14	20.09 –> GEM
JUL 4	22.10 –> CAN
JUL 19	02.44 –> LEO
AUG 4	02.38 –> VIR
AUG 26	18.04 –> LIB
SEP 20	02.13 –> VIR
OCT 11	04.45 –> LIB
OCT 29	14.35 –> SCO
NOV 17	05.31 –> SAG
DEC 6	20.57 –> CAP

VENUS
mth dy time –> sign

JAN 1	00.00 –> CAP
JAN 24	00.22 –> AQU
FEB 16	22.11 –> PIS
MAR 12	22.33 –> ARI
APR 6	02.57 –> TAU
APR 30	12.37 –> GEM
MAY 25	04.36 –> CAN
JUN 19	04.39 –> LEO
JUL 14	16.34 –> VIR
AUG 10	00.54 –> LIB
SEP 7	04.06 –> SCO
OCT 12	02.45 –> SAG
NOV 22	07.43 –> SCO

MARS
mth dy time –> sign

JAN 1	00.00 –> CAP
FEB 6	18.21 –> AQU
MAR 17	05.55 –> PIS
APR 24	17.27 –> ARI
JUN 3	03.15 –> TAU
JUL 14	12.54 –> GEM
AUG 28	11.27 –> CAN
OCT 20	14.44 –> LEO

SATURN
mth dy time –> sign

JAN 1	00.00 –> CAP

JUPITER
mth dy time –> sign

JAN 1	00.00 –> GEM
JUN 26	22.42 –> CAN

MOON   MOON

dy	jan	feb	mar	apr	may	jun	jul	aug	sep	oct	nov	dec	dy
1	18.29	PIS	PIS	TAU	GEM	LEO	VIR	SCO	20.35	15.09	PIS	ARI	1
2	AQU	PIS	06.08	TAU	13.54	LEO	09.47	SCO	CAP	AQU	23.34	18.32	2
3	AQU	00.23	ARI	03.42	CAN	00.37	LIB	04.24	CAP	AQU	ARI	TAU	3
4	07.04	ARI	15.19	GEM	16.32	VIR	14.56	SAG	08.27	03.48	APR	TAU	4
5	PIS	09.49	TAU	08.11	LEO	04.04	SCO	14.34	AQU	PIS	09.37	01.32	5
6	18.27	TAU	22.16	CAN	19.11	LIB	22.49	CAP	21.06	15.52	TAU	GEM	6
7	ARI	16.08	GEM	11.09	VIR	09.30	SAG	CAP	PIS	ARI	16.58	05.31	7
8	ARI	GEM	GEM	LEO	22.30	SCO	SAG	02.26	PIS	ARI	GEM	CAN	8
9	02.59	18.55	02.34	13.11	LIB	16.56	08.49	AQU	09.21	02.14	22.05	07.53	9
10	TAU	CAN	CAN	VIR	LIB	SAG	CAP	15.03	ARI	TAU	CAN	LEO	10
11	07.34	19.00	04.25	15.17	03.06	SAG	20.23	PIS	20.18	10.29	CAN	10.04	11
12	GEM	LEO	LEO	LIB	SCO	02.20	AQU	PIS	TAU	GEM	01.45	VIR	12
13	08.35	18.14	04.54	18.45	09.39	CAP	AQU	03.32	TAU	16.29	LEO	13.05	13
14	CAN	VIR	VIR	SCO	SAG	13.39	08.57	ARI	05.01	CAN	04.42	LIB	14
15	07.37	18.50	05.43	SCO	18.39	AQU	PIS	14.38	GEM	20.19	VIR	17.19	15
16	LEO	LIB	LIB	00.49	CAP	AQU	21.26	TAU	10.42	LEO	07.27	SCO	16
17	06.57	22.45	08.46	SAG	CAP	02.12	ARI	22.46	CAN	22.26	LIB	22.54	17
18	VIR	SCO	SCO	10.07	06.03	PIS	ARI	GEM	13.18	VIR	10.36	SAG	18
19	08.44	SCO	15.24	CAP	AQU	14.15	07.54	GEM	23.43	SCO	SAG	SAG	19
20	LIB	06.49	SAG	21.58	18.34	ARI	TAU	03.02	13.45	LIB	15.00	06.11	20
21	14.25	SAG	SAG	AQU	PIS	23.25	14.39	CAN	VIR	LIB	SAG	CAP	21
22	SCO	18.13	01.40	AQU	PIS	TAU	GEM	03.58	13.43	01.32	21.42	15.43	22
23	23.56	CAP	CAP	10.23	05.55	TAU	17.22	LEO	LIB	SCO	CAP	AQU	23
24	SAG	CAP	14.05	PIS	TAU	05.00	CAN	03.13	15.07	05.23	CAP	AQU	24
25	SAG	06.57	AQU	21.10	14.15	GEM	17.19	VIR	SCO	SAG	07.23	03.35	25
26	11.53	AQU	AQU	ARI	TAU	06.57	LEO	02.58	19.34	12.27	AQU	PIS	26
27	CAP	19.13	02.24	ARI	19.07	CAN	16.34	LIB	SAG	CAP	19.32	16.29	27
28	CAP	PIS	PIS	05.08	GEM	07.06	VIR	05.11	SAG	22.54	PIS	ARI	28
29	00.35		PIS	13.00	TAU	LEO	17.18	SCO	03.48	AQU	PIS	ARI	29
30	AQU		ARI	10.26	CAN	07.28	LIB	11.04	CAP	AQU	08.06	03.51	30
31	12.59		21.24		22.45		21.05	SAG		11.23		TAU	31

SUN
mth dy time –> sign

JAN 1	00.00 –> CAP
JAN 21	00.18 –> AQU
FEB 19	14.40 –> PIS
MAR 21	14.06 –> ARI
APR 21	01.40 –> TAU
MAY 22	01.15 –> GEM
JUN 22	09.28 –> CAN
JUL 23	20.21 –> LEO
AUG 24	03.10 –> VIR
SEP 24	00.23 –> LIB
OCT 24	09.15 –> SCO
NOV 23	06.25 –> SAG
DEC 22	19.30 –> CAP

MERCURY
mth dy time –> sign

JAN 1	00.00 –> CAP
FEB 11	12.27 –> AQU
MAR 2	17.28 –> PIS
MAR 18	19.31 –> ARI
APR 3	13.38 –> TAU
JUN 11	07.26 –> GEM
JUN 26	13.49 –> CAN
JUL 10	19.56 –> LEO
JUL 28	23.24 –> VIR
OCT 4	18.27 –> LIB
OCT 22	02.08 –> SCO
NOV 10	04.27 –> SAG
DEC 2	00.00 –> CAP
DEC 20	07.59 –> SAG

VENUS
mth dy time –> sign

JAN 1	00.00 –> SCO
JAN 3	20.02 –> SAG
FEB 6	12.25 –> CAP
MAR 5	21.45 –> AQU
MAR 31	19.04 –> PIS
APR 26	02.10 –> ARI
MAY 21	02.38 –> TAU
JUN 14	23.04 –> GEM
JUL 9	15.35 –> CAN
AUG 3	03.29 –> LEO
AUG 27	10.42 –> VIR
SEP 20	14.15 –> LIB
OCT 14	15.45 –> SCO
NOV 7	16.32 –> SAG
DEC 1	17.29 –> CAP
DEC 25	19.44 –> AQU

MARS
mth dy time –> sign

JAN 1	00.00 –> LEO
JAN 16	14.28 –> CAN
MAR 30	03.47 –> LEO
JUN 10	14.58 –> VIR
AUG 1	16.37 –> LIB
SEP 17	08.43 –> SCO
OCT 30	12.46 –> SAG
DEC 10	03.11 –> CAP

SATURN
mth dy time –> sign

JAN 1	00.00 –> CAP

JUPITER
mth dy time –> sign

JAN 1	00.00 –> CAN
JUL 17	07.52 –> LEO

MOON

dy	jan	feb	mar	apr	may	jun	jul	aug	sep	oct	nov	dec	dy
1	11.34	CAN	14.25	VIR	11.26	SAG	18.56	PIS	20.59	15.03	CAN	LEO	1
2	GEM	03.24	LEO	00.49	SCO	03.07	AQU	PIS	TAU	GEM	13.39	00.16	2
3	15.21	LEO	14.21	LIB	13.14	CAP	AQU	01.10	TAU	GEM	LEO	VIR	3
4	CAN	02.56	VIR	00.50	SAG	10.23	05.10	ARI	08.43	00.38	18.08	03.44	4
5	16.32	VIR	13.32	SCO	17.35	AQU	PIS	14.05	GEM	CAN	VIR	LIB	5
6	LEO	02.54	LIB	02.52	CAP	21.01	17.40	TAU	17.15	06.49	20.03	05.43	6
7	17.06	LIB	14.03	SAG	CAP	PIS	ARI	TAU	CAN	LEO	LIB	SCO	7
8	VIR	05.04	SCO	08.20	01.37	PIS	ARI	01.01	21.47	09.34	20.21	07.04	8
9	18.48	SCO	17.30	CAP	AQU	09.44	06.14	GEM	LEO	VIR	SCO	SAG	9
10	LIB	10.21	SAG	17.40	13.02	ARI	TAU	08.10	23.04	09.50	20.39	09.18	10
11	22.40	SAG	SAG	AQU	PIS	21.54	16.14	CAN	VIR	LIB	SAG	CAP	11
12	SCO	18.39	00.39	AQU	PIS	TAU	GEM	11.31	22.43	09.17	22.52	14.10	12
13	SCO	CAP	CAP	05.49	01.57	TAU	22.30	LEO	LIB	SCO	CAP	AQU	13
14	04.50	CAP	11.03	PIS	ARI	07.22	CAN	12.25	22.40	09.51	CAP	22.50	14
15	SAG	05.14	AQU	18.48	13.54	GEM	CAN	VIR	SCO	SAG	04.40	PIS	15
16	13.02	AQU	23.26	ARI	TAU	13.38	01.41	12.45	SCO	13.18	AQU	PIS	16
17	CAP	17.23	PIS	ARI	23.26	CAN	LEO	LIB	00.39	CAP	14.32	10.49	17
18	23.04	PIS	PIS	06.50	GEM	17.36	03.22	14.10	SAG	20.39	PIS	ARI	18
19	AQU	PIS	12.24	TAU	GEM	LEO	VIR	SCO	05.48	AQU	PIS	23.45	19
20	AQU	06.21	ARI	16.56	06.26	20.32	05.06	17.47	CAP	AQU	03.08	TAU	20
21	10.55	ARI	ARI	GEM	CAN	VIR	LIB	SAG	14.18	07.32	ARI	TAU	21
22	PIS	18.54	00.44	GEM	11.27	23.23	07.56	23.58	AQU	PIS	16.00	10.59	22
23	23.55	TAU	TAU	00.42	LEO	LIB	SCO	CAP	AQU	20.21	TAU	GEM	23
24	ARI	TAU	11.19	CAN	15.07	LIB	12.18	CAP	01.28	ARI	TAU	19.22	24
25	ARI	05.13	GEM	06.04	VIR	02.34	SAG	08.38	PIS	ARI	03.12	CAN	25
26	12.10	GEM	19.04	LEO	17.51	SCO	18.22	AQU	14.09	09.12	GEM	CAN	26
27	TAU	11.47	CAN	09.10	LIB	06.26	CAP	19.27	ARI	TAU	12.09	01.16	27
28	21.18	CAN	23.29	VIR	20.08	SAG	CAP	PIS	ARI	20.48	CAN	LEO	28
29	GEM		LEO	10.35	SCO	11.35	02.24	PIS	03.07	GEM	19.06	05.41	29
30	GEM		LEO	LIB	22.48	CAP	AQU	07.56	TAU	GEM	LEO	VIR	30
31	02.09		00.58		SAG		12.45	ARI		06.26		09.17	31

1932

SUN
mth dy time –> sign

JAN 1	00.00	–> CAP
JAN 21	06.07	–> AQU
FEB 19	20.28	–> PIS
MAR 20	19.54	–> ARI
APR 20	07.28	–> TAU
MAY 21	07.06	–> GEM
JUN 21	15.22	–> CAN
JUL 23	02.18	–> LEO
AUG 23	09.06	–> VIR
SEP 23	06.16	–> LIB
OCT 23	15.04	–> SCO
NOV 22	12.10	–> SAG
DEC 22	01.15	–> CAP

MERCURY
mth dy time –> sign

JAN 1	00.00	–> SAG
JAN 14	12.47	–> CAP
FEB 5	02.36	–> AQU
FEB 23	00.50	–> PIS
MAR 9	20.21	–> ARI
MAY 15	22.49	–> TAU
JUN 2	23.04	–> GEM
JUN 16	22.30	–> CAN
JUL 2	08.16	–> LEO
JUL 27	20.37	–> VIR
AUG 10	07.31	–> LEO
SEP 9	07.19	–> VIR
SEP 26	01.15	–> LIB
OCT 13	15.41	–> SCO
NOV 2	20.28	–> SAG

VENUS
mth dy time –> sign

JAN 1	00.00	–> AQU
JAN 19	01.52	–> PIS
FEB 12	16.58	–> ARI
MAR 9	02.07	–> TAU
APR 5	00.19	–> GEM
MAY 6	09.04	–> CAN
JUL 13	10.33	–> GEM
JUL 28	12.36	–> CAN
SEP 8	19.44	–> LEO
OCT 7	05.46	–> VIR
NOV 2	04.01	–> LIB
NOV 27	00.06	–> SCO
DEC 21	07.43	–> SAG

MARS
mth dy time –> sign

JAN 1	00.00	–> CAP
JAN 18	00.35	–> AQU
FEB 25	02.36	–> PIS
APR 3	07.02	–> ARI
MAY 12	10.53	–> TAU
JUN 22	09.19	–> GEM
AUG 4	19.52	–> CAN
SEP 20	19.43	–> LEO
NOV 13	21.25	–> VIR

SATURN
mth dy tim –> sign

JAN 1	00.00	–> CAP
FEB 24	02.47	–> AQU
AUG 13	11.14	–> CAP
NOV 20	02.09	–> AQU

JUPITER
mth dy time –> sign

JAN 1	00.00	–> LEO
AUG 11	07.16	–> VIR

MOON

dy	jan	feb	mar	apr	may	jun	jul	aug	sep	oct	nov	dec	dy
1	LIB	SAG	07.06	AQU	22.46	TAU	GEM	15.57	VIR	18.44	SAG	16.46	1
2	12.24	SAG	CAP	05.05	ARI	TAU	GEM	LEO	08.32	SCO	04.54	AQU	2
3	SCO	01.39	14.00	PIS	ARI	06.32	00.07	21.15	LIB	19.02	CAP	22.08	3
4	15.15	CAP	AQU	16.53	11.46	GEM	CAN	VIR	10.06	SAG	08.06	PIS	4
5	SAG	07.48	23.15	ARI	TAU	17.21	08.18	VIR	SCO	21.00	AQU	PIS	5
6	18.37	AQU	PIS	ARI	TAU	CAN	LEO	00.56	12.00	CAP	15.06	07.35	6
7	CAP	16.15	PIS	05.44	00.20	CAN	14.33	LIB	SAG	CAP	PIS	ARI	7
8	23.43	PIS	10.35	TAU	GEM	02.14	VIR	03.49	15.11	01.44	PIS	19.41	8
9	AQU	PIS	ARI	18.27	11.34	LEO	19.12	SCO	CAP	AQU	01.24	TAU	9
10	AQU	03.17	23.19	GEM	CAN	09.06	LIB	06.32	20.16	09.26	ARI	TAU	10
11	07.49	ARI	TAU	GEM	20.47	VIR	22.27	SAG	AQU	PIS	13.33	08.26	11
12	PIS	16.05	TAU	05.47	LEO	13.41	SCO	09.38	AQU	19.36	TAU	GEM	12
13	19.07	TAU	12.03	CAN	LEO	LIB	SCO	CAP	03.31	ARI	TAU	20.28	13
14	ARI	TAU	GEM	14.22	03.13	16.00	00.38	13.54	PIS	ARI	02.13	CAN	14
15	ARI	04.27	22.46	LEO	VIR	SCO	SAG	AQU	13.01	07.24	GEM	CAN	15
16	08.02	GEM	CAN	19.21	06.32	16.45	02.35	20.13	ARI	TAU	14.32	07.12	16
17	TAU	14.02	CAN	VIR	LIB	SAG	CAP	PIS	ARI	20.03	CAN	LEO	17
18	19.47	CAN	05.56	21.00	07.15	17.31	05.44	PIS	00.33	GEM	CAN	16.09	18
19	GEM	19.49	LEO	LIB	SCO	CAP	AQU	05.18	TAU	GEM	01.35	VIR	19
20	GEM	LEO	09.18	20.33	06.48	20.12	11.34	ARI	13.14	08.26	LEO	22.32	20
21	04.22	22.25	VIR	SCO	SAG	AQU	PIS	16.56	GEM	CAN	10.08	LIB	21
22	CAN	VIR	09.56	19.57	07.12	AQU	20.52	TAU	GEM	18.57	VIR	LIB	22
23	09.39	23.22	LIB	SAG	CAP	02.25	ARI	TAU	01.13	LEO	15.08	01.53	23
24	LEO	LIB	09.35	21.15	10.31	PIS	ARI	05.33	CAN	LEO	LIB	SCO	24
25	12.47	LIB	SCO	CAP	AQU	12.34	08.54	GEM	10.32	02.02	16.38	02.42	25
26	VIR	00.20	10.07	CAP	17.57	ARI	TAU	16.50	LEO	VIR	SCO	SAG	26
27	15.07	SCO	SAG	02.04	PIS	ARI	21.26	CAN	16.07	05.15	15.58	02.31	27
28	LIB	02.38	13.08	AQU	PIS	01.08	GEM	CAN	VIR	LIB	SAG	CAP	28
29	17.43		SAG	CAP	10.55	05.09	GEM	01.03	18.22	05.30	15.16	03.32	29
30	SCO		19.30	PIS	ARI	13.35	08.07	LEO	LIB	SCO	CAP	AQU	30
31	21.07		AQU		18.05		CAN	05.58		04.40		07.16	31

SUN

mth dy   time –> sign

JAN   1 00.00 –> CAP
JAN 20   11.53 –> AQU
FEB 19   02.16 –> PIS
MAR 21   01.42 –> ARI
APR 20   13.18 –> TAU
MAY 21   12.57 –> GEM
JUN 21   21.12 –> CAN
JUL 23   08.05 –> LEO
AUG 23   14.52 –> VIR
SEP 23   12.01 –> LIB
OCT 23   20.48 –> SCO
NOV 22   17.53 –> SAG
DEC 22   06.58 –> CAP

SATURN

mth dy   time –> sign

JAN 1   00.00 –> AQU

MERCURY

mth dy   time –> sign

JAN 1   00.00 –> SAG
JAN 8   10.25 –> CAP
JAN 27   22.39 –> AQU
FEB 14   05.06 –> PIS
MAR 3   10.49 –> ARI
MAR 25   21.49 –> PIS
APR 17   15.27 –> ARI
MAY 10 07.42 –> TAU
MAY 25 14.27 –> GEM
JUN 8   14.12 –> CAN
JUN 27   01.11 –> LEO
SEP 2   05.44 –> VIR
SEP 18   03.48 –> LIB
OCT 6   15.04 –> SCO
OCT 30   04.27 –> SAG
NOV 16   02.07 –> SCO
DEC 12   03.43 –> SAG

VENUS

mth dy   time –> sign

JAN 1   00.00 –> SAG
JAN 14   09.56 –> CAP
FEB 7   10.30 –> AQU
MAR 3   11.24 –> PIS
MAR 27   13.58 –> ARI
APR 20   19.00 –> TAU
MAY 15   02.47 –> GEM
JUN 8   13.01 –> CAN
JUL 3   01.29 –> LEO
JUL 27   16.45 –> VIR
AUG 21   12.23 –> LIB
SEP 15   14.54 –> SCO
OCT 11   04.32 –> SAG
NOV 6   16.03 –> CAP
DEC 5   18.00 –> AQU

MARS

mth dy   time –> sign

JAN 1   00.00 –> VIR
JUL 6   22.02 –> LIB
AUG 26   06.34 –> SCO
OCT 9   11.34 –> SAG
NOV 19   07.18 –> CAP
DEC 28   03.42 –> AQU

JUPITER

mth dy   time –> sign

JAN 1   00.00 –> VIR
SEP 10   05.10 –> LIB

MOON

dy	jan	feb	mar	apr	may	jun	jul	aug	sep	oct	nov	dec	dy
1	PIS	10.40	TAU	GEM	23.06	VIR	LIB	SAG	07.00	PIS	13.53	06.45	1
2	15.13	TAU	TAU	03.50	LEO	23.15	10.57	21.40	AQU	22.51	TAU	GEM	2
3	ARI	23.05	07.17	CAN	LEO	LIB	SCO	CAP	09.44	ARI	TAU	18.53	3
4	ARI	GEM	GEM	15.16	08.41	LIB	12.32	22.22	PIS	ARI	00.02	CAN	4
5	02.36	GEM	19.43	LEO	VIR	02.25	SAG	AQU	14.15	06.18	GEM	CAN	5
6	TAU	11.13	CAN	23.33	14.17	SCO	12.15	AQU	ARI	TAU	12.05	07.49	6
7	15.19	CAN	CAN	VIR	LIB	02.32	CAP	00.10	21.35	16.18	CAN	LEO	7
8	GEM	21.16	06.18	VIR	16.07	SAG	12.05	PIS	TAU	GEM	CAN	20.00	8
9	GEM	LEO	LEO	04.00	SCO	01.33	AQU	04.40	TAU	GEM	00.58	VIR	9
10	03.16	LEO	13.42	LIB	15.43	CAP	14.01	ARI	08.01	04.29	LEO	VIR	10
11	CAN	04.33	VIR	05.32	SAG	01.41	PIS	12.45	GEM	CAN	12.24	05.18	11
12	13.26	VIR	18.03	SCO	15.15	AQU	19.31	TAU	20.25	17.02	VIR	LIB	12
13	LEO	09.59	LIB	05.52	CAP	04.49	ARI	23.57	CAN	LEO	20.13	10.27	13
14	21.42	LIB	20.27	SAG	16.46	PIS	ARI	GEM	CAN	LEO	LIB	SCO	14
15	VIR	13.46	SCO	06.53	AQU	11.50	04.49	GEM	08.30	03.24	23.52	11.48	15
16	VIR	SCO	22.18	CAP	21.34	ARI	TAU	LEO	VIR	SCO	SAG	16
17	04.03	16.42	SAG	10.02	PIS	22.12	16.44	CAN	18.13	10.07	SCO	11.08	17
18	LIB	SAG	SAG	AQU	PIS	TAU	GEM	CAN	VIR	LIB	00.34	CAP	18
19	08.24	19.22	00.47	15.45	05.45	TAU	GEM	00.22	VIR	13.27	SAG	10.37	19
20	SCO	CAP	CAP	PIS	ARI	10.25	05.25	LEO	00.51	SCO	00.23	AQU	20
21	10.54	22.29	04.39	PIS	16.26	GEM	CAN	10.07	LIB	14.54	CAP	12.15	21
22	SAG	AQU	AQU	00.14	TAU	23.06	17.19	VIR	05.00	SAG	01.21	PIS	22
23	12.18	AQU	10.16	ARI	TAU	CAN	LEO	17.29	SCO	16.13	AQU	17.15	23
24	CAP	02.56	PIS	10.31	04.31	CAN	LEO	LIB	07.49	CAP	04.50	ARI	24
25	13.56	PIS	17.49	TAU	GEM	11.17	03.35	22.44	SAG	18.48	PIS	ARI	25
26	AQU	09.42	ARI	22.18	17.12	LEO	VIR	SCO	10.23	AQU	11.13	01.42	26
27	17.31	ARI	ARI	GEM	CAN	22.01	11.44	SCO	CAP	23.17	ARI	TAU	27
28	PIS	19.20	03.32	GEM	CAN	VIR	LIB	02.21	13.27	PIS	20.03	12.43	28
29	PIS		TAU	10.58	05.33	VIR	17.21	SAG	AQU	PIS	TAU	GEM	29
30	00.21		15.13	CAN	LEO	06.11	SCO	04.52	17.27	05.40	TAU	GEM	30
31	ARI		GEM		16.06		20.27	CAP		ARI		01.07	31

MOON

1934

SUN
mth dy   time –> sign

JAN 1   00.00 –> CAP
JAN 20 17.37 –> AQU
FEB 19 08.02 –> PIS
MAR 21 07.27 –> ARI
APR 20 19.00 –> TAU
MAY 21 18.35 –> GEM
JUN 22 02.48 –> CAN
JUL 23 13.42 –> LEO
AUG 23 20.32 –> VIR
SEP 23 17.45 –> LIB
OCT 24 02.36 –> SCO
NOV 22 23.44 –> SAG
DEC 22 12.49 –> CAP

MERCURY
mth dy   time –> sign

JAN 1   18.40 –> CAP
JAN 20 11.44 –> AQU
FEB 6   17.24 –> PIS
APR 15 04.13 –> ARI
MAY 2   18.45 –> TAU
MAY 16 23.43 –> GEM
JUN 1   08.22 –> CAN
AUG 9   13.49 –> LEO
AUG 25 02.18 –> VIR
SEP 10 11.29 –> LIB
SEP 30 14.46 –> SCO
DEC 6   06.42 –> SAG
DEC 25 14.59 –> CAP

VENUS
mth dy   time –> sign

JAN 1   00.00 –> AQU
APR 6   09.22 –> PIS
MAY 6   08.54 –> ARI
JUN 2   10.11 –> TAU
JUN 28 09.38 –> GEM
JUL 23 18.21 –> CAN
AUG 17 15.45 –> LEO
SEP 11 03.32 –> VIR
OCT 5   07.56 –> LIB
OCT 29 07.37 –> SCO
NOV 22 04.59 –> SAG
DEC 16 01.39 –> CAP

MARS
mth dy   time –> sign

JAN 1   00.00 –> AQU
FEB 4   04.13 –> PIS
MAR 14 09.08 –> ARI
APR 22 15.40 –> TAU
JUN 2   16.21 –> GEM
JUL 15 21.33 –> CAN
AUG 30 13.43 –> LEO
OCT 18 04.59 –> VIR
DEC 11 09.32 –> LIB

SATURN
mth dy   time –> sign

JAN 1   00.00 –> AQU

JUPITER
mth dy · time –> sign

JAN 1   00.00 –> LIB
SEP 11 04.55 –> SCO

MOON

dy	jan	feb	mar	apr	may	jun	jul	aug	sep	oct	nov	dec	dy
1	CAN	08.00	VIR	13.35	01.02	11.55	PIS	13.25	GEM	CAN	08.36	04.39	1
2	13.56	VIR	VIR	SCO	SAG	AQU	PIS	TAU	15.40	11.44	VIR	LIB	2
3	LEO	17.59	00.02	17.37	02.53	14.06	00.39	21.48	CAN	LEO	19.41	13.06	3
4	LEO	LIB	LIB	SAG	CAP	PIS	ARI	GEM	CAN	LEO	LIB	SCO	4
5	02.09	LIB	06.59	20.45	05.06	18.31	06.47	GEM	04.32	00.31	LIB	17.52	5
6	VIR	01.31	SCO	CAP	AQU	ARI	TAU	09.13	LEO	VIR	03.32	SAG	6
7	12.20	SCO	11.58	23.43	08.26	ARI	15.55	CAN	17.16	11.20	SCO	20.09	7
8	LIB	06.14	SAG	AQU	PIS	01.17	GEM	22.08	VIR	LIB	08.33	CAP	8
9	19.11	SAG	15.22	AQU	13.09	TAU	GEM	LEO	VIR	19.31	SAG	21.34	9
10	SCO	08.23	CAP	02.52	ARI	10.14	03.20	LEO	04.23	SCO	11.57	AQU	10
11	22.18	CAP	17.36	PIS	19.24	GEM	CAN	10.59	LIB	SCO	CAP	23.31	11
12	SAG	08.57	AQU	06.40	TAU	21.14	16.07	VIR	13.19	01.32	14.52	PIS	12
13	22.37	AQU	19.25	ARI	TAU	CAN	LEO	22.33	SCO	SAG	AQU	PIS	13
14	CAP	09.27	PIS	11.55	03.38	CAN	LEO	LIB	20.03	06.04	17.56	02.51	14
15	21.56	PIS	22.00	TAU	GEM	09.53	05.07	LIB	SAG	CAP	PIS	ARI	15
16	AQU	11.39	ARI	19.41	14.17	LEO	VIR	07.51	SAG	09.32	21.26	07.56	16
17	22.17	ARI	ARI	GEM	CAN	22.51	16.47	SCO	00.36	AQU	ARI	TAU	17
18	PIS	17.03	02.46	GEM	CAN	VIR	LIB	14.12	CAP	12.10	ARI	14.58	18
19	PIS	TAU	TAU	06.26	02.55	VIR	LIB	SAG	03.06	PIS	01.46	GEM	19
20	01.28	TAU	10.51	CAN	LEO	09.59	01.31	17.27	AQU	14.28	TAU	GEM	20
21	ARI	02.16	GEM	19.10	15.35	LIB	SCO	CAP	04.14	ARI	07.47	00.11	21
22	08.26	GEM	22.13	LEO	VIR	17.25	06.28	18.18	PIS	17.34	GEM	CAN	22
23	TAU	14.22	CAN	LEO	VIR	SCO	SAG	AQU	05.13	TAU	16.25	11.37	23
24	18.54	CAN	CAN	07.20	01.43	20.49	08.03	18.08	ARI	22.58	CAN	LEO	24
25	GEM	CAN	11.03	VIR	LIB	SAG	CAP	PIS	07.47	GEM	CAN	LEO	25
26	GEM	03.13	LEO	16.32	07.52	21.24	07.43	18.44	TAU	GEM	03.54	00.32	26
27	07.24	LEO	22.44	LIB	SCO	CAP	AQU	ARI	13.33	07.46	LEO	VIR	27
28	CAN	14.46	VIR	22.07	10.28	21.02	07.20	21.55	GEM	CAN	16.52	12.59	28
29	20.12		VIR	SCO	SAG	AQU	PIS	TAU	23.14	19.42	VIR	LIB	29
30	LEO		07.37	SCO	11.12	21.38	08.45	TAU	CAN	LEO	VIR	22.41	30
31	LEO		LIB		CAP		ARI	04.55		LEO		SCO	31

SUN

mth dy	time –> sign
JAN 1	00.00 –> CAP
JAN 20	23.28 –> AQU
FEB 19	13.52 –> PIS
MAR 21	13.18 –> ARI
APR 21	00.50 –> TAU
MAY 22	00.25 –> GEM
JUN 22	08.38 –> CAN
JUL 23	19.33 –> LEO
AUG 24	02.24 –> VIR
SEP 23	23.38 –> LIB
OCT 24	08.29 –> SCO
NOV 23	05.35 –> SAG
DEC 22	18.37 –> CAP

MERCURY

mth dy	time –> sign
JAN 1	00.00 –> CAP
JAN 13	01.20 –> AQU
FEB 1	11.17 –> PIS
FEB 15	03.02 –> AQU
MAR 18	21.53 –> PIS
APR 8	18.39 –> ARI
APR 24	12.29 –> TAU
MAY 8	17.20 –> GEM
MAY 29	19.26 –> CAN
JUN 20	17.58 –> GEM
JUL 13	22.21 –> CAN
AUG 2	01.48 –> LEO
AUG 16	20.39 –> VIR
SEP 3	09.33 –> LIB
SEP 28	15.52 –> SCO
OCT 12	18.03 –> LIB
NOV 10	01.24 –> SCO
NOV 29	07.05 –> SAG
DEC 18	08.29 –> CAP

VENUS

mth dy	time –> sign
JAN 1	00.00 –> CAP
JAN 8	22.44 –> AQU
FEB 1	21.37 –> PIS
FEB 26	00.30 –> ARI
MAR 22	10.29 –> TAU
APR 16	07.37 –> GEM
MAY 11	22.02 –> CAN
JUN 7	19.11 –> LEO
JUL 7	20.33 –> VIR
NOV 9	16.34 –> LIB
DEC 8	14.36 –> SCO

MARS

mth dy	time –> sign
JAN 1	00.00 –> LIB
JUL 29	17.32 –> SCO
SEP 16	12.59 –> SAG
OCT 28	18.22 –> CAP
DEC 7	04.33 –> AQU

SATURN

mth dy	time –> sign
JAN 1	00.00 –> AQU
FEB 14	14.08 –> PIS

JUPITER

mth dy	time –> sign
JAN 1	00.00 –> SCO
NOV 9	02.56 –> SAG

MOON

dy	jan	feb	mar	apr	may	jun	jul	aug	sep	oct	nov	dec	dy
1	SCO	CAP	CAP	PIS	ARI	GEM	CAN	09.07	LIB	SCO	CAP	AQU	1
2	04.27	18.26	05.16	15.31	02.09	20.44	14.13	VIR	16.22	08.41	CAP	14.03	2
3	SAG	AQU	AQU	ARI	TAU	CAN	LEO	21.55	SCO	SAG	04.38	PIS	3
4	06.44	17.47	05.13	16.18	05.26	CAN	LEO	LIB	SCO	17.02	AQU	16.53	4
5	CAP	PIS	PIS	TAU	GEM	06.19	02.08	LIB	02.48	CAP	08.20	ARI	5
6	07.04	17.49	04.40	19.35	11.50	LEO	VIR	09.57	SAG	22.20	PIS	19.03	6
7	AQU	ARI	ARI	GEM	CAN	18.25	14.52	SCO	10.08	AQU	09.54	TAU	7
8	07.17	20.22	05.43	GEM	21.55	VIR	LIB	19.25	CAP	AQU	ARI	21.36	8
9	PIS	TAU	TAU	02.49	LEO	VIR	LIB	SAG	13.44	00.27	10.29	GEM	9
10	09.03	TAU	10.11	CAN	LEO	06.59	02.15	SAG	AQU	PIS	TAU	GEM	10
11	ARI	02.35	GEM	13.52	10.26	LIB	SCO	01.10	14.15	00.20>ARI	11.52	01.54	11
12	13.24	GEM	18.52	LEO	VIR	17.35	10.27	CAP	PIS	23.54	GEM	CAN	12
13	TAU	12.24	CAN	LEO	22.48	SCO	SAG	03.22	13.20	TAU	15.56	09.07	13
14	20.43	CAN	CAN	02.47	LIB	SCO	15.03	AQU	ARI	TAU	CAN	LEO	14
15	GEM	CAN	06.48	VIR	LIB	00.57	CAP	03.19	13.10	01.17	23.51	19.33	15
16	GEM	00.35	LEO	15.01	08.54	SAG	16.53	PIS	TAU	GEM	LEO	VIR	16
17	06.37	LEO	19.51	LIB	SCO	05.21	AQU	02.55	15.48	06.21	LEO	VIR	17
18	CAN	13.33	VIR	LIB	16.13	CAP	17.30	ARI	GEM	CAN	11.10	07.58	18
19	18.27	VIR	VIR	01.09	SAG	07.56	PIS	04.07	22.27	15.35	VIR	LIB	19
20	LEO	VIR	08.08	SCO	21.20	AQU	18.33	TAU	CAN	LEO	23.52	20.03	20
21	LEO	02.02	LIB	09.06	CAP	09.56	ARI	08.25	CAN	LIB	LIB	SCO	21
22	07.19	LIB	18.44	SAG	CAP	PIS	21.21	GEM	08.50	03.44	LIB	SCO	22
23	VIR	13.04	SCO	15.13	01.08	12.21	TAU	16.17	LEO	VIR	11.36	05.44	23
24	19.59	SCO	SCO	CAP	AQU	ARI	TAU	CAN	21.18	16.31	SCO	SAG	24
25	LIB	21.40	03.24	19.43	04.13	15.54	02.42	CAN	VIR	LIB	21.08	12.27	25
26	LIB	SAG	SAG	AQU	PIS	TAU	GEM	03.00	VIR	LIB	SAG	CAP	26
27	06.46	SAG	09.49	22.40	06.59	21.06	10.43	LEO	10.05	04.15	SAG	16.46	27
28	SCO	03.04	CAP	PIS	ARI	GEM	CAN	15.20	LIB	SCO	04.28	AQU	28
29	14.11		13.41	PIS	09.59	GEM	21.04	VIR	22.06	14.17	CAP	19.42	29
30	SAG		AQU	00.26	TAU	04.26	LEO	VIR	SCO	SAG	10.00	PIS	30
31	17.47		15.14		14.11		LEO	04.08		22.31		22.15	31

1936

SUN
mth dy   time –> sign

JAN 1	00.00 –> CAP
JAN 21	05.12 –> AQU
FEB 19	19.33 –> PIS
MAR 20	18.58 –> ARI
APR 20	06.31 –> TAU
MAY 21	06.06 –> GEM
JUN 21	14.22 –> CAN
JUL 23	01.18 –> LEO
AUG 23	08.11 –> VIR
SEP 23	05.26 –> LIB
OCT 23	14.18 –> SCO
NOV 22	11.25 –> SAG
DEC 22	00.27 –> CAP

MERCURY
mth dy   time –> sign

JAN 1	00.00 –> CAP
JAN 6	03.32 –> AQU
MAR 13	06.40 –> PIS
MAR 31	05.08 –> ARI
APR 15	01.45 –> TAU
MAY 1	01.30 –> GEM
JUL 8	20.47 –> CAN
JUL 23	15.39 –> LEO
AUG 7	22.59 –> VIR
AUG 27	17.43 –> LIB
NOV 2	11.00 –> SCO
NOV 21	00.39 –> SAG
DEC 10	06.40 –> CAP

VENUS
mth dy   time –> sign

JAN 1	00.00 –> SCO
JAN 3	14.16 –> SAG
JAN 28	14.00 –> CAP
FEB 22	04.14 –> AQU
MAR 17	14.53 –> PIS
APR 11	00.41 –> ARI
MAY 5	10.53 –> TAU
MAY 29	21.39 –> GEM
JUN 23	08.16 –> CAN
JUL 17	17.51 –> LEO
AUG 11	02.11 –> VIR
SEP 4	10.02 –> LIB
SEP 28	18.36 –> SCO
OCT 23	05.00 –> SAG
NOV 16	18.36 –> CAP
DEC 11	14.51 –> AQU

MARS
mth dy   time –> sign

JAN 1	00.00 –> AQU
JAN 14	13.59 –> PIS
FEB 22	04.09 –> ARI
APR 1	21.30 –> TAU
MAY 13	09.17 –> GEM
JUN 25	21.53 –> CAN
AUG 10	09.43 –> LEO
SEP 26	14.51 –> VIR
NOV 14	14.52 –> LIB

SATURN
mth dy   time –> sign

JAN 1	00.00 –> PIS

JUPITER
mth dy   time –> sign

JAN 1	00.00 –> SAG
DEC 2	08.39 –> CAP

MOON

dy	jan	feb	mar	apr	may	jun	jul	aug	sep	oct	nov	dec	dy
1	ARI	10.39	22.25	LEO	VIR	14.11	09.27	CAP	PIS	ARI	GEM	CAN	1
2	ARI	GEM	CAN	LEO	18.43	SCO	SAG	09.25	22.43	08.25	20.00	09.43	2
3	01.11	16.58	CAN	00.07	LIB	SCO	18.34	AQU	ARI	TAU	CAN	LEO	3
4	TAU	CAN	07.20	VIR	LIB	01.37	CAP	12.36	23.04	08.37	CAN	16.31	4
5	05.04	CAN	LEO	12.31	07.16	SAG	CAP	PIS	TAU	GEM	00.37	VIR	5
6	GEM	01.26	18.18	LIB	SCO	11.03	00.56	14.21	TAU	11.29	LEO	VIR	6
7	10.29	LEO	VIR	LIB	18.54	CAP	AQU	ARI	00.54	CAN	09.00	02.55	7
8	CAN	11.48	VIR	01.05	SAG	18.17	05.10	16.11	GEM	17.45	VIR	LIB	8
9	18.02	VIR	06.26	SCO	SAG	AQU	PIS	TAU	05.16	LEO	20.15	15.28	9
10	LEO	23.45	LIB	13.03	04.57	23.27	08.10	19.12	CAN	LEO	LIB	SCO	10
11	LEO	LIB	19.03	SAG	CAP	PIS	ARI	GEM	12.13	03.01	LIB	SCO	11
12	04.05	LIB	SCO	23.23	12.47	PIS	10.46	23.52	LEO	VIR	08.52	04.07	12
13	VIR	12.24	SCO	CAP	AQU	02.47	TAU	CAN	21.20	14.19	SCO	SAG	13
14	16.10	SCO	07.06	CAP	17.52	ARI	13.38	CAN	VIR	LIB	21.33	15.25	14
15	LIB	23.56	SAG	06.49	PIS	04.48	GEM	06.20	VIR	LIB	SAG	CAP	15
16	LIB	SAG	16.51	AQU	20.14	TAU	17.28	LEO	08.12	02.47	SAG	CAP	16
17	04.38	SAG	CAP	10.38	ARI	06.29	CAN	14.44	LIB	SCO	09.20	00.42	17
18	SCO	08.21	22.52	PIS	20.47	GEM	22.58	VIR	20.32	15.38	CAP	AQU	18
19	15.11	CAP	AQU	11.20	TAU	09.08	LEO	VIR	SCO	SAG	19.11	07.43	19
20	SAG	12.47	AQU	ARI	21.12	CAN	LEO	01.17	SCO	SAG	AQU	PIS	20
21	22.19	AQU	00.59	10.37	GEM	14.06	06.54	LIB	09.24	03.37	AQU	12.26	21
22	CAP	13.55	PIS	TAU	23.19	LEO	VIR	13.36	SAG	CAP	02.04	ARI	22
23	CAP	PIS	00.31>ARI	10.37	CAN	22.15	17.30	SCO	20.53	13.00	PIS	15.06	23
24	02.02	13.35	23.37	GEM	CAN	VIR	LIB	SCO	CAP	AQU	05.37	TAU	24
25	AQU	ARI	TAU	13.22	04.41	VIR	LIB	02.09	CAP	18.28	ARI	16.24	25
26	03.35	13.51	TAU	CAN	LEO	09.23	05.54	SAG	04.53	PIS	06.29	GEM	26
27	PIS	TAU	00.31	20.03	13.48	LIB	SCO	12.35	AQU	20.09	TAU	17.36	27
28	04.36	16.30	GEM	LEO	VIR	21.53	17.56	CAP	08.39	ARI	06.11	CAN	28
29	ARI	GEM	04.52	LEO	VIR	SCO	SAG	19.12	PIS	19.34	GEM	20.14	29
30	06.37		CAN	06.22	01.38	SCO	SAG	AQU	09.10	TAU	06.40	LEO	30
31	TAU		13.04		LIB		03.24	22.06		18.49		LEO	31

212

SUN
mth dy   time –> sign

JAN 1   00.00 –> CAP
JAN 20   11.01 –> AQU
FEB 19   01.21 –> PIS
MAR 21   00.45 –> ARI
APR 20   12.19 –> TAU
MAY 21   11.57 –> GEM
JUN 21   20.12 –> CAN
JUL 23   07.07 –> LEO
AUG 23   13.58 –> VIR
SEP 23   11.13 –> LIB
OCT 23   20.07 –> SCO
NOV 22   17.17 –> SAG
DEC 22   06.22 –> CAP

MERCURY
mth dy   time –> sign

JAN 1   16.41 –> AQU
JAN 9   21.28 –> CAP
FEB 14   00.26 –> AQU
MAR 6   14.06 –> PIS
MAR 23   03.41 –> ARI
APR 7   01.09 –> TAU
JUN 13   22.28 –> GEM
JUL 1   02.21 –> CAN
JUL 15   04.11 –> LEO
JUL 31   21.07 –> VIR
OCT 8   10.12 –> LIB
OCT 26   01.14 –> SCO
NOV 13   19.25 –> SAG
DEC 3   23.51 –> CAP

VENUS
mth dy   time –> sign

JAN 1   00.00 –> AQU
JAN 6   03.18 –> PIS
FEB 2   10.39 –> ARI
MAR 9   13.19 –> TAU
APR 14   04.19 –> ARI
JUN 4   06.41 –> TAU
JUL 7   21.13 –> GEM
AUG 4   20.14 –> CAN
AUG 31   00.08 –> LEO
SEP 25   04.03 –> VIR
OCT 19   16.33 –> LIB
NOV 12   19.43 –> SCO
DEC 6   18.06 –> SAG
DEC 30   14.42 –> CAP

MARS
mth dy   time –> sign

JAN 1   00.00 –> LIB
JAN 5   20.39 –> SCO
MAR 13   03.16 –> SAG
MAY 14   22.52 –> SCO
AUG 8   22.14 –> SAG
SEP 30   09.08 –> CAP
NOV 11   18.31 –> AQU
DEC 21   17.46 –> PIS

SATURN
mth dy   time –> sign

JAN 1   00.00 –> PIS
APR 25   06.29 –> ARI
OCT 18   03.40 –> PIS

JUPITER
mth dy   time –> sign

JAN 1   00.00 –> CAP
DEC 20   04.05 –> AQU

MOON   MOON

dy	jan	feb	mar	apr	may	jun	jul	aug	sep	oct	nov	dec	dy
1	01.45	LIB	15.23	SAG	CAP	08.58	ARI	09.29	21.21	08.29	LIB	SCO	1
2	VIR	07.10	SCO	SAG	18.08	PIS	ARI	GEM	LEO	VIR	07.48	02.05	2
3	10.55	SCO	SCO	00.16	AQU	14.22	00.34	11.34	LEO	15.31	SCO	SAG	3
4	LIB	19.59	04.08	CAP	AQU	ARI	TAU	CAN	01.34	LIB	19.46	15.07	4
5	22.58	SAG	SAG	10.39	01.57	16.36	02.15	13.35	VIR	LIB	SAG	CAP	5
6	SCO	SAG	16.23	AQU	PIS	TAU	GEM	LEO	07.48	00.55	SAG	CAP	6
7	SCO	07.34	CAP	16.59	05.47	16.46	02.53	16.54	LIB	SCO	08.50	03.40	7
8	11.43	CAP	CAP	PIS	ARI	GEM	CAN	VIR	16.59	12.44	CAP	AQU	8
9	SAG	16.00	01.36	19.28	06.32	16.31	03.59	22.58	SCO	SAG	21.19	14.21	9
10	22.53	AQU	AQU	ARI	TAU	CAN	LEO	LIB	SCO	SAG	AQU	PIS	10
11	CAP	21.10	06.50	19.39	05.56	17.44	07.15	LIB	04.59	01.47	AQU	21.55	11
12	CAP	PIS	PIS	TAU	GEM	LEO	VIR	08.37	SAG	CAP	07.07	ARI	12
13	07.25	PIS	09.00	19.34	06.00	22.01	14.04	SCO	17.52	13.37	PIS	ARI	13
14	AQU	00.12	ARI	GEM	CAN	VIR	LIB	20.59	CAP	AQU	12.59	01.50	14
15	13.28	ARI	09.54	21.02	08.27	VIR	LIB	SAG	CAP	22.03	ARI	TAU	15
16	PIS	02.34	TAU	CAN	LEO	06.08	00.36	SAG	04.51	PIS	15.12	02.42	16
17	17.48	TAU	11.19	CAN	14.19	LIB	SCO	09.37	AQU	PIS	TAU	GEM	17
18	ARI	05.22	GEM	01.11	VIR	17.31	13.20	CAP	12.19	02.32	15.10	02.03	18
19	21.07	GEM	14.25	LEO	23.34	SCO	SAG	20.05	PIS	ARI	GEM	CAN	19
20	TAU	09.04	CAN	08.16	LIB	SCO	SAG	AQU	16.31	04.09	14.47	01.48	20
21	23.54	CAN	19.35	VIR	LIB	06.25	01.50	AQU	ARI	TAU	CAN	LEO	21
22	GEM	13.51	LEO	17.51	11.18	SAG	CAP	03.28	18.49	04.40	15.55	03.57	22
23	GEM	LEO	LEO	LIB	SCO	18.58	12.20	PIS	TAU	GEM	LEO	VIR	23
24	02.38	20.04	02.44	LIB	SCO	CAP	AQU	08.23	20.46	05.47	19.55	09.53	24
25	CAN	VIR	VIR	05.21	00.10	CAP	20.21	ARI	GEM	CAN	VIR	LIB	25
26	06.08	VIR	11.47	SCO	SAG	05.54	PIS	11.57	23.24	08.42	VIR	19.45	26
27	LEO	04.26	LIB	18.05	12.53	AQU	PIS	TAU	CAN	LEO	03.22	SCO	27
28	11.30	LIB	22.51	SAG	CAP	14.37	02.15	15.01	CAN	14.01	LIB	SCO	28
29	VIR		SCO	SAG	CAP	PIS	ARI	GEM	03.14	VIR	13.46	08.12	29
30	19.49		SCO	06.56	00.13	20.50	06.31	18.03	LEO	21.47	SCO	SAG	30
31	LIB		11.32		AQU		TAU	CAN		LIB		21.17	31

213

1938

SUN
mth dy time –> sign

JAN 1	00.00	–> CAP
JAN 20	16.59	–> AQU
FEB 19	07.20	–> PIS
MAR 21	06.43	–> ARI
APR 20	18.15	–> TAU
MAY 21	17.50	–> GEM
JUN 22	02.04	–> CAN
JUL 23	12.57	–> LEO
AUG 23	19.46	–> VIR
SEP 23	17.00	–> LIB
OCT 24	01.54	–> SCO
NOV 22	23.06	–> SAG
DEC 22	12.13	–> CAP

SATURN
mth dy time –> sign

JAN 1	00.00	–> PIS
JAN 14	10.32	–> ARI

MERCURY
mth dy time –> sign

JAN 1	00.00	–> CAP
JAN 6	21.37	–> SAG
JAN 12	22.30	–> CAP
FEB 8	13.17	–> AQU
FEB 27	03.01	–> PIS
MAR 15	00.03	–> ARI
APR 1	13.24	–> TAU
APR 23	13.56	–> ARI
MAY 16	17.46	–> TAU
JUN 8	00.32	–> GEM
JUN 22	13.09	–> CAN
JUL 7	03.21	–> LEO
JUL 26	22.55	–> VIR
SEP 3	02.59	–> LEO
SEP 10	15.38	–> VIR
OCT 1	04.19	–> LIB
OCT 18	12.43	–> SCO
NOV 6	23.33	–> SAG

VENUS
mth dy time –> sign

JAN 1	00.00	–> CAP
JAN 23	11.16	–> AQU
FEB 16	09.00	–> PIS
MAR 12	09.20	–> ARI
APR 5	13.46	–> TAU
APR 29	23.35	–> GEM
MAY 24	15.56	–> CAN
JUN 18	16.37	–> LEO
JUL 14	05.45	–> VIR
AUG 9	16.26	–> LIB
SEP 7	01.36	–> SCO
OCT 13	18.49	–> SAG
NOV 15	16.07	–> SCO

MARS
mth dy time –> sign

JAN 1	00.00	–> PIS
JAN 30	12.44	–> ARI
MAR 12	07.48	–> TAU
APR 23	18.39	–> GEM
JUN 7	01.28	–> CAN
JUL 22	22.26	–> LEO
SEP 7	20.23	–> VIR
OCT 25	06.20	–> LIB
DEC 11	23.26	–> SCO

JUPITER
mth dy time –> sign

JAN 1	00.00	–> AQU
MAY 14	07.46	–> PIS
JUL 30	03.01	–> AQU
DEC 29	18.34	–> PIS

MOON

dy	jan	feb	mar	apr	may	jun	jul	aug	sep	oct	nov	dec	dy
1	CAP	AQU	09.13	ARI	15.45	CAN	12.24	LIB	00.28	CAP	AQU	PIS	1
2	CAP	01.58	PIS	04.43	GEM	02.09	VIR	06.49	SAG	CAP	05.09	00.02	2
3	09.31	PIS	16.16	TAU	16.50	LEO	16.09	SCO	12.30	08.58	PIS	ARI	3
4	AQU	09.54	ARI	07.33	CAN	04.21	LIB	17.02	CAP	AQU	14.35	07.01	4
5	20.07	ARI	21.29	GEM	18.42	VIR	23.49	SAG	CAP	20.27	ARI	TAU	5
6	PIS	15.58	TAU	10.07	LEO	09.35	SCO	SAG	01.10	PIS	20.41	10.18	6
7	PIS	TAU	TAU	CAN	22.17	LIB	SCO	05.33	AQU	PIS	TAU	GEM	7
8	04.29	20.08	01.33	13.04	VIR	18.01	10.45	CAP	12.28	05.22	TAU	11.08	8
9	ARI	GEM	GEM	LEO	VIR	SCO	SAG	18.15	PIS	ARI	00.03	CAN	9
10	10.06	22.26	04.46	16.51	04.06	SCO	23.22	AQU	21.40	11.43	GEM	11.17	10
11	TAU	CAN	CAN	VIR	LIB	04.57	CAP	AQU	ARI	TAU	01.59	LEO	11
12	12.50	23.33	07.23	22.02	12.16	SAG	CAP	05.45	ARI	16.10	CAN	12.37	12
13	GEM	LEO	LEO	LIB	SCO	17.21	12.05	PIS	04.54	GEM	03.50	VIR	13
14	13.21	LEO	10.05	LIB	22.40	CAP	AQU	15.34	TAU	19.31	LEO	16.27	14
15	CAN	00.57	VIR	05.21	SAG	CAP	23.55	ARI	10.23	CAN	06.38	LIB	15
16	13.09	VIR	14.08	SCO	SAG	06.07	PIS	23.25	GEM	22.19	VIR	23.13	16
17	LEO	04.28	LIB	15.19	10.51	AQU	PIS	TAU	14.09	LEO	11.03	SCO	17
18	14.12	LIB	20.53	SAG	CAP	18.02	10.02	TAU	CAN	LEO	LIB	SCO	18
19	VIR	11.37	SCO	SAG	23.37	PIS	ARI	04.51	16.26	01.09	17.26	08.31	19
20	18.27	SCO	SCO	03.31	AQU	PIS	17.31	GEM	LEO	VIR	SCO	SAG	20
21	LIB	22.33	07.01	CAP	AQU	03.40	TAU	07.40	18.01	04.43	SCO	19.39	21
22	LIB	SAG	SAG	16.11	11.08	ARI	21.43	CAN	VIR	LIB	01.56	CAP	22
23	02.55	SAG	19.32	AQU	PIS	09.50	GEM	08.27	20.19	10.00	SAG	CAP	23
24	SCO	11.28	CAP	AQU	19.35	TAU	22.55	LEO	LIB	SCO	12.37	07.59	24
25	14.51	CAP	CAP	02.53	ARI	12.25	CAN	08.43	LIB	17.54	CAP	AQU	25
26	SAG	23.36	07.56	PIS	ARI	GEM	22.26	VIR	00.57	SAG	CAP	20.41	26
27	SAG	AQU	AQU	10.08	00.17	12.27	LEO	10.26	SCO	SAG	00.58	PIS	27
28	03.58	AQU	AQU	ARI	TAU	CAN	22.17	LIB	09.02	04.39	PIS	PIS	28
29	CAP		PIS	14.02	01.52	11.45	VIR	15.26	SAG	CAP	13.30	08.14	29
30	16.00		PIS	TAU	GEM	LEO	VIR	SCO	20.20	17.08	PIS	ARI	30
31	AQU		00.33		01.52		00.35	SCO		AQU		16.48	31

SUN

mth dy	time –> sign
JAN 1	00.00 –> CAP
JAN 20	22.51 –> AQU
FEB 19	13.09 –> PIS
MAR 21	12.28 –> ARI
APR 20	23.55 –> TAU
MAY 21	23.27 –> GEM
JUN 22	07.39 –> CAN
JUL 23	18.37 –> LEO
AUG 24	01.31 –> VIR
SEP 23	22.49 –> LIB
OCT 24	07.46 –> SCO
NOV 23	04.59 –> SAG
DEC 22	18.06 –> CAP

MERCURY

mth dy	time –> sign
JAN 1	00.00 –> SAG
JAN 12	07.57 –> CAP
FEB 1	17.57 –> AQU
FEB 19	08.10 –> PIS
MAR 7	09.14 –> ARI
MAY 14	13.43 –> TAU
MAY 31	02.45 –> GEM
JUN 13	23.01 –> CAN
JUN 30	06.41 –> LEO
SEP 7	04.58 –> VIR
SEP 23	07.48 –> LIB
OCT 11	05.20 –> SCO
NOV 1	07.03 –> SAG
DEC 3	07.22 –> SCO
DEC 13	19.16 –> SAG

VENUS

mth dy	time –> sign
JAN 1	00.00 –> SCO
JAN 4	21.48 –> SAG
FEB 6	09.20 –> CAP
MAR 5	13.29 –> AQU
MAR 31	08.34 –> PIS
APR 25	14.28 –> ARI
MAY 20	14.13 –> TAU
JUN 14	10.11 –> GEM
JUL 9	02.25 –> CAN
AUG 2	14.11 –> LEO
AUG 26	21.24 –> VIR
SEP 20	01.02 –> LIB
OCT 14	02.41 –> SCO
NOV 7	03.41 –> SAG
DEC 1	04.52 –> CAP
DEC 25	07.25 –> AQU

MARS

mth dy	time –> sign
JAN 1	00.00 –> SCO
JAN 29	09.49 –> SAG
MAR 21	07.25 –> CAP
MAY 25	00.19 –> AQU
JUL 21	19.30 –> CAP
SEP 24	01.14 –> AQU
NOV 19	15.56 –> PIS

JUPITER

mth dy	time –> sign
JAN 1	00.00 –> PIS
MAY 11	14.08 –> ARI
OCT 30	00.44 –> PIS
DEC 20	17.04 –> ARI

SATURN

mth dy	time –> sign
JAN 1	00.00 –> ARI
JUL 6	05.47 –> TAU
OCT 22	05.16 –> ARI

MOON

dy	jan	feb	mar	apr	may	jun	jul	aug	sep	oct	nov	dec	dy
1	TAU	09.22	CAN	04.39	LIB	07.15	CAP	AQU	ARI	TAU	13.41	LEO	1
2	21.19	CAN	19.30	VIR	17.36	SAG	CAP	04.41	ARI	TAU	CAN	LEO	2
3	GEM	09.06	LEO	05.48	SCO	15.50	09.54	PIS	10.47	01.38	18.01	02.23	3
4	22.20	LEO	19.17	LIB	23.11	CAP	AQU	17.22	TAU	GEM	LEO	VIR	4
5	CAN	08.02	VIR	08.21	SAG	CAP	22.17	ARI	20.02	08.16	20.57	05.22	5
6	21.32	VIR	19.25	SCO	SAG	02.40	PIS	ARI	GEM	CAN	VIR	LIB	6
7	LEO	08.29	LIB	13.47	07.34	AQU	PIS	04.47	GEM	12.10	23.03	08.57	7
8	21.08	LIB	21.59	SAG	CAP	15.04	10.50	TAU	01.52	LIB	SCO	SCO	8
9	VIR	12.22	SCO	22.47	18.41	PIS	ARI	13.06	CAN	13.46	LIB	13.32	9
10	23.10	SCO	SCO	CAP	AQU	PIS	21.27	GEM	04.12	VIR	01.14	SAG	10
11	LIB	20.24	04.23	CAP	AQU	03.10	TAU	17.21	LEO	14.15	SCO	19.51	11
12	LIB	SAG	SAG	10.33	07.09	ARI	TAU	CAN	04.09	LIB	04.41	CAP	12
13	04.54	SAG	14.35	AQU	PIS	12.43	04.21	18.09	VIR	15.18	SAG	CAP	13
14	SCO	07.41	CAP	23.04	18.41	TAU	GEM	LEO	03.39	SCO	10.42	04.42	14
15	14.10	CAP	CAP	PIS	ARI	18.32	07.16	17.19	LIB	18.36	CAP	AQU	15
16	SAG	20.22	03.01	PIS	ARI	GEM	CAN	VIR	04.43	SAG	20.00	16.14	16
17	SAG	AQU	AQU	10.13	03.28	21.06	07.30	17.03	SCO	SAG	AQU	PIS	17
18	01.44	AQU	15.31	ARI	TAU	CAN	LEO	LIB	09.02	01.22	AQU	PIS	18
19	CAP	08.52	PIS	18.57	09.06	21.58	07.07	19.20	SAG	CAP	08.00	05.03	19
20	14.15	PIS	PIS	TAU	GEM	LEO	VIR	SCO	17.11	11.40	PIS	ARI	20
21	AQU	20.23	02.41	TAU	12.23	22.56	08.10	SCO	CAP	AQU	20.36	16.32	21
22	AQU	ARI	ARI	01.16	CAN	VIR	LIB	01.14	CAP	AQU	ARI	TAU	22
23	02.51	ARI	11.58	GEM	14.33	VIR	12.04	SAG	04.24	00.05	ARI	TAU	23
24	PIS	06.19	TAU	05.43	LEO	01.30	SCO	10.33	AQU	PIS	07.23	00.37	24
25	14.42	TAU	19.15	CAN	16.51	LIB	19.10	CAP	17.00	12.28	TAU	GEM	25
26	ARI	13.47	GEM	08.55	VIR	06.25	SAG	22.09	PIS	ARI	15.09	05.03	26
27	ARI	GEM	GEM	LEO	20.06	SCO	SAG	AQU	PIS	23.09	GEM	CAN	27
28	00.29	18.07	00.19	11.26	LIB	13.39	04.51	AQU	05.22	TAU	20.11	07.05	28
29	TAU		CAN	VIR	LIB	SAG	CAP	10.42	ARI	TAU	CAN	LEO	29
30	06.50		03.15	14.02	00.47	22.53	16.15	PIS	16.29	07.31	23.34	08.29	30
31		GEM		LEO		SCO		AQU	23.15	GEM		VIR	31

1940

SUN

mth dy	time –> sign
JAN 1	00.00 –> CAP
JAN 21	04.44 –> AQU
FEB 19	19.04 –> PIS
MAR 20	18.24 –> ARI
APR 20	05.51 –> TAU
MAY 21	05.23 –> GEM
JUN 21	13.36 –> CAN
JUL 23	00.34 –> LEO
AUG 23	07.29 –> VIR
SEP 23	04.46 –> LIB
OCT 23	13.39 –> SCO
NOV 22	10.49 –> SAG
DEC 21	23.54 –> CAP

MERCURY

mth dy	time –> sign
JAN 1	00.00 –> SAG
JAN 6	07.56 –> CAP
JAN 25	10.15 –> AQU
FEB 11	14.01 –> PIS
MAR 4	10.10 –> ARI
MAR 8	01.26 –> PIS
APR 17	04.56 –> ARI
MAY 6	21.14 –> TAU
MAY 21	13.58 –> GEM
JUN 4	22.29 –> CAN
JUN 26	14.32 –> LEO
JUL 21	01.39 –> CAN
AUG 11	17.05 –> LEO
AUG 29	11.11 –> VIR
SEP 14	.11.34 –> LIB
OCT 3	12.14 –> SCO
DEC 9	12.45 –> SAG
DEC 29	09.35 –> CAP

VENUS

mth dy	time –> sign
JAN 1	00.00 –> AQU
JAN 18	14.00 –> PIS
FEB 12	05.51 –> ARI
MAR 8	16.25 –> TAU
APR 4	18.10 –> GEM
MAY 6	18.46 –> CAN
JUL 5	16.17 –> GEM
AUG 1	02.19 –> CAN
SEP 8	16.59 –> LEO
OCT 6	21.10 –> VIR
NOV 1	17.23 –> LIB
NOV 26	12.32 –> SCO
DEC 20	19.36 –> SAG

MARS

mth dy	time –> sign
JAN 1	00.00 –> PIS
JAN 4	00.05 –> ARI
FEB 17	01.54 –> TAU
APR 1	18.41 –> GEM
MAY 17	14.45 –> CAN
JUL 3	10.32 –> LEO
AUG 19	15.58 –> VIR
OCT 5	14.21 –> LIB
NOV 20	17.16 –> SCO

SATURN

mth dy	time –> sign
JAN 1	00.00 –> ARI
MAR 20	09.42 –> TAU

JUPITER

mth dy	time –> sign
JAN 1	00.00 –> ARI
MAY 16	07.54 –> TAU

MOON

MOON

dy	jan	feb	mar	apr	may	jun	jul	aug	sep	oct	nov	dec	dy
1	10.43	SCO	SAG	07.13	01.56	ARI	TAU	CAN	12.57	LIB	10.21	CAP	1
2	LIB	01.36	15.02	AQU	PIS	10.44	05.15	CAN	VIR	23.12	SAG	CAP	2
3	14.36	SAG	CAP	19.11	14.52	TAU	GEM	01.20	12.54	SCO	12.22	03.12	3
4	SCO	09.27	CAP	PIS	ARI	20.49	12.10	LEO	LIB	23.54	CAP	AQU	4
5	20.12	CAP	01.07	PIS	ARI	GEM	CAN	02.50	13.16	SAG	18.03	11.35	5
6	SAG	19.21	AQU	08.10	03.12	GEM	16.12	VIR	SCO	SAG	AQU	PIS	6
7	SAG	AQU	13.07	ARI	TAU	04.02	LEO	03.50	15.36	03.28	AQU	23.26	7
8	03.30	AQU	PIS	20.39	13.34	CAN	18.44	LIB	SAG	CAP	03.46	ARI	8
9	CAP	06.58	PIS	TAU	GEM	09.00	VIR	05.46	20.45	10.44	PIS	ARI	9
10	12.42	PIS	02.01	TAU	21.33	LEO	21.07	SCO	CAP	AQU	16.13	12.27	10
11	AQU	19.49	ARI	07.32	CAN	12.41	LIB	09.29	21.18	21.18	ARI	TAU	11
12	AQU	ARI	14.44	GEM	CAN	VIR	LIB	SAG	04.51	PIS	ARI	TAU	12
13	00.03	ARI	TAU	16.04	03.22	15.43	00.07	15.15	AQU	PIS	15.13	00.08	13
14	PIS	08.36	TAU	CAN	LEO	LIB	SCO	CAP	15.25	09.50	TAU	GEM	14
15	12.55	TAU	01.53	21.44	07.17	18.31	04.05	23.07	PIS	ARI	17.00	09.20	15
16	ARI	19.10	GEM	LEO	VIR	SCO	SAG	AQU	PIS	22.49	GEM	CAN	16
17	ARI	GEM	09.57	LEO	09.40	21.34	09.17	AQU	03.43	TAU	GEM	16.16	17
18	01.15	GEM	CAN	00.34	LIB	SAG	CAP	09.10	ARI	02.52	CAN	LEO	18
19	TAU	01.46	14.15	VIR	11.12	SAG	16.22	PIS	16.45	10.59	CAN	21.35	19
20	10.32	CAN	LEO	01.23	SCO	01.44	AQU	21.14	TAU	GEM	10.38	VIR	20
21	GEM	04.19	15.20	LIB	13.00	CAP	AQU	ARI	TAU	21.18	LEO	VIR	21
22	15.35	LEO	VIR	01.33	SAG	08.15	01.58	ARI	05.05	16.11	VIR	01.37	22
23	CAN	04.11	14.47	SCO	16.35	AQU	PIS	10.17	GEM	CAN	VIR	LIB	23
24	17.10	VIR	LIB	02.48	CAP	17.55	14.01	TAU	14.57	04.51	19.25	04.30	24
25	LEO	03.29	14.33	SAG	23.19	PIS	ARI	22.13	CAN	LEO	LIB	SCO	25
26	17.12	LIB	SCO	06.50	AQU	PIS	ARI	GEM	21.09	09.09	20.44	06.36	26
27	VIR	04.13	16.31	CAP	AQU	06.13	02.56	GEM	LEO	VIR	SCO	SAG	27
28	17.43	SCO	SAG	14.39	09.39	ARI	TAU	06.53	23.41	10.37	21.18	08.58	28
29	LIB	07.54	21.59	AQU	PIS	18.52	14.04	CAN	VIR	LIB	SAG	CAP	29
30	20.17		CAP	AQU	22.18	TAU	GEM	11.31	23.46	10.25	22.50	13.09	30
31	SCO		CAP		ARI		21.32	LEO		SCO		AQU	31

SUN

mth dy	time -> sign
JAN 1	00.00 -> CAP
JAN 20	10.34 -> AQU
FEB 19	00.56 -> PIS
MAR 21	00.20 -> ARI
APR 20	11.50 -> TAU
MAY 21	11.23 -> GEM
JUN 21	19.33 -> CAN
JUL 23	06.26 -> LEO
AUG 23	13.17 -> VIR
SEP 23	10.33 -> LIB
OCT 23	19.27 -> SCO
NOV 22	16.38 -> SAG
DEC 22	05.44 -> CAP

MERCURY

mth dy	time -> sign
JAN 1	00.00 -> CAP
JAN 16	22.36 -> AQU
FEB 3	13.08 -> PIS
MAR 7	02.22 -> AQU
MAR 16	12.27 -> PIS
APR 12	07.19 -> ARI
APR 28	23.09 -> TAU
MAY 13	00.51 -> GEM
MAY 29	17.32 -> CAN
AUG 6	05.57 -> LEO
AUG 21	05.18 -> VIR
SEP 6	23.58 -> LIB
SEP 28	09.21 -> SCO
OCT 29	30.34 -> LIB
NOV 11	20.11 -> SCO
DEC 3	00.11 -> SAG
DEC 22	03.54 -> CAP

VENUS

mth dy	time -> sign
JAN 1	00.00 -> SAG
JAN 13	21.29 -> CAP
FEB 6	21.49 -> AQU
MAR 2	22.33 -> PIS
MAR 27	00.57 -> ARI
APR 20	05.53 -> TAU
MAY 14	13.36 -> GEM
JUN 7	23.53 -> CAN
JUL 2	12.33 -> LEO
JUL 27	04.12 -> VIR
AUG 21	00.29 -> LIB
SEP 15	04.01 -> SCO
OCT 10	19.22 -> SAG
NOV 6	10.17 -> CAP
DEC 5	23.04 -> AQU

MARS

mth dy	time -> sign
JAN 1	00.00 -> SCO
JAN 4	19.42 -> SAG
FEB 17	23.32 -> CAP
APR 2	11.45 -> AQU
MAY 16	05.05 -> PIS
JUL 2	05.16 -> ARI

JUPITER

mth dy	time -> sign
JAN 1	00.00 -> TAU
MAY 26	12.48 -> GEM

SATURN

mth dy	time -> sign
JAN 1	00.00 -> TAU

MOON

dy	jan	feb	mar	apr	may	jun	jul	aug	sep	oct	nov	dec	dy
1	20.35	ARI	ARI	08.06	01.56	LEO	11.17	22.49	CAP	AQU	ARI	TAU	1
2	PIS	ARI	12.23	GEM	CAN	00.38	LIB	SAG	11.39	00.18	ARI	22.00	2
3	PIS	04.41	TAU	19.44	11.34	VIR	14.33	SAG	AQU	PIS	03.19	GEM	3
4	07.34	TAU	TAU	CAN	LEO	05.17	SCO	01.17	17.52	09.37	TAU	GEM	4
5	ARI	17.09	01.12	CAN	18.06	LIB	16.13	CAP	PIS	ARI	15.52	10.22	5
6	20.28	GEM	GEM	04.26	VIR	07.13	SAG	04.32	PIS	20.52	GEM	CAN	6
7	TAU	GEM	12.04	LEO	21.11	SCO	17.21	AQU	02.28	TAU	GEM	21.43	7
8	TAU	02.57	CAN	09.21	LIB	07.23	CAP	09.51	ARI	TAU	04.26	LEO	8
9	08.27	CAN	19.19	VIR	21.34	SAG	19.36	PIS	13.32	09.23	CAN	LEO	9
10	GEM	09.07	LEO	10.54	SCO	07.31	AQU	18.13	TAU	GEM	15.49	07.12	10
11	17.33	LEO	22.51	LIB	20.49	CAP	AQU	ARI	TAU	21.53	LEO	VIR	11
12	CAN	12.21	VIR	10.31	SAG	09.41	00.42	ARI	02.06	CAN	LEO	13.46	12
13	23.39	VIR	23.51	SCO	21.03	AQU	PIS	05.32	GEM	CAN	00.29	LIB	13
14	LEO	14.07	LIB	10.07	CAP	15.33	09.34	TAU	14.09	08.29	VIR	16.51	14
15	LEO	LIB	LIB	SAG	CAP	PIS	ARI	18.09	CAN	LEO	05.21	SCO	15
16	03.45	15.52	00.03	11.38	00.15	PIS	21.30	GEM	23.36	15.36	LIB	17.10	16
17	VIR	SCO	SCO	CAP	AQU	01.30	TAU	GEM	LEO	VIR	06.40	SAG	17
18	07.00	18.37	01.08	16.31	07.33	ARI	TAU	05.37	LEO	18.54	SCO	16.26	18
19	LIB	SAG	SAG	AQU	PIS	14.03	10.09	CAN	05.29	LIB	05.53	CAP	19
20	10.04	22.54	04.25	AQU	18.34	TAU	GEM	14.15	VIR	19.25	SAG	16.53	20
21	SCO	CAP	CAP	01.07	ARI	TAU	21.15	LEO	08.17	SCO	05.11	AQU	21
22	13.16	CAP	10.34	PIS	ARI	02.44	CAN	19.53	LIB	19.00	CAP	20.33	22
23	SAG	05.01	AQU	12.34	07.26	GEM	CAN	VIR	09.23	SAG	06.46	PIS	23
24	17.01	AQU	19.30	ARI	TAU	13.51	05.48	23.21	SCO	19.40	AQU	PIS	24
25	CAP	13.18	PIS	ARI	20.10	CAN	LEO	LIB	10.24	CAP	12.09	04.24	25
26	22.06	PIS	PIS	01.22	GEM	22.55	12.03	LIB	SAG	23.02	PIS	ARI	26
27	AQU	23.54	06.39	TAU	GEM	LEO	VIR	01.48	12.44	AQU	21.26	15.43	27
28	AQU	ARI	ARI	14.11	07.36	LEO	16.41	SCO	CAP	AQU	ARI	TAU	28
29	05.34		19.13	GEM	CAN	06.03	LIB	04.13	17.17	05.51	ARI	TAU	29
30	PIS		TAU	GEM	17.15	VIR	20.09	SAG	AQU	PIS	09.18	04.27	30
31	16.02		TAU		LEO		SCO	07.18		15.38		GEM	31

1942

SUN

mth dy	time –> sign
JAN 1	00.00 –> CAP
JAN 20	16.24 –> AQU
FEB 19	06.46 –> PIS
MAR 21	06.11 –> ARI
APR 20	17.39 –> TAU
MAY 21	17.08 –> GEM
JUN 22	01.16 –> CAN
JUL 23	12.07 –> LEO
AUG 23	18.58 –> VIR
SEP 23	16.16 –> LIB
OCT 24	01.15 –> SCO
NOV 22	22.31 –> SAG
DEC 22	11.39 –> CAP

MERCURY

mth dy	time –> sign
JAN 1	00.00 –> CAP
JAN 9	15.24 –> AQU
MAR 17	00.10 –> PIS
APR 5	07.06 –> ARI
APR 20	13.42 –> TAU
MAY 5	04.37 –> GEM
JUL 12	20.24 –> CAN
JUL 29	04.24 –> LEO
AUG 13	01.48 –> VIR
AUG 31	08.27 –> LIB
NOV 7	01.44 –> SCO
NOV 25	20.26 –> SAG
DEC 14	22.22 –> CAP

VENUS

mth dy	time –> sign
JAN 1	00.00 –> AQU
APR 6	13.14 –> PIS
MAY 6	02.25 –> ARI
JUN 2	00.26 –> TAU
JUN 27	22.18 –> GEM
JUL 23	06.10 –> CAN
AUG 17	03.04 –> LEO
SEP 10	14.38 –> VIR
OCT 4	18.58 –> LIB
OCT 28	18.41 –> SCO
NOV 21	16.07 –> SAG
DEC 15	12.53 –> CAP

MARS

mth dy	time –> sign
JAN 1	00.00 –> ARI
JAN 11	22.21 –> TAU
MAR 7	08.04 –> GEM
APR 26	06.18 –> CAN
JUN 14	03.55 –> LEO
AUG 1	08.27 –> VIR
SEP 17	10.10 –> LIB
NOV 1	22.36 –> SCO
DEC 15	16.51 –> SAG

SATURN

mth dy	time –> sign
JAN 1	00.00 –> TAU
MAY 8	19.40 –> GEM

JUPITER

mth dy	time –> sign
JAN 1	00.00 –> GEM
JUN 10	10.36 –> CAN

MOON

dy	jan	feb	mar	apr	may	jun	jul	aug	sep	oct	nov	dec	dy
1	16.41	LEO	LEO	LIB	SCO	CAP	AQU	ARI	20.40	17.03	LEO	VIR	1
2	CAN	18.57	03.06	19.54	06.03	15.59	03.46	ARI	GEM	CAN	LEO	18.55	2
3	CAN	VIR	VIR	SCO	SAG	AQU	PIS	01.47	GEM	CAN	01.19	LIB	3
4	03.32	VIR	08.23	21.04	06.04	19.14	09.10	TAU	09.00	05.35	VIR	LIB	4
5	LEO	01.18	LIB	SAG	CAP	PIS	ARI	12.54	CAN	LEO	09.21	00.06	5
6	12.42	LIB	11.50	22.41	07.56	PIS	18.22	GEM	21.15	16.13	LIB	SCO	6
7	VIR	05.56	SCO	CAP	AQU	02.11	TAU	GEM	LEO	VIR	13.27	01.34	7
8	19.48	SCO	14.28	CAP	12.44	ARI	TAU	01.30	LEO	23.33	SCO	SAG	8
9	LIB	09.06	SAG	01.56	PIS	12.16	06.10	CAN	07.31	LIB	14.47	01.07	9
10	LIB	SAG	17.08	AQU	20.31	TAU	GEM	13.39	VIR	LIB	SAG	CAP	10
11	00.24	11.19	CAP	07.19	ARI	TAU	18.51	LEO	15.05	03.46	15.18	00.57	11
12	SCO	CAP	20.30	PIS	ARI	00.11	CAN	LEO	LIB	SCO	CAP	AQU	12
13	02.31	13.27	AQU	14.49	06.37	GEM	CAN	00.09	20.19	06.10	16.48	02.56	13
14	SAG	AQU	AQU	ARI	TAU	12.50	07.08	VIR	SCO	SAG	AQU	PIS	14
15	03.07	16.51	01.09	ARI	18.15	CAN	LEO	08.31	23.58	08.13	20.28	08.04	15
16	CAP	PIS	PIS	00.18	GEM	CAN	18.08	LIB	SAG	CAP	PIS	ARI	16
17	03.52	22.46	07.41	TAU	GEM	01.19	VIR	14.38	SAG	11.01	PIS	16.16	17
18	AQU	ARI	ARI	11.37	06.49	LEO	VIR	SCO	02.48	AQU	02.30	TAU	18
19	06.43	ARI	16.39	GEM	CAN	12.33	03.02	18.35	CAP	15.05	ARI	TAU	19
20	PIS	07.57	TAU	GEM	19.21	VIR	LIB	SAG	05.27	PIS	10.38	02.46	20
21	13.08	TAU	TAU	00.10	LEO	21.04	09.02	20.46	AQU	20.37	TAU	GEM	21
22	ARI	19.47	04.00	CAN	LEO	LIB	SCO	CAP	08.34	ARI	20.35	14.46	22
23	23.18	GEM	GEM	12.21	06.07	LIB	11.58	22.07	PIS	ARI	GEM	CAN	23
24	TAU	GEM	16.33	LEO	VIR	01.50	SAG	AQU	12.57	03.52	GEM	CAN	24
25	TAU	08.15	CAN	22.02	13.22	SCO	12.38	23.55	ARI	TAU	08.17	03.35	25
26	11.44	CAN	CAN	VIR	LIB	03.09	CAP	PIS	19.34	13.18	CAN	LEO	26
27	GEM	19.06	04.04	VIR	16.32	SAG	12.37	PIS	TAU	GEM	21.09	16.10	27
28	GEM	LEO	LEO	03.50	SCO	02.30	AQU	03.39	TAU	GEM	LEO	VIR	28
29	00.03		12.36	LIB	16.39	CAP	13.49	ARI	05.05	01.00	LEO	VIR	29
30	CAN		VIR	05.59	SAG	02.00	PIS	10.29	GEM	CAN	09.29	02.44	30
31	10.37		17.36		15.43		17.55	TAU		13.48		LIB	31

SUN

mth dy	time -> sign
JAN 1	00.00 -> CAP
JAN 20	22.19 -> AQU
FEB 19	12.40 -> PIS
MAR 21	12.03 -> ARI
APR 20	23.31 -> TAU
MAY 21	23.03 -> GEM
JUN 22	07.12 -> CAN
JUL 23	18.04 -> LEO
AUG 24	00.55 -> VIR
SEP 23	22.12 -> LIB
OCT 24	07.08 -> SCO
NOV 23	04.21 -> SAG
DEC 22	17.29 -> CAP

SATURN

mth dy	time -> sign
JAN 1	00.00 -> GEM

MERCURY

mth dy	time -> sign
JAN 1	00.00 -> CAP
JAN 3	08.27 -> AQU
JAN 27	23.43 -> CAP
FEB 15	19.00 -> AQU
MAR 11	04.59 -> PIS
MAR 28	11.19 -> ARI
APR 12	04.57 -> TAU
APR 30	15.56 -> GEM
MAY 26	10.22 -> TAU
JUN 14	00.46 -> GEM
JUL 6	09.05 -> CAN
JUL 20	16.08 -> LEO
AUG 5	10.33 -> VIR
AUG 27	00.36 -> LIB
SEP 25	09.56 -> VIR
OCT 11	23.26 -> LIB
OCT 30	23.37 -> SCO
NOV 18	13.39 -> SAG
DEC 8	01.47 -> CAP

VENUS

mth dy	time -> sign
JAN 1	00.00 -> CAP
JAN 8	10.03 -> AQU
FEB 1	09.02 -> PIS
FEB 25	12.04 -> ARI
MAR 21	22.24 -> TAU
APR 15	20.12 -> GEM
MAY 11	11.56 -> CAN
JUN 7	12.09 -> LEO
JUL 7	23.56 -> VIR
NOV 9	18.25 -> LIB
DEC 8	07.44 -> SCO

MARS

mth dy	time -> sign
JAN 1	00.00 -> SAG
JAN 26	19.10 -> CAP
MAR 8	12.42 -> AQU
APR 17	10.25 -> PIS
MAY 27	09.25 -> ARI
JUL 7	23.05 -> TAU
AUG 23	23.58 -> GEM

JUPITER

mth dy	time -> sign
JAN 1	00.00 -> CAN
JUN 30	21.46 -> LEO

MOON

dy	jan	feb	mar	apr	may	jun	jul	aug	sep	oct	nov	dec	dy
1	09.39	23.15	07.19	18.27	04.39	TAU	17.13	LEO	18.33	10.04	SAG	13.01	1
2	SCO	CAP	CAP	PIS	ARI	00.29	CAN	LEO	LIB	SCO	03.37	AQU	2
3	12.33	23.10	08.56	21.17	09.57	GEM	CAN	00.45	LIB	17.03	CAP	15.36	3
4	SAG	AQU	AQU	ARI	TAU	10.45	05.39	VIR	04.20	SAG	07.09	PIS	4
5	12.35	23.07	09.54	ARI	17.16	CAN	LEO	12.51	SCO	22.11	AQU	19.00	5
6	CAP	PIS	PIS	01.37	GEM	23.03	18.45	LIB	11.38	CAP	10.16	ARI	6
7	11.42	PIS	11.41	TAU	GEM	LEO	VIR	22.40	SAG	CAP	PIS	23.30	7
8	AQU	01.00	ARI	08.41	03.17	LEO	VIR	SCO	16.13	01.39	13.10	TAU	8
9	12.03	ARI	15.53	GEM	CAN	12.03	06.44	SCO	CAP	AQU	ARI	TAU	9
10	PIS	06.17	TAU	19.03	15.39	VIR	LIB	05.08	18.18	03.44	16.32	05.32	10
11	15.21	TAU	23.39	CAN	LEO	23.22	15.40	SAG	AQU	PIS	TAU	GEM	11
12	ARI	15.25	GEM	CAN	LEO	LIB	SCO	08.09	18.46	05.12	21.31	13.46	12
13	22.22	GEM	GEM	07.39	04.21	LIB	20.37	CAP	PIS	ARI	GEM	CAN	13
14	TAU	GEM	10.51	LEO	VIR	06.59	SAG	08.36	19.09	07.26	GEM	CAN	14
15	TAU	03.24	CAN	19.59	14.44	SCO	22.07	AQU	ARI	TAU	05.22	00.37	15
16	08.39	CAN	23.41	VIR	LIB	10.36	CAP	08.06	21.14	12.07	CAN	LEO	16
17	GEM	16.18	LEO	VIR	21.19	SAG	21.46	PIS	TAU	16.27	13.22	17
18	20.53	LEO	LEO	05.41	SCO	11.29	AQU	08.32	TAU	20.28	LEO	VIR	18
19	CAN	LEO	11.43	LIB	SCO	CAP	21.30	ARI	02.42	CAN	LEO	VIR	19
20	CAN	04.20	VIR	12.04	00.33	11.33	PIS	11.39	GEM	CAN	05.21	01.55	20
21	09.44	VIR	21.21	SCO	SAG	AQU	23.08	TAU	12.10	08.12	VIR	LIB	21
22	LEO	14.30	LIB	15.56	02.00	12.36	ARI	18.34	CAN	LEO	17.19	11.46	22
23	22.03	LIB	LIB	SAG	CAP	PIS	ARI	GEM	CAN	21.10	LIB	SCO	23
24	VIR	22.25	04.23	18.39	03.23	15.52	03.53	GEM	00.34	VIR	LIB	17.44	24
25	VIR	SCO	SCO	CAP	AQU	ARI	TAU	05.07	LEO	VIR	02.09	SAG	25
26	08.47	SCO	09.23	21.21	05.58	21.52	12.04	CAN	13.30	SCO	20.24	26
27	LIB	03.59	SAG	AQU	PIS	TAU	GEM	17.49	VIR	LIB	07.35	CAP	27
28	16.51	SAG	13.05	AQU	10.16	TAU	23.04	LEO	VIR	17.14	SAG	21.21	28
29	SCO		CAP	00.36	ARI	06.27	CAN	LEO	00.56	SCO	10.43	AQU	29
30	21.34		15.57	PIS	16.25	GEM	CAN	06.47	LIB	23.14	CAP	22.17	30
31	SAG		AQU		TAU		11.43	VIR		SAG		PIS	31

MOON

1944

SUN
mth dy   time –> sign

JAN 1   00.00 –> CAP
JAN 21   04.07 –> AQU
FEB 19   18.27 –> PIS
MAR 20   17.49 –> ARI
APR 20   05.18 –> TAU
MAY 21   04.51 –> GEM
JUN 21   13.02 –> CAN
JUL 22   23.56 –> LEO
AUG 23   06.46 –> VIR
SEP 23   04.02 –> LIB
OCT 23   12.56 –> SCO
NOV 22   10.08 –> SAG
DEC 21   23.15 –> CAP

MERCURY
mth dy   time –> sign

JAN 1   00.00 –> CAP
FEB 12   14.17 –> AQU
MAR 3   02.45 –> PIS
MAR 19   07.43 –> ARI
APR 3   17.29 –> TAU
JUN 11   11.46 –> GEM
JUN 27   03.39 –> CAN
JUL 11   07.41 –> LEO
JUL 28   23.44 –> VIR
OCT 5   03.17 –> LIB
OCT 22   11.33 –> SCO
NOV 10   11.09 –> SAG
DEC 1   15.31 –> CAP
DEC 23   23.21 –> SAG

VENUS
mth dy   time –> sign

JAN 1   00.00 –> SCO
JAN 3   04.43 –> SAG
JAN 28   03.11 –> CAP
FEB 21   16.40 –> AQU
MAR 17   02.46 –> PIS
APR 10   12.09 –> ARI
MAY 4   22.04 –> TAU
MAY 29   08.39 –> GEM
JUN 22   19.12 –> CAN
JUL 17   04.47 –> LEO
AUG 10   13.13 –> VIR
SEP 3   21.17 –> LIB
SEP 28   06.12 –> SCO
OCT 22   17.07 –> SAG
NOV 16   07.26 –> CAP
DEC 11   04.47 –> AQU

MARS
mth dy   time –> sign

JAN 1   00.00 –> GEM
MAR 28   09.54 –> CAN
MAY 22   14.16 –> LEO
JUL 12   02.55 –> VIR
AUG 29   00.23 –> LIB
OCT 13   12.09 –> SCO
NOV 25   16.11 –> SAG

SATURN
mth dy   time –> sign

JAN 1   00.00 –> GEM
JUN 20   07.50 –> CAN

JUPITER
mth dy   time –> sign

JAN 1   00.00 –> LEO
JUL 26   01.05 –> VIR

MOON

dy	jan	feb	mar	apr	may	jun	jul	aug	sep	oct	nov	dec	dy
1	PIS	TAU	00.06	CAN	23.04	LIB	SCO	14.42	AQU	14.30	TAU	15.17	1
2	00.34	17.17	GEM	02.54	VIR	LIB	23.38	CAP	04.14	ARI	01.28	CAN	2
3	ARI	GEM	08.38	LEO	VIR	06.32	SAG	17.10	PIS	13.46	GEM	21.53	3
4	04.58	GEM	CAN	15.49	11.39	SCO	SAG	AQU	03.27	TAU	05.04	LEO	4
5	TAU	02.40	20.19	VIR	LIB	14.27	04.42	17.35	ARI	14.59	CAN	LEO	5
6	11.44	CAN	LEO	VIR	22.18	SAG	CAP	PIS	03.28	GEM	12.44	08.04	6
7	GEM	14.20	LEO	04.22	SCO	19.41	07.14	17.43	TAU	19.56	LEO	VIR	7
8	20.48	LEO	19.18	LIB	SCO	CAP	AQU	ARI	06.13	CAN	23.59	20.28	8
9	CAN	LEO	VIR	15.12	06.27	23.12	08.39	19.19	GEM	CAN	VIR	LIB	9
10	CAN	03.08	21.55	SCO	SAG	AQU	PIS	TAU	12.47	05.03	VIR	LIB	10
11	07.57	VIR	LIB	SCO	12.33	AQU	10.18	23.38	CAN	LEO	12.45	08.42	11
12	LEO	15.54	LIB	00.02	CAP	01.58	ARI	GEM	22.50	17.04	LIB	SCO	12
13	20.38	LIB	09.12	SAG	17.10	PIS	13.16	GEM	LEO	VIR	LIB	18.50	13
14	VIR	LIB	SCO	06.56	AQU	04.41	TAU	07.03	LEO	VIR	00.48	SAG	14
15	VIR	03.24	18.31	CAP	20.35	ARI	18.11	CAN	11.00	05.55	SCO	SAG	15
16	09.29	SCO	SAG	11.46	PIS	07.52	GEM	17.08	VIR	LIB	11.02	02.22	16
17	LIB	12.15	SAG	AQU	23.03	TAU	GEM	LEO	23.48	18.03	SAG	CAP	17
18	20.27	SAG	01.13	14.28	ARI	12.11	01.21	LEO	LIB	SCO	19.20	07.44	18
19	SCO	17.33	CAP	PIS	ARI	GEM	CAN	05.00	LIB	SCO	CAP	AQU	19
20	SCO	CAP	04.55	15.35	01.15	18.28	10.51	VIR	12.11	04.50	CAP	11.39	20
21	03.53	19.27	AQU	ARI	TAU	CAN	LEO	17.45	SCO	SAG	01.47	PIS	21
22	SAG	AQU	05.59	16.29	04.26	CAN	22.24	LIB	23.16	13.48	AQU	14.42	22
23	07.26	19.09	PIS	TAU	GEM	03.25	VIR	LIB	SAG	CAP	06.18	ARI	23
24	CAP	PIS	05.42	18.59	10.04	LEO	VIR	06.13	SAG	20.19	PIS	17.24	24
25	08.09	18.31	ARI	GEM	CAN	14.58	11.08	SCO	07.55	AQU	08.57	TAU	25
26	AQU	ARI	06.01	GEM	19.04	VIR	LIB	16.52	CAP	23.53	ARI	20.26	26
27	07.48	19.36	TAU	00.49	LEO	VIR	23.16	SAG	13.10	PIS	10.22	GEM	27
28	PIS	TAU	08.58	CAN	LEO	03.40	SCO	SAG	AQU	PIS	TAU	GEM	28
29	08.15	TAU	GEM	10.36	06.58	LIB	SCO	00.12	14.58	00.54	11.55	00.44	29
30	ARI		15.59	LEO	VIR	15.10	08.50	CAP	PIS	ARI	GEM	CAN	30
31	11.07		CAN		19.37		SAG	03.44		00.45		07.19	31

MOON

SUN

mth dy   time –> sign

JAN 1	00.00 –>	CAP
JAN 20	09.54 –>	AQU
FEB 19	00.14 –>	PIS
MAR 20	23.37 –>	ARI
APR 20	11.07 –>	TAU
MAY 21	10.40 –>	GEM
JUN 21	18.52 –>	CAN
JUL 23	05.45 –>	LEO
AUG 23	12.35 –>	VIR
SEP 23	09.50 –>	LIB
OCT 23	18.44 –>	SCO
NOV 22	15.55 –>	SAG
DEC 22	05.03 –>	CAP

MERCURY

mth dy   time –> sign

JAN 1	00.00 –>	SAG
JAN 14	03.04 –>	CAP
FEB 5	09.20 –>	AQU
FEB 23	11.26 –>	PIS
MAR 11	06.45 –>	ARI
MAY 16	15.21 –>	TAU
JUN 4	10.30 –>	GEM
JUN 18	12.27 –>	CAN
JUL 3	15.39 –>	LEO
JUL 26	14.48 –>	VIR
AUG 17	08.35 –>	LEO
SEP 10	07.20 –>	VIR
SEP 27	12.08 –>	LIB
OCT 15	00.13 –>	SCO
NOV 3	23.06 –>	SAG

VENUS

mth dy   time –> sign

JAN 1	00.00 –>	AQU
JAN 5	19.18 –>	PIS
FEB 2	08.07 –>	ARI
MAR 11	11.17 –>	TAU
APR 7	19.15 –>	ARI
JUN 4	22.57 –>	TAU
JUL 7	16.20 –>	GEM
AUG 4	10.59 –>	CAN
AUG 30	13.05 –>	LEO
SEP 24	16.06 –>	VIR
OCT 19	04.09 –>	LIB
NOV 12	07.05 –>	SCO
DEC 6	05.22 –>	SAG
DEC 30	01.56 –>	CAP

MARS

mth dy   time –> sign

JAN 1	00.00 –>	SAG
JAN 5	19.31 –>	CAP
FEB 14	09.58 –>	AQU
MAR 25	03.43 –>	PIS
MAY 2	20.29 –>	ARI
JUN 11	11.52 –>	TAU
JUL 23	08.59 –>	GEM
SEP 7	20.56 –>	CAN
NOV 11	21.05 –>	LEO
DEC 26	15.04 –>	CAN

JUPITER

mth dy   time –> sign

JAN 1	00.00 –>	VIR
AUG 25	06.06 –>	LIB

SATURN

mth dy   time –> sign

JAN 1	00.00 –>	CAN

MOON

dy	jan	feb	mar	apr	may	jun	jul	aug	sep	oct	nov	dec	dy
1	LEO	12.46	LIB	SCO	19.40	AQU	PIS	TAU	CAN	LEO	10.08	04.43	1
2	16.49	LIB	LIB	03.08	CAP	15.25	00.29	11.23	CAN	17.34	LIB	SCO	2
3	VIR	LIB	08.32	SAG	CAP	PIS	ARI	GEM	03.19	VIR	22.29	17.30	3
4	VIR	01.22	SCO	13.51	04.06	18.51	03.04	15.23	LEO	VIR	SCO	SAG	4
5	04.44	SCO	20.45	CAP	AQU	ARI	TAU	CAN	11.36	04.16	SCO	SAG	5
6	LIB	12.57	SAG	21.28	09.21	20.23	05.20	20.52	VIR	LIB	11.18	05.23	6
7	17.13	SAG	SAG	AQU	PIS	TAU	GEM	LEO	21.48	16.24	SAG	CAP	7
8	SCO	21.29	06.37	AQU	11.25	21.15	08.10	LEO	LIB	23.35	15.34	8
9	SCO	CAP	CAP	01.10	ARI	GEM	CAN	04.24	LIB	SCO	CAP	AQU	9
10	03.55	CAP	12.40	PIS	11.24	23.02	12.43	VIR	09.48	05.17	CAP	23.20	10
11	SAG	02.12	AQU	01.38	TAU	CAN	LEO	14.21	SCO	SAG	09.59	PIS	11
12	11.28	AQU	14.50	ARI	11.12	CAN	19.58	LIB	22.37	17.33	AQU	PIS	12
13	CAP	03.52	PIS	00.40	GEM	03.20	VIR	LIB	SAG	CAP	17.05	04.15	13
14	15.57	PIS	14.32	TAU	12.51	LEO	VIR	02.24	SAG	CAP	PIS	ARI	14
15	AQU	04.12	ARI	00.31	CAN	11.07	06.13	SCO	10.11	03.07	20.24	06.30	15
16	18.27	ARI	13.54	GEM	17.57	VIR	LIB	14.56	CAP	AQU	ARI	TAU	16
17	PIS	05.05	TAU	03.13	LEO	22.06	18.29	SAG	08.34	20.48	07.03	17
18	20.21	TAU	15.04	CAN	LEO	LIB	SCO	SAG	AQU	PIS	TAU	GEM	18
19	ARI	08.01	GEM	09.52	02.56	LIB	SCO	01.31	22.19	10.09	20.02	07.27	19
20	22.48	GEM	19.31	LEO	VIR	10.36	06.36	CAP	PIS	ARI	GEM	CAN	20
21	TAU	13.42	CAN	20.03	14.43	SCO	SAG	08.32	23.11	09.30	20.14	09.30	21
22	TAU	CAN	CAN	VIR	LIB	22.27	16.29	AQU	ARI	TAU	CAN	LEO	22
23	02.35	21.58	03.32	VIR	LIB	SAG	CAP	12.05	22.53	08.49	23.12	14.44	23
24	GEM	LEO	LEO	08.15	03.21	SAG	23.16	PIS	TAU	GEM	LEO	VIR	24
25	08.05	LEO	14.11	LIB	SCO	08.14	AQU	13.30	23.32	10.11	LEO	23.45	25
26	CAN	08.13	VIR	20.52	15.11	CAP	AQU	ARI	GEM	CAN	05.59	LIB	26
27	15.33	VIR	VIR	SCO	SAG	15.36	03.26	14.34	GEM	14.55	VIR	LIB	27
28	LEO	19.57	02.15	SCO	SAG	AQU	PIS	TAU	02.38	LEO	16.18	11.43	28
29	LEO		LIB	08.56	01.24	20.51	06.07	16.47	CAN	23.12	LIB	SCO	29
30	01.09		14.50	SAG	CAP	PIS	ARI	GEM	08.47	VIR	LIB	SCO	30
31	VIR		SCO		09.35		08.29	21.00		VIR		00.32	31

SUN

mth dy	time –> sign
JAN 1	00.00 –> CAP
JAN 20	15.45 –> AQU
FEB 19	06.08 –> PIS
MAR 21	05.32 –> ARI
APR 20	17.02 –> TAU
MAY 21	16.34 –> GEM
JUN 22	00.44 –> CAN
JUL 23	11.37 –> LEO
AUG 23	18.26 –> VIR
SEP 23	15.41 –> LIB
OCT 24	00.35 –> SCO
NOV 22	21.46 –> SAG
DEC 22	10.54 –> CAP

MERCURY

mth dy	time –> sign
JAN 1	00.00 –> SAG
JAN 9	14.10 –> CAP
JAN 29	07.22 –> AQU
FEB 15	15.43 –> PIS
MAR 4	09.27 –> ARI
APR 1	18.16 –> PIS
APR 16	14.54 –> ARI
MAY 11	14.29 –> TAU
MAY 27	04.13 –> GEM
JUN 10	02.00 –> CAN
JUN 27	19.07 –> LEO
SEP 3	16.29 –> VIR
SEP 19	14.34 –> LIB
OCT 7	21.21 –> SCO
OCT 30	11.23 –> SAG
NOV 20	20.16 –> SCO
DEC 13	00.03 –> SAG

VENUS

mth dy	time –> sign
JAN 1	00.00 –> CAP
JAN 22	22.28 –> AQU
FEB 15	20.12 –> PIS
MAR 11	20.32 –> ARI
APR 5	01.01 –> TAU
ARI 29	10.59 –> GEM
MAY 24	03.40 –> CAN
JUN 18	05.00 –> LEO
JUL 13	19.22 –> VIR
AUG 9	08.35 –> LIB
SEP 7	00.16 –> SCO
OCT 16	10.45 –> SAG
NOV 8	08.56 –> SCO

MARS

mth dy	time –> sign
JAN 1	00.00 –> CAN
APR 22	19.31 –> LEO
JUN 20	08.32 –> VIR
AUG 9	13.17 –> LIB
SEP 24	16.35 –> SCO
NOV 6	18.22 –> SAG
DEC 17	10.56 –> CAP

SATURN

mth dy	time –> sign
JAN 1	00.00 –> CAN
AUG 2	14.42 –> LEO

JUPITER

mth dy	time –> sign
JAN 1	00.00 –> LIB
SEP 25	10.19 –> SCO

MOON

dy	jan	feb	mar	apr	may	jun	jul	aug	sep	oct	nov	dec	dy
1	SAG	05.23	AQU	09.16	TAU	06.29	LEO	12.05	SCO	SAG	10.36	04.30	1
2	12.11	AQU	20.25	ARI	20.03	CAN	20.45	LIB	17.31	14.29	AQU	PIS	2
3	CAP	11.32	PIS	09.56	GEM	07.39	VIR	21.23	SAG	CAP	20.32	12.05	3
4	21.38	PIS	23.23	TAU	20.23	LEO	VIR	SCO	SAG	CAP	PIS	ARI	4
5	AQU	15.38	ARI	10.25	CAN	11.57	03.21	SCO	06.24	02.27	PIS	15.48	5
6	AQU	ARI	ARI	GEM	23.04	VIR	LIB	09.36	CAP	AQU	03.28	TAU	6
7	04.47	18.47	01.08	12.21	LEO	19.57	13.41	SAG	17.41	11.09	ARI	16.30	7
8	PIS	TAU	TAU	CAN	LEO	LIB	SCO	22.23	AQU	PIS	04.49	GEM	8
9	09.56	21.45	03.12	16.37	04.57	LIB	SCO	CAP	AQU	16.05	TAU	15.50	9
10	ARI	GEM	GEM	LEO	VIR	07.04	02.20	CAP	01.46	ARI	05.07	CAN	10
11	13.25	GEM	06.28	23.20	13.53	SCO	SAG	09.23	PIS	18.20	GEM	15.46	11
12	TAU	00.59	CAN	VIR	LIB	19.50	15.05	AQU	06.49	TAU	05.15	LEO	12
13	15.42	CAN	11.14	VIR	LIB	SAG	CAP	17.41	ARI	19.37	CAN	18.09	13
14	GEM	04.50	LEO	18.13	01.08	SAG	CAP	PIS	10.03	GEM	06.53	VIR	14
15	17.32	LEO	17.32	LIB	SCO	08.39	02.17	23.37	TAU	21.23	LEO	VIR	15
16	CAN	10.03	VIR	19.03	13.46	CAP	AQU	ARI	12.45	CAN	11.05	00.07	16
17	20.04	VIR	VIR	SCO	SAG	20.16	11.15	ARI	GEM	CAN	VIR	LIB	17
18	LEO	17.36	01.40	SCO	SAG	AQU	PIS	03.59	15.42	00.35	18.12	09.43	18
19	LEO	LIB	LIB	07.30	02.42	AQU	17.59	TAU	CAN	LIB	LIB	SCO	19
20	00.40	LIB	12.04	SAG	CAP	05.43	ARI	07.22	19.13	05.35	LIB	21.48	20
21	VIR	04.05	SCO	20.28	14.31	PIS	22.35	GEM	LEO	VIR	03.58	SAG	21
22	08.31	SCO	SCO	CAP	AQU	12.19	TAU	10.06	23.38	12.33	SCO	SAG	22
23	LIB	16.41	00.30	CAP	23.39	ARI	TAU	CAN	VIR	LIB	15.44	10.50	23
24	19.40	SAG	SAG	07.56	PIS	15.56	01.18	12.38	VIR	21.41	SAG	CAP	24
25	SCO	SAG	13.18	AQU	PIS	TAU	GEM	LEO	05.40	SCO	SAG	23.29	25
26	SCO	05.01	CAP	15.54	05.05	17.07	02.44	15.54	LIB	SCO	04.40	AQU	26
27	08.27	CAP	23.51	PIS	ARI	GEM	CAN	VIR	14.12	09.03	CAP	AQU	27
28	SAG	14.34	AQU	19.45	07.03	17.10	03.57	21.15	SCO	SAG	17.30	10.43	28
29	20.18		AQU	ARI	TAU	CAN	LEO	LIB	SCO	21.59	AQU	PIS	29
30	CAP		06.26	20.31	06.54	17.47	06.32	LIB	01.32	CAP	AQU	19.31	30
31	CAP		PIS		GEM		VIR	05.49		CAP		ARI	31

SUN

mth dy	time -> sign
JAN 1	00.00 -> CAP
JAN 20	21.31 -> AQU
FEB 19	11.52 -> PIS
MAR 21	11.13 -> ARI
APR 20	22.39 -> TAU
MAY 21	22.09 -> GEM
JUN 22	06.19 -> CAN
JUL 23	17.14 -> LEO
AUG 24	00.09 -> VIR
SEP 23	21.29 -> LIB
OCT 24	06.26 -> SCO
NOV 23	03.38 -> SAG
DEC 22	16.43 -> CAP

MERCURY

mth dy	time -> sign
JAN 1	00.00 -> SAG
JAN 3	01.46 -> CAP
JAN 21	21.06 -> AQU
FEB 8	01.32 -> PIS
APR 16	04.31 -> ARI
MAY 4	06.03 -> TAU
MAY 18	13.33 -> GEM
JUN 2	13.40 -> CAN
AUG 10	17.40 -> LEO
AUG 26	14.50 -> VIR
SEP 11	20.54 -> LIB
OCT 1	15.26 -> SCO
DEC 7	12.32 -> SAG
DEC 26	23.18 -> CAP

VENUS

mth dy	time -> sign
JAN 1	00.00 -> SCO
JAN 5	16.45 -> SAG
FEB 6	05.41 -> CAP
MAR 5	05.09 -> AQU
MAR 30	22.15 -> PIS
APR 25	03.03 -> ARI
MAY 20	02.06 -> TAU
JUN 13	21.35 -> GEM
JUL 8	13.30 -> CAN
AUG 2	01.06 -> LEO
AUG 26	08.17 -> VIR
SEP 19	12.01 -> LIB
OCT 13	13.49 -> SCO
NOV 6	14.59 -> SAG
NOV 30	16.23 -> CAP
DEC 24	19.13 -> AQU

MARS

mth dy	time -> sign
JAN 1	00.00 -> CAP
JAN 25	11.44 -> AQU
MAR 4	16.47 -> PIS
APR 11	23.02 -> ARI
MAY 21	03.40 -> TAU
JUL 1	03.34 -> GEM
AUG 13	21.26 -> CAN
OCT 1	02.31 -> LEO
DEC 1	11.44 -> VIR

JUPITER

mth dy	time -> sign
JAN 1	00.00 -> SCO
OCT 24	03.00 -> SAG

SATURN

mth dy	time -> sign
JAN 1	00.00 -> LEO

MOON

dy	jan	feb	mar	apr	may	jun	jul	aug	sep	oct	nov	dec	dy
1	ARI	GEM	20.59	LEO	19.24	SCO	SAG	07.50	PIS	ARI	GEM	CAN	1
2	01.06	13.38	CAN	08.30	LIB	18.54	13.03	AQU	12.02	02.15	17.32	02.30	2
3	TAU	CAN	23.00	VIR	LIB	SAG	CAP	19.49	ARI	TAU	CAN	LEO	3
4	03.26	14.01	LEO	12.39	02.35	SAG	CAP	PIS	20.10	07.44	20.03	04.23	4
5	GEM	LEO	LEO	LIB	SCO	06.51	01.50	PIS	TAU	GEM	LEO	VIR	5
6	03.28	14.42	00.46	18.56	12.09	CAP	AQU	06.20	TAU	11.47	22.55	08.14	6
7	CAN	VIR	VIR	SCO	SAG	19.38	14.03	ARI	02.18	CAN	VIR	LIB	7
8	02.53	17.39	03.51	SCO	23.55	AQU	PIS	14.43	GEM	14.41	VIR	14.24	8
9	LEO	LIB	LIB	04.12	CAP	AQU	PIS	TAU	06.12	LEO	02.42	SCO	9
10	03.45	LIB	09.51	SAG	CAP	07.47	00.34	20.17	CAN	16.57	LIB	22.49	10
11	VIR	00.28	SCO	16.08	12.41	PIS	ARI	GEM	08.03	VIR	08.02	SAG	11
12	07.54	SCO	19.34	CAP	AQU	17.34	08.12	22.49	LEO	19.31	SCO	SAG	12
13	LIB	11.15	SAG	CAP	AQU	ARI	TAU	CAN	08.51	LIB	15.33	09.14	13
14	16.15	SAG	SAG	04.51	00.20	23.45	12.16	23.06	VIR	23.45	SAG	CAP	14
15	SCO	SAG	08.00	AQU	PIS	TAU	GEM	LEO	10.16	SCO	SAG	21.16	15
16	SCO	00.12	CAP	15.47	08.56	TAU	13.14	22.49	LIB	SCO	01.37	AQU	16
17	04.03	CAP	20.35	PIS	ARI	02.21	CAN	VIR	14.11	CAP	06.53	AQU	17
18	SAG	12.38	AQU	23.25	13.51	GEM	12.34	VIR	SCO	SAG	13.45	09.59	18
19	17.10	AQU	AQU	ARI	TAU	02.32	LEO	00.04	21.49	17.14	AQU	PIS	19
20	CAP	22.57	06.57	ARI	15.51	CAN	12.19	LIB	SAG	CAP	AQU	21.37	20
21	CAP	PIS	PIS	03.56	GEM	02.06	VIR	04.44	SAG	CAP	02.16	ARI	21
22	05.37	PIS	14.23	TAU	16.27	LEO	14.33	SCO	08.58	05.39	PIS	ARI	22
23	AQU	06.57	ARI	06.27	CAN	03.01	LIB	13.34	CAP	AQU	12.53	06.11	23
24	16.23	ARI	19.29	GEM	17.18	VIR	20.41	SAG	21.38	17.45	ARI	TAU	24
25	PIS	13.08	TAU	08.22	LEO	06.51	SCO	SAG	AQU	PIS	20.06	10.47	25
26	PIS	TAU	23.16	CAN	19.50	LIB	SCO	01.31	AQU	PIS	TAU	GEM	26
27	01.10	17.47	GEM	10.44	VIR	14.17	06.40	CAP	09.24	03.31	23.55	12.03	27
28	ARI	GEM	GEM	LEO	VIR	SCO	SAG	14.18	PIS	ARI	GEM	CAN	28
29	07.45		02.26	14.15	00.54	SCO	19.01	AQU	18.58	10.16	GEM	11.41	29
30	TAU		CAN	VIR	LIB	00.46	CAP	AQU	ARI	TAU	01.31	LEO	30
31		11.52		05.22		08.42	CAP	02.03		14.36		11.47	31

1948

SUN
mth dy   time -> sign

JAN 1   00.00 -> CAP
JAN 21   03.18 -> AQU
FEB 19   17.37 -> PIS
MAR 20   16.57 -> ARI
APR 20   04.25 -> TAU
MAY 21   03.57 -> GEM
JUN 21   12.11 -> CAN
JUL 22   23.08 -> LEO
AUG 23   06.03 -> VIR
SEP 23   03.22 -> LIB
OCT 23   12.28 -> SCO
NOV 22   09.29 -> SAG
DEC 21   22.33 -> CAP

MERCURY
mth dy   time -> sign

JAN 1   00.00 -> CAP
JAN 14   10.06 -> AQU
FEB 2   00.47 -> PIS
FEB 20   11.05 -> AQU
MAR 18   08.14 -> PIS
APR 9   02.26 -> ARI
APR 25   01.38 -> TAU
MAY 9   04.38 -> GEM
MAY 28   10.50 -> CAN
JUN 28   17.57 -> GEM
JUL 11   20.56 -> CAN
AUG 2   13.54 -> LEO
AUG 17   08.44 -> VIR
SEP 3   15.47 -> LIB
SEP 27   07.19 -> SCO
OCT 17   03.33 -> LIB
NOV 10   02.19 -> SCO
NOV 29   15.09 -> SAG
DEC 18   16.47 -> CAP

VENUS
mth dy   time -> sign

JAN 1   00.00 -> AQU
JAN 18   02.14 -> PIS
FEB 11   18.51 -> ARI
MAR 8   07.00 -> TAU
APR 4   12.40 -> GEM
MAY 7   08.27 -> CAN
JUN 29   07.58 -> GEM
AUG 3   02.14 -> CAN
SEP 8   13.40 -> LEO
OCT 6   12.25 -> VIR
NOV 1   06.42 -> LIB
NOV 26   00.55 -> SCO
DEC 20   07.28 -> SAG

MARS
mth dy   time -> sign

JAN 1   00.00 -> VIR
FEB 12   10.28 -> LEO
MAY 18   20.54 -> VIR
JUL 17   05.26 -> LIB
SEP 3   13.58 -> SCO
OCT 17   05.43 -> SAG
NOV 26   21.59 -> CAP

SATURN
mth dy   time -> sign

JAN 1   00.00 -> LEO
SEP 19   04.37 -> VIR

JUPITER
mth dy   time -> sign

JAN 1   00.00 -> SAG
NOV 15   10.38 -> CAP

MOON

dy	jan	feb	mar	apr	may	jun	jul	aug	sep	oct	nov	dec	dy
1	VIR	02.27	17.41	CAP	AQU	15.55	10.40	GEM	LEO	VIR	SCO	SAG	1
2	14.10	SCO	SAG	23.18	19.44	ARI	TAU	07.20	18.20	04.30	18.10	09.16	2
3	LIB	10.26	SAG	AQU	PIS	ARI	17.48	CAN	VIR	LIB	SAG	CAP	3
4	19.51	SAG	03.50	AQU	PIS	01.43	GEM	08.13	17.35	04.58	23.39	17.32	4
5	SCO	21.30	CAP	11.56	07.28	TAU	21.07	LEO	LIB	SCO	CAP	AQU	5
6	SCO	CAP	16.14	PIS	ARI	08.06	CAN	07.32	18.34	07.55	CAP	AQU	6
7	04.40	CAP	AQU	23.28	16.48	GEM	21.53	VIR	SCO	SAG	08.41	04.46	7
8	SAG	09.59	AQU	ARI	TAU	11.28	LEO	07.30	22.52	14.31	AQU	PIS	8
9	15.41	AQU	04.53	ARI	23.20	CAN	22.03	LIB	SAG	CAP	20.34	17.30	9
10	CAP	22.37	PIS	08.58	GEM	13.11	VIR	09.56	SAG	CAP	PIS	ARI	10
11	CAP	PIS	16.33	TAU	GEM	LEO	23.31	SCO	06.56	00.42	PIS	ARI	11
12	03.54	PIS	ARI	16.20	03.38	14.49	LIB	15.49	CAP	AQU	09.12	05.09	12
13	AQU	10.37	ARI	GEM	CAN	VIR	LIB	SAG	17.58	13.03	ARI	TAU	13
14	16.35	ARI	02.40	21.41	06.39	17.33	03.28	SAG	AQU	PIS	20.24	13.44	14
15	PIS	21.08	TAU	CAN	LEO	LIB	SCO	00.51	AQU	PIS	TAU	GEM	15
16	PIS	TAU	10.45	CAN	09.14	22.03	10.11	CAP	06.27	01.36	TAU	19.01	16
17	04.44	TAU	GEM	01.16	VIR	SCO	SAG	12.02	PIS	ARI	05.02	CAN	17
18	ARI	04.56	16.14	LEO	12.07	SCO	19.13	AQU	19.02	12.54	GEM	22.03	18
19	14.42	GEM	CAN	03.30	LIB	04.28	CAP	AQU	ARI	TAU	11.11	LEO	19
20	TAU	09.09	18.58	VIR	15.56	SAG	CAP	00.23	ARI	22.15	CAN	LEO	20
21	21.01	CAN	LEO	05.16	SCO	12.51	06.02	PIS	06.45	GEM	15.32	00.19	21
22	GEM	10.07	19.42	LIB	21.22	CAP	AQU	13.05	TAU	GEM	LEO	VIR	22
23	23.23	LEO	VIR	07.49	SAG	23.15	18.13	ARI	16.40	05.21	18.48	02.59	23
24	CAN	09.22	20.01	SCO	SAG	AQU	PIS	ARI	GEM	CAN	VIR	LIB	24
25	23.00	VIR	LIB	12.31	05.08	AQU	PIS	01.03	23.46	10.10	21.33	06.39	25
26	LEO	09.05	21.49	SAG	CAP	11.23	06.57	TAU	CAN	LEO	LIB	SCO	26
27	21.56	LIB	SCO	20.21	15.31	PIS	ARI	10.40	CAN	12.53	LIB	11.29	27
28	VIR	11.24	SCO	CAP	AQU	23.56	18.34	GEM	03.35	VIR	00.19	SAG	28
29	22.29	SCO	02.46	CAP	AQU	ARI	TAU	16.34	LEO	14.16	SCO	17.47	29
30	LIB		SAG	07.16	03.46	ARI	TAU	CAN	LEO	LIB	03.52	CAP	30
31	LIB		11.34		PIS		03.01	18.41		15.31		CAP	31

MOON

SUN

mth dy	time –> sign
JAN 1	00.00 –> CAP
JAN 20	09.09 –> AQU
FEB 18	23.27 –> PIS
MAR 20	22.48 –> ARI
APR 20	10.17 –> TAU
MAY 21	09.50 –> GEM
JUN 21	18.03 –> CAN
JUL 23	04.57 –> LEO
AUG 23	11.48 –> VIR
SEP 23	09.06 –> LIB
OCT 23	18.03 –> SCO
NOV 22	15.16 –> SAG
DEC 22	04.23 –> CAP

MERCURY

mth dy	time –> sign
JAN 1	00.00 –> CAP
JAN 6	08.53 –> AQU
MAR 14	09.52 –> PIS
APR 1	16.02 –> ARI
APR 16	14.55 –> TAU
MAY 2	02.19 –> GEM
JUL 10	03.19 –> CAN
JUL 25	05.20 –> LEO
AUG 9	09.04 –> VIR
AUG 28	15.48 –> LIB
NOV 3	18.58 –> SCO
NOV 22	09.07 –> SAG
DEC 11	13.37 –> CAP

VENUS

mth dy	time –> sign
JAN 1	00.00 –> SAG
JAN 13	09.01 –> CAP
FEB 6	09.06 –> AQU
MAR 2	09.38 –> PIS
MAR 26	11.54 –> ARI
APR 19	16.44 –> TAU
MAY 14	00.26 –> GEM
JUN 7	10.47 –> CAN
JUL 1	23.41 –> LEO
JUL 26	15.44 –> VIR
AUG 20	12.39 –> LIB
SEP 14	17.12 –> SCO
OCT 10	10.18 –> SAG
NOV 6	04.53 –> CAP
DEC 6	06.06 –> AQU

MARS

mth dy	time –> sign
JAN 1	00.00 –> CAP
JAN 4	17.50 –> AQU
FEB 11	18.06 –> PIS
MAR 21	22.02 –> ARI
APR 30	02.33 –> TAU
JUN 10	00.57 –> GEM
JUL 23	05.54 –> CAN
SEP 7	04.52 –> LEO
OCT 27	00.58 –> VIR
DEC 26	05.24 –> LIB

SATURN

mth dy	time –> sign
JAN 1	00.00 –> VIR
APR 3	03.41 –> LEO
MAY 29	12.56 –> VIR

JUPITER

mth dy	time –> sign
JAN 1	00.00 –> CAP
APR 12	19.16 –> AQU
JUN 27	18.30 –> CAP
NOV 30	20.08 –> AQU

MOON

dy	jan	feb	mar	apr	may	jun	jul	aug	sep	oct	nov	dec	dy
1	02.07 PIS	15.36	TAU	GEM	00.36	VIR	SCO	12.05	01.13	PIS	ARI		1
2	AQU	09.04	ARI	22.03	12.43	LEO	13.22	SCO	CAP	AQU	05.34	01.22	2
3	12.58	ARI	ARI	GEM	CAN	04.53	LIB	01.25	19.37	11.19	ARI	13.28	3
4	PIS	21.57	04.33	GEM	19.11	VIR	16.22	SAG	AQU	PIS	18.37	13.28	4
5	PIS	TAU	TAU	07.10	LEO	07.57	SCO	06.36	AQU	23.27	TAU	GEM	5
6	01.40	TAU	16.05	CAN	23.11	LIB	19.45	CAP	05.26	ARI	TAU	23.31	6
7	ARI	08.40	GEM	12.59	VIR	10.13	SAG	13.34	PIS	ARI	06.55	CAN	7
8	14.03	GEM	GEM	LEO	VIR	SCO	SAG	AQU	17.13	12.26	GEM	CAN	8
9	TAU	15.22	00.21	15.32	01.07	12.23	00.02	22.45	ARI	TAU	17.35	07.27	9
10	23.31	CAN	CAN	VIR	LIB	SAG	CAP	PIS	ARI	TAU	CAN	LEO	10
11	GEM	18.00	04.33	15.48	01.54	15.40	06.09	PIS	06.12	01.02	CAN	13.31	11
12	GEM	LEO	LEO	LIB	SCO	CAP	AQU	10.20	TAU	02.00	02.00	VIR	12
13	04.57	18.05	05.24	15.27	02.57	21.26	15.01	ARI	18.47	11.51	LEO	17.45	13
14	CAN	VIR	VIR	SCO	SAG	AQU	PIS	23.18	GEM	CAN	07.42	LIB	14
15	07.08	17.44	04.40	16.23	05.57	AQU	PIS	TAU	GEM	19.35	VIR	20.13	15
16	LEO	LIB	LIB	SAG	CAP	06.38	02.43	TAU	04.51	LEO	10.35	SCO	16
17	07.52	18.53	04.25	20.16	12.19	PIS	11.23	CAN	23.42	LIB	21.32	17
18	VIR	SCO	SCO	CAP	AQU	18.45	15.36	GEM	11.04	VIR	11.18	SAG	18
19	09.03	22.49	06.30	CAP	22.26	ARI	TAU	20.15	LEO	VIR	SCO	23.00	19
20	LIB	SAG	SAG	03.59	PIS	ARI	TAU	CAN	13.34	00.48	11.15	CAP	20
21	11.59	SAG	12.04	AQU	PIS	07.30	02.57	CAN	VIR	LIB	SAG	CAP	21
22	SCO	05.50	CAP	15.08	11.02	TAU	GEM	01.07	13.41	00.18	12.19	02.24	22
23	17.09	CAP	21.10	PIS	ARI	18.20	10.52	LEO	LIB	SCO	CAP	AQU	23
24	SAG	15.26	AQU	PIS	23.42	GEM	CAN	02.55	13.20	00.08	16.24	09.20	24
25	SAG	AQU	AQU	04.01	TAU	GEM	15.19	VIR	SCO	SAG	AQU	PIS	25
26	00.21	AQU	08.50	ARI	TAU	02.01	LEO	03.24	14.21	02.10	AQU	20.05	26
27	CAP	02.54	PIS	16.41	10.27	CAN	17.36	LIB	SAG	CAP	00.35	ARI	27
28	09.26	PIS	21.41	TAU	GEM	07.00	VIR	04.19	18.07	07.50	PIS	ARI	28
29	AQU		ARI	TAU	18.38	LEO	19.20	SCO	CAP	AQU	12.18	08.58	29
30	20.26		ARI	03.48	CAN	10.27	LIB	07.00	CAP	17.21	ARI	TAU	30
31	PIS		10.29		CAN		21.44	SAG		PIS		21.13	31

1950

SUN

mth dy	time –> sign
JAN 1	00.00 –> CAP
JAN 20	15.00 –> AQU
FEB 19	05.17 –> PIS
MAR 21	04.35 –> ARI
APR 20	15.59 –> TAU
MAY 21	15.27 –> GEM
JUN 21	23.36 –> CAN
JUL 23	10.30 –> LEO
AUG 23	17.20 –> VIR
SEP 23	14.44 –> LIB
OCT 23	23.45 –> SCO
NOV 22	21.02 –> SAG
DEC 22	10.14 –> CAP

MERCURY

mth dy	time –> sign
JAN 1	12.40 –> AQU
JAN 15	07.35 –> CAP
FEB 14	19.12 –> AQU
MAR 7	22.05 –> PIS
MAR 24	15.52 –> ARI
APR 8	11.13 –> TAU
JUN 14	14.33 –> GEM
JUL 2	14.57 –> CAN
JUL 16	17.08 –> LEO
AUG 2	02.44 –> VIR
AUG 27	14.17 –> LIB
SEP 10	19.15 –> VIR
OCT 9	14.40 –> LIB
OCT 27	10.36 –> SCO
NOV 15	03.10 –> SAG
DEC 5	01.57 –> CAP

VENUS

mth dy	time –> sign
JAN 1	00.00 –> AQU
APR 6	15.13 –> PIS
MAY 5	19.19 –> ARI
JUN 1	14.19 –> TAU
JUN 27	10.45 –> GEM
JUL 22	17.50 –> CAN
AUG 16	14.18 –> LEO
SEP 10	01.37 –> VIR
OCT 4	05.51 –> LIB
OCT 28	05.33 –> SCO
NOV 21	03.03 –> SAG
DEC 14	23.54 –> CAP

MARS

mth dy	time –> sign
JAN 1	00.00 –> LIB
MAR 28	11.06 –> VIR
JUN 11	20.27 –> LIB
AUG 10	16.48 –> SCO
SEP 25	19.48 –> SAG
NOV 6	06.40 –> CAP
DEC 15	08.59 –> AQU

SATURN

mth dy	time –> sign
JAN 1	00.00 –> VIR
NOV 20	15.51 –> LIB

JUPITER

mth dy	time –> sign
JAN 1	00.00 –> AQU
APR 15	08.59 –> PIS
SEP 15	02.21 –> AQU
DEC 1	19.58 –> PIS

MOON

dy	jan	feb	mar	apr	may	jun	jul	aug	sep	oct	nov	dec	dy
1	GEM	22.34	08.30	VIR	11.37	21.27	09.19	PIS	02.19	GEM	CAN	21.53	1
2	GEM	LEO	LEO	00.40	SCO	CAP	AQU	07.03	TAU	GEM	05.38	VIR	2
3	06.56	LEO	12.24	LIB	10.50	23.18	13.51	ARI	14.45	10.59	LEO	VIR	3
4	CAN	02.37	VIR	00.35	SAG	AQU	PIS	18.06	GEM	CAN	14.21	04.29	4
5	13.58	VIR	14.00	SCO	11.08	AQU	22.24	TAU	GEM	21.40	VIR	LIB	5
6	LEO	05.19	LIB	0.37	CAP	04.57	ARI	TAU	02.54	LEO	19.10	07.19	6
7	19.06	LIB	14.55	SAG	14.22	PIS	ARI	06.44	CAN	LEO	LIB	SCO	7
8	VIR	07.50	SCO	02.29	AQU	14.44	10.13	GEM	12.34	04.54	20.29	07.17	8
9	23.08	SCO	16.37	CAP	21.34	ARI	TAU	18.27	LEO	VIR	SCO	SAG	9
10	LIB	10.51	SAG	07.24	PIS	ARI	23.02	CAN	18.55	08.29	19.51	06.16	10
11	LIB	SAG	20.07	AQU	PIS	03.12	GEM	CAN	VIR	LIB	SAG	CAP	11
12	02.28	14.45	CAP	15.38	08.18	TAU	GEM	03.36	22.28	09.31	19.25	06.34	12
13	SCO	CAP	CAP	PIS	ARI	16.05	10.33	LEO	LIB	SCO	CAP	AQU	13
14	05.16	19.57	01.52	PIS	20.59	GEM	CAN	10.03	LIB	09.44	21.14	10.10	14
15	SAG	AQU	AQU	02.32	TAU	GEM	19.52	VIR	00.27	SAG	AQU	PIS	15
16	08.06	AQU	09.59	ARI	TAU	03.45	LEO	14.31	SCO	10.55	AQU	17.58	16
17	CAP	03.11	PIS	15.00	09.52	CAN	LEO	LIB	02.12	CAP	02.38	ARI	17
18	12.07	PIS	20.21	TAU	GEM	13.37	03.05	17.49	SAG	14.27	PIS	ARI	18
19	AQU	13.01	ARI	TAU	21.50	LEO	VIR	SCO	04.49	AQU	11.39	05.09	19
20	18.41	ARI	ARI	03.54	CAN	21.31	08.34	20.36	CAP	20.53	ARI	TAU	20
21	PIS	ARI	08.32	GEM	CAN	VIR	LIB	SAG	08.59	PIS	23.08	17.49	21
22	PIS	01.12	TAU	16.02	08.06	VIR	12.27	23.23	AQU	PIS	TAU	GEM	22
23	04.37	TAU	21.28	CAN	LEO	03.09	SCO	CAP	15.09	05.59	TAU	GEM	23
24	ARI	14.03	GEM	CAN	15.50	LIB	14.55	CAP	PIS	ARI	11.38	06.18	24
25	17.08	GEM	GEM	01.51	VIR	06.19	SAG	02.53	23.32	17.03	GEM	CAN	25
26	TAU	GEM	09.17	LEO	20.26	SCO	16.39	AQU	ARI	TAU	GEM	17.45	26
27	TAU	01.03	CAN	08.30	LIB	07.26	CAP	08.02	ARI	TAU	00.13	LEO	27
28	05.43	CAN	18.04	VIR	22.01	SAG	18.55	PIS	10.08	CAN	05.22	LEO	28
29	GEM		LEO	11.25	SCO	07.48	AQU	15.44	TAU	GEM	12.02	03.41	29
30	15.50		23.01	LIB	21.43	CAP	23.19	ARI	22.26	LEO	18.03	VIR	30
31	CAN		VIR		SAG		PIS	ARI		CAN		11.20	31

SUN

mth dy	time –> sign
JAN 1	00.00 –> CAP
JAN 20	20.52 –> AQU
FEB 19	11.10 –> PIS
MAR 21	10.26 –> ARI
APR 20	20.48 –> TAU
MAY 21	21.15 –> GEM
JUN 22	05.25 –> CAN
JUL 23	16.21 –> LEO
AUG 23	23.16 –> VIR
SEP 23	20.37 –> LIB
OCT 24	05.36 –> SCO
NOV 23	02.51 –> SAG
DEC 22	16.00 –> CAP

MERCURY

mth dy	time –> sign
JAN 1	00.00 –> CAP
FEB 9	17.50 –> AQU
FEB 28	13.04 –> PIS
MAR 16	11.53 –> ARI
APR 2	03.27 –> TAU
MAY 1	21.25 –> ARI
MAY 15	01.40 –> TAU
JUN 9	08.43 –> GEM
JUN 24	03.13 –> CAN
JUL 8	13.39 –> LEO
JUL 27	15.24 –> VIR
OCT 2	14.25 –> LIB
OCT 19	21.53 –> SCO
NOV 8	04.59 –> SAG
DEC 1	20.41 –> CAP
DEC 12	12.39 –> SAG

VENUS

mth dy	time –> sign
JAN 1	00.00 –> CAP
JAN 7	21.10 –> AQU
JAN 31	20.14 –> PIS
FEB 24	23.27 –> ARI
MAR 21	10.06 –> TAU
APR 15	08.33 –> GEM
MAY 11	01.42 –> CAN
JUN 7	05.10 –> LEO
JUL 8	04.54 –> VIR
NOV 9	18.48 –> LIB
DEC 8	00.19 –> SCO

MARS

mth dy	time –> sign
JAN 1	00.00 –> AQU
JAN 22	13.05 –> PIS
MAR 1	22.03 –> ARI
APR 10	09.37 –> TAU
MAY 21	15.32 –> GEM
JUL 3	23.42 –> CAN
AUG 18	10.55 –> LEO
OCT 5	00.20 –> VIR
NOV 24	06.11 –> LIB

SATURN

mth dy	time –> sign
JAN 1	00.00 –> LIB
MAR 7	12.16 –> VIR
AUG 13	16.45 –> LIB

JUPITER

mth dy	time –> sign
JAN 1	00.00 –> PIS
APR 21	14.57 –> APR

MOON

dy	jan	feb	mar	apr	may	jun	jul	aug	sep	oct	nov	dec	dy
1	LIB	01.16	SAG	AQU	PIS	02.33	GEM	CAN	VIR	LIB	05.20	CAP	1
2	15.58	SAG	09.29	22.44	11.26	TAU	GEM	03.07	VIR	18.23	SAG	15.45	2
3	SCO	02.52	CAP	PIS	ARI	14.03	08.27	LEO	05.32	SCO	06.40	AQU	3
4	17.38	CAP	12.11	PIS	20.46	GEM	CAN	14.18	LIB	21.48	CAP	18.08	4
5	SAG	04.04	AQU	05.16	TAU	GEM	21.00	VIR	11.49	SAG	08.43	PIS	5
6	17.32	AQU	15.45	ARI	TAU	02.31	LEO	23.34	SCO	SAG	AQU	23.18	6
7	CAP	06.29	PIS	13.52	07.51	CAN	LEO	LIB	16.11	00.30	12.32	ARI	7
8	17.35	PIS	21.16	TAU	GEM	15.12	08.36	LIB	SAG	CAP	PIS	ARI	8
9	AQU	11.43	ARI	TAU	20.13	LEO	VIR	06.24	9.06	03.19	17.52	07.04	9
10	19.56	ARI	ARI	00.41	CAN	LEO	18.04	SCO	CAP	AQU	ARI	TAU	10
11	PIS	20.33	05.33	GEM	CAN	02.46	LIB	10.31	21.11	06.46	ARI	16.54	11
12	PIS	TAU	TAU	13.04	08.49	VIR	LIB	SAG	AQU	PIS	01.07	GEM	12
13	02.05	TAU	16.36	CAN	LEO	11.31	00.19	12.18	23.21	11.19	TAU	GEM	13
14	ARI	08.18	GEM	CAN	19.44	LIB	SCO	CAP	PIS	ARI	10.15	04.22	14
15	12.10	GEM	GEM	01.18	VIR	16.17	03.03	12.53	PIS	17.37	GEM	CAN	15
16	TAU	20.51	05.06	LEO	VIR	SCO	SAG	AQU	02.47	TAU	21.27	17.05	16
17	TAU	CAN	CAN	11.07	03.05	17.26	03.14	13.52	ARI	TAU	CAN	LEO	17
18	00.36	CAN	16.44	VIR	LIB	SAG	CAP	PIS	08.41	02.22	CAN	LEO	18
19	GEM	08.01	LEO	17.13	06.23	16.38	02.41	16.58	TAU	GEM	10.12	05.52	19
20	13.06	LEO	LEO	LIB	SCO	CAP	AQU	ARI	17.47	13.42	LEO	VIR	20
21	CAN	16.43	01.39	19.55	06.44	16.04	03.29	23.26	GEM	CAN	22.35	16.41	21
22	CAN	VIR	VIR	SCO	SAG	AQU	PIS	TAU	GEM	CAN	VIR	LIB	22
23	00.12	23.01	07.21	20.40	06.07	17.49	07.21	TAU	05.34	02.25	VIR	23.38	23
24	LEO	LIB	LIB	SAG	CAP	PIS	ARI	09.27	CAN	LEO	08.09	SCO	24
25	09.26	LIB	10.36	21.19	06.41	23.13	15.07	GEM	18.08	14.01	LIB	SCO	25
26	VIR	03.31	SCO	CAP	AQU	ARI	TAU	21.44	LEO	VIR	13.32	02.27	26
27	16.46	SCO	12.40	23.32	10.05	ARI	TAU	CAN	LEO	22.25	SCO	SAG	27
28	LIB	06.49	SAG	AQU	PIS	08.17	02.07	CAN	05.05	LIB	15.20	02.24	28
29	22.04		14.51	AQU	16.53	TAU	GEM	10.10	VIR	LIB	SAG	CAP	29
30	SCO		CAP	04.13	ARI	19.51	14.42	LEO	13.08	SCO	15.22	01.36	30
31	SCO		18.02		ARI		CAN	21.00		SCO		AQU	31

1952

SUN

mth dy	time –> sign
JAN 1	00.00 –> CAP
JAN 21	02.38 –> AQU
FEB 19	16.57 –> PIS
MAR 20	16.13 –> ARI
APR 20	03.37 –> TAU
MAY 21	03.04 –> GEM
JUN 21	11.12 –> CAN
JUL 22	22.07 –> LEO
AUG 23	05.03 –> VIR
SEP 23	02.24 –> LIB
OCT 23	11.22 –> SCO
NOV 22	08.36 –> SAG
DEC 21	21.43 –> CAP

MERCURY

mth dy	time –> sign
JAN 1	00.00 –> SAG
JAN 13	06.44 –> CAP
FEB 3	01.38 –> AQU
FEB 20	18.54 –> PIS
MAR 7	17.10 –> ARI
MAY 14	14.43 –> TAU
MAY 31	15.26 –> GEM
JUN 14	12.22 –> CAN
JUN 30	10.27 –> LEO
SEP 7	12.02 –> VIR
SEP 23	18.45 –> LIB
OCT 11	13.05 –> SCO
NOV 1	05.34 –> SAG

VENUS

mth dy	time –> sign
JAN 1	00.00 –> SCO
JAN 2	18.44 –> SAG
JAN 27	15.58 –> CAP
FEB 21	04.42 –> AQU
MAR 16	14.18 –> PIS
APR 9	23.17 –> ARI
MAY 4	08.55 –> TAU
MAY 28	19.19 –> GEM
JUN 22	05.46 –> CAN
JUL 16	15.23 –> LEO
AUG 9	23.58 –> VIR
SEP 3	08.17 –> LIB
SEP 27	17.36 –> SCO
OCT 22	05.02 –> SAG
NOV 15	20.03 –> CAP
DEC 10	18.31 –> AQU

MARS

mth dy	time –> sign
JAN 1	00.00 –> LIB
JAN 20	01.33 –> SCO
AUG 27	18.53 –> SAG
OCT 12	04.45 –> CAP
NOV 21	19.40 –> AQU
DEC 30	21.35 –> PIS

SATURN

mth dy	time –> sign
JAN 1	00.00 –> LIB

JUPITER

mth dy	time –> sign
JAN 1	00.00 –> ARI
APR 28	20.50 –> TAU

MOON

dy	jan	feb	mar	apr	may	jun	jul	aug	sep	oct	nov	dec	dy
1	02.10	19.51	TAU	07.39	04.12	VIR	LIB	SAG	09.03	PIS	06.58	GEM	1
2	PIS	TAU	12.36	CAN	LEO	12.26	05.25	22.27	AQU	19.34	TAU	GEM	2
3	05.42	TAU	GEM	20.10	16.57	LIB	SCO	CAP	09.00	ARI	11.02	03.08	3
4	ARI	04.55	23.40	LEO	VIR	20.19	10.27	22.41	PIS	21.05	GEM	CAN	4
5	12.43	GEM	CAN	LEO	VIR	SCO	SAG	AQU	08.57	TAU	18.12	13.23	5
6	TAU	16.44	CAN	08.40	03.39	SCO	12.02	22.05	ARI	TAU	CAN	LEO	6
7	22.42	CAN	12.30	VIR	LIB	00.21	CAP	PIS	10.48	01.15	CAN	LEO	7
8	GEM	CAN	LEO	18.56	10.49	SAG	11.54	22.33	TAU	GEM	04.56	01.57	8
9	GEM	05.36	LEO	LIB	SCO	01.46	AQU	ARI	16.06	09.16	LEO	VIR	9
10	10.34	LEO	00.51	LIB	14.50	CAP	11.59	ARI	GEM	CAN	17.47	14.35	10
11	CAN	18.02	VIR	02.13	SAG	02.26	PIS	01.46	GEM	20.50	VIR	LIB	11
12	23.19	VIR	11.16	SCO	17.09	AQU	13.56	TAU	01.24	LEO	VIR	LIB	12
13	LEO	VIR	LIB	07.08	CAP	04.00	ARI	08.36	CAN	LEO	05.57	00.39	13
14	LEO	05.00	19.20	SAG	19.14	PIS	18.45	GEM	13.38	09.51	LIB	SCO	14
15	12.00	LIB	SCO	10.41	AQU	07.29	TAU	18.52	LEO	VIR	15.18	07.00	15
16	VIR	13.45	SCO	CAP	22.05	ARI	TAU	CAN	LEO	21.44	SCO	SAG	16
17	23.19	SCO	01.15	13.43	PIS	13.11	02.37	CAN	02.41	LIB	21.33	10.17	17
18	LIB	19.42	SAG	AQU	PIS	TAU	GEM	07.19	VIR	LIB	SAG	CAP	18
19	LIB	SAG	05.19	16.40	02.07	21.03	13.05	LEO	14.41	07.10	SAG	12.02	19
20	07.44	22.49	CAP	PIS	ARI	GEM	CAN	20.22	LIB	SCO	01.40	AQU	20
21	SCO	CAP	07.55	19.56	07.29	GEM	CAN	LIB	LIB	14.12	CAP	13.45	21
22	12.22	23.48	AQU	ARI	TAU	07.04	01.20	VIR	00.43	SAG	04.52	PIS	22
23	SAG	AQU	09.39	ARI	14.37	CAN	LEO	08.42	SCO	19.28	AQU	16.30	23
24	13.39	AQU	PIS	00.15	GEM	19.02	14.24	LIB	08.33	CAP	07.55	ARI	24
25	CAP	00.01	11.34	TAU	GEM	LEO	VIR	19.10	SAG	23.28	PIS	20.46	25
26	13.06	PIS	ARI	06.40	00.06	LEO	VIR	SCO	14.06	AQU	11.09	TAU	26
27	AQU	01.11	15.05	GEM	CAN	08.06	02.54	SCO	CAP	AQU	ARI	TAU	27
28	12.45	ARI	TAU	16.06	11.59	VIR	LIB	02.53	17.24	02.23	14.54	02.48	28
29	PIS	05.02	21.36	CAN	LEO	20.18	13.04	SAG	AQU	PIS	TAU	GEM	29
30	14.33		GEM	CAN	LEO	LIB	SCO	07.24	18.52	04.34	19.53	10.53	30
31	ARI		GEM		00.57		19.37	CAP		ARI		CAN	31

SUN

mth dy	time -> sign
JAN 1	00.00 -> CAP
JAN 20	08.21 -> AQU
FEB 18	22.42 -> PIS
MAR 20	22.00 -> ARI
APR 20	09.25 -> TAU
MAY 21	08.53 -> GEM
JUN 21	17.00 -> CAN
JUL 23	03.52 -> LEO
AUG 23	10.45 -> VIR
SEP 23	08.06 -> LIB
OCT 23	17.06 -> SCO
NOV 22	14.22 -> SAG
DEC 22	03.32 -> CAP

MERCURY

mth dy	time -> sign
JAN 1	00.00 -> SAG
JAN 6	13.24 -> CAP
JAN 25	19.11 -> AQU
FEB 11	23.57 -> PIS
MAR 2	19.23 -> ARI
MAR 15	21.01 -> PIS
APR 17	16.47 -> ARI
MAY 8	06.23 -> TAU
MAY 23	03.58 -> GEM
JUN 6	08.23 -> CAN
JUN 26	11.00 -> LEO
JUL 28	13.40 -> CAN
AUG 11	14.04 -> LEO
AUG 30	22.59 -> VIR
SEP 15	21.45 -> LIB
OCT 4	16.40 -> SCO
OCT 31	15.51 -> SAG
NOV 6	22.18 -> SCO
DEC 30	17.14 -> CAP
DEC 10	14.48 -> SAG

VENUS

mth dy	time -> sign
JAN 1	00.00 -> AQU
JAN 5	11.11 -> PIS
FEB 2	05.54 -> ARI
MAR 14	18.58 -> TAU
MAR 31	04.50 -> ARI
JUN 5	10.33 -> TAU
JUL 7	10.29 -> GEM
AUG 4	01.08 -> CAN
AUG 30	01.35 -> LEO
SEP 24	03.48 -> VIR
OCT 18	15.27 -> LIB
NOV 11	18.12 -> SCO
DEC 5	16.24 -> SAG
DEC 29	12.54 -> CAP

MARS

mth dy	time -> sign
JAN 1	00.00 -> PIS
FEB 8	01.07 -> ARI
MAR 20	06.54 -> TAU
MAY 1	06.08 -> GEM
JUN 14	03.49 -> CAN
JUL 29	19.25 -> LEO
SEP 14	17.59 -> VIR
NOV 1	14.19 -> LIB
DEC 20	11.22 -> SCO

SATURN

mth dy	time -> sign
JAN 1	00.00 -> LIB
OCT 22	15.36 -> SCO

JUPITER

mth dy	time -> sign
JAN 1	00.00 -> TAU
MAY 9	15.33 -> GEM

MOON

dy	jan	feb	mar	apr	may	jun	jul	aug	sep	oct	nov	dec	dy
1	21.17	VIR	VIR	05.19	SAG	14.45	00.08	10.57	GEM	18.53	VIR	LIB	1
2	LEO	VIR	11.41	SCO	SAG	AQU	PIS	TAU	03.30	LEO	VIR	21.30	2
3	LEO	05.31	LIB	14.58	03.55	18.12	02.23	15.10	CAN	LEO	01.51	SCO	3
4	09.41	LIB	23.31	SAG	CAP	PIS	ARI	GEM	13.05	06.40	LIB	SCO	4
5	VIR	17.21	SCO	22.29	09.12	21.01	05.23	21.59	LEO	VIR	14.12	08.09	5
6	22.36	SCO	SCO	CAP	AQU	ARI	TAU	CAN	LEO	SCO	SAG	6	
7	LIB	SCO	09.20	CAP	12.46	23.41	09.42	CAN	00.47	SCO	16.33	7	
8	LIB	02.20	SAG	03.27	PIS	TAU	GEM	07.16	VIR	LIB	01.06	CAP	8
9	09.44	SAG	16.10	AQU	14.49	TAU	15.54	LEO	13.27	07.56	SAG	22.59	9
10	SCO	07.32	CAP	05.49	ARI	03.03	CAN	18.33	LIB	SCO	10.18	AQU	10
11	17.14	CAP	19.37	PIS	16.12	GEM	CAN	VIR	LIB	19.19	CAP	AQU	11
12	SAG	09.16	AQU	06.19	TAU	08.17	00.28	VIR	02.05	SAG	17.31	03.46	12
13	20.55	AQU	20.17	ARI	18.27	CAN	LEO	07.08	SCO	SAG	AQU	PIS	13
14	CAP	08.58	PIS	06.31	GEM	16.27	11.28	LIB	13.32	04.51	22.17	07.06	14
15	21.57	PIS	19.39	TAU	23.16	LEO	VIR	19.43	SAG	CAP	PIS	ARI	15
16	AQU	08.30	ARI	08.27	CAN	LEO	VIR	SCO	22.21	11.34	PIS	09.22	16
17	22.07	ARI	19.44	GEM	CAN	03.36	00.04	SCO	CAP	AQU	00.35	TAU	17
18	PIS	09.51	TAU	13.53	07.47	VIR	LIB	06.30	CAP	14.55	ARI	11.27	18
19	23.08	TAU	22.35	CAN	LEO	16.16	12.17	SAG	03.30	PIS	01.15	GEM	19
20	ARI	14.27	GEM	23.27	19.31	LIB	SCO	13.53	AQU	15.27	TAU	14.40	20
21	ARI	GEM	GEM	LEO	VIR	LIB	21.59	CAP	05.06	ARI	01.54	CAN	21
22	02.20	22.47	05.29	LEO	VIR	03.57	SAG	17.29	PIS	14.47	GEM	20.23	22
23	TAU	CAN	CAN	11.53	08.16	SCO	SAG	AQU	04.30	TAU	04.31	LEO	23
24	08.21	CAN	16.14	VIR	LIB	12.47	04.06	18.12	ARI	15.04	CAN	LEO	24
25	GEM	10.05	LEO	VIR	19.32	SAG	CAP	PIS	03.45	GEM	10.40	05.24	25
26	17.07	LEO	LEO	00.40	SCO	18.29	07.03	17.46	TAU	18.24	LEO	VIR	26
27	CAN	22.51	05.04	LIB	SCO	CAP	AQU	ARI	05.01	CAN	20.41	17.11	27
28	CAN	VIR	VIR	11.52	04.08	21.51	08.07	18.10	GEM	CAN	VIR	LIB	28
29	04.06		17.51	SCO	SAG	AQU	PIS	TAU	09.56	01.55	VIR	LIB	29
30	LEO		LIB	20.52	10.17	AQU	08.56	21.07	CAN	LEO	09.06	05.43	30
31	16.35		LIB		CAP		ARI	GEM		13.04		SCO	31

1954

SUN
mth dy time –> sign

JAN 1	00.00 –>	CAP
JAN 20	14.11 –>	AQU
FEB 19	04.32 –>	PIS
MAR 21	03.53 –>	ARI
APR 20	15.19 –>	TAU
MAY 21	14.47 –>	GEM
JUN 21	22.54 –>	CAN
JUL 23	09.45 –>	LEO
AUG 23	16.36 –>	VIR
SEP 23	13.55 –>	LIB
OCT 23	22.56 –>	SCO
NOV 22	20.14 –>	SAG
DEC 22	09.25 –>	CAP

MERCURY
mth dy time –> sign

JAN 1	00.00 –>	CAP
JAN 18	07.43 –>	AQU
FEB 4	18.03 –>	PIS
APR 13	11.34 –>	ARI
APR 30	11.26 –>	TAU
MAY 14	13.57 –>	GEM
MAY 30	16.13 –>	CAN
AUG 7	14.43 –>	LEO
AUG 22	17.42 –>	VIR
SEP 8	08.05 –>	LIB
SEP 29	04.06 –>	SCO
NOV 4	12.37 –>	LIB
NOV 11	10.23 –>	SCO
DEC 4	07.03 –>	SAG
DEC 23	12.10 –>	CAP

VENUS
mth dy time –> sign

JAN 1	00.00 –>	CAP
JAN 22	09.21 –>	AQU
FEB 15	07.01 –>	PIS
MAR 11	07.21 –>	ARI
APR 4	11.55 –>	TAU
APR 28	22.03 –>	GEM
MAY 23	15.04 –>	CAN
JUN 17	17.04 –>	LEO
JUL 13	08.43 –>	VIR
AUG 9	00.34 –>	LIB
SEP 6	23.28 –>	SCO
OCT 23	22.07 –>	SAG
OCT 27	10.42 –>	SCO

MARS
mth dy time –> sign

JAN 1	00.00 –>	SCO
FEB 9	19.17 –>	SAG
ARI 12	16.28 –>	CAP
JUL 3	07.27 –>	SAG
AUG 24	13.23 –>	CAP
OCT 21	12.03 –>	AQU
DEC 4	07.41 –>	PIS

SATURN
mth dy time –> sign

JAN 1	00.00 –>	SCO

JUPITER
mth dy time –> sign

JAN 1	00.00 –>	GEM
MAY 24	04.44 –>	CAN

MOON

dy	jan	feb	mar	apr	may	jun	jul	aug	sep	oct	nov	dec	dy
1	16.39	CAP	CAP	PIS	ARI	GEM	CAN	VIR	22.48	18.41	CAP	AQU	1
2	SAG	15.38	02.07	15.40	01.42	12.46	02.16	VIR	SCO	SAG	CAP	14.38	2
3	SAG	AQU	AQU	ARI	TAU	CAN	LEO	03.14	SCO	SAG	00.22	PIS	3
4	00.45	18.03	04.32	14.43	01.06	16.34	08.56	LIB	11.32	07.04	AQU	19.35	4
5	CAP	PIS	PIS	TAU	GEM	LEO	VIR	15.03	SAG	CAP	07.34	ARI	5
6	06.09	19.14	04.40	14.40	02.30	LEO	18.53	SCO	23.10	16.45	PIS	21.23	6
7	AQU	ARI	ARI	GEM	CAN	00.06	LIB	SCO	CAP	AQU	10.42	TAU	7
8	09.43	20.47	04.32	17.29	07.29	VIR	LIB	03.32	CAP	22.17	ARI	21.16	8
9	PIS	TAU	TAU	CAN	LEO	10.59	07.04	SAG	07.31	PIS	10.48	GEM	9
10	12.27	23.54	06.06	CAN	16.23	LIB	SCO	14.20	AQU	23.58	TAU	21.06	10
11	ARI	GEM	GEM	00.05	VIR	23.30	19.19	CAP	11.55	ARI	09.50	CAN	11
12	15.10	GEM	10.37	LEO	VIR	SCO	SAG	21.54	PIS	23.32	GEM	22.48	12
13	TAU	05.10	CAN	10.03	04.03	SCO	SAG	AQU	13.22	TAU	09.59	LEO	13
14	18.29	CAN	18.17	VIR	LIB	11.37	05.40	AQU	ARI	23.10	CAN	LEO	14
15	GEM	12.35	LEO	21.57	16.42	SAG	CAP	02.17	13.44	GEM	13.03	03.54	15
16	23.01	LEO	LEO	LIB	SCO	22.05	13.19	PIS	TAU	GEM	LEO	VIR	16
17	CAN	22.00	04.21	LIB	SCO	CAP	AQU	04.37	14.55	00.50	19.52	12.51	17
18	CAN	VIR	VIR	10.32	04.53	CAP	18.33	ARI	GEM	CAN	VIR	LIB	18
19	05.24	VIR	15.57	SCO	SAG	06.26	PIS	06.26	18.13	05.41	VIR	LIB	19
20	LEO	09.14	LIB	22.55	15.49	AQU	22.07	TAU	CAN	LEO	06.02	00.43	20
21	14.14	LIB	LIB	SAG	CAP	12.37	ARI	08.56	CAN	13.44	LIB	SCO	21
22	VIR	21.43	04.26	SAG	CAP	PIS	ARI	GEM	00.04	VIR	18.13	13.35	22
23	VIR	SCO	SCO	10.11	00.48	16.43	00.52	12.50	LEO	VIR	SCO	SAG	23
24	01.30	SCO	16.56	CAP	AQU	ARI	TAU	CAN	08.11	00.12	SCO	SAG	24
25	LIB	10.00	SAG	19.02	07.08	19.09	03.30	18.22	VIR	LIB	07.01	01.40	25
26	14.03	SAG	SAG	AQU	PIS	TAU	GEM	LEO	18.11	12.11	SAG	CAP	26
27	SCO	19.58	03.55	AQU	10.31	20.41	06.41	LEO	LIB	SCO	19.24	12.00	27
28	SCO	CAP	CAP	00.21	ARI	GEM	CAN	01.44	LIB	SCO	CAP	AQU	28
29	01.42		11.37	PIS	11.33	22.35	11.10	VIR	05.52	00.59	CAP	20.09	29
30	SAG		AQU	02.08	TAU	CAN	LEO	11.12	SCO	SAG	06.19	PIS	30
31	10.26		15.16		11.41		17.50	LIB		13.36		PIS	31

SUN

mth dy	time –> sign
JAN 1	00.00 –> CAP
JAN 20	20.02 –> AQU
FEB 19	10.19 –> PIS
MAR 21	09.35 –> ARI
APR 20	20.58 –> TAU
MAY 21	20.24 –> GEM
JUN 22	04.31 –> CAN
JUL 23	15.25 –> LEO
AUG 23	22.19 –> VIR
SEP 23	19.41 –> LIB
OCT 24	04.43 –> SCO
NOV 23	02.01 –> SAG
DEC 22	15.11 –> CAP

MERCURY

mth dy	time –> sign
JAN 1	00.00 –> CAP
JAN 10	23.05 –> AQU
MAR 17	20.49 –> PIS
APR 6	16.14 –> ARI
APR 22	02.57 –> TAU
MAY 6	13.05 –> GEM
JUL 13	14.44 –> CAN
JUL 30	17.22 –> LEO
AUG 14	13.08 –> VIR
SEP 1	12.06 –> LIB
NOV 8	06.57 –> SCO
NOV 27	04.34 –> SAG
DEC 16	06.07 –> CAP

VENUS

mth dy	time –> sign
JAN 1	00.00 –> SCO
JAN 6	06.48 –> SAG
FEB 6	01.15 –> CAP
MAR 4	20.21 –> AQU
MAR 30	11.30 –> PIS
APR 24	15.13 –> ARI
MAY 19	13.35 –> TAU
JUN 13	08.38 –> GEM
JUL 8	00.15 –> CAN
AUG 1	11.43 –> LEO
AUG 25	18.52 –> VIR
SEP 18	22.41 –> LIB
OCT 13	00.39 –> SCO
NOV 6	02.02 –> SAG
NOV 30	03.42 –> CAP
DEC 24	06.53 –> AQU

MARS

mth dy	time –> sign
JAN 1	00.00 –> PIS
JAN 15	04.33 –> ARI
FEB 26	10.22 –> TAU
APR 10	23.09 –> GEM
MAY 26	00.50 –> CAN
JUL 11	09.22 –> LEO
AUG 27	10.13 –> VIR
OCT 13	11.19 –> LIB
NOV 29	01.33 –> SCO

JUPITER

mth dy	time –> sign
JAN 1	00.00 –> CAN
JUN 13	00.07 –> LEO
NOV 17	03.59 –> VIR

SATURN

mth dy	time –> sign
JAN 1	00.00 –> SCO

MOON

dy	jan	feb	mar	apr	may	jun	jul	aug	sep	oct	nov	dec	dy
1	01.56	14.02	GEM	08.20	VIR	20.54	15.34	CAP	15.23	05.46	19.23	05.46	1
2	ARI	GEM	22.40	LEO	VIR	SCO	SAG	22.52	PIS	ARI	GEM	CAN	2
3	05.24	16.36	CAN	14.31	04.26	SCO	SAG	AQU	21.24	08.52	20.11	06.07	3
4	TAU	CAN	CAN	VIR	LIB	09.23	04.29	AQU	ARI	TAU	CAN	LEO	4
5	07.04	19.28	02.48	22.33	15.04	SAG	CAP	08.04	ARI	10.59	22.20	08.50	5
6	GEM	LEO	LEO	LIB	SCO	22.21	16.18	PIS	01.36	GEM	LEO	VIR	6
7	08.00	23.43	08.09	LIB	SCO	CAP	AQU	15.00	TAU	13.23	LEO	14.48	7
8	CAN	VIR	VIR	08.38	03.19	CAP	AQU	ARI	04.58	CAN	02.36	LIB	8
9	09.41	VIR	15.20	SCO	SAG	10.30	02.08	20.03	GEM	16.41	VIR	23.59	9
10	LEO	06.33	LIB	20.41	16.19	AQU	PIS	TAU	08.01	LEO	09.15	SCO	10
11	13.43	LIB	LIB	SAG	CAP	20.32	09.33	23.33	CAN	21.11	LIB	SCO	11
12	VIR	16.38	01.04	SAG	CAP	PIS	ARI	GEM	11.02	VIR	18.12	11.34	12
13	21.15	SCO	SCO	09.40	04.29	PIS	14.20	GEM	LEO	VIR	SCO	SAG	13
14	LIB	SCO	13.13	CAP	AQU	03.24	TAU	01.50	14.33	03.13	SCO	SAG	14
15	LIB	05.07	SAG	21.20	13.53	ARI	16.43	CAN	VIR	LIB	05.17	00.23	15
16	08.14	SAG	SAG	AQU	PIS	06.50	GEM	03.34	19.35	11.23	SAG	CAP	16
17	SCO	17.34	02.01	AQU	19.21	TAU	17.30	LEO	LIB	SCO	17.59	13.19	17
18	21.01	CAP	CAP	05.28	ARI	07.36	CAN	05.57	LIB	22.07	CAP	AQU	18
19	SAG	CAP	12.47	PIS	21.12	GEM	18.03	VIR	03.18	SAG	CAP	AQU	19
20	SAG	03.33	AQU	09.29	TAU	07.15	LEO	10.34	SCO	SAG	06.58	01.02	20
21	09.09	AQU	19.45	ARI	20.56	CAN	20.06	LIB	14.11	10.52	AQU	PIS	21
22	CAP	10.09	PIS	10.29	GEM	07.36	VIR	18.37	SAG	CAP	18.10	10.05	22
23	18.58	PIS	23.09	TAU	20.33	LEO	VIR	SCO	SAG	23.33	PIS	ARI	23
24	AQU	14.06	ARI	10.24	CAN	10.26	01.16	SCO	03.01	AQU	PIS	15.33	24
25	AQU	ARI	ARI	GEM	21.52	VIR	LIB	06.03	CAP	AQU	01.47	TAU	25
26	02.11	16.46	00.31	11.09	LEO	16.55	10.19	SAG	15.07	09.37	ARI	17.33	26
27	PIS	TAU	TAU	CAN	LEO	LIB	SCO	18.57	AQU	PIS	05.27	GEM	27
28	07.19	19.24	01.42	14.09	02.16	LIB	22.24	CAP	AQU	15.46	TAU	17.17	28
29	ARI		GEM	LEO	VIR	03.04	SAG	CAP	00.12	ARI	06.11	CAN	29
30	11.06		04.05	19.58	10.08	SCO	SAG	06.35	PIS	18.30	GEM	16.36	30
31	TAU		CAN		LIB		11.18	AQU		TAU		LEO	31

1956

SUN
mth dy   time –> sign

JAN 1   00.00 –> CAP
JAN 21 01.48 –> AQU
FEB 19 16.05 –> PIS
MAR 20 15.20 –> ARI
APR 20 02.43 –> TAU
MAY 21 02.12 –> GEM
JUN 21 10.24 –> CAN
JUL 22 21.20 –> LEO
AUG 23 04.15 –> VIR
SEP 23 01.35 –> LIB
OCT 23 10.34 –> SCO
NOV 22 07.50 –> SAG
DEC 21 20.59 –> CAP

MERCURY
mth dy   time –> sign

JAN 1   00.00 –> CAP
JAN 4   09.16 –> AQU
FEB 2   12.18 –> CAP
FEB 15 06.34 –> AQU
MAR 11 10.28 –> PIS
MAR 28 22.41 –> ARI
APR 12 17.10 –> TAU
APR 29 22.42 –> GEM
JUL 6   19.02 –> CAN
JUL 21 05.35 –> LEO
AUG 5   19.06 –> VIR
AUG 26 13.29 –> LIB
SEP 29 21.25 –> VIR
OCT 11 07.28 –> LIB
OCT 31 08.19 –> SCO
NOV 18 21.42 –> SAG
DEC 8   07.11 –> CAP

VENUS
mth dy   time –> sign

JAN 1   00.00 –> AQU
JAN 17 14.22 –> PIS
FEB 11 07.47 –> ARI
MAR 7   21.32 –> TAU
APR 4   07.23 –> GEM
MAY 8   02.17 –> CAN
JUN 23 12.10 –> GEM
AUG 4   09.48 –> CAN
SEP 8   09.23 –> LEO
OCT 6   03.12 –> VIR
OCT 31 19.40 –> LIB
NOV 25 13.01 –> SCO
DEC 19 19.07 –> SAG

MARS
mth dy   time –> sign

JAN 1   00.00 –> SCO
JAN 14 02.28 –> SAG
FEB 28 20.05 –> CAP
APR 14 23.40 –> AQU
JUN 3   07.51 –> PIS
DEC 6   11.24 –> ARI

SATURN
mth dy   time –> sign

JAN 1   00.00 –> SCO
JAN 12 18.47 –> SAG
MAY 14 03.46 –> SCO
OCT 10 15.13 –> SAG

JUPITER
mth dy   time –> sign

JAN 1   00.00 –> VIR
JAN 18 02.04 –> LEO
JUL 7   19.02 –> VIR
DEC 13 02.17 –> LIB

MOON

dy	jan	feb	mar	apr	may	jun	jul	aug	sep	oct	nov	dec	dy
1	17.31	LIB	SCO	SAG	CAP	PIS	ARI	11.16	23.14	08.24	22.24	12.59	1
2	VIR	13.33	SCO	04.37	01.27	PIS	22.26	GEM	LEO	VIR	SCO	SAG	2
3	21.44	SCO	08.09	CAP	AQU	07.04	TAU	13.32	23.20	10.01	SCO	22.36	3
4	LIB	SCO	SAG	17.24	13.15	ARI	TAU	CAN	VIR	LIB	04.56	CAP	4
5	LIB	00.13	20.32	AQU	PIS	13.22	02.26	13.27	VIR	13.19	SAG	CAP	5
6	06.00	SAG	CAP	AQU	22.05	TAU	GEM	LEO	00.04	SCO	14.24	10.16	6
7	SCO	13.08	CAP	04.37	ARI	16.09	03.20	12.50	LIB	19.46	CAP	AQU	7
8	17.32	CAP	09.19	PIS	ARI	GEM	CAN	VIR	03.26	SAG	CAP	22.57	8
9	SAG	CAP	AQU	12.46	03.24	16.42	02.42	13.50	SCO	SAG	02.19	PIS	9
10	SAG	01.52	20.11	ARI	TAU	CAN	LEO	LIB	10.46	05.48	AQU	PIS	10
11	06.33	AQU	PIS	18.03	06.00	16.45	02.34	18.20	SAG	CAP	14.51	10.37	11
12	CAP	12.52	PIS	TAU	GEM	LEO	VIR	SCO	21.46	18.09	PIS	ARI	12
13	19.19	PIS	04.26	21.30	07.21	18.03	04.54	SCO	CAP	AQU	PIS	19.15	13
14	AQU	21.48	ARI	GEM	CAN	VIR	LIB	03.00	CAP	AQU	01.36	TAU	14
15	AQU	ARI	10.32	GEM	08.52	21.58	10.56	SAG	10.28	06.25	ARI	TAU	15
16	06.47	ARI	TAU	00.15	LEO	LIB	SCO	14.47	AQU	PIS	09.12	00.06	16
17	PIS	04.48	15.11	CAN	11.40	LIB	20.38	CAP	22.33	16.35	TAU	GEM	17
18	16.17	TAU	GEM	03.00	VIR	05.03	SAG	CAP	PIS	ARI	13.45	01.52	18
19	ARI	09.50	18.47	LEO	16.25	SCO	SAG	03.38	PIS	ARI	GEM	CAN	19
20	23.11	GEM	CAN	06.17	LIB	14.55	08.40	AQU	08.47	00.07	16.17	02.11	20
21	TAU	12.50	21.31	VIR	23.26	SAG	CAP	15.47	ARI	TAU	CAN	LEO	21
22	TAU	CAN	LEO	10.36	SCO	SAG	21.28	PIS	17.01	05.28	18.10	02.56	22
23	03.05	14.10	23.53	LIB	SCO	02.43	AQU	PIS	TAU	GEM	LEO	VIR	23
24	GEM	LEO	VIR	16.44	08.46	CAP	AQU	02.29	23.25	09.23	20.32	05.39	24
25	04.20	15.05	VIR	SCO	SAG	15.26	09.50	ARI	GEM	CAN	VIR	LIB	25
26	CAN	VIR	03.00	SCO	20.11	AQU	PIS	11.23	GEM	12.27	VIR	11.09	26
27	04.06	17.20	LIB	01.25	CAP	AQU	20.54	TAU	04.00	LEO	00.11	SCO	27
28	LEO	LIB	08.18	SAG	CAP	03.54	ARI	17.59	CAN	15.09	LIB	19.20	28
29	04.17	22.45	SCO	12.44	08.52	PIS	ARI	GEM	06.49	VIR	05.34	SAG	29
30	VIR		16.56	CAP	AQU	14.43	05.40	21.51	LEO	18.10	SCO	SAG	30
31	06.56		SAG		21.09		TAU	CAN		LIB		05.37	31

232

SUN

mth dy time –> sign

JAN 1   00.00 –> CAP
JAN 20 07.39 –> AQU
FEB 18 21.58 –> PIS
MAR 20 21.16 –> ARI
APR 20 08.41 –> TAU
MAY 21 08.10 –> GEM
JUN 21 16.20 –> CAN
JUL 23 03.15 –> LEO
AUG 23 10.07 –> VIR
SEP 23 07.26 –> LIB
OCT 23 16.24 –> SCO
NOV 22 13.39 –> SAG
DEC 22 02.49 –> CAP

MERCURY

mth dy time –> sign

JAN 1   00.00 –> CAP
FEB 12 14.30 –> AQU
MAR 4   11.34 –> PIS
MAR 20 19.48 –> ARI
APR 19 03.29 –> TAU
JUN 12 13.40 –> GEM
JUN 28 17.08 –> CAN
JUL 12 19.41 –> LEO
JUL 30 01.44 –> VIR
OCT 6   11.09 –> LIB
OCT 23 20.50 –> SCO
NOV 11 18.00 –> SAG
DEC 2   11.19 –> CAP
DEC 28 17.30 –> SAG

VENUS

mth dy time –> sign

JAN 1   00.00 –> SAG
JAN 12 20.23 –> CAP
FEB 5   20.16 –> AQU
MAR 1   20.39 –> PIS
MAR 25 22.46 –> ARI
APR 4   23.38 –> TAU
MAY 13 11.08 –> GEM
JUN 6   21.35 –> CAN
JUL 1   10.42 –> LEO
JUL 26 03.10 –> VIR
AUG 20 00.44 –> LIB
SEP 14 06.20 –> SCO
OCT 10 01.16 –> SAG
NOV 5   23.46 –> CAP
DEC 6   15.26 –> AQU

MARS

mth dy time –> sign

JAN 1   00.00 –> ARI
JAN 28 14.19 –> TAU
MAR 17 21.34 –> GEM
MAY 4   15.22 –> CAN
JUN 21 12.18 –> LEO
AUG 8   05.27 –> VIR
SEP 24 04.31 –> LIB
NOV 8   21.04 –> SCO
DEC 23 01.29 –> SAG

JUPITER

mth dy time –> sign

JAN 1   00.00 –> LIB
FEB 19 15.37 –> VIR
AUG 7   02.11 –> LIB

SATURN

mth dy time –> sign

JAN 1   00.00 –> SAG

MOON

dy	jan	feb	mar	apr	may	jun	jul	aug	sep	oct	nov	dec	dy
1	CAP	12.20	PIS	23.11	13.47	CAN	13.23	LIB	SAG	CAP	09.18	05.56	1
2	17.24	PIS	PIS	TAU	GEM	04.45	VIR	01.00	21.05	14.04	PIS	ARI	2
3	AQU	PIS	06.31	TAU	19.08	LEO	15.16	SCO	CAP	AQU	22.00	17.48	3
4	AQU	00.42	ARI	07.30	CAN	06.59	LIB	06.47	CAP	AQU	ARI	TAU	4
5	06.04	ARI	17.20	GEM	22.53	VIR	19.10	SAG	07.50	02.17	ARI	TAU	5
6	PIS	11.37	TAU	13.37	LEO	09.45	SCO	15.23	AQU	PIS	09.38	03.00	6
7	18.23	TAU	TAU	CAN	LEO	LIB	SCO	CAP	20.04	14.57	TAU	GEM	7
8	ARI	19.34	02.03	17.24	01.37	13.41	01.20	CAP	PIS	ARI	19.09	09.16	8
9	ARI	GEM	GEM	LEO	VIR	SCO	SAG	02.01	PIS	ARI	GEM	CAN	9
10	04.26	23.39	07.45	19.13	03.57	19.09	09.35	AQU	08.45	02.48	GEM	13.23	10
11	TAU	CAN	CAN	VIR	LIB	SAG	CAP	14.02	ARI	TAU	02.24	LEO	11
12	10.44	CAN	10.12	20.08	06.48	SAG	19.43	PIS	20.57	13.01	CAN	16.28	12
13	GEM	00.19>LEO	LEO	LIB	SCO	02.36	AQU	PIS	TAU	GEM	07.36	VIR	13
14	13.05	23.17	10.20	21.45	11.13	CAP	AQU	02.46	TAU	20.54	LEO	19.23	14
15	CAN	VIR	VIR	SCO	SAG	12.23	07.32	ARI	07.26	CAN	11.07	LIB	15
16	12.50	22.50	09.59	SCO	18.13	AQU	PIS	15.00	GEM	CAN	VIR	22.35	16
17	LEO	17
17	LEO	LIB	LIB	01.43	CAP	AQU	20.14	TAU	14.49	01.59	13.25	SCO	17
18	12.03	LIB	11.15	SAG	CAP	00.15	ARI	TAU	CAN	LEO	LIB	SCO	18
19	VIR	01.06	SCO	09.08	04.12	PIS	ARI	00.51	18.31	04.23	15.17	02.30	19
20	12.55	SCO	15.54	CAP	AQU	12.46	07.58	GEM	LEO	VIR	SCO	SAG	20
21	LIB	07.23	SAG	19.53	16.20	ARI	TAU	06.48	19.11	05.03	17.52	07.47	21
22	17.02	SAG	SAG	AQU	PIS	23.38	16.34	CAN	VIR	LIB	SAG	CAP	22
23	SCO	17.27	00.34	AQU	PIS	TAU	GEM	08.51	18.33	05.31	22.29	15.19	23
24	SCO	CAP	CAP	08.23	04.34	TAU	21.05	LEO	LIB	SCO	CAP	AQU	24
25	00.52	CAP	12.17	PIS	ARI	07.07	CAN	08.26	18.40	07.33	CAP	AQU	25
26	SAG	05.42	AQU	20.22	14.43	GEM	22.16	VIR	SCO	SAG	06.16	01.41	26
27	11.32	AQU	AQU	ARI	TAU	11.00	LEO	07.41	21.27	12.41	AQU	PIS	27
28	CAP	18.25	01.00	ARI	21.47	CAN	21.59	LIB	SAG	CAP	17.16	14.13	28
29	23.42		PIS	06.18	GEM	12.31	VIR	08.45	SAG	21.32	PIS	ARI	29
30	AQU		12.55	TAU	GEM	LEO	22.20	SCO	03.59	AQU	PIS	ARI	30
31	AQU		ARI		02.05		LIB	13.07		AQU		02.37	31

1958

SUN
mth dy time –> sign

JAN 1	00.00 –>	CAP
JAN 20	13.29 –>	AQU
FEB 19	03.48 –>	PIS
MAR 21	03.06 –>	ARI
APR 20	14.27 –>	TAU
MAY 21	13.51 –>	GEM
JUN 21	21.57 –>	CAN
JUL 23	08.50 –>	LEO
AUG 23	15.46 –>	VIR
SEP 23	13.09 –>	LIB
OCT 23	22.12 –>	SCO
NOV 22	19.29 –>	SAG
DEC 22	08.40 –>	CAP

MERCURY
mth dy time –> sign

JAN 1	00.00 –>	SAG
JAN 14	10.03 –>	CAP
FEB 6	15.21 –>	AQU
FEB 24	21.44 –>	PIS
MAR 12	17.31 –>	ARI
APR 2	19.17 –>	TAU
APR 10	13.42 –>	ARI
MAY 17	01.53 –>	TAU
JUN 5	20.59 –>	GEM
JUN 20	02.20 –>	CAN
JUL 4	23.46 –>	LEO
JUL 26	10.08 –>	VIR
AUG 23	14.36 –>	LEO
SEP 11	01.08 –>	VIR
SEP 28	22.46 –>	LIB
OCT 16	08.52 –>	SCO
NOV 5	02.36 –>	SAG

VENUS
mth dy time –> sign

JAN 1	00.00 –>	AQU
APR 6	16.00 –>	PIS
MAY 5	11.59 –>	ARI
JUN 1	04.07 –>	TAU
JUN 26	23.08 –>	GEM
JUL 22	05.26 –>	CAN
AUG 16	01.28 –>	LEO
SEP 9	12.36 –>	VIR
OCT 3	16.44 –>	LIB
OCT 27	16.26 –>	SCO
NOV 20	13.59 –>	SAG
DEC 14	10.55 –>	CAP

MARS
mth dy time –> sign

JAN 1	00.00 –>	SAG
FEB 3	18.56 –>	CAP
MAR 17	07.10 –>	AQU
APR 27	02.30 –>	PIS
JUN 7	06.21 –>	ARI
JUL 21	07.03 –>	TAU
SEP 21	05.26 –>	GEM
OCT 29	00.01 –>	TAU

JUPITER
mth dy time –> sign

JAN 1	00.00 –>	LIB
JAN 13	12.52 –>	SCO
MAR 20	19.13 –>	LIB
SEP 7	08.52 –>	SCO

SATURN
mth dy time –> sign

JAN 1	00.00 –>	SAG

MOON

dy	jan	feb	mar	apr	may	jun	jul	aug	sep	oct	nov	dec	dy
1	TAU	04.40	CAN	06.01	LIB	02.53	CAP	12.11	ARI	TAU	08.09	LEO	1
2	12.21	CAN	18.27	VIR	16.14	SAG	19.44	PIS	19.24	14.50	CAN	LEO	2
3	GEM	07.37	LEO	05.54	SCO	05.23	AQU	23.14	TAU	GEM	17.02	05.18	3
4	18.22	LEO	19.15	LIB	16.43	CAP	AQU	ARI	TAU	GEM	LEO	VIR	4
5	CAN	08.11	VIR	05.16	SAG	10.34	03.57	ARI	08.07	02.00	22.45	09.31	5
6	21.21	VIR	18.35	SCO	19.21	AQU	PIS	12.04	GEM	CAN	VIR	LIB	6
7	LEO	08.23	LIB	06.07	CAP	19.24	15.18	TAU	18.22	09.50	VIR	11.28	7
8	22.59	LIB	18.34	SAG	CAP	PIS	ARI	TAU	CAN	LEO	01.16	SCO	8
9	VIR	10.03	SCO	10.00	01.29	PIS	ARI	00.16	CAN	13.49	LIB	12.02	9
10	VIR	SCO	20.56	CAP	AQU	07.20	04.09	GEM	00.42	VIR	01.30	SAG	10
11	00.52	14.11	SAG	17.41	11.27	ARI	TAU	09.25	LEO	14.44	SCO	12.46	11
12	LIB	SAG	SAG	AQU	PIS	20.12	15.46	CAN	03.19	LIB	01.03	CAP	12
13	04.02	20.55	02.36	AQU	23.58	TAU	GEM	14.43	VIR	14.11	SAG	15.38	13
14	SCO	CAP	CAP	04.38	ARI	TAU	GEM	LEO	03.44	SCO	01.54	AQU	14
15	08.49	CAP	11.28	PIS	ARI	07.31	00.15	17.07	LIB	14.09	CAP	22.12	15
16	SAG	05.51	AQU	17.23	12.50	GEM	CAN	VIR	03.49	SAG	05.53	PIS	16
17	15.13	AQU	22.41	ARI	TAU	16.04	05.31	18.17	SCO	16.23	AQU	PIS	17
18	CAP	16.39	PIS	ARI	TAU	CAN	LEO	LIB	05.16	CAP	13.56	08.45	18
19	23.22	PIS	PIS	06.16	00.14	22.04	08.42	19.50	SAG	22.04	PIS	ARI	19
20	AQU	PIS	11.17	TAU	GEM	LEO	VIR	SCO	09.13	AQU	PIS	21.38	20
21	AQU	05.02	ARI	18.03	09.23	LEO	11.11	22.48	CAP	AQU	01.28	TAU	21
22	09.42	ARI	ARI	GEM	CAN	02.22	LIB	SAG	16.03	07.19	ARI	TAU	22
23	PIS	18.05	00.16	GEM	16.14	VIR	13.57	SAG	AQU	PIS	14.30	10.09	23
24	22.03	TAU	TAU	03.46	LEO	05.42	SCO	03.38	AQU	19.10	TAU	GEM	24
25	ARI	TAU	12.20	CAN	21.00	LIB	17.25	CAP	01.33	ARI	TAU	20.33	25
26	ARI	05.52	GEM	10.44	VIR	08.30	SAG	10.28	PIS	ARI	03.00	CAN	26
27	10.56	GEM	21.53	LEO	23.55	SCO	21.53	AQU	13.07	08.07	GEM	CAN	27
28	TAU	14.17	CAN	14.40	LIB	11.11	CAP	19.25	ARI	TAU	13.51	04.33	28
29	21.47		CAN	VIR	LIB	SAG	CAP	PIS	ARI	20.49	CAN	LEO	29
30	GEM		03.45	16.06	01.33	14.32	03.52	PIS	01.58	GEM	22.41	10.41	30
31	GEM		LEO		SCO		AQU	06.35		GEM		VIR	31

SUN
mth dy   time –> sign

JAN 1	00.00 –> CAP
JAN 20	19.19 –> AQU
FEB 19	09.38 –> PIS
MAR 21	08.55 –> ARI
APR 20	20.17 –> TAU
MAY 21	19.42 –> GEM
JUN 22	03.50 –> CAN
JUL 23	14.45 –> LEO
AUG 23	21.43 –> VIR
SEP 23	19.09 –> LIB
OCT 24	04.11 –> SCO
NOV 23	01.27 –> SAG
DEC 22	14.35 –> CAP

MERCURY
mth dy   time –> sign

JAN 1	00.00 –> SAG
JAN 10	16.48 –> CAP
JAN 30	15.41 –> AQU
FEB 17	02.15 –> PIS
MAR 5	11.53 –> ARI
MAY 12	19.48 –> TAU
MAY 28	17.35 –> GEM
JUN 11	14.11 –> CAN
JUN 28	16.31 –> LEO
SEP 5	02.28 –> VIR
SEP 21	01.20 –> LIB
OCT 9	04.02 –> SCO
OCT 31	01.16 –> SAG
NOV 25	11.53 –> SCO
DEC 13	15.42 –> SAG

VENUS
mth dy   time –> sign

JAN 1	00.00 –> CAP
JAN 7	08.17 –> AQU
JAN 31	07.28 –> PIS
FEB 24	10.53 –> ARI
MAR 20	21.55 –> TAU
APR 14	21.08 –> GEM
MAY 10	15.45 –> CAN
JUN 6	22.43 –> LEO
JUL 8	12.08 –> VIR
SEP 20	03.04 –> LEO
SEP 25	08.06 –> VIR
NOV 9	18.10 –> LIB
DEC 7	16.41 –> SCO

MARS
mth dy   time –> sign

JAN 1	00.00 –> TAU
FEB 10	13.57 –> GEM
APR 10	09.46 –> CAN
JUN 1	02.26 –> LEO
JUL 20	11.03 –> VIR
SEP 5	22.46 –> LIB
OCT 21	09.40 –> SCO
DEC 3	18.09 –> SAG

JUPITER
mth dy   time –> sign

JAN 1	00.00 –> SCO
FEB 10	13.44 –> SAG
APR 24	14.10 –> SCO
OCT 5	14.40 –> SAG

SATURN
mth dy   time –> sign

JAN 1	00.00 –> SAG
JAN 5	13.32 –> CAP

MOON   MOON

dy	jan	feb	mar	apr	may	jun	jul	aug	sep	oct	nov	dec	dy
1	15.21	SCO	08.33	22.41	11.58	ARI	TAU	07.23	LEO	22.08	SCO	20.11	1
2	LIB	03.11	SAG	AQU	PIS	16.37	12.05	CAN	08.31	LIB	10.02	CAP	2
3	18.42	SAG	12.05	AQU	22.19	TAU	GEM	17.09	VIR	23.54	SAG	20.35	3
4	SCO	06.29	CAP	06.23	ARI	TAU	GEM	LEO	12.56	SCO	10.05	AQU	4
5	20.55	CAP	17.16	PIS	ARI	05.35	00.03	LEO	LIB	SCO	CAP	AQU	5
6	SAG	10.40	AQU	16.33	10.39	GEM	CAN	00.29	15.53	00.54	12.14	00.16	6
7	22.50	AQU	AQU	ARI	TAU	17.44	10.08	VIR	SCO	SAG	AQU	PIS	7
8	CAP	16.50	00.25	ARI	23.34	CAN	LEO	05.56	18.20	02.38	17.35	07.59	8
9	CAP	PIS	PIS	04.32	GEM	CAN	18.15	LIB	SAG	CAP	PIS	ARI	9
10	01.52	PIS	09.54	TAU	GEM	04.19	VIR	09.59	21.04	06.12	PIS	18.56	10
11	AQU	01.55	ARI	17.25	11.57	LEO	VIR	SCO	CAP	AQU	02.10	TAU	11
12	07.39	ARI	21.37	GEM	CAN	12.50	00.26	12.58	CAP	12.06	ARI	TAU	12
13	PIS	13.47	TAU	GEM	22.40	VIR	LIB	SAG	00.43	PIS	13.04	07.24	13
14	17.10	TAU	TAU	05.48	LEO	18.42	04.33	15.8	AQU	20.20	TAU	GEM	14
15	ARI	TAU	10.30	CAN	LEO	LIB	SCO	CAP	05.54	ARI	TAU	20.00	15
16	ARI	02.39	GEM	15.55	06.38	21.38	06.42	17.53	PIS	ARI	01.16	CAN	16
17	05.33	GEM	22.28	LEO	VIR	SCO	SAG	AQU	13.16	06.40	GEM	CAN	17
18	TAU	13.50	CAN	22.27	11.06	22.14	07.42	21.59	ARI	TAU	13.56	07.58	18
19	18.16	CAN	CAN	VIR	LIB	SAG	CAP	PIS	23.12	18.40	CAN	LEO	19
20	GEM	20.38	07.22	VIR	12.24	22.01	09.05	PIS	TAU	GEM	CAN	18.29	20
21	GEM	LEO	LEO	01.19	SCO	CAP	AQU	04.51	TAU	GEM	02.04	VIR	21
22	04.47	LEO	12.28	LIB	11.51	23.00	12.41	ARI	11.16	07.22	LEO	VIR	22
23	CAN	02.06	VIR	01.34	SAG	AQU	PIS	14.58	GEM	CAN	12.08	02.29	23
24	12.13	VIR	14.27	SCO	11.24	AQU	19.53	TAU	23.49	19.03	VIR	LIB	24
25	LEO	04.29	LIB	00.59	CAP	03.09	ARI	TAU	CAN	LEO	18.41	07.00	25
26	17.13	LIB	14.53	SAG	13.09	PIS	ARI	03.18	CAN	LEO	LIB	SCO	26
27	VIR	06.14	SCO	01.32	AQU	11.28	06.43	GEM	10.36	03.48	21.21	08.15	27
28	20.54	SCO	15.31	CAP	18.42	ARI	TAU	15.33	LEO	VIR	SCO	SAG	28
29	LIB		SAG	04.55	PIS	23.11	19.23	CAN	18.04	08.41	21.12	07.38	29
30	LIB		17.49	AQU	PIS	TAU	GEM	CAN	VIR	LIB	SAG	CAP	30
31	00.05		CAP		04.18		GEM	01.33		10.14		07.15	31

235

1960

SUN

mth	dy	time -> sign
JAN	1	00.00 -> CAP
JAN	21	01.10 -> AQU
FEB	19	15.26 -> PIS
MAR	20	14.42 -> ARI
APR	20	02.06 -> TAU
MAY	21	01.33 -> GEM
JUN	21	09.42 -> CAN
JUL	22	20.37 -> LEO
AUG	23	03.34 -> VIR
SEP	23	00.59 -> LIB
OCT	23	10.02 -> SCO
NOV	22	07.19 -> SAG
DEC	21	20.26 -> CAP

MERCURY

mth	dy	time -> sign
JAN	1	00.00 -> SAG
JAN	4	08.24 -> CAP
JAN	23	06.16 -> AQU
FEB	9	10.13 -> PIS
APR	16	02.22 -> ARI
MAY	4	16.45 -> TAU
MAY	19	03.27 -> GEM
JUN	2	20.31 -> CAN
JUL	1	01.13 -> LEO
JUL	6	01.23 -> CAN
AUG	10	17.49 -> LEO
AUG	27	03.11 -> VIR
SEP	12	06.29 -> LIB
OCT	1	17.17 -> SCO
DEC	7	17.30 -> SAG
DEC	27	07.21 -> CAP

VENUS

mth	dy	time -> sign
JAN	1	00.00 -> SCO
JAN	2	08.43 -> SAG
JAN	27	04.46 -> CAP
FEB	20	16.47 -> AQU
MAR	16	01.53 -> PIS
APR	9	10.32 -> ARI
MAY	3	19.56 -> TAU
MAY	28	06.11 -> GEM
JUN	21	16.34 -> CAN
JUL	16	02.11 -> LEO
AUG	9	10.54 -> VIR
SEP	2	19.29 -> LIB
SEP	27	05.13 -> SCO
OCT	21	17.12 -> SAG
NOV	15	08.57 -> CAP
DEC	10	08.35 -> AQU

MARS

mth	dy	time -> sign
JAN	1	00.00 -> SAG
JAN	14	04.59 -> CAP
FEB	23	04.11 -> AQU
APR	2	06.24 -> PIS
MAY	11	07.19 -> ARI
JUN	20	09.05 -> TAU
AUG	2	04.32 -> GEM
SEP	21	04.06 -> CAN

JUPITER

mth	dy	time -> sign
JAN	1	00.00 -> SAG
MAR	1	13.10 -> CAP
JUN	10	01.53 -> SAG
OCT	26	03.01 -> CAP

SATURN

mth	dy	time -> sign
JAN	1	00.00 -> CAP

MOON

dy	jan	feb	mar	apr	may	jun	jul	aug	sep	oct	nov	dec	dy
1	AQU	00.39	18.18	GEM	CAN	16.38	08.46	SCO	CAP	22.14	ARI	TAU	1
2	09.19	ARI	TAU	GEM	21.59	VIR	LIB	02.04	12.35	PIS	15.27	07.01	2
3	PIS	09.16	TAU	01.46	LEO	VIR	15.08	SAG	AQU	PIS	TAU	GEM	3
4	15.21	TAU	05.08	CAN	LEO	01.31	SCO	03.25	13.51	01.46	23.44	17.52	4
5	ARI	20.58	GEM	14.01	08.59	LIB	17.42	CAP	PIS	ARI	GEM	CAN	5
6	ARI	GEM	17.37	LEO	VIR	06.20	SAG	03.21	16.26	07.09	GEM	CAN	6
7	01.22	GEM	CAN	LEO	16.30	SCO	17.34	AQU	ARI	TAU	10.26	06.21	7
8	TAU	09.37	CAN	00.02	LIB	07.31	CAP	03.42	21.44	15.16	CAN	LEO	8
9	13.45	CAN	05.25	VIR	20.07	SAG	16.43	PIS	TAU	GEM	22.59	19.13	9
10	GEM	21.08	LEO	06.35	SCO	06.48	AQU	06.21	TAU	GEM	LEO	VIR	10
11	GEM	LEO	14.47	LIB	20.55	CAP	17.19	ARI	06.31	02.18	LEO	VIR	11
12	02.23	LEO	VIR	10.01	SAG	06.23	PIS	12.36	GEM	CAN	11.24	06.10	12
13	CAN	06.35	21.19	SCO	20.50	AQU	21.07	TAU	18.10	14.55	VIR	LIB	13
14	13.59	VIR	LIB	11.37	CAP	08.17	ARI	22.29	CAN	LEO	21.07	13.13	14
15	LEO	13.55	LIB	SAG	21.51	PIS	ARI	GEM	CAN	LEO	LIB	SCO	15
16	LEO	LIB	01.37	13.01	AQU	13.42	04.48	GEM	06.46	02.40	LIB	16.07	16
17	00.03	19.24	SCO	CAP	AQU	ARI	TAU	10.43	LEO	VIR	02.53	SAG	17
18	VIR	SCO	04.37	15.32	01.23	22.33	15.40	CAN	18.07	11.32	SCO	16.16	18
19	08.14	23.12	SAG	AQU	PIS	TAU	GEM	23.17	VIR	LIB	05.17	CAP	19
20	LIB	SAG	07.14	19.55	07.55	TAU	GEM	LEO	VIR	17.06	SAG	15.49	20
21	13.59	SAG	CAP	PIS	ARI	09.46	04.09	LEO	02.58	SCO	06.02	AQU	21
22	SCO	01.39	10.10	PIS	17.00	GEM	CAN	10.41	LIB	20.16	CAP	16.47	22
23	17.02	CAP	AQU	02.23	TAU	22.10	16.46	VIR	09.18	SAG	07.04	PIS	23
24	SAG	03.42	14.02	ARI	TAU	CAN	LEO	20.09	SCO	22.28	AQU	20.34	24
25	17.59	AQU	PIS	10.50	03.55	CAN	LEO	LIB	13.42	CAP	09.49	ARI	25
26	CAP	06.04	19.29	TAU	GEM	10.51	04.31	LIB	SAG	CAP	PIS	ARI	26
27	18.19	PIS	ARI	21.16	16.06	LEO	VIR	03.23	16.54	00.57	14.51	03.30	27
28	AQU	10.38	ARI	GEM	CAN	22.53	14.33	SCO	CAP	AQU	ARI	TAU	28
29	19.56	ARI	03.13	09.22	CAN	VIR	LIB	08.19	19.32	04.26	22.00	13.01	29
30	PIS		TAU	CAN	04.50	VIR	21.55	SAG	AQU	PIS	TAU	GEM	30
31	PIS		13.32		LEO		SCO	11.09		09.11		GEM	31

SUN

mth dy time –> sign

JAN 1 00.00 –> CAP
JAN 20 07.01 –> AQU
FEB 18 21.17 –> PIS
MAR 20 20.32 –> ARI
APR 20 07.55 –> TAU
MAY 21 07.22 –> GEM
JUN 21 15.30 –> CAN
JUL 23 02.24 –> LEO
AUG 23 09.19 –> VIR
SEP 23 06.43 –> LIB
OCT 23 15.47 –> SCO
NOV 22 13.08 –> SAG
DEC 22 02.19 –> CAP

MERCURY

mth dy time –> sign

JAN 1 00.00 –> CAP
JAN 14 18.59 –> AQU
FEB 1 21.39 –> PIS
FEB 24 20.22 –> AQU
MAR 18 10.16 –> PIS
APR 10 09.22 –> ARI
APR 26 14.34 –> TAU
MAY 10 16.34 –> GEM
MAY 28 17.23 –> CAN
AUG 4 01.15 –> LEO
AUG 18 20.52 –> VIR
SEP 4 22.32 –> LIB
SEP 27 12.16 –> SCO
OCT 22 02.29 –> LIB
NOV 10 23.53 –> SCO
NOV 30 22.55 –> SAG
DEC 20 01.04 –> CAP

VENUS

mth dy time –> sign

JAN 1 00.00 –> AQU
JAN 5 03.31 –> PIS
FEB 2 04.46 –> ARI
JUN 5 19.25 –> TAU
JUL 7 04.32 –> GEM
AUG 3 15.28 –> CAN
AUG 29 14.18 –> LEO
SEP 23 15.43 –> VIR
OCT 18 19.58 –> LIB
NOV 11 05.33 –> SCO
DEC 5 03.40 –> SAG
DEC 29 00.07 –> CAP

MARS

mth dy time –> sign

JAN 1 00.00 –> CAN
FEB 5 00.22 –> GEM
FEB 7 05.26 –> CAN
MAY 6 01.13 –> LEO
JUN 28 23.47 –> VIR
AUG 17 00.42 –> LIB
OCT 1 20.02 –> SCO
NOV 13 21.50 –> SAG
DEC 24 17.50 –> CAP

JUPITER

mth dy time –> sign

JAN 1 00.00 –> CAP
MAR 15 08.01 –> AQU
AUG 12 08.55 –> CAP
NOV 4 02.49 –> AQU

SATURN

mth dy time –> sign

JAN 1 00.00 –> CAP

MOON   MOON

dy	jan	feb	mar	apr	may	jun	jul	aug	sep	oct	nov	dec	dy
1	00.22	LEO	14.12	LIB	SCO	CAP	AQU	ARI	05.52	CAN	LEO	VIR	1
2	CAN	07.48	VIR	16.36	05.25	17.45	02.52	16.19	GEM	CAN	06.17	03.08	2
3	12.54	VIR	VIR	SCO	SAG	AQU	PIS	TAU	15.00	09.43	VIR	LIB	3
4	LEO	19.27	01.21	22.34	08.40	19.50	04.12	23.04	CAN	LEO	18.42	13.30	4
5	LEO	LIB	LIB	SAG	CAP	PIS	ARI	GEM	CAN	22.45	LIB	SCO	5
6	01.48	LIB	10.24	SAG	11.24	23.23	10.01	GEM	03.01	VIR	LIB	20.24	6
7	VIR	04.51	SCO	02.42	AQU	ARI	TAU	08.56	LEO	VIR	04.40	SAG	7
8	13.31	SCO	17.04	CAP	14.23	ARI	17.27	CAN	16.05	11.04	SCO	SAG	8
9	LIB	11.01	SAG	06.03	PIS	04.38	GEM	20.59	VIR	LIB	11.51	00.31	9
10	22.09	SAG	21.19	AQU	17.56	TAU	GEM	LEO	VIR	21.19	SAG	CAP	10
11	SCO	13.50	CAP	08.31	ARI	11.40	03.13	LEO	04.33	SCO	16.59	03.11	11
12	SCO	CAP	23.29	PIS	22.25	GEM	CAN	10.00	LIB	SCO	CAP	AQU	12
13	02.40	14.14	AQU	10.55	TAU	20.50	14.56	VIR	15.23	05.21	20.59	05.41	13
14	SAG	AQU	AQU	ARI	TAU	CAN	LEO	22.44	SCO	SAG	AQU	PIS	14
15	03.41	13.53	00.26	14.16	04.34	CAN	LEO	LIB	23.54	11.24	AQU	08.44	15
16	CAP	PIS	PIS	TAU	GEM	08.16	03.55	LIB	SAG	CAP	00.18	ARI	16
17	02.55	14.41	01.32	19.55	13.17	LEO	VIR	09.44	SAG	15.37	PIS	12.39	17
18	AQU	ARI	ARI	GEM	CAN	21.12	16.39	SCO	05.42	AQU	03.10	TAU	18
19	02.32	18.21	04.25	GEM	CAN	VIR	LIB	17.44	CAP	1810	ARI	17.47	19
20	PIS	TAU	TAU	04.50	00.45	VIR	LIB	SAG	08.43	PIS	06.03	GEM	20
21	04.26	TAU	10.32	CAN	LEO	09.32	03.04	22.07	AQU	19.35	TAU	GEM	21
22	ARI	01.51	GEM	16.43	13.38	LIB	SCO	CAP	09.36	ARI	09.59	00.50	22
23	09.51	GEM	20.22	LEO	VIR	18.51	09.42	23.25	PIS	21.07	GEM	CAN	23
24	TAU	12.49	CAN	LEO	VIR	SCO	SAG	AQU	09.40	TAU	16.20	10.26	24
25	18.50	CAN	CAN	05.31	01.18	SCO	12.28	23.02	ARI	TAU	CAN	LEO	25
26	GEM	CAN	08.48	VIR	LIB	00.05	CAP	PIS	10.42	00.24	CAN	22.29	26
27	GEM	01.34	LEO	16.34	09.34	SAG	12.41	22.49	TAU	GEM	02.01	VIR	27
28	06.22	LEO	21.30	LIB	SCO	02.00	AQU	ARI	14.32	07.03	LEO	VIR	28
29	CAN		VIR	LIB	14.11	CAP	12.13	ARI	GEM	CAN	14.25	11.26	29
30	19.05		VIR	00.27	SAG	02.18	PIS	00.37	22.19	17.30	VIR	LIB	30
31		LEO		08.21		16.20		12.56	TAU		LEO		22.42	31

1962

SUN
mth dy time –> sign

JAN 1 00.00 –> CAP
JAN 20 12.58 –> AQU
FEB 19 03.15 –> PIS
MAR 21 02.29 –> ARI
APR 20 13.51 –> TAU
MAY 21 13.16 –> GEM
JUN 21 21.24 –> CAN
JUL 23 08.18 –> LEO
AUG 23 15.13 –> VIR
SEP 23 12.35 –> LIB
OCT 23 21.40 –> SCO
NOV 22 19.02 –> SAG
DEC 22 08.16 –> CAP

MERCURY
mth dy time –> sign

JAN 1 00.00 –> CAP
JAN 7 15.08 –> AQU
MAR 15 11.43 –> PIS
APR 3 02.32 –> ARI
APR 18 04.10 –> TAU
MAY 3 06.05 –> GEM
JUL 11 07.36 –> CAN
JUL 26 18.50 –> LEO
AUG 10 19.29 –> VIR
AUG 29 15.48 –> LIB
NOV 5 02.20 –> SCO
NOV 23 17.31 –> SAG
DEC 12 20.51 –> CAP

VENUS
mth dy time –> sign

JAN 1 00.00 –> CAP
JAN 21 20.31 –> AQU
FEB 14 18.09 –> PIS
MAR 10 18.28 –> ARI
APR 3 23.05 –> TAU
APR 28 09.23 –> GEM
MAY 23 02.46 –> CAN
JUN 17 05.31 –> LEO
JUL 12 22.32 –> VIR
AUG 8 17.14 –> LIB
SEP 7 00.11 –> SCO

MARS
mth dy time –> sign

JAN 1 00.00 –> CAP
FEB 1 23.07 –> AQU
MAR 12 07.59 –> PIS
APR 19 16.58 –> ARI
MAY 28 23.47 –> TAU
JUL 9 03.50 –> GEM
AUG 22 11.37 –> CAN
OCT 11 23.54 –> LEO

SATURN
mth dy time –> sign

JAN 1 00.00 –> CAP
JAN 3 19.01 –> AQU

JUPITER
mth dy time –> sign

JAN 1 00.00 –> AQU
MAR 25 22.07 –> PIS

MOON   MOON

dy	jan	feb	mar	apr	may	jun	jul	aug	sep	oct	nov	dec	dy
1	SCO	21.09	06.38	20.42	06.12	17.40	06.19	LEO	03.01	SCO	SAG	14.26	1
2	SCO	CAP	CAP	PIS	ARI	GEM	CAN	07.57	LIB	SCO	01.17	AQU	2
3	06.23	22.57	09.52	20.41	06.49	21.56	13.55	VIR	15.46	09.40	CAP	19.53	3
4	SAG	AQU	AQU	ARI	TAU	CAN	LEO	20.17	SCO	SAG	09.02	PIS	4
5	10.24	22.53	10.16	20.25	08.16	CAN	LEO	LIB	SCO	19.35	AQU	23.17	5
6	CAP	PIS	PIS	TAU	GEM	05.23	00.22	LIB	03.26	CAP	13.52	ARI	6
7	12.00	22.50	09.32	22.00	12.28	LEO	VIR	08.56	SAG	CAP	PIS	ARI	7
8	AQU	ARI	ARI	GEM	CAN	16.12	12.48	SCO	12.20	02.21	15.45	00.59	8
9	12.53	ARI	09.40	GEM	20.35	VIR	LIB	19.48	CAP	AQU	ARI	TAU	9
10	PIS	00.35	TAU	03.12	LEO	VIR	LIB	SAG	17.26	05.29	15.45	02.07	10
11	14.34	TAU	12.35	CAN	LEO	04.51	01.05	SAG	AQU	PIS	TAU	GEM	11
12	ARI	05.18	GEM	12.36	08.11	LIB	SCO	03.17	19.02	05.40	15.43	04.21	12
13	18.01	GEM	19.25	LEO	VIR	16.45	11.00	CAP	PIS	ARI	GEM	CAN	13
14	TAU	13.20	CAN	LEO	21.03	SCO	SAG	07.07	ARI	04.43	17.49	09.20	14
15	23.42	CAN	CAN	00.57	LIB	SCO	17.32	AQU	ARI	TAU	CAN	LEO	15
16	GEM	CAN	05.56	VIR	LIB	02.03	CAP	08.17	18.01	04.50	23.40	17.59	16
17	GEM	00.04	LEO	13.54	08.43	SAG	21.07	PIS	TAU	GEM	LEO	VIR	17
18	07.39	LEO	18.33	LIB	SCO	08.30	AQU	08.25	19.29	08.05	LEO	VIR	18
19	CAN	12.26	VIR	LIB	18.02	CAP	23.00	ARI	GEM	CAN	09.33	05.41	19
20	17.50	VIR	VIR	01.37	SAG	12.49	PIS	09.20	GEM	15.30	VIR	LIB	20
21	LEO	VIR	07.28	SCO	SAG	AQU	PIS	TAU	00.26	LEO	21.58	18.18	21
22	LEO	01.21	LIB	11.27	01.08	15.59	00.34	12.28	CAN	LEO	LIB	SCO	22
23	05.53	LIB	19.28	SAG	CAP	PIS	ARI	GEM	09.07	02.31	LIB	SCO	23
24	VIR	13.36	SCO	19.20	06.31	18.43	02.57	18.34	LEO	VIR	10.33	05.32	24
25	18.52	SCO	SCO	CAP	AQU	ARI	TAU	CAN	20.31	15.13	SCO	SAG	25
26	LIB	23.46	05.48	CAP	10.29	21.34	06.57	CAN	VIR	LIB	21.43	14.19	26
27	LIB	SAG	SAG	01.08	PIS	TAU	GEM	03.30	VIR	LIB	SAG	CAP	27
28	06.54	SAG	13.46	AQU	13.15	TAU	13.00	LEO	09.08	03.48	SAG	20.42	28
29	SCO		CAP	04.40	ARI	01.09	CAN	14.36	LIB	SCO	07.00	AQU	29
30	15.59		18.43	PIS	15.17	GEM	21.21	VIR	21.49	15.19	CAP	AQU	30
31	SAG		AQU		TAU		LEO	VIR		SAG		01.20	31

SUN

mth dy time –> sign

JAN 1   00.00 –> CAP
JAN 20 18.54 –> AQU
FEB 19 09.09 –> PIS
MAR 21 08.20 –> ARI
APR 20 19.36 –> TAU
MAY 21 18.58 –> GEM
JUN 22 03.04 –> CAN
JUL 23 13.59 –> LEO
AUG 23 20.58 –> VIR
SEP 23 18.23 –> LIB
OCT 24 03.29 –> SCO
NOV 23 00.50 –> SAG
DEC 22 14.02 –> CAP

SATURN

mth dy time –> sign

JAN 1   00.00 –> AQU

MERCURY

mth dy time –> sign

JAN 1   00.00 –> CAP
JAN 2   01.11 –> AQU
JAN 20 04.59 –> CAP
FEB 15 10.09 –> AQU
MAR 9   05.26 –> PIS
MAR 26 03.52 –> ARI
APR 9   22.04 –> TAU
MAY 3   04.17 –> GEM
MAY 10 20.39 –> TAU
JUN 14 23.20 –> GEM
JUL 4   03.00 –> CAN
JUL 18 06.19 –> LEO
AUG 3   09.20 –> VIR
AUG 26 20.33 –> LIB
SEP 16 20.29 –> VIR
OCT 10 16.44 –> LIB
OCT 28 19.54 –> SCO
NOV 16 11.07 –> SAG
DEC 6   05.17 –> CAP

VENUS

mth dy time –> sign

JAN 1   00.00 –> SCO
JAN 6   17.35 –> SAG
FEB 5   20.35 –> CAP
MAR 4   11.42 –> AQU
MAR 30 01.00 –> PIS
APR 24 03.39 –> ARI
MAY 19 01.21 –> TAU
JUN 12 19.57 –> GEM
JUL 7   11.18 –> CAN
JUL 31 22.39 –> LEO
AUG 25 05.49 –> VIR
SEP 18 09.43 –> LIB
OCT 12 11.50 –> SCO
NOV 5   13.25 –> SAG
NOV 29 15.21 –> CAP
DEC 23 18.53 –> AQU

MARS

mth dy time –> sign

JAN 1   00.00 –> LEO
JUN 3   06.30 –> VIR
JUL 27 04.15 –> LIB
SEP 12 09.11 –> SCO
OCT 25 17.32 –> SAG
DEC 5   09.03 –> CAP

JUPITER

mth dy time –> sign

JAN 1   00.00 –> PIS
APR 4   03.19 –> ARI

MOON

dy	jan	feb	mar	apr	may	jun	jul	aug	sep	oct	nov	dec	dy
1	PIS	TAU	21.39	CAN	LEO	00.09	SCO	SAG	AQU	PIS	00.42>TAU	GEM	1
2	04.48	16.03	GEM	14.45	06.13	LIB	SCO	03.12	AQU	1348	23.48	10.45	2
3	ARI	GEM	GEM	LEO	VIR	12.38	08.11	CAP	01.37	ARI	GEM	CAN	3
4	07.33	20.40	02.08	LEO	17.42	SCO	SAG	11.25	PIS	13.50	GEM	12.20	4
5	TAU	CAN	CAN	00.20	LIB	SCO	19.03	AQU	03.52	TAU	00.08	LEO	5
6	10.14	CAN	09.15	VIR	LIB	01.01	CAP	16.46	ARI	13.58	CAN	17.26	6
7	GEM	03.06	LEO	11.49	06.16	SAG	CAP	PIS	05.02	GEM	03.24	VIR	7
8	13.41	LEO	18.34	LIB	SCO	12.07	03.36	20.07	TAU	16.01	LEO	VIR	8
9	CAN	11.36	VIR	LIB	18.42	CAP	AQU	ARI	06.46	CAN	10.14	02.21	9
10	19.01	VIR	VIR	00.14	SAG	21.22	09.53	22.37	GEM	20.54	VIR	LIB	10
11	LEO	22.18	05.35	SCO	SAG	AQU	PIS	TAU	10.08	LEO	20.07	14.04	11
12	LEO	LIB	LIB	12.48	06.13	AQU	14.16	TAU	CAN	LEO	LIB	SCO	12
13	03.07	LIB	17.51	SAG	CAP	04.20	ARI	01.16	15.30	04.34	LIB	SCO	13
14	VIR	10.38	SCO	SAG	15.51	PIS	17.15	GEM	LEO	VIR	07.57	02.53	14
15	14.05	SCO	SCO	00.27	AQU	08.46	TAU	04.39	22.47	14.24	SCO	SAG	15
16	LIB	22.57	06.27	CAP	22.32	ARI	19.27	CAN	VIR	LIB	20.40	15.21	16
17	LIB	SAG	SAG	09.34	PIS	10.54	GEM	09.17	VIR	LIB	SAG	CAP	17
18	02.35	SAG	17.35	AQU	PIS	TAU	21.45	LEO	08.00	01.52	SAG	CAP	18
19	SCO	09.00	CAP	14.53	01.47	11.44	CAN	15.40	LIB	SCO	09.23	02.29	19
20	14.20	CAP	CAP	PIS	ARI	GEM	CAN	VIR	19.10	14.32	CAP	AQU	20
21	SAG	15.23	01.21	16.30	02.21	12.46	01.15	VIR	SCO	SAG	20.51	11.28	21
22	23.23	AQU	AQU	ARI	TAU	CAN	LEO	00.25	SCO	SAG	AQU	PIS	22
23	CAP	18.17	05.04	15.51	01.53	15.44	07.06	LIB	07.50	03.21	AQU	17.41	23
24	CAP	PIS	PIS	TAU	GEM	LEO	VIR	11.39	SAG	CAP	05.32	ARI	24
25	05.14	19.05	05.37	15.06	02.29	21.56	16.02	SCO	20.15	14.20	PIS	20.57	25
26	AQU	ARI	ARI	GEM	CAN	VIR	LIB	SCO	CAP	AQU	10.25	TAU	26
27	08.35	19.38	04.57	16.27	05.58	VIR	LIB	00.15	CAP	21.36	ARI	21.58	27
28	PIS	TAU	TAU	CAN	LEO	07.41	03.38	SAG	06.03	PIS	11.49	GEM	28
29	10.44		05.13	21.25	13.22	LIB	SCO	11.57	AQU	PIS	TAU	22.07	29
30	ARI		GEM	LEO	VIR	19.48	16.08	CAP	11.46	00.40	11.14	CAN	30
31	12.55		08.14		VIR		SAG	20.37		ARI		23.09	31

1964

SUN
mth dy time –> sign

JAN 1	00.00 –> CAP
JAN 21	00.41 –> AQU
FEB 19	14.57 –> PIS
MAR 20	14.10 –> ARI
APR 20	01.27 –> TAU
MAY 21	00.50 –> GEM
JUN 21	08.57 –> CAN
JUL 22	19.53 –> LEO
AUG 23	02.51 –> VIR
SEP 23	00.17 –> LIB
OCT 23	09.21 –> SCO
NOV 22	06.39 –> SAG
DEC 21	19.50 –> CAP

MERCURY
mth dy time –> sign

JAN 1	00.00 –> CAP
FEB 10	21.30 –> AQU
FEB 29	22.50 –> PIS
MAR 16	23.55 –> ARI
APR 2	00.58 –> TAU
JUN 9	15.45 –> GEM
JUN 24	17.17 –> CAN
JUL 9	00.39 –> LEO
JUL 27	11.35 –> VIR
OCT 3	00.12 –> LIB
OCT 20	07.11 –> SCO
NOV 8	11.02 –> SAG
NOV 30	19.30 –> CAP
DEC 16	14.31 –> SAG

VENUS
mth dy time –> sign

JAN 1	00.00 –> AQU
JAN 17	02.53 –> PIS
FEB 10	21.10 –> ARI
MAR 7	12.38 –> TAU
APR 4	03.03 –> GEM
MAY 9	03.15 –> CAN
JUN 17	18.17 –> GEM
AUG 5	08.52 –> CAN
SEP 8	04.53 –> LEO
OCT 5	18.10 –> VIR
OCT 31	08.54 –> LIB
NOV 25	01.25 –> SCO
DEC 19	07.02 –> SAG

MARS
mth dy time –> sign

JAN 1	00.00 –> CAP
JAN 13	06.14 –> AQU
FEB 20	07.33 –> PIS
MAR 29	11.24 –> ARI
MAY 7	14.41 –> TAU
JUN 17	11.43 –> GEM
JUL 30	18.23 –> CAN
SEP 15	05.22 –> LEO
NOV 6	03.20 –> VIR

SATURN
mth dy time –> sign

JAN 1	00.00 –> AQU
MAR 24	04.17 –> PIS
SEP 16	21.04 –> AQU
DEC 16	05.39 –> PIS

JUPITER
mth dy time –> sign

JAN 1	00.00 –> ARI
APR 12	06.53 –> TAU

MOON   MOON

dy	jan	feb	mar	apr	may	jun	jul	aug	sep	oct	nov	dec	dy
1	LEO	19.25	LIB	09.41	05.42	AQU	PIS	TAU	00.13	LEO	00.24	SCO	1
2	LEO	LIB	13.54	SAG	CAP	11.01	00.52	15.28	CAN	12.42	LIB	SCO	2
3	02.48	LIB	SCO	22.36	18.06	PIS	ARI	GEM	02.36	VIR	08.25	01.24	3
4	VIR	05.12	SCO	CAP	AQU	18.03	05.42	17.13	LEO	17.44	SCO	SAG	4
5	10.10	SCO	01.47	CAP	AQU	ARI	TAU	CAN	05.12	LIB	18.43	13.53	5
6	LIB	17.35	SAG	10.24	03.43	21.20	07.43	18.11	VIR	LIB	SAG	CAP	6
7	21.04	SAG	14.35	AQU	PIS	TAU	GEM	LEO	09.19	00.57	SAG	CAP	7
8	SCO	SAG	CAP	18.47	09.15	21.50	07.57	19.50	LIB	SCO	07.06	02.57	8
9	SCO	06.11	CAP	PIS	ARI	GEM	CAN	VIR	16.20	11.02	CAP	AQU	9
10	09.49	CAP	01.35	23.08	11.09	21.16	08.01	23.51	SCO	SAG	20.08	15.00	10
11	SAG	16.39	AQU	ARI	TAU	CAN	LEO	LIB	SCO	23.32	AQU	PIS	11
12	22.14	AQU	ARI	11.01	21.35	09.44	LIB	02.47	CAP	AQU	PIS	12
13	CAP	AQU	PIS	00.37	GEM	LEO	VIR	07.31	SAG	CAP	07.28	00.12	13
14	CAP	00.09	13.15	TAU	10.53	LEO	14.41	SCO	15.30	12.15	PIS	ARI	14
15	08.48	PIS	ARI	01.06	CAN	00.27	LIB	18.44	CAP	AQU	15.10	05.32	15
16	AQU	05.10	15.30	GEM	12.31	VIR	23.32	SAG	CAP	22.33	ARI	TAU	16
17	17.04	ARI	TAU	02.23	LEO	06.54	SCO	SAG	03.47	PIS	18.57	07.21	17
18	PIS	08.45	17.26	CAN	17.02	LIB	SCO	07.38	AQU	PIS	TAU	GEM	18
19	23.10	TAU	GEM	05.40	VIR	16.49	11.28	CAP	13.22	05.05	19.58	07.02	19
20	ARI	11.48	20.11	LEO	VIR	SCO	SAG	19.39	PIS	ARI	GEM	CAN	20
21	ARI	GEM	CAN	11.17	00.41	SCO	SAG	AQU	19.44	08.24	20.04	06.31	21
22	03.23	14.49	CAN	VIR	LIB	05.03	00.27	AQU	ARI	TAU	CAN	LEO	22
23	TAU	CAN	00.15	19.08	10.58	SAG	CAP	05.13	23.46	10.03	20.59	07.41	23
24	06.05	18.11	LEO	LIB	SCO	18.02	12.30	PIS	TAU	GEM	LEO	VIR	24
25	GEM	LEO	05.42	LIB	23.03	CAP	AQU	12.15	TAU	11.37	LEO	12.04	25
26	07.51	22.30	VIR	05.01	SAG	CAP	22.36	ARI	02.46	CAN	00.02	LIB	26
27	CAN	VIR	12.48	SCO	SAG	06.22	PIS	17.24	GEM	14.14	VIR	20.11	27
28	09.45	VIR	LIB	16.46	12.00	AQU	PIS	TAU	05.39	LEO	05.54	SCO	28
29	LEO	04.46	LIB	22.03	SAG	CAP	16.56	06.25	21.16	CAN	18.25	LIB	SCO	29
30	13.09		SCO	SAG	CAP	PIS	ARI	GEM	08.52	VIR	14.31	07.20	30
31	VIR		SCO		00.32		12.00	GEM		VIR		SAG	31

240

SUN
mth dy time –> sign

JAN 1	00.00 –> CAP
JAN 20	06.29 –> AQU
FEB 18	20.48 –> PIS
MAR 20	20.05 –> ARI
APR 20	07.26 –> TAU
MAY 21	06.50 –> GEM
JUN 21	14.56 –> CAN
JUL 23	01.48 –> LEO
AUG 23	08.43 –> VIR
SEP 23	06.06 –> LIB
OCT 23	15.10 –> SCO
NOV 22	12.30 –> SAG
DEC 22	01.40 –> CAP

MERCURY
mth dy time –> sign

JAN 1	00.00 –> SAG
JAN 13	03.12 –> CAP
FEB 3	09.02 –> AQU
FEB 21	05.40 –> PIS
MAR 9	02.19 –> ARI
MAY 15	13.19 –> TAU
JUN 2	03.47 –> GEM
JUN 16	02.04 –> CAN
JUL 1	15.55 –> LEO
JUL 31	08.08 –> VIR
AUG 3	04.57 –> LEO
SEP 8	17.14 –> VIR
SEP 25	05.49 –> LIB
OCT 12	21.15 –> SCO
NOV 2	06.04 –> SAG

VENUS
mth dy time –> sign

JAN 1	00.00 –> SAG
JAN 12	08.01 –> CAP
FEB 5	07.42 –> AQU
MAR 1	07.55 –> PIS
MAR 25	09.54 –> ARi
APR 18	14.31 –> TAU
MAY 12	22.08 –> GEM
JUN 6	08.39 –> CAN
JUN 30	21.59 –> LEO
JUL 25	14.52 –> VIR
AUG 19	13.06 –> LIB
SEP 13	19.50 –> SCO
OCT 9	16.46 –> SAG
NOV 5	19.36 –> CAP
DEC 7	04.37 –> AQU

MARS
mth dy time –> sign

JAN 1	00.00 –> VIR
JUN 29	01.12 –> LIB
AUG 20	12.16 –> SCO
OCT 4	06.46 –> SAG
NOV 14	07.19 –> CAP
DEC 23	05.36 –> AQU

JUPITER
mth dy time –> sign

JAN 1	00.00 –> TAU
APR 22	14.33 –> GEM
SEP 21	04.39 –> CAN
NOV 17	03.08 –> GEM

SATURN
mth dy time –> sign

JAN 1	00.00 –> PIS

MOON

dy	jan	feb	mar	apr	may	jun	jul	aug	sep	oct	nov	dec	dy
1	20.06 AQU	AQU	02.19	TAU	07.05	LEO	03.54	SCO	18.29	AQU	PIS	1
2	CAP	AQU	09.38 ARI	20.26	CAN	17.11	LIB	00.00	CAP	AQU	23.22	2
3	CAP	02.56 PIS	08.29	GEM	07.47	VIR	08.20	SAG	CAP	03.23	ARI	3
4	09.04	PIS	18.45	TAU	22.39	LEO	19.43	SCO	10.51	06.48	PIS	ARI	4
5	AQU	12.43	ARI	12.55	CAN	09.33	LIB	16.49	CAP	AQU	14.21	08.11	5
6	21.06	ARI	ARI	GEM	CAN	VIR	LIB	SAG	23.34	19.14	ARI	TAU	6
7	PIS	20.24	01.49	16.24	00.50	13.29	01.38	SAG	AQU	PIS	22.29	13.27	7
8	PIS	TAU	TAU	CAN	LEO	LIB	SCO	04.22	AQU	PIS	TAU	GEM	8
9	07.08	TAU	07.14	19.23	03.47	20.04	10.53	CAP	11.56	05.54	TAU	15.57	9
10	ARI	01.36	GEM	LEO	VIR	SCO	SAG	17.09	PIS	ARI	03.54	CAN	10
11	14.10	GEM	11.03	22.14	08.04	SCO	22.29	AQU	22.50	14.16	GEM	17.08	11
12	TAU	04.14	CAN	VIR	LIB	05.10	CAP	AQU	ARI	TAU	07.29	LEO	12
13	17.48	CAN	13.23	VIR	14.10	SAG	CAP	05.37	ARI	20.40	CAN	18.35	13
14	GEM	04.54	LEO	01.38	SCO	16.20	11.08	PIS	07.56	GEM	10.13	VIR	14
15	18.35	LEO	14.55	LIB	22.32	CAP	AQU	16.57	TAU	GEM	LEO	21.33	15
16	CAN	05.05	VIR	06.42	SAG	CAP	23.45	ARI	15.06	01.27	12.54	LIB	16
17	17.57	VIR	17.04	SCO	SAG	04.51	PIS	ARI	GEM	CAN	VIR	LIB	17
18	LEO	06.45	LIB	14.31	09.20	AQU	PIS	02.27	20.01	04.51	16.10	02.40	18
19	17.55	LIB	21.32	SAG	CAP	17.29	11.13	TAU	CAN	LEO	LIB	SCO	19
20	VIR	11.45	SCO	SAG	21.50	PIS	ARI	09.20	22.35	07.13	20.37	10.01	20
21	20.28	SCO	SCO	01.24	AQU	PIS	20.14	GEM	LEO	VIR	SCO	SAG	21
22	LIB	20.57	05.37	CAP	AQU	04.29	TAU	13.04	23.30	09.21	SCO	19.27	22
23	LIB	SAG	SAG	14.04	10.14	ARI	TAU	CAN	VIR	LIB	02.56	CAP	23
24	03.01	SAG	17.07	AQU	PIS	12.16	01.48	14.01	VIR	12.31	SAG	CAP	24
25	SCO	09.17	CAP	AQU	20.19	TAU	GEM	LEO	00.15	SCO	11.45	06.44	25
26	13.32	CAP	CAP	02.02	ARI	16.18	03.53	13.36	LIB	18.09	CAP	AQU	26
27	SAG	22.14	05.59	PIS	ARI	GEM	CAN	VIR	02.47	SAG	23.03	19.17	27
28	SAG	AQU	AQU	11.12	02.48	17.20	03.37	13.52	SCO	SAG	AQU	PIS	28
29	02.21		17.32	ARI	TAU	CAN	LEO	LIB	08.42	03.05	AQU	PIS	29
30	CAP		PIS	17.03	05.58	16.59	02.55	16.54	SAG	CAP	11.40	07.40	30
31	15.17		PIS		GEM		VIR	SCO		14.49		ARI	31

1966

SUN
mth dy time –> sign

JAN 1 00.00 –> CAP
JAN 20 12.20 –> AQU
FEB 19 02.38 –> PIS
MAR 21 01.53 –> ARI
APR 20 13.12 –> TAU
MAY 21 12.32 –> GEM
JUN 21 20.33 –> CAN
JUL 23 07.23 –> LEO
AUG 23 14.18 –> VIR
SEP 23 11.43 –> LIB
OCT 23 20.51 –> SCO
NOV 22 18.14 –> SAG
DEC 22 07.28 –> CAP

MERCURY
mth dy time –> sign

JAN 1 00.00 –> SAG
JAN 7 18.26 –> CAP
JAN 27 04.10 –> AQU
FEB 13 10.18 –> PIS
MAR 3 02.58 –> ARI
MAR 22 02.33 –> PIS
APR 17 21.32 –> ARI
MAY 9 14.48 –> TAU
MAY 24 17.59 –> GEM
JUN 7 19.11 –> CAN
JUN 26 19.05 –> LEO
SEP 1 10.35 –> VIR
SEP 17 08.19 –> LIB
OCT 5 22.03 –> SCO
OCT 30 07.38 –> SAG
NOV 13 03.25 –> SCO
DEC 11 15.27 –> SAG

VENUS
mth dy time –> sign

JAN 1 00.00 –> AQU
FEB 6 12.46 –> CAP
FEB 25 10.55 –> AQU
APR 6 15.53 –> PIS
MAY 5 04.33 –> ARI
MAY 31 18.00 –> TAU
JUN 26 11.40 –> GEM
JUL 21 17.12 –> CAN
AUG 15 12.47 –> LEO
SEP 8 23.40 –> VIR
OCT 3 03.44 –> LIB
OCT 27 03.28 –> SCO
NOV 20 01.07 –> SAG
DEC 13 22.09 –> CAP

MARS
mth dy time –> sign

JAN 1 00.00 –> AQU
JAN 30 07.02 –> PIS
MAR 9 12.55 –> ARI
APR 17 20.35 –> TAU
MAY 28 22.07 –> GEM
JUL 11 03.15 –> CAN
AUG 25 15.52 –> LEO
OCT 12 18.37 –> VIR
DEC 4 00.55 –> LIB

JUPITER
mth dy time –> sign

JAN 1 00.00 –> GEM
MAY 5 14.52 –> CAN
SEP 27 13.20 –> LEO

SATURN
mth dy time –> sign

JAN 1 00.00 –> PIS

MOON

dy	jan	feb	mar	apr	may	jun	jul	aug	sep	oct	nov	dec	dy
1	17.46	GEM	22.48	LEO	19.31	SCO	23.51	AQU	22.27	16.47	GEM	CAN	1
2	TAU	13.41	CAN	10.31	LIB	09.38	CAP	AQU	ARI	TAU	17.43	05.02	2
3	TAU	CAN	CAN	VIR	21.23	SAG	CAP	03.36	ARI	TAU	CAN	LEO	3
4	00.06	14.14	00.57	10.40	SCO	16.10	09.14	PIS	10.59	03.43	23.36	08.48	4
5	GEM	LEO	LEO	LIB	SCO	CAP	AQU	16.15	TAU	GEM	LEO	VIR	5
6	02.40	13.11	00.36>VIR	11.30	00.52	CAP	20.39	ARI	21.52	12.12	LEO	11.43	6
7	CAN	VIR	23.48	SCO	SAG	01.21	PIS	ARI	GEM	CAN	03.10	LIB	7
8	02.50	12.50	LIB	14.54	07.12	AQU	PUS	04.38	GEM	17.25	VIR	14.18	8
9	LEO	LIB	LIB	SAG	CAP	12.57	09.16	05.26	LEO	04.54	SCO	9
10	02.34	15.15	00.47	22.02	16.52	PIS	ARI	14.38	CAN	19.27	LIB	17.13	10
11	VIR	SCO	SCO	CAP	AQU	PIS	21.03	GEM	09.01	VIR	05.53	SAG	11
12	03.53	21.33	05.18	CAP	AQU	01.26	TAU	20.41	LEO	19.29	SCO	21.30	12
13	LIB	SAG	SAG	08.42	04.55	ARI	TAU	CAN	09.25	LIB	07.37	CAP	13
14	08.08	SAG	13.55	AQU	PIS	12.29	05.51	22.50	VIR	19.21	SAG	CAP	14
15	SCO	07.26	CAP	21.13	17.15	TAU	GEM	LEO	08.33	SCO	11.37	04.19	15
16	15.39	CAP	CAP	PIS	ARI	20.26	10.44	22.35	LIB	20.59	CAP	AQU	16
17	SAG	19.25	01.35	PIS	ARI	GEM	CAN	VIR	08.34	SAG	19.03	14.17	17
18	SAG	AQU	AQU	09.27	03.49	GEM	12.27	22.05	SCO	SAG	AQU	PIS	18
19	01.45	AQU	14.18	ARI	TAU	01.05	LEO	LIB	11.21	01.55	AQU	PIS	19
20	CAP	08.05	PIS	20.00	11.40	CAN	12.47	23.24	SAG	CAP	05.53	02.39	20
21	13.26	PIS	PIS	TAU	GEM	03.29	VIR	SCO	17.53	10.41	PIS	ARI	21
22	AQU	20.30	02.33	TAU	17.00	LEO	13.38	SCO	CAP	AQU	18.31	15.07	22
23	33333333AQU	ARI	ARI	04.27	CAN	05.08	LIB	03.51	CAP	22.20	ARI	TAU	23
24	01.58	ARI	13.32	GEM	20.37	VIR	16.32	SAG	03.48	PIS	ARI	TAU	24
25	PIS	07.53	TAU	10.48	LEO	07.23	SCO	11.37	AQU	PIS	06.37	01.13	25
26	14.33	TAU	22.41	CAN	23.22	LIB	22.04	CAP	15.48	11.03	TAU	GEM	26
27	ARI	17.03	GEM	15.09	VIR	11.04	SAG	21.56	PIS	ARI	16.31	07.58	27
28	ARI	GEM	GEM	LEO	VIR	SCO	SAG	AQU	PIS	23.05	GEM	CAN	28
29	01.43		05.23	17.50	02.00	16.31	06.04	AQU	04.29	TAU	23.50	11.57	29
30	TAU		CAN	VIR	LIB	SAG	CAP	09.48	ARI	TAU	CAN	LEO	30
31	09.43		09.12		05.11		16.02	PIS		09.28		14.33	31

SUN

mth dy	time -> sign
JAN 1	00.00 -> CAP
JAN 20	18.08 -> AQU
FEB 19	08.24 -> PIS
MAR 21	07.37 -> ARI
APR 20	18.55 -> TAU
MAY 21	18.18 -> GEM
JUN 22	02.23 -> CAN
JUL 23	13.16 -> LEO
AUG 23	20.12 -> VIR
SEP 23	17.38 -> LIB
OCT 24	02.44 -> SCO
NOV 23	00.05 -> SAG
DEC 22	13.17 -> CAP

MERCURY

mth dy	time -> sign
JAN 1	00.52 -> CAP
JAN 19	17.06 -> AQU
FEB 6	00.37 -> PIS
APR 14	14.38 -> ARI
MAY 1	23.26 -> TAU
MAY 16	03.27 -> GEM
MAY 31	18.02 -> CAN
AUG 8	22.09 -> LEO
AUG 24	06.17 -> VIR
SEP 9	16.53 -> LIB
SEP 30	01.46 -> SCO
DEC 5	13.41 -> SAG
DEC 24	20.33 -> CAP

VENUS

mth dy	time -> sign
JAN 1	00.00 -> CAP
JAN 6	19.36 -> AQU
JAN 30	18.54 -> PIS
FEB 23	22.30 -> ARI
MAR 20	09.56 -> TAU
APR 14	09.55 -> GEM
MAY 10	06.05 -> CAN
JUN 6	16.48 -> LEO
JUL 8	22.11 -> VIR
SEP 9	11.57 -> LEO
OCT 1	18.08 -> VIR
NOV 9	16.32 -> LIB
DEC 7	08.48 -> SCO

MARS

mth dy	time -> sign
JAN 1	00.00 -> LIB
FEB 12	12.20 -> SCO
MAR 31	06.10 -> LIB
JUL 19	22.56 -> SCO
SEP 10	01.44 -> SAG
OCT 23	02.15 -> CAP
DEC 1	20.12 -> AQU

JUPITER

mth dy	time -> sign
JAN 1	00.00 -> LEO
JAN 16	03.47 -> CAN
MAY 23	08.21 -> LEO
OCT 19	10.51 -> VIR

SATURN

mth dy	time -> sign
JAN 1	00.00 -> PIS
MAR 3	21.31 -> ARI

MOON

dy	jan	feb	mar	apr	may	jun	jul	aug	sep	oct	nov	dec	dy
1	VIR	01.44	SCO	00.11	AQU	20.07	16.43	GEM	14.08	03.38	15.26	02.10	1
2	17.04	SCO	11.53	CAP	AQU	ARI	TAU	22.32	LEO	VIR	SCO	SAG	2
3	LIB	05.55	SAG	07.49	00.47	ARI	TAU	CAN	17.07	04.34	14.51	02.25	3
4	20.16	SAG	17.35	AQU	PIS	09.04	04.39	CAN	VIR	LIB	SAG	CAP	4
5	SCO	12.10	CAP	18.29	13.10	TAU	GEM	04.26	18.03	04.14	15.44	04.57	5
6	SCO	CAP	CAP	PIS	ARI	20.52	13.47	LEO	LIB	SCO	CAP	AQU	6
7	00.28	20.17	02.03	PIS	ARI	GEM	CAN	07.36	18.44	04.32	19.45	11.19	7
8	SAG	AQU	AQU	06.57	02.09	GEM	19.58	VIR	SCO	SAG	AQU	PIS	8
9	05.53	AQU	12.41	ARI	TAU	06.18	LEO	09.34	20.40	07.04	AQU	21.43	9
10	CAP	06.19	PIS	19.56	14.08	CAN	LEO	LIB	SAG	CAP	03.42	ARI	10
11	13.05	PIS	PIS	TAU	GEM	13.19	00.07	11.44	SAG	12.45	PIS	ARI	11
12	AQU	18.17	00.53	08.15	GEM	LEO	VIR	SCO	00.43	AQU	14.58	10.32	12
13	22.45	ARI	ARI	GEM	00.11	18.24	03.20	14.52	CAP	21.38	ARI	TAU	13
14	PIS	ARI	13.54	GEM	CAN	VIR	LIB	SAG	07.08	PIS	ARI	23.18	14
15	PIS	07.19	TAU	18.37	07.49	21.58	06.17	19.18	AQU	PIS	03.52	GEM	15
16	10.48	TAU	TAU	CAN	LEO	LIB	SCO	CAP	15.53	08.58	TAU	GEM	16
17	ARI	19.16	02.19	CAN	12.52	LIB	09.22	CAP	PIS	ARI	16.40	10.23	17
18	23.39	GEM	GEM	01.54	VIR	00.25	SAG	01.17	PIS	21.41	GEM	CAN	18
19	TAU	GEM	12.10	LEO	15.31	SCO	12.59	AQU	02.46	TAU	GEM	19.21	19
20	TAU	03.48	CAN	05.42	LIB	02.20	CAP	09.18	ARI	TAU	04.13	LEO	20
21	10.38	CAN	18.04	VIR	16.30	SAG	17.59	PIS	15.20	10.38	CAN	LEO	21
22	GEM	08.04	LEO	06.41	SCO	04.46	AQU	19.47	TAU	GEM	13.47	02.21	22
23	17.51	LEO	20.08	LIB	17.06	CAP	AQU	ARI	TAU	22.27	LEO	VIR	23
24	CAN	09.04	VIR	06.19	SAG	09.11	01.28	ARI	04.21	CAN	20.46	07.27	24
25	21.20	VIR	19.50	SCO	18.58	AQU	PIS	08.21	GEM	CAN	VIR	LIB	25
26	LEO	08.44	LIB	06.27	CAP	16.49	12.00	TAU	15.45	07.40	VIR	10.36	26
27	22.36	LIB	19.10	SAG	23.44	PIS	ARI	21.08	CAN	LEO	00.48	SCO	27
28	VIR	09.09	SCO	08.54	AQU	PIS	ARI	GEM	23.41	13.19	LIB	12.09	28
29	23.33		20.08	CAP	AQU	03.52	00.40	GEM	LEO	VIR	02.13	SAG	29
30	LIB		SAG	14.57	08.18	ARI	TAU	07.34	LEO	15.31	SCO	13.11	30
31	LIB		SAG		PIS		13.00	CAN		LIB		CAP	31

1968

SUN
mth dy time -> sign

JAN 1	00.00	-> CAP
JAN 20	23.54	-> AQU
FEB 19	14.09	-> PIS
MAR 20	13.22	-> ARI
APR 20	00.41	-> TAU
MAY 21	00.06	-> GEM
JUN 21	08.13	-> CAN
JUL 22	19.08	-> LEO
AUG 23	02.03	-> VIR
SEP 22	23.26	-> LIB
OCT 23	08.30	-> SCO
NOV 22	05.49	-> SAG
DEC 21	19.00	-> CAP

MERCURY
mth dy time -> sign

JAN 1	00.00	-> CAP
JAN 12	07.19	-> AQU
FEB 1	12.58	-> PIS
FEB 11	18.54	-> AQU
MAR 17	14.46	-> PIS
APR 7	01.01	-> ARI
APR 22	16.18	-> TAU
MAY 6	22.56	-> GEM
MAY 29	22.44	-> CAN
JUN 13	22.32	-> GEM
JUL 13	01.30	-> CAN
JUL 31	06.11	-> LEO
AUG 15	00.54	-> VIR
SEP 1	16.59	-> LIB
SEP 28	14.41	-> SCO
OCT 7	22.45	-> LIB
NOV 8	11.00	-> SCO
NOV 27	12.47	-> SAG
DEC 16	14.11	-> CAP

VENUS
mth dy time -> sign

JAN 1	22.38	-> SAG
JAN 26	17.35	-> CAP
FEB 20	04.55	-> AQU
MAR 15	13.32	-> PIS
APR 8	21.49	-> ARI
MAY 3	06.57	-> TAU
MAY 27	17.02	-> GEM
JUN 21	03.21	-> CAN
JUL 15	12.59	-> LEO
AUG 8	21.49	-> VIR
SEP 2	06.39	-> LIB
SEP 26	16.46	-> SCO
OCT 21	05.17	-> SAG
NOV 14	21.48	-> CAP
DEC 9	22.40	-> AQU

MARS
mth dy time -> sign

JAN 1	00.00	-> AQU
JAN 9	09.50	-> PIS
FEB 17	03.17	-> ARI
MAR 27	23.43	-> TAU
MAY 8	14.15	-> GEM
JUN 21	05.03	-> CAN
AUG 5	17.07	-> LEO
SEP 21	18.39	-> VIR
NOV 9	06.10	-> LIB
DEC 29	22.08	-> SC0

JUPITER
mth dy time -> sign

JAN 1	00.00	-> VIR
FEB 27	03.34	-> LEO
JUN 15	14.44	-> VIR
NOV 15	22.43	-> LIB

SATURN
mth dy time -> sign

JAN 1	00.00	-> ARI

MOON

dy	jan	feb	mar	apr	may	jun	jul	aug	sep	oct	nov	dec	dy
1	15.24	PIS	ARI	TAU	GEM	LEO	VIR	02.11	13.22	AQU	16.51	08.58	1
2	AQU	14.39	ARI	06.40	01.50	LEO	16.10	SCO	CAP	AQU	ARI	TAU	2
3	20.35	ARI	10.27	GEM	CAN	03.52	LIB	05.11	16.19	03.21	ARI	21.06	3
4	PIS	ARI	TAU	19.13	12.54	VIR	20.20	SAG	AQU	PIS	03.01	GEM	4
5	PIS	02.15	23.17	CAN	LEO	09.49	SCO	06.57	20.27	10.35	TAU	GEM	5
6	05.45	TAU	GEM	CAN	20.58	LIB	22.05	CAP	PIS	ARI	14.48	09.43	6
7	ARI	15.09	GEM	05.28	VIR	12.30	SAG	08.37	PIS	20.07	GEM	CAN	7
8	18.02	GEM	11.21	LEO	VIR	SCO	22.24	AQU	02.49	TAU	GEM	22.02	8
9	TAU	GEM	CAN	12.04	01.21	12.42	CAP	11.45	ARI	TAU	03.26	LEO	9
10	TAU	02.34	20.27	VIR	LIB	SAG	23.03	PIS	12.06	07.43	CAN	LEO	10
11	06.54	CAN	LEO	15.01	02.30	12.05	AQU	17.53	TAU	GEM	15.45	08.59	11
12	GEM	10.50	LEO	LIB	SCO	CAP	AQU	ARI	23.54	20.23	LEO	VIR	12
13	17.54	LEO	01.51	15.32	01.53	12.46	02.03	ARI	GEM	CAN	LEO	17.08	13
14	CAN	16.02	VIR	SCO	SAG	AQU	PIS	03.36	GEM	CAN	01.55	LIB	14
15	CAN	VIR	04.23	15.23	01.30	16.42	08.51	TAU	12.28	08.08	VIR	21.31	15
16	02.09	19.21	LIB	SAG	CAP	PIS	ARI	15.51	CAN	LEO	08.26	SCO	16
17	LEO	LIB	05.33	16.23	03.22	PIS	19.30	GEM	23.25	16.58	LIB	22.27	17
18	08.11	22.00	SCO	CAP	AQU	00.50	TAU	GEM	LEO	VIR	11.06	SAG	18
19	VIR	SCO	06.54	19.57	08.53	ARI	TAU	04.15	LEO	22.05	SCO	21.32	19
20	12.47	SCO	SAG	AQU	PIS	12.25	08.13	CAN	07.15	LIB	11.04	CAP	20
21	LIB	00.48	09.34	AQU	18.14	TAU	GEM	14.40	VIR	LIB	SAG	20.59	21
22	16.28	SAG	CAP	02.45	ARI	TAU	20.31	LEO	12.00	00.05	10.20	AQU	22
23	SCO	04.12	14.16	PIS	ARI	01.22	CAN	22.21	LIB	SCO	CAP	23.01	23
24	19.23	CAP	AQU	12.32	06.15	GEM	CAN	VIR	14.39	00.32	11.02	PIS	24
25	SAG	08.37	21.15	ARI	TAU	13.43	06.55	VIR	SCO	SAG	AQU	PIS	25
26	21.57	AQU	PIS	ARI	19.12	CAN	LEO	03.45	16.30	01.13	14.52	05.02	26
27	CAP	14.42	PIS	00.22	GEM	CAN	15.10	LIB	SAG	CAP	PIS	ARI	27
28	CAP	PIS	06.32	TAU	GEM	00.30	VIR	07.38	18.44	03.43	22.26	14.57	28
29	01.06	23.14	ARI	13.11	07.43	LEO	21.32	SCO	CAP	AQU	ARI	TAU	29
30	AQU		17.55	GEM	CAN	09.26	LIB	10.40	22.11	08.54	ARI	TAU	30
31	06.16		TAU		08.53		LIB	SAG		PIS		03.11	31

SUN

mth dy	time -> sign
JAN 1	00.00 -> CAP
JAN 20	05.38 -> AQU
FEB 18	19.55 -> PIS
MAR 20	19.08 -> ARI
APR 20	06.27 -> TAU
MAY 21	05.50 -> GEM
JUN 21	13.55 -> CAN
JUL 23	00.48 -> LEO
AUG 23	07.43 -> VIR
SEP 23	05.07 -> LIB
OCT 23	14.11 -> SCO
NOV 22	11.31 -> SAG
DEC 22	00.44 -> CAP

MERCURY

mth dy	time -> sign
JAN 1	00.00 -> CAP
JAN 4	12.19 -> AQU
MAR 12	15.19 -> PIS
MAR 30	09.58 -> ARI
APR 14	05.55 -> TAU
APR 30	15.18 -> GEM
JUL 8	03.58 -> CAN
JUL 22	19.11 -> LEO
AUG 7	04.21 -> VIR
AUG 27	06.50 -> LIB
OCT 7	02.57 -> VIR
OCT 9	16.55 -> LIB
NOV 1	16.54 -> SCO
NOV 20	06.00 -> SAG
DEC 9	13.21 -> CAP

VENUS

mth dy	time -> sign
JAN 1	00.00 -> AQU
JAN 4	20.07 -> PIS
FEB 2	04.45 -> ARI
JUN 6	01.48 -> TAU
JUL 6	22.04 -> GEM
AUG 3	05.30 -> CAN
AUG 29	02.48 -> LEO
SEP 23	03.26 -> VIR
OCT 17	14.17 -> LIB
NOV 10	16.40 -> SCO
DEC 4	14.41 -> SAG
DEC 28	11.04 -> CAP

MARS

mth dy	time -> sign
JAN 1	00.00 -> SCO
FEB 25	06.21 -> SAG
SEP 21	06.35 -> CAP
NOV 4	18.51 -> AQU
DEC 15	14.22 -> PIS

JUPITER

mth dy	time -> sign
JAN 1	00.00 -> LIB
MAR 30	21.37 -> VIR
JUL 15	13.29 -> LIB
DEC 15	15.56 -> SCO

SATURN

mth dy	time -> sign
JAN 1	00.00 -> ARI
APR 29	22.22 -> TAU

MOON

dy	jan	feb	mar	apr	may	jun	jul	aug	sep	oct	nov	dec	dy
1	GEM	10.29	LEO	20.03	09.49	21.07	06.49	19.55	TAU	GEM	11.35	08.14	1
2	15.53	LEO	LEO	LIB	SCO	CAP	AQU	ARI	19.23	14.52	LEO	VIR	2
3	CAN	20.40	04.07	LIB	11.19	21.03	07.26	ARI	GEM	CAN	LEO	19.17	3
4	CAN	VIR	VIR	00.22	SAG	AQU	PIS	02.02	GEM	CAN	00.00	LIB	4
5	03.54	VIR	11.34	SCO	11.57	23.13	11.16	TAU	06.57	03.25	VIR	LIB	5
6	LEO	05.00	LIB	02.57	CAP	PIS	ARI	11.49	CAN	LEO	09.59	02.30	6
7	14.42	LIB	16.56	SAG	13.28	PIS	18.53	GEM	19.36	15.21	LIB	SCO	7
8	VIR	11.18	SCO	05.04	AQU	04.36	TAU	23.57	LEO	VIR	16.18	05.42	8
9	23.32	SCO	20.48	CAP	17.04	ARI	TAU	CAN	LEO	VIR	SCO	SAG	9
10	LIB	15.23	SAG	07.46	PIS	13.06	05.31	CAN	07.20	00.48	19.30	06.20	10
11	LIB	SAG	23.40	AQU	23.09	TAU	GEM	12.38	VIR	LIB	SAG	CAP	11
12	05.32	17.28	CAP	11.41	ARI	23.48	17.47	LEO	17.01	07.19	21.08	06.27	12
13	SCO	CAP	CAP	PIS	ARI	GEM	CAN	LEO	LIB	SCO	CAP	AQU	13
14	08.19	18.30	02.09	17.13	07.28	GEM	CAN	00.32	LIB	11.33	22.53	07.56	14
15	SAG	AQU	AQU	ARI	TAU	11.52	06.29	VIR	00.25	SAG	AQU	PIS	15
16	08.39	20.03	05.04	ARI	17.41	CAN	LEO	10.51	SCO	14.35	AQU	11.56	16
17	CAP	PIS	PIS	00.43	GEM	CAN	18.42	LIB	05.42	CAP	01.52	ARI	17
18	08.17	23.48	09.27	TAU	GEM	00.35	VIR	18.54	SAG	17.21	PIS	18.35	18
19	AQU	ARI	ARI	10.28	05.30	LEO	VIR	SCO	09.14	AQU	06.32	TAU	19
20	09.21	ARI	16.20	GEM	CAN	12.53	05.20	SCO	CAP	20.26	ARI	TAU	20
21	PIS	07.02	TAU	22.17	18.12	VIR	LIB	00.12	11.31	PIS	12.52	03.28	21
22	13.43	TAU	TAU	CAN	LEO	23.03	13.04	SAG	AQU	PIS	TAU	GEM	22
23	ARI	17.41	02.12	CAN	LEO	LIB	SCO	02.49	13.22	00.17	20.59	14.08	23
24	22.13	GEM	GEM	10.51	06.07	LIB	17.10	CAP	PIS	ARI	GEM	CAN	24
25	TAU	GEM	14.18	LEO	VIR	05.31	SAG	03.36	15.55	05.32	GEM	CAN	25
26	TAU	06.11	CAN	21.57	15.07	SCO	18.09	AQU	ARI	TAU	07.10	02.21	26
27	09.53	CAN	CAN	VIR	LIB	08.00	CAP	04.03	20.29	13.00	CAN	LEO	27
28	GEM	18.12	02.37	VIR	20.05	SAG	17.35	PIS	TAU	GEM	19.22	15.20	28
29	22.36		LEO	05.43	SCO	07.44	AQU	05.57	TAU	23.13	LEO	VIR	29
30	CAN		12.54	LIB	21.30	CAP	17.30	ARI	04.05	CAN	LEO	VIR	30
31	CAN		VIR		SAG		PIS	10.50		CAN		03.18	31

1970

SUN
mth dy time –> sign

JAN 1   00.00 –> CAP
JAN 20 11.24 –> AQU
FEB 19 01.42 –> PIS
MAR 21 00.56 –> ARI
APR 20 12.15 –> TAU
MAY 21 11.37 –> GEM
JUN 21 19.43 –> CAN
JUL 23 06.37 –> LEO
AUG 23 13.34 –> VIR
SEP 23 10.59 –> LIB
OCT 23 20.04 –> SCO
NOV 22 17.25 –> SAG
DEC 22 06.36 –> CAP

MERCURY
mth dy time –> sign

JAN 1   00.00 –> CAP
FEB 4   04.24 –> AQU
FEB 4   11.53 –> CAP
FEB 13 13.08 –> AQU
MAR 5   20.10 –> PIS
MAR 22 07.59 –> ARI
APR 6   07.40 –> TAU
JUN 13 12.46 –> GEM
JUN 30 06.22 –> CAN
JUL 14 08.06 –> LEO
JUL 31 05.21 –> VIR
OCT 7   18.04 –> LIB
OCT 25 06.16 –> SCO
NOV 13 01.17 –> SAG
DEC 3   10.14 –> CAP

VENUS
mth dy time –> sign

JAN 1   00.00 –> CAP
JAN 21 07.26 –> AQU
FEB 14 05.04 –> PIS
MAR 10 05.25 –> ARI
APR 3   10.05 –> TAU
APR 27 20.33 –> GEM
MAY 22 14.19 –> CAN
JUN 16 17.49 –> LEO
JUL 12 12.16 –> VIR
AUG 8   10.00 –> LIB
SEP 7   01.54 –> SCO

MARS
mth dy time –> sign

JAN 1   00.00 –> PIS
JAN 24 21.30 –> ARI
MAR 7   01.28 –> TAU
APR 18 18.59 –> GEM
JUN 2   06.51 –> CAN
JUL 18 06.43 –> LEO
SEP 3   04.57 –> VIR
OCT 20 10.57 –> LIB
DEC 6   16.34 –> SCO

JUPITER
mth dy time –> sign

JAN 1   00.00 –> SCO
APR 30 06.44 –> LIB
AUG 15 17.57 –> SCO

SATURN
mth dy time –> sign

JAN 1   00.00 –> TAU

MOON

dy	jan	feb	mar	apr	may	jun	jul	aug	sep	oct	nov	dec	dy
1	LIB	01.50	SAG	AQU	PIS	TAU	GEM	10.44	VIR	LIB	02.24	CAP	1
2	12.03	SAG	12.54	AQU	09.32	TAU	17.21	LEO	18.25	11.35	SAG	18.45	2
3	SCO	04.21	CAP	00.01	ARI	02.10	CAN	23.34	LIB	SCO	08.32	AQU	3
4	16.33	CAP	14.34	PIS	13.05	GEM	CAN	VIR	LIB	20.31	CAP	21.55	4
5	SAG	04.19	AQU	01.32	TAU	10.25	04.26	VIR	SAG	13.11	PIS		5
6	17.30	AQU	14.49	ARI	18.17	CAN	LEO	12.32	SCO	SAG	AQU	PIS	6
7	CAP	03.37	PIS	04.02	GEM	21.17	17.11	LIB	14.58	03.10	16.33	01.03	7
8	16.47	PIS	15.16	TAU	GEM	LEO	VIR	23.57	SAG	CAP	PIS	ARI	8
9	AQU	04.17	ARI	09.02	02.17	LEO	VIR	SCO	20.51	07.26	18.52	04.24	9
10	16.37	ARI	17.43	GEM	CAN	10.02	06.02	SCO	CAP	AQU	ARI	TAU	10
11	PIS	07.59	TAU	17.33	13.22	VIR	LIB	08.07	23.34	09.30	20.50	08.33	11
12	18.48	TAU	23.37	CAN	LEO	22.28	16.41	SAG	AQU	PIS	TAU	GEM	12
13	ARI	15.29	GEM	CAN	02.10	LIB	SCO	12.25	23.57	10.12	23.48	14.32	13
14	ARI	GEM	GEM	05.15	VIR	LIB	23.26	CAP	PIS	ARI	GEM	CAN	14
15	00.20	GEM	09.18	LEO	VIR	08.01	SAG	13.31	PIS	11.00	GEM	23.21	15
16	TAU	02.17	CAN	18.07	14.02	SCO	SAG	AQU	ARI	TAU	05.23	LEO	16
17	09.07	CAN	21.39	VIR	LIB	13.39	02.19	13.01	ARI	13.43	CAN	LEO	17
18	GEM	14.53	LEO	VIR	22.49	SAG	CAP	PIS	00.21	GEM	14.36	11.04	18
19	20.13	LEO	LEO	05.35	SCO	16.04	02.44	12.50	TAU	19.59	LEO	VIR	19
20	CAN	LEO	10.30	LIB	SCO	CAP	AQU	ARI	04.02	CAN	LEO	VIR	20
21	CAN	03.42	VIR	14.15	04.11	17.00	02.36	14.46	GEM	CAN	02.50	00.01	21
22	08.40	VIR	21.56	SCO	SAG	AQU	PIS	TAU	11.41	06.12	VIR	LIB	22
23	LEO	15.30	LIB	20.15	07.13	18.11	03.42	20.03	CAN	LEO	15.39	11.27	23
24	21.33	LIB	LIB	SAG	CAP	PIS	ARI	GEM	22.54	18.57	LIB	SCO	24
25	VIR	LIB	07.10	SAG	09.26	20.52	07.18	GEM	LEO	VIR	LIB	19.27	25
26	VIR	01.23	SCO	00.26	AQU	ARI	TAU	04.58	LEO	VIR	02.25	SAG	26
27	09.42	SCO	14.07	CAP	11.59	ARI	13.53	CAN	11.53	07.37	SCO	SAG	27
28	LIB	08.38	SAG	03.43	PIS	01.35	GEM	16.38	VIR	LIB	10.02	00.01	28
29	19.34		19.00	AQU	15.27	TAU	23.14	LEO	VIR	18.15	SAG	CAP	29
30	SCO		CAP	06.37	ARI	08.24	CAN	LEO	00.33	SCO	15.05	02.24	30
31	SCO		22.08		20.03		CAN	05.36		SCO		AQU	31

SUN

mth dy	time –> sign
JAN 1	00.00 –> CAP
JAN 20	17.13 –> AQU
FEB 19	07.27 –> PIS
MAR 21	06.38 –> ARI
APR 20	17.54 –> TAU
MAY 21	17.15 –> GEM
JUN 22	01.19 –> CAN
JUL 23	12.15 –> LEO
AUG 23	19.15 –> VIR
SEP 23	16.45 –> LIB
OCT 24	01.53 –> SCO
NOV 22	23.14 –> SAG
DEC 22	12.24 –> CAP

MERCURY

mth dy	time –> sign
JAN 1	00.00 –> CAP
JAN 2	23.36 –> SAG
JAN 14	02.16 –> CAP
FEB 7	20.52 –> AQU
FEB 26	07.57 –> PIS
MAR 14	04.45 –> ARI
APR 1	14.12 –> TAU
APR 18	21.52 –> ARI
MAY 17	03.32 –> TAU
JUN 7	06.45 –> GEM
JUN 21	16.25 –> CAN
JUL 6	08.53 –> LEO
JUL 26	17.03 –> VIR
AUG 29	20.41 –> LEO
SEP 11	06.45 –> VIR
SEP 30	09.19 –> LIB
OCT 17	17.49 –> SCO
NOV 6	06.59 –> SAG

VENUS

mth dy	time –> sign
JAN 1	00.00 –> SCO
JAN 7	01.00 –> SAG
FEB 5	14.57 –> CAP
MAR 4	02.24 –> AQU
MAR 29	14.02 –> PIS
APR 23	15.44 –> ARI
MAY 18	12.48 –> TAU
JUN 12	06.58 –> GEM
JUL 6	22.02 –> CAN
JUL 31	09.15 –> LEO
AUG 24	16.25 –> VIR
SEP 17	20.26 –> LIB
OCT 11	22.43 –> SCO
NOV 5	00.30 –> SAG
NOV 29	02.41 –> CAP
DEC 23	06.33 –> AQU

MARS

mth dy	time –> sign
JAN 1	00.00 –> SCO
JAN 23	01.34 –> SAG
MAR 12	10.11 –> CAP
MAY 3	20.58 –> AQU
NOV 6	12.31 –> PIS
DEC 26	18.04 –> ARI

JUPITER

mth dy	time –> sign
JAN 1	00.00 –> SCO
JAN 14	08.49 –> SAG
JUN 5	02.13 –> SCO
SEP 11	15.34 –> SAG

SATURN

mth dy	time –> sign
JAN 1	00.00 –> TAU
JUN 18	16.08 –> GEM

MOON

dy	jan	feb	mar	apr	may	jun	jul	aug	sep	oct	nov	dec	dy
1	04.08	15.49	TAU	16.51	09.34	VIR	LIB	08.49	CAP	19.36	ARI	16.25	1
2	PIS	TAU	TAU	CAN	LEO	17.26	13.46	SAG	07.04	PIS	05.55	GEM	2
3	06.26	20.34	03.01	CAN	21.03	LIB	SCO	16.32	AQU	19.40	TAU	17.51	3
4	ARI	GEM	GEM	02.05	VIR	LIB	23.59	CAP	08.51	ARI	05.27	CAN	4
5	10.00	GEM	09.47	LEO	VIR	05.36	SAG	20.47	PIS	18.42	GEM	22.17	5
6	TAU	04.07	CAN	14.16	09.59	SCO	SAG	AQU	08.43	TAU	07.15	LEO	6
7	15.08	CAN	19.55	VIR	LIB	15.28	07.03	22.34	ARI	18.53	CAN	LEO	7
8	GEM	14.06	LEO	VIR	22.03	SAG	CAP	PIS	08.37	GEM	12.56	06.40	8
9	22.09	LEO	LEO	03.17	SCO	22.45	11.26	23.27	TAU	22.10	LEO	VIR	9
10	CAN	LEO	08.10	LIB	SCO	CAP	AQU	ARI	10.25	CAN	22.44	18.19	10
11	CAN	01.58	VIR	15.28	08.08	CAP	14.14	ARI	GEM	CAN	VIR	LIB	11
12	07.24	VIR	21.06	SCO	SAG	04.03	PIS	00.55	15.21	05.30	VIR	LIB	12
13	LEO	14.50	LIB	SCO	16.09	AQU	16.32	TAU	CAN	LEO	11.05	07.01	13
14	18.57	LIB	LIB	02.03	CAP	08.01	ARI	04.10	23.38	16.16	LIB	SCO	14
15	VIR	LIB	09.31	SAG	22.19	PIS	19.10	GEM	LEO	VIR	23.49	18.37	15
16	VIR	03.22	SCO	10.38	AQU	11.06	TAU	09.50	LEO	VIR	SCO	SAG	16
17	07.53	SCO	20.23	CAP	AQU	ARI	22.47	CAN	10.29	04.47	SCO	SAG	17
18	LIB	13.45	SAG	16.46	02.39	13.39	GEM	17.57	VIR	11.30	11.30	04.07	18
19	20.04	SAG	SAG	AQU	PIS	TAU	GEM	LEO	22.47	17.31	SAG	CAP	19
20	SCO	20.37	04.37	20.07	05.11	16.24	03.56	LEO	LIB	SCO	21.36	11.32	20
21	SCO	CAP	CAP	PIS	ARI	GEM	CAN	04.19	LIB	SCO	CAP	AQU	21
22	05.15	23.43	09.28	21.08	06.31	20.30	11.16	VIR	11.33	CAP	05.31	17.10	22
23	SAG	AQU	AQU	ARI	TAU	CAN	LEO	16.22	SCO	SAG	05.52	PIS	23
24	10.32	AQU	11.07	21.06	08.01	CAN	21.09	LIB	23.43	16.05	AQU	21.09	24
25	CAP	00.05>PIS	PIS	TAU	GEM	03.12	VIR	LIB	SAG	CAP	11.48	ARI	25
26	12.36	23.30	10.45	21.58	11.26	LEO	VIR	05.09	SAG	CAP	PIS	23.45	26
27	AQU	ARI	ARI	GEM	CAN	13.06	09.12	SCO	09.53	00.11	15.03	TAU	27
28	13.02	23.54	10.16	GEM	18.16	VIR	LIB	16.56	CAP	AQU	ARI	TAU	28
29	PIS		TAU	01.43	LEO	VIR	21.50	SAG	16.39	04.56	16.08	01.38	29
30	13.36		11.43	CAN	LEO	01.22	SCO	SAG	AQU	PIS	TAU	GEM	30
31	ARI		GEM		04.48		SCO	01.54		06.26		04.01	31

1972

SUN
mth dy time –> sign

JAN 1	00.00	–> CAP
JAN 20	23.00	–> AQU
FEB 19	13.12	–> PIS
MAR 20	12.21	–> ARI
APR 19	23.38	–> TAU
MAY 20	22.59	–> GEM
JUN 21	07.06	–> CAN
JUL 22	18.03	–> LEO
AUG 23	01.03	–> VIR
SEP 22	22.33	–> LIB
OCT 23	07.42	–> SCO
NOV 22	05.03	–> SAG
DEC 21	18.13	–> CAP

MERCURY
mth dy time –> sign

JAN 1	00.00	–> SAG
JAN 11	18.18	–> CAP
JAN 31	23.47	–> AQU
FEB 18	12.53	–> PIS
MAR 5	16.59	–> ARI
MAY 12	23.45	–> TAU
MAY 29	06.46	–> GEM
JUN 12	02.56	–> CAN
JUN 28	16.52	–> LEO
SEP 5	11.36	–> VIR
SEP 21	12.12	–> LIB
OCT 9	11.11	–> SCO
OCT 30	19.27	–> SAG
NOV 29	07.08	–> SCO
DEC 12	23.21	–> SAG

VENUS
mth dy time –> sign

JAN 1	00.00	–> AQU
JAN 16	15.02	–> PIS
FEB 10	10.08	–> ARI
MAR 7	03.26	–> TAU
APR 3	22.48	–> GEM
MAY 10	13.51	–> CAN
JUN 11	20.08	–> GEM
AUG 6	01.26	–> CAN
SEP 7	23.27	–> LEO
OCT 5	08.34	–> VIR
OCT 30	21.40	–> LIB
NOV 24	13.23	–> SCO
DEC 18	18.34	–> SAG

MARS
mth dy time –> sign

JAN 1	00.00	–> ARI
FEB 10	14.04	–> TAU
MAR 27	04.30	–> GEM
MAY 12	13.14	–> CAN
JUN 28	16.09	–> LEO
AUG 15	00.59	–> VIR
SEP 30	23.23	–> LIB
NOV 15	22.17	–> SCO
DEC 30	16.12	–> SAG

SATURN
mth dy time –> sign

JAN 1	00.00	–> GEM
JAN 10	03.44	–> TAU
FEB 21	14.51	–> GEM

JUPITER
mth dy time –> sign

JAN 1	00.00	–> SAG
FEB 6	19.37	–> CAP
JUL 24	16.43	–> SAG
SEP 25	18.20	–> CAP

MOON

dy	jan	feb	mar	apr	may	jun	jul	aug	sep	oct	nov	dec	dy
1	CAN	00.56	19.00	SCO	SAG	12.15	01.18	14.57	GEM	12.25	VIR	LIB	1
2	08.22	VIR	LIB	SCO	20.29	AQU	PIS	TAU	02.11	LEO	10.27	03.42	2
3	LEO	11.06	LIB	02.27	CAP	19.52	06.22	17.33	CAN	19.31	LIB	SCO	3
4	15.50	LIB	07.00	SAG	CAP	PIS	ARI	GEM	06.54	VIR	21.46	16.22	4
5	VIR	23.18	SCO	14.20	06.35	PIS	09.25	20.18	LEO	VIR	SCO	SAG	5
6	VIR	SCO	19.36	CAP	AQU	00.27	TAU	CAN	13.15	04.35	SCO	SAG	6
7	02.33	SCO	SAG	23.37	13.28	ARI	11.05	23.56	VIR	LIB	10.16	05.06	7
8	LIB	11.38	SAG	AQU	PIS	02.14	GEM	LEO	21.36	15.27	SAG	CAP	8
9	15.03	SAG	06.49	AQU	16.35	TAU	12.29	LEO	LIB	SCO	23.11	16.53	9
10	SCO	21.50	CAP	04.58	ARI	02.24	CAN	05.23	LIB	SCO	CAP	AQU	10
11	SCO	CAP	14.42	PIS	16.47	GEM	15.05	VIR	08.15	03.52	CAP	AQU	11
12	02.57	CAP	AQU	06.32	TAU	02.45	LEO	13.27	SCO	SAG	11.02	02.32	12
13	SAG	04.36	18.39	ARI	15.57	CAN	20.16	LIB	20.42	16.44	AQU	PIS	13
14	12.26	AQU	PIS	05.54	GEM	05.10	VIR	LIB	SAG	CAP	19.56	08.59	14
15	CAP	08.11	19.37	TAU	16.16	LEO	VIR	00.19	SAG	CAP	PIS	ARI	15
16	19.04	PIS	ARI	05.16	CAN	11.03	04.49	SCO	09.07	03.51	PIS	11.59	16
17	AQU	09.51	19.27	GEM	19.38	VIR	LIB	12.49	CAP	AQU	00.44	TAU	17
18	23.28	ARI	TAU	06.46	LEO	20.39	16.15	SAG	19.04	11.12	ARI	12.24	18
19	PIS	11.11	20.12	CAN	LEO	LIB	SCO	SAG	AQU	PIS	01.53	GEM	19
20	PIS	TAU	GEM	11.47	02.56	LIB	SCO	00.38	AQU	14.22	TAU	11.57	20
21	02.35	13.35	23.26	LEO	VIR	08.43	04.46	CAP	01.09	ARI	01.05	CAN	21
22	ARI	GEM	CAN	20.24	13.36	SCO	SAG	09.43	PIS	14.37	GEM	12.34	22
23	05.17	17.52	CAN	VIR	LIB	21.14	16.10	AQU	03.44	00.31	LEO	16.03	23
24	TAU	CAN	05.46	VIR	LIB	SAG	CAP	15.28	TAU	14.02	CAN	VIR	24
25	08.14	CAN	LEO	07.34	02.01	SAG	CAP	PIS	04.27	02.12	VIR		25
26	GEM	00.15	14.47	LIB	SCO	08.36	01.07	18.40	TAU	14.44	LEO	23.21	26
27	12.01	LEO	VIR	19.56	14.33	CAP	AQU	ARI	05.14	CAN	07.24	LIB	27
28	CAN	08.39	VIR	SCO	SAG	18.02	07.29	20.43	GEM	18.14	VIR	LIB	28
29	17.21	VIR	01.42	SCO	SAG	AQU	PIS	TAU	07.39	16.15	16.15	10.10	29
30	LEO		LIB	08.31	02.13	AQU	11.50	22.56	CAN	LEO	LIB	SCO	30
31	LEO		13.48		CAP		ARI	GEM		00.59		22.51	31

SUN

mth dy	time -> sign
JAN 1	00.00 -> CAP
JAN 20	04.49 -> AQU
FEB 18	19.02 -> PIS
MAR 20	18.13 -> ARI
APR 20	05.30 -> TAU
MAY 21	04.54 -> GEM
JUN 21	13.01 -> CAN
JUL 22	23.56 -> LEO
AUG 23	06.54 -> VIR
SEP 23	04.21 -> LIB
OCT 23	13.30 -> SCO
NOV 22	10.54 -> SAG
DEC 22	00.08 -> CAP

MERCURY

mth dy	time -> sign
JAN 1	00.00 -> SAG
JAN 4	14.41 -> CAP
JAN 23	15.23 -> AQU
FEB 9	19.30 -> PIS
APR 16	21.18 -> ARI
MAY 6	02.55 -> TAU
MAY 20	17.24 -> GEM
JUN 4	04.42 -> CAN
JUN 27	06.41 -> LEO
JUL 16	08.03 -> CAN
AUG 11	12.21 -> LEO
AUG 28	15.22 -> VIR
SEP 13	16.16 -> LIB
OCT 2	20.12 -> SCO
DEC 8	21.29 -> SAG
DEC 28	15.15 -> CAP

VENUS

mth dy	time -> sign
JAN 1	00.00 -> SAG
JAN 11	19.14 -> CAP
FEB 4	18.43 -> AQU
FEB 28	18.45 -> PIS
MAR 24	20.34 -> ARI
APR 18	01.05 -> TAU
MAY 12	08.42 -> GEM
JUN 5	19.20 -> CAN
JUN 30	08.55 -> LEO
JUL 25	02.13 -> VIR
AUG 19	01.10 -> LIB
SEP 13	09.05 -> SCO
OCT 9	08.08 -> SAG
NOV 5	15.39 -> CAP
DEC 7	21.37 -> AQU

MARS

mth dy	time -> sign
JAN 1	00.00 -> SAG
FEB 12	05.51 -> CAP
MAR 26	20.59 -> AQU
MAY 8	04.09 -> PIS
JUN 20	20.54 -> ARI
AUG 12	14.56 -> TAU
OCT 29	22.56 -> ARI
DEC 24	08.09 -> TAU

SATURN

mth dy	time -> sign
JAN 1	00.00 -> GEM
AUG 1	22.20 -> CAN

JUPITER

mth dy	time -> sign
JAN 1	00.00 -> CAP
FEB 23	09.29 -> AQU

MOON

dy	jan	feb	mar	apr	may	jun	jul	aug	sep	oct	nov	dec	dy
1	SAG	CAP	14.22	PIS	ARI	GEM	21.55	VIR	05.17	SAG	CAP	AQU	1
2	SAG	05.55	AQU	12.48	01.01	11.21	LEO	13.12	SCO	SAG	08.58	04.32	2
3	11.30	AQU	22.31	ARI	TAU	CAN	23.31	LIB	15.24	12.02	AQU	PIS	3
4	CAP	14.22	PIS	14.58	01.16	11.49	VIR	20.35	SAG	CAP	20.26	13.50	4
5	22.47	PIS	PIS	TAU	GEM	LEO	VIR	SCO	SAG	CAP	PIS	ARI	5
6	AQU	20.29	03.37	16.12	01.35	14.51	04.23	SCO	04.01	00.48	PIS	19.08	6
7	AQU	ARI	ARI	GEM	CAN	VIR	LIB	07.37	CAP	AQU	04.19	TAU	7
8	08.03	ARI	06.51	18.04	03.36	21.16	13.05	SAG	16.30	11.23	ARI	20.58	8
9	PIS	00.53	TAU	CAN	LEO	LIB	SCO	20.30	AQU	PIS	08.25	GEM	9
10	14.57	TAU	09.31	21.31	08.13	LIB	SCO	CAP	AQU	18.29	TAU	20.52	10
11	ARI	04.10	GEM	LEO	VIR	06.52	00.48	CAP	02.40	ARI	09.59	CAN	11
12	19.24	GEM	12.29	LEO	15.31	SCO	SAG	08.52	PIS	22.36	GEM	20.44	12
13	TAU	06.44	CAN	02.46	LIB	18.43	13.45	AQU	09.56	TAU	10.46	LEO	13
14	21.41	CAN	16.07	VIR	LIB	SAG	CAP	19.14	ARI	TAU	CAN	22.20	14
15	GEM	09.12	LEO	09.50	01.09	SAG	CAP	PIS	14.59	01.09	12.20	VIR	15
16	22.39	LEO	20.42	LIB	SCO	07.37	02.15	PIS	TAU	GEM	LEO	VIR	16
17	CAN	12.31	VIR	18.51	12.41	CAP	AQU	03.15	18.48	03.28	15.41	02.53	17
18	23.40	VIR	VIR	SCO	SAG	20.19	13.07	ARI	GEM	CAN	VIR	LIB	18
19	LEO	17.58	02.48	SCO	SAG	AQU	PIS	09.14	22.01	06.25	21.15	10.44	19
20	LEO	LIB	LIB	06.02	01.30	AQU	21.43	TAU	CAN	LEO	LIB	SCO	20
21	02.23	LIB	11.15	SAG	CAP	07.29	ARI	13.26	CAN	10.19	LIB	21.20	21
22	VIR	02.35	SCO	18.49	14.17	PIS	ARI	GEM	00.56	VIR	05.06	SAG	22
23	08.16	SCO	22.26	CAP	AQU	15.48	03.41	16.08	LEO	15.28	SCO	SAG	23
24	LIB	14.14	SAG	CAP	AQU	ARI	TAU	CAN	03.58	LIB	15.11	09.41	24
25	17.52	SAG	SAG	07.21	01.05	20.37	06.58	17.49	VIR	22.28	SAG	CAP	25
26	SCO	SAG	11.16	AQU	PIS	TAU	GEM	LEO	08.00	SCO	SAG	22.43	26
27	SCO	03.04	CAP	17.09	08.14	22.18	08.10	19.33	LIB	SCO	03.13	AQU	27
28	06.10	CAP	23.12	PIS	ARI	GEM	CAN	VIR	14.18	07.57	CAP	AQU	28
29	SAG		AQU	22.53	11.28	22.08	08.29	22.52	SCO	SAG	16.17	11.10	29
30	18.54		AQU	ARI	TAU	CAN	LEO	LIB	23.47	19.57	AQU	PIS	30
31	CAP		07.55		11.53		09.34	LIB		CAP		21.34	31

1974

SUN

mth dy time –> sign

JAN 1 00.00 –> CAP
JAN 20 10.46 –> AQU
FEB 19 00.59 –> PIS
MAR 21 00.07 –> ARI
APR 20 11.19 –> TAU
MAY 21 10.36 –> GEM
JUN 21 18.38 –> CAN
JUL 23 05.30 –> LEO
AUG 23 12.29 –> VIR
SEP 23 09.59 –> LIB
OCT 23 19.11 –> SCO
NOV 22 16.39 –> SAG
DEC 22 05.57 –> CAP

MERCURY

mth dy time –> sign

JAN 1 00.00 –> CAP
JAN 16 03.57 –> AQU
FEB 2 22.42 –> PIS
MAR 2 17.49 –> AQU
MAR 17 20.11 –> PIS
APR 11 15.20 –> ARI
APR 28 03.10 –> TAU
MAY 12 04.55 –> GEM
MAY 29 08.03 –> CAN
AUG 5 11.41 –> LEO
AUG 20 09.04 –> VIR
SEP 6 05.48 –> LIB
SEP 28 00.20 –> SCO
OCT 26 23.22 –> LIB
NOV 11 16.05 –> SCO
DEC 2 06.17 –> SAG
DEC 21 09.17 –> CAP

VENUS

mth dy time –> sign

JAN 1 00.00 –> AQU
JAN 29 19.51 –> CAP
FEB 28 14.25 –> AQU
APR 6 14.17 –> PIS
MAY 4 20.21 –> ARI
MAY 31 07.19 –> TAU
JUN 25 23.44 –> GEM
JUL 21 04.34 –> CAN
AUG 14 23.47 –> LEO
SEP 8 10.28 –> VIR
OCT 2 14.27 –> LIB
OCT 26 14.12 –> SCO
NOV 19 11.57 –> SAG
DEC 13 09.06 –> CAP

MARS

mth dy time –> sign

JAN 1 00.00 –> TAU
FEB 27 10.11 –> GEM
APR 20 08.18 –> CAN
JUN 9 00.54 –> LEO
JUL 27 14.04 –> VIR
SEP 12 19.08 –> LIB
OCT 28 07.04 –> SCO
DEC 10 22.06 –> SAG

SATURN

mth dy time –> sign

JAN 1 00.00 –> CAN
JAN 7 20.27 –> GEM
APR 18 22.33 –> CAN

JUPITER

mth dy time –> sign

JAN 1 00.00 –> AQU
MAR 8 11.12 –> PIS

MOON

dy	jan	feb	mar	apr	may	jun	jul	aug	sep	oct	nov	dec	dy
1	ARI	16.53	GEM	11.40	VIR	11.10	01.20	CAP	01.29	ARI	18.23	06.22	1
2	ARI	GEM	GEM	LEO	23.39	SCO	SAG	06.46	PIS	ARI	GEM	CAN	2
3	04.38	19.05	02.59	13.56	LIB	19.21	12.19	AQU	12.58	04.39	23.01	08.31	3
4	TAU	CAN	CAN	VIR	LIB	SAG	CAP	19.26	ARI	TAU	CAN	LEO	4
5	08.00	19.11	04.49	16.22	04.43	SAG	CAP	PIS	22.50	12.00	CAN	10.40	5
6	GEM	LEO	LEO	LIB	SCO	05.48	00.41	PIS	TAU	GEM	02.30	VIR	6
7	08.28	18.52	05.33	20.25	12.05	CAP	AQU	07.15	TAU	17.30	LEO	13.42	7
8	CAN	VIR	VIR	SCO	SAG	18.02	13.25	ARI	06.36	CAN	05.18	L1B	8
9	07.42	20.10	06.52	SCO	22.15	AQU	PIS	17.13	GEM	21.03	VIR	18.13	9
10	LEO	LIB	LIB	03.27	CAP	AQU	PIS	TAU	11.39	LEO	07.58	SCO	10
11	07.41	LIB	10.40	SAG	CAP	06.43	01.10	TAU	CAN	22.56	LIB	SCO	11
12	VIR	00.58	SCO	13.56	10.34	PIS	ARI	00.15	13.54	VIR	11.23	00.34	12
13	10.21	SCO	18.20	CAP	AQU	17.52	10.21	GEM	LEO	VIR	SCO	SAG	13
14	LIB	10.01	SAG	CAP	23.33	ARI	TAU	03.49	14.12	00.11	16.39	09.04	14
15	16.54	SAG	SAG	02.34	PIS	ARI	15.54	CAN	VIR	LIB	SAG	CAP	15
16	SCO	22.16	05.41	AQU	PIS	01.46	GEM	04.26	14.17	02.23	SAG	19.48	16
17	SCO	CAP	CAP	14.44	09.19	TAU	17.56	LEO	LIB	SCO	00.42	AQU	17
18	03.12	CAP	18.38	PIS	ARI	05.59	CAN	03.42	16.14	07.14	CAP	AQU	18
19	SAG	11.21	AQU	PIS	16.10	GEM	17.43	VIR	SCO	SAG	11.39	08.12	19
20	15.47	AQU	AQU	00.20	TAU	07.21	LEO	03.45	21.46	15.44	AQU	PIS	20
21	CAP	23.15	06.33	ARI	19.54	CAN	17.10	LIB	SAG	CAP	AQU	20.35	21
22	CAP	PIS	PIS	06.53	GEM	07.30	VIR	06.37	SAG	CAP	00.11	ARI	22
23	04.50	PIS	16.02	TAU	21.46	LEO	18.19	SCO	07.22	AQU	PIS	ARI	23
24	AQU	09.12	ARI	11.11	CAN	08.11	LIB	13.34	CAP	AQU	11.59	06.44	24
25	17.00	ARI	23.09	GEM	23.12	VIR	22.45	SAG	19.38	15.57	ARI	TAU	25
26	PIS	17.11	TAU	14.17	LEO	10.57	SCO	SAG	AQU	PIS	21.05	13.15	26
27	PIS	TAU	TAU	CAN	LEO	LIB	SCO	00.15	AQU	PIS	TAU	GEM	27
28	03.32	23.10	04.33	17.03	01.25	16.40	07.00	CAP	08.14	03.13	TAU	16.15	28
29	ARI		GEM	LEO	VIR	SCO	SAG	12.52	PIS	ARI	02.58	CAN	29
30	11.41		08.40	20.00	05.16	SCO	18.11	AQU	19.25	12.00	GEM	17.05	30
31	TAU		CAN		LIB		CAP	AQU		TAU		LEO	31

SUN
mth dy time –> sign

JAN 1 00.00 –> CAP
JAN 20 16.36 –> AQU
FEB 19 06.50 –> PIS
MAR 21 05.56 –> ARI
APR 20 17.07 –> TAU
MAY 21 16.24 –> GEM
JUN 22 00.26 –> CAN
JUL 23 11.22 –> LEO
AUG 23 18.24 –> VIR
SEP 23 15.55 –> LIB
OCT 24 01.06 –> SCO
NOV 22 22.31 –> SAG
DEC 22 11.46 –> CAP

MERCURY
mth dy time –> sign

JAN 1 00.00 –> CAP
JAN 8 21.58 –> AQU
MAR 16 11.50 –> PIS
APR 4 12.28 –> ARI
APR 19 17.20 –> TAU
MAY 4 11.55 –> GEM
JUL 12 08.56 –> CAN
JUL 28 08.05 –> LEO
AUG 12 06.12 –> VIR
AUG 30 17.20 –> LIB
NOV 6 08.58 –> SCO
NOV 25 01.44 –> SAG
DEC 14 04.10 –> CAP

VENUS
mth dy time –> sign

JAN 1 00.00 –> CAP
JAN 6 06.40 –> AQU
JAN 30 06.05 –> PIS
FEB 23 09.53 –> ARI
MAR 19 21.42 –> TAU
APR 13 22.26 –> GEM
MAY 9 20.12 –> CAN
JUN 6 10.54 –> LEO
JUL 9 11.06 –> VIR
SEP 2 15.34 –> LEO
OCT 4 05.19 –> VIR
NOV 9 13.52 –> LIB
DEC 7 00.29 –> SCO

MARS
mth dy time –> sign

JAN 1 00.00 –> SAG
JAN 21 18.49 –> CAP
MAR 3 05.32 –> AQU
APR 11 19.15 –> PIS
MAY 21 08.14 –> ARI
JUL 1 03.53 –> TAU
AUG 14 20.47 –> GEM
OCT 17 08.44 –> CAN
NOV 25 18.30 –> GEM

SATURN
mth dy time –> sign

JAN 1 00.00 –> CAN
SEP 17 04.56 –> LEO

JUPITER
mth dy time –> sign

JAN 1 00.00 –> PIS
MAR 18 16.47 –> ARI

MOON

dy	jan	feb	mar	apr	may	jun	jul	aug	sep	oct	nov	dec	dy
1	17.32	LIB	14.33	SAG	CAP	01.32	ARI	TAU	CAN	LEO	LIB	SCO	1
2	VIR	05.53	SCO	11.08	05.34	PIS	ARI	04.02	23.08	10.03	20.07	07.33	2
3	19.21	SCO	19.05	CAP	AQU	14.01	09.54	GEM	LEO	VIR	SCO	SAG	3
4	LIB	12.10	SAG	21.45	17.34	ARI	TAU	10.17	23.29	09.39	21.10	10.58	4
5	23.39	SAG	SAG	AQU	PIS	ARI	18.58	CAN	VIR	LIB	SAG	CAP	5
6	SCO	21.42	03.39	AQU	PIS	01.19	GEM	12.44	22.38	09.09	SAG	17.12	6
7	SCO	CAP	CAP	10.17	06.03	TAU	GEM	LEO	LIB	SCO	00.45	AQU	7
8	06.39	CAP	15.09	PIS	ARI	09.49	00.23	12.53	22.46	10.35	CAP	AQU	8
9	SAG	09.16	AQU	22.44	17.03	GEM	CAN	VIR	SCO	SAG	07.59	02.52	9
10	15.58	AQU	AQU	ARI	TAU	15.21	02.50	12.51	SCO	15.29	AQU	PIS	10
11	CAP	21.45	03.49	ARI	TAU	CAN	LEO	LIB	01.41	CAP	18.42	15.06	11
12	CAP	PIS	PIS	09.53	01.44	18.45	03.55	14.30	SAG	CAP	PIS	ARI	12
13	03.03	PIS	16.18	TAU	GEM	LEO	VIR	SCO	08.11	00.10	PIS	ARI	13
14	AQU	10.22	ARI	19.14	08.08	21.11	05.21	18.59	CAP	AQU	07.17	03.39	14
15	15.23	ARI	ARI	GEM	CAN	VIR	LIB	SAG	17.51	11.40	ARI	TAU	15
16	PIS	22.09	03.52	GEM	12.38	23.41	08.23	SAG	AQU	PIS	19.38	14.12	16
17	PIS	TAU	TAU	02.27	LEO	LIB	SCO	02.25	AQU	PIS	TAU	GEM	17
18	04.03	TAU	13.43	CAN	15.45	LIB	13.32	CAP	05.32	00.20	TAU	21.49	18
19	ARI	07.35	GEM	07.14	VIR	02.59	SAG	12.09	PIS	ARI	06.14	CAN	19
20	15.21	GEM	20.48	LEO	18.05	SCO	20.46	AQU	18.07	12.43	GEM	CAN	20
21	TAU	13.18	CAN	09.42	LIB	07.34	CAP	23.32	ARI	TAU	14.36	02.54	21
22	23.23	CAN	CAN	VIR	20.25	SAG	CAP	PIS	ARI	23.51	CAN	LEO	22
23	GEM	15.13	00.31	10.41	SCO	13.56	05.56	PIS	06.43	GEM	20.48	06.28	23
24	GEM	LEO	LEO	LIB	23.51	CAP	AQU	12.02	TAU	GEM	LEO	VIR	24
25	03.20	14.37	01.21	11.39	SAG	22.33	16.58	ARI	18.13	08.57	LEO	09.27	25
26	CAN	VIR	VIR	SCO	SAG	AQU	PIS	ARI	GEM	CAN	01.04	LIB	26
27	04.00	13.38	00.51	14.20	05.31	AQU	PIS	00.45	GEM	15.20	VIR	12.28	27
28	LEO	LIB	LIB	SAG	CAP	09.33	05.27	TAU	03.07	LEO	03.48	SCO	28
29	03.14		01.08	20.08	14.09	PIS	ARI	11.53	CAN	18.47	LIB	15.53	29
30	VIR		SCO	CAP	AQU	22.02	17.53	GEM	08.20	VIR	05.36	SAG	30
31	03.13		04.09		AQU		TAU	19.35		19.55		20.16	31

1976

SUN
mth dy time –> sign

JAN 1 00.00 –> CAP
JAN 20 22.25 –> AQU
FEB 19 12.40 –> PIS
MAR 20 11.50 –> ARI
APR 19 23.03 –> TAU
MAY 20 22.21 –> GEM
JUN 21 06.24 –> CAN
JUL 22 17.18 –> LEO
AUG 23 00.18 –> VIR
SEP 22 21.48 –> LIB
OCT 23 06.58 –> SCO
NOV 22 04.22 –> SAG
DEC 21 17.36 –> CAP

SATURN
mth dy time –> sign

JAN 1 00.00 –> LEO
JAN 14 13.17 –> CAN
JUN 5 05.08 –> LEO

MERCURY
mth dy time –> sign

JAN 1 00.00 –> CAP
JAN 2 20.22 –> AQU
JAN 25 01.31 –> CAP
FEB 15 19.03 –> AQU
MAR 9 12.02 –> PIS
MAR 26 15.36 –> ARI
APR 10 09.30 –> TAU
APR 29 23.11 –> GEM
MAY 19 19.21 –> TAU
JUN 13 19.20 –> GEM
JUL 4 14.18 –> CAN
JUL 18 19.35 –> LEO
AUG 3 16.41 –> VIR
AUG 25 20.52 –> LIB
SEP 21 07.15 –> VIR
OCT 10 14.47 –> LIB
OCT 29 04.55 –> SCO
NOV 16 19.02 –> SAG
DEC 6 09.25 –> CAP

VENUS
mth dy time –> sign

JAN 1 12.14 –> SAG
JAN 26 06.09 –> CAP
FEB 19 16.50 –> AQU
MAR 15 00.59 –> PIS
APR 8 08.57 –> ARI
MAY 2 17.49 –> TAU
MAY 27 03.43 –> GEM
JUN 20 13.56 –> CAN
JUL 14 23.36 –> LEO
AUG 8 08.36 –> VIR
SEP 1 17.45 –> LIB
SEP 26 04.17 –> SCO
OCT 20 17.22 –> SAG
NOV 14 10.42 –> CAP
DEC 9 12.53 –> AQU

MARS
mth dy time –> sign

JAN 1 00.00 –> GEM
MAR 18 13.15 –> CAN
MAY 16 11.11 –> LEO
JUL 6 23.27 –> VIR
AUG 24 05.55 –> LIB
OCT 8 20.23 –> SCO
NOV 20 23.53 –> SAG

JUPITER
mth dy time –> sign

JAN 1 00.00 –> ARI
MAR 26 10.26 –> TAU
AUG 23 10.26 –> GEM
OCT 16 20.24 –> TAU

MOON

dy	jan	feb	mar	apr	may	jun	jul	aug	sep	oct	nov	dec	dy
1	CAP	19.47	PIS	09.34	04.05	CAN	15.46	LIB	SAG	CAP	PIS	ARI	1
2	CAP	PIS	14.22	TAU	GEM	04.37	VIR	03.55	16.29	03.49	PIS	23.41	2
3	02.33	PIS	ARI	22.15	14.53	LEO	19.34	SCO	CAP	AQU	04.46	TAU	3
4	AQU	07.17	ARI	GEM	CAN	10.21	LIB	07.03	22.20	12.10	ARI	TAU	4
5	11.35	ARI	03.18	GEM	23.09	VIR	22.33	SAG	AQU	PIS	17.23	12.38	5
6	PIS	20.13	TAU	09.06	LEO	14.00	SCO	10.54	AQU	22.50	TAU	GEM	6
7	23.21	TAU	15.56	CAN	LEO	LIB	SCO	CAP	06.11	ARI	TAU	GEM	7
8	ARI	TAU	GEM	16.36	04.21	15.58	01.05	15.57	PIS	ARI	06.21	00.21	8
9	ARI	08.16	GEM	LEO	VIR	SCO	SAG	AQU	16.18	11.11	GEM	CAN	9
10	12.10	GEM	01.59	20.16	06.39	17.06	03.49	23.00	ARI	TAU	18.28	10.12	10
11	TAU	16.59	CAN	VIR	LIB	SAG	CAP	PIS	ARI	TAU	CAN	LEO	11
12	23.19	CAN	07.55	20.54	07.03	18.45	07.53	PIS	04.30	00.14	CAN	17.55	12
13	GEM	21.32	LEO	LIB	SCO	CAP	AQU	08.49	TAU	GEM	04.36	VIR	13
14	GEM	LEO	09.59	20.14	07.04	22.31	14.36	ARI	17.32	12.24	LEO	23.13	14
15	07.00	22.59	VIR	SCO	SAG	AQU	PIS	21.05	GEM	CAN	11.46	LIB	15
16	CAN	VIR	09.44	20.15	08.31	AQU	PIS	TAU	GEM	21.49	VIR	LIB	16
17	11.15	23.14	LIB	SAG	CAP	05.43	00.40	TAU	05.07	LEO	15.34	02.01	17
18	LEO	LIB	09.18	22.43	13.02	PIS	ARI	09.54	CAN	LEO	LIB	SCO	18
19	13.25	LIB	SCO	CAP	AQU	16.32	13.11	GEM	13.10	03.25	16.31	02.54	19
20	VIR	00.14	10.34	CAP	21.27	ARI	TAU	20.34	LEO	VIR	SCO	SAG	20
21	15.10	SCO	SAG	04.47	PIS	ARI	TAU	CAN	17.16	05.26	16.03	03.12	21
22	LIB	03.18	14.48	AQU	PIS	05.21	01.40	CAN	VIR	LIB	SAG	CAP	22
23	17.48	SAG	CAP	14.28	09.07	TAU	GEM	03.30	18.28	05.17	16.03	04.48	23
24	SCO	08.54	22.19	PIS	ARI	17.37	11.39	LEO	SCO	SCO	CAP	AQU	24
25	21.51	CAP	AQU	PIS	22.07	GEM	CAN	07.03	18.34	04.49	18.30	09.36	25
26	SAG	16.48	AQU	02.37	TAU	GEM	18.19	VIR	SCO	SAG	AQU	PIS	26
27	SAG	AQU	08.34	ARI	TAU	03.29	LEO	08.42	19.21	05.55	AQU	18.32	27
28	03.24	AQU	PIS	15.37	10.22	CAN	22.23	LIB	SAG	CAP	00.47	ARI	28
29	CAP	02.42	20.37	TAU	GEM	10.39	VIR	10.05	22.13	10.05	PIS	ARI	29
30	10.34		ARI	TAU	20.39	LEO	VIR	SCO	CAP	AQU	11.01	06.43	30
31	AQU		ARI		CAN		01.13	12.28		17.53		TAU	31

SUN
mth dy time -> sign

JAN 1   00.00 -> CAP
JAN 20 04.15 -> AQU
FEB 18 18.30 -> PIS
MAR 20 17.43 -> ARI
APR 20 04.57 -> TAU
MAY 21 04.14 -> GEM
JUN 21 12.14 -> CAN
JUL 22 23.04 -> LEO
AUG 23 06.00 -> VIR
SEP 23 03.29 -> LIB
OCT 23 12.41 -> SCO
NOV 22 10.07 -> SAG
DEC 21 23.24 -> CAP

MERCURY
mth dy time -> sign

JAN 1   00.00 -> CAP
FEB 10 23.55 -> AQU
MAR 2   08.09 -> PIS
MAR 18 11.56 -> ARI
APR 3   02.46 -> TAU
JUN 10 21.06 -> GEM
JUN 26 07.07 -> CAN
JUL 10 12.00 -> LEO
JUL 28 10.15 -> VIR
OCT 4   09.17 -> LIB
OCT 21 16.24 -> SCO
NOV 9   17.20 -> SAG
DEC 1   06.44 -> CAP
DEC 21 07.18 -> SAG

VENUS
mth dy time -> sign

JAN 1   00.00 -> AQU
JAN 4   13.02 -> PIS
FEB 2   05.54 -> ARI
JUN 6   06.10 -> TAU
JUL 6   15.09 -> GEM
AUG 2   19.19 -> CAN
AUG 28 15.10 -> LEO
SEP 22 15.05 -> VIR
OCT 17 01.37 -> LIB
NOV 10 03.52 -> SCO
DEC 4   01.49 -> SAG
DEC 27 22.09 -> CAP

MARS
mth dy time -> sign

JAN 1   00.41 -> CAP
FEB 9   11.57 -> AQU
MAR 20 02.19 -> PIS
APR 27 15.46 -> ARI
JUN 6   03.00 -> TAU
JUL 17 15.13 -> GEM
SEP 1   00.20 -> CAN
OCT 26 18.56 -> LEO

JUPITER
mth dy time -> sign

JAN 1   0.00 -> TAU
APR 3   15.43 -> GEM
AUG 20 12.43 -> CAN
DEC 30 23.50 -> GEM

SATURN
mth dy time -> sign

JAN 1   00.00 -> LEO
NOV 17 02.42 -> VIR

MOON

dy	jan	feb	mar	apr	may	jun	jul	aug	sep	oct	nov	dec	dy
1	19.43	CAN	CAN	01.25	LIB	02.54	CAP	01.23	ARI	20.33	CAN	LEO	1
2	GEM	CAN	09.25	VIR	16.23	SAG	12.56	PIS	00.52	GEM	CAN	23.05	2
3	GEM	00.11	LEO	04.39	SCO	02.07	AQU	06.54	TAU	GEM	05.03	VIR	3
4	07.12	LEO	15.19	LIB	15.59	CAP	15.31	ARI	12.27	09.09	LEO	VIR	4
5	CAN	06.17	VIR	05.40	SAG	02.44	PIS	16.18	GEM	CAN	15.16	07.17	5
6	16.20	VIR	18.34	SCO	15.54	AQU	22.03	TAU	GEM	20.58	VIR	LIB	6
7	LEO	10.36	LIB	06.09	CAP	06.35	ARI	TAU	01.03	LEO	21.51	11.33	7
8	23.23	LIB	20.37	SAG	18.00	PIS	ARI	04.29	CAN	LEO	LIB	SCO	8
9	VIR	14.04	SCO	07.40	AQU	14.34	08.33	GEM	12.14	05.58	LIB	12.22	9
10	VIR	SCO	22.42	CAP	23.29	ARI	TAU	17.04	LEO	VIR	00.42	SAG	10
11	04.48	17.11	SAG	11.24	PIS	ARI	21.15	CAN	20.34	11.29	SCO	11.26	11
12	LIB	SAG	SAG	AQU	PIS	01.56	GEM	CAN	VIR	LIB	01.03	CAP	12
13	08.44	20.14	01.40	17.49	08.29	TAU	GEM	03.57	VIR	14.11	SAG	10.59	13
14	SCO	CAP	CAP	PIS	ARI	14.50	09.50	02.07	SCO	00.50	AQU	14
15	11.18	23.45	06.00	PIS	20.04	GEM	CAN	12.26	LIB	15.27	CAP	13.09	15
16	SAG	AQU	AQU	02.52	TAU	GEM	20.51	VIR	05.45	SAG	02.00	PIS	16
17	13.02	AQU	12.06	ARI	TAU	03.28	LEO	18.49	SCO	16.51	AQU	19.11	17
18	CAP	04.45	PIS	14.02	08.50	CAN	LEO	LIB	08.28	CAP	05.58	ARI	18
19	15.12	PIS	20.23	TAU	GEM	14.53	05.58	23.35	SAG	19.36	PIS	ARI	19
20	AQU	12.22	ARI	TAU	21.35	LEO	VIR	SCO	11.04	AQU	13.13	04.54	20
21	19.30	ARI	ARI	02.37	CAN	LEO	13.09	SCO	CAP	AQU	ARI	TAU	21
22	PIS	23.06	07.05	GEM	CAN	00.29	LIB	03.03	14.12	00.26	23.09	16.51	22
23	PIS	TAU	TAU	15.25	09.13	VIR	18.13	SAG	AQU	PIS	TAU	GEM	23
24	03.19	TAU	19.39	CAN	LEO	07.35	SCO	05.30	18.30	07.34	TAU	GEM	24
25	ARI	11.50	GEM	CAN	18.31	LIB	21.04	CAP	PIS	ARI	10.48	05.30	25
26	14.41	GEM	GEM	02.43	VIR	11.42	SAG	07.41	PIS	16.53	GEM	CAN	26
27	TAU	GEM	08.16	LEO	VIR	SCO	22.15	AQU	00.40	TAU	23.20	17.52	27
28	TAU	00.02	CAN	10.52	00.28	13.02	CAP	10.46	ARI	TAU	CAN	LEO	28
29	03.37	CAN	18.40	VIR	LIB	SAG	23.04	PIS	09.21	04.08	CAN	LEO	29
30	GEM		LEO	15.13	VIR	02.56	12.48	AQU	16.11	TAU	GEM	11.53	05.13	30
31	15.20		LEO		SCO		AQU	ARI		16.40		VIR	31

1978

SUN
mth dy time –> sign

JAN 1	00.00 –> CAP
JAN 20	10.04 –> AQU
FEB 19	00.21 –> PIS
MAR 20	23.34 –> ARI
APR 20	10.50 –> TAU
MAY 21	10.08 –> GEM
JUN 21	18.09 –> CAN
JUL 23	05.00 –> LEO
AUG 23	11.57 –> VIR
SEP 23	09.26 –> LIB
OCT 23	18.37 –> SCO
NOV 22	16.05 –> SAG
DEC 22	05.21 –> CAP

MERCURY
mth dy time –> sign

JAN 1	00.00 –> SAG
JAN 13	20.07 –> CAP
FEB 4	15.55 –> AQU
FEB 22	16.11 –> PIS
MAR 10	12.10 –> ARI
MAY 16	08.20 –> TAU
JUN 3	15.26 –> GEM
JUN 17	15.49 –> CAN
JUL 2	22.28 –> LEO
JUL 27	06.09 –> VIR
AUG 13	07.06 –> LEO
SEP 9	19.23 –> VIR
SEP 26	16.40 –> LIB
OCT 14	05.30 –> SCO
NOV 3	07.48 –> SAG

VENUS
mth dy time –> sign

JAN 1	00.00 –> CAP
JAN 20	18.29 –> AQU
FEB 13	16.07 –> PIS
MAR 9	16.29 –> ARI
APR 2	21.14 –> TAU
APR 27	07.54 –> GEM
MAY 22	02.04 –> CAN
JUN 16	06.19 –> LEO
JUL 12	02.14 –> VIR
AUG 8	03.09 –> LIB
SEP 7	05.08 –> SCO

MARS
mth dy time –> sign

JAN 1	00.00 –> LEO
JAN 26	02.00 –> CAN
APR 10	18.50 –> LEO
JUN 14	02.38 –> VIR
AUG 4	09.07 –> LIB
SEP 19	20.57 –> SCO
NOV 2	01.20 –> SAG
DEC 12	17.39 –> CAP

SATURN
mth dy time –> sign

JAN 1	00.00 –> VIR
JAN 5	00.45 –> LEO
JUL 26	12.02 –> VIR

JUPITER
mth dy time –> sign

JAN 1	00.00 –> GEM
APR 12	00.13 –> CAN
SEP 5	08.31 –> LEO

MOON

dy	jan	feb	mar	apr	may	jun	jul	aug	sep	oct	nov	dec	dy
1	14.31 SCO	13.02 CAP	09.00 ARI	19.37 CAN	20.46	14.17 SCO	20.44						1
2	LIB	07.13 SAG	00.05 PIS	03.50	GEM	CAN	VIR	LIB	10.03 CAP				2
3	20.35 SAG	15.58 AQU	14.27 TAU	GEM	02.10 VIR	21.48 SAG	21.35						3
4	SCO	08.50 CAP	03.20 ARI	13.53	07.33 LEO	07.15 SCO	12.40 AQU						4
5	22.03 CAP	17.50 PIS	21.52 GEM	14.29	GEM	SCO	CAP	23.36					5
6	SAG	09.04 AQU	07.51 TAU	GEM	20.13 VIR	15.38	03.06	15.04 PIS					6
7	22.55 AQU	19.45 ARI	TAU	01.30 LEO	VIR	SCO	SAG	AQU	PIS				7
8	CAP	09.47 PIS	14.21 CAN	07.18	LEO	01.30 LIB	21.39 SAG	06.52	18.06	03.39			8
9	22.05 PIS	23.08 TAU	GEM	14.07	08.44 VIR	SAG	CAP	PIS	ARI				9
10	AQU	12.56 ARI	23.27 LEO	18.41	VIR	10.11 SAG	09.42	22.11	09.50				10
11	22.50 ARI	ARI	GEM	CAN	LEO	19.48 SCO	01.20 AQU	ARI	TAU				11
12	PIS	19.50 TAU	05.18 GEM	CAN	02.35 LIB	15.43 CAP	12.12 ARI	03.35	17.54				12
13	PIS	TAU	TAU	10.59 VIR	07.17 LIB	SAG	03.08 PIS	03.35	GEM				13
14	03.05 TAU	14.48 CAN	LEO	12.55	03.47 AQU	18.03	15.06 TAU	10.45	GEM				14
15	ARI	06.24 GEM	23.30 LIB	19.15	SCO	CAP	04.09 ARI	03.50					15
16	11.30 GEM	GEM	LEO	VIR	19.28	07.50 SCO	18.15 PIS	19.22	GEM	CAN			16
17	TAU	18.56 LEO	02.49 LEO	VIR	SCO	SAG	05.50 AQU	TAU	20.16	15.37			17
18	23.06 CAN	CAN	10.44 VIR	04.24	22.01 SAG	08.33 AQU	18.04 ARI	TAU	CAN	LEO			18
19	GEM	CAN	15.12 VIR	LIB	SAG	CAP	PIS	09.43	02.05 CAN	LEO			19
20	GEM	07.09 LEO	18.53	09.39	21.52 TAU	07.41	19.29	GEM	08.09	04.34			20
21	11.50 LEO	LEO	LIB	SCO	CAP	AQU	ARI	16.56	11.52 LEO	VIR			21
22	CAN	17.39 VIR	01.49 VIR	23.39	11.31 SAG	21.07 AQU	07.26 ARI	GEM	CAN	20.57	16.40		22
23	CAN	VIR	VIR	SCO	SAG	AQU	PIS	00.06 GEM	CAN	VIR	LIB		23
24	00.02 VIR	09.41 LIB	SCO	11.41	21.57 PIS	09.46 TAU	03.31 CAN	00.04	VIR	08.07	LIB		24
25	LEO	02.03 LIB	02.00 CAP	PIS	ARI	08.31 CAN	LEO	08.07	01.32				25
26	10.56 LIB	15.01 SAG	12.10 PIS	15.50	GEM	16.01 LIB	SCO						26
27	VIR	08.28 SCO	03.27 AQU	01.53	TAU	19.59 LEO	VIR	15.38	06.07				27
28	20.08 SCO	18.37 CAP	14.37 ARI	TAU	CAN	LEO	22.51 SCO	SAG					28
29	LIB	SAG	05.28 PIS	09.21	01.31 CAN	04.11 LIB	19.23 SAG	07.15					29
30	LIB	21.23 AQU	19.52 TAU	GEM	08.40 VIR	LIB	SAG	CAP					30
31	03.03	CAP		ARI		13.28 LEO			05.52		06.53		31

SUN

mth dy	time	->	sign
JAN 1	00.00	->	CAP
JAN 20	16.00	->	AQU
FEB 19	06.13	->	PIS
MAR 21	05.20	->	ARI
APR 20	16.35	->	TAU
MAY 21	15.54	->	GEM
JUN 21	23.56	->	CAN
JUL 23	10.48	->	LEO
AUG 23	17.47	->	VIR
SEP 23	15.17	->	LIB
OCT 24	00.28	->	SCO
NOV 22	21.54	->	SAG
DEC 22	11.10	->	CAP

MERCURY

mth dy	time	->	sign
JAN 1	00.00	->	SAG
JAN 8	22.33	->	CAP
JAN 28	12.50	->	AQU
FEB 14	20.38	->	PIS
MAR 3	21.32	->	ARI
MAR 28	10.40	->	PIS
APR 17	12.48	->	ARI
MAY 10	22.03	->	TAU
MAY 26	07.44	->	GEM
JUN 9	06.32	->	CAN
JUN 27	09.51	->	LEO
SEP 2	21.39	->	VIR
SEP 18	18.59	->	LIB
OCT 7	03.55	->	SCO
OCT 30	07.06	->	SAG
NOV 18	03.08	->	SCO
DEC 12	13.34	->	SAG

VENUS

mth dy	time	->	sign
JAN 1	00.00	->	SCO
JAN 7	06.38	->	SAG
FEB 5	09.16	->	CAP
MAR 9	17.19	->	AQU
MAR 29	03.17	->	PIS
APR 23	04.03	->	ARI
MAY 18	00.29	->	TAU
JUN 11	18.14	->	GEM
JUL 6	09.02	->	CAN
JUL 30	20.07	->	LEO
AUG 24	03.16	->	VIR
SEP 17	07.21	->	LIB
OCT 11	09.48	->	SCO
NOV 4	11.50	->	SAG
NOV 28	14.20	->	CAP
DEC 22	18.25	->	AQU

MARS

mth dy	time	->	sign
JAN 1	00.00	->	CAP
JAN 20	17.08	->	AQU
FEB 27	20.25	->	PIS
APR 7	01.08	->	ARI
MAY 16	04.25	->	TAU
JUN 26	01.55	->	GEM
AUG 8	13.29	->	CAN
SEP 24	21.21	->	LEO
NOV 19	21.36	->	VIR

JUPITER

mth dy	time	->	sign
JAN 1	00.00	->	LEO
FEB 28	23.31	->	CAN
APR 20	08.33	->	LEO
SEP 29	10.24	->	VIR

SATURN

mth dy	time	->	sign
JAN 1	00.00	->	VIR

MOON

dy	jan	feb	mar	apr	may	jun	jul	aug	sep	oct	nov	dec	dy
1	AQU	ARI	ARI	GEM	CAN	22.41	19.08	SCO	11.33	AQU	10.09	TAU	1
2	07.08	22.03	07.09	GEM	CAN	VIR	LIB	22.05	CAP	AQU	ARI	23.02	2
3	PIS	TAU	TAU	06.24	01.56	VIR	LIB	SAG	13.59	00.23	11.16	GEM	3
4	09.41	TAU	12.58	CAN	LEO	11.12	05.57	SAG	AQU	PIS	TAU	GEM	4
5	ARI	05.33	GEM	17.58	14.41	LIB	SCO	02.23	14.03	00.28	13.26	04.01	5
6	15.17	GEM	22.34	LEO	VIR	21.05	12.55	CAP	PIS	ARI	GEM	CAN	6
7	TAU	16.06	CAN	LEO	VIR	SCO	SAG	03.28	13.29	00.45	18.24	12.09	7
8	23.42	CAN	CAN	06.52	02.47	SCO	16.07	AQU	ARI	TAU	CAN	LEO	8
9	GEM	CAN	10.47	VIR	LIB	03.14	CAP	03.05	14.12	03.07	CAN	23.33	9
10	GEM	04.25	LEO	18.45	12.10	SAG	16.59	PIS	TAU	GEM	03.14	VIR	10
11	10.14	LEO	23.42	LIB	SCO	06.23	AQU	03.10	17.54	09.09	LEO	VIR	11
12	CAN	17.18	VIR	LIB	18.25	CAP	17.23	ARI	GEM	CAN	15.20	12.29	12
13	22.16	VIR	VIR	04.16	SAG	08.06	PIS	05.21	GEM	19.12	VIR	LIB	13
14	LEO	VIR	11.41	SCO	22.25	AQU	18.57	TAU	01.27	LEO	VIR	LIB	14
15	LEO	05.37	LIB	11.18	CAP	09.56	ARI	10.41	CAN	LEO	04.16	00.08	15
16	11.10	LIB	21.49	SAG	CAP	PIS	22.43	GEM	12.25	07.51	LIB	SCO	16
17	VIR	16.12	SCO	16.23	01.26	12.52	TAU	19.17	LEO	VIR	15.29	08.36	17
18	23.40	SCO	SCO	CAP	AQU	ARI	TAU	CAN	LEO	20.44	SCO	SAG	18
19	LIB	23.51	05.38	22.02	04.18	17.18	04.59	CAN	01.15	LIB	23.56	13.54	19
20	LIB	SAG	SAG	AQU	PIS	TAU	GEM	06.28	VIR	LIB	SAG	CAP	20
21	09.51	SAG	10.56	22.41	07.30	23.23	13.40	LEO	14.11	08.02	SAG	17.13	21
22	SCO	04.00	CAP	PIS	ARI	GEM	CAN	19.11	LIB	SCO	06.01	AQU	22
23	16.08	CAP	13.52	PIS	11.20	GEM	CAN	VIR	LIB	17.09	CAP	19.50	23
24	SAG	05.12	AQU	00.51	TAU	07.24	00.30	VIR	01.54	SAG	10.37	PIS	24
25	18.27	AQU	15.04	ARI	16.28	CAN	LEO	08.13	SCO	SAG	AQU	22.40	25
26	CAP	04.52	PIS	03.27	GEM	17.47	13.01	LIB	11.36	00.11	14.17	ARI	26
27	18.12	PIS	15.47	TAU	23.51	LEO	VIR	20.12	SAG	CAP	PIS	ARI	27
28	AQU	04.54	ARI	07.49	CAN	LEO	VIR	SCO	18.40	05.16	17.17	02.08	28
29	17.25		17.36	GEM	CAN	06.14	02.06	SCO	CAP	AQU	ARI	TAU	29
30	PIS		TAU	15.11	10.08	VIR	LIB	05.39	22.49	08.29	19.54	06.32	30
31	18.11		22.08		LEO		13.46	SAG		PIS		GEM	31

1980

SUN
mth dy time –> sign

JAN 1   00.00 –> CAP
JAN 20 21.48 –> AQU
FEB 19 12.02 –> PIS
MAR 20 11.10 –> ARI
APR 19 22.23 –> TAU
MAY 20 21.42 –> GEM
JUN 21 05.47 –> CAN
JUL 22 16.42 –> LEO
AUG 22 23.41 –> VIR
SEP 22 21.09 –> LIB
OCT 23 06.18 –> SCO
NOV 22 03.42 –> SAG
DEC 21 16.56 –> CAP

MERCURY
mth dy time –> sign

JAN 1   00.00 –> SAG
JAN 2   08.03 –> CAP
JAN 21 02.18 –> AQU
FEB 7   08.07 –> PIS
APR 14 15.58 –> ARI
MAY 2   10.56 –> TAU
MAY 16 17.07 –> GEM
MAY 21 22.06 –> CAN
AUG 9   03.30 –> LEO
AUG 24 18.47 –> VIR
SEP 10 02.00 –> LIB
SEP 30 01.16 –> SCO
DEC 5   19.45 –> SAG
DEC 25 04.47 –> CAP

VENUS
mth dy time –> sign

JAN 1   00.00 –> AQU
JAN 16 03.37 –> PIS
FEB 9   23.40 –> ARI
MAR 6   18.54 –> TAU
APR 3   19.46 –> GEM
MAY 12 20.52 –> CAN
JUN 5   05.44 –> GEM
AUG 6   14.25 –> CAN
SEP 7   17.57 –> LEO
OCT 4   23.07 –> VIR
OCT 30 10.38 –> LIB
NOV 24 01.35 –> SCO
DEC 18 06.21 –> SAG

MARS
mth dy time –> sign

JAN 1   00.00 –> VIR
MAR 11 20.46 –> LEO
MAY 4   02.27 –> VIR
JUL 10 17.59 –> LIB
AUG 29 05.50 –> SCO
OCT 12 06.27 –> SAG
NOV 22 01.43 –> CAP
DEC 30 22.30 –> AQU

SATURN
mth dy time –> sign

JAN 1   00.00 –> VIR
SEP 21 10.48 –> LIB

JUPITER
mth dy time –> sign

JAN 1   00.00 –> VIR
OCT 27 10.11 –> LIB

MOON

dy	jan	feb	mar	apr	may	jun	jul	aug	sep	oct	nov	dec	dy
1	12.29	LEO	VIR	LIB	22.22	CAP	AQU	ARI	01.50	CAN	12.18	07.13	1
2	CAN	15.21	VIR	05.21	SAG	19.29	05.48	16.55	GEM	19.57	VIR	LIB	2
3	20.47	VIR	10.40	SCO	SAG	AQU	PIS	TAU	06.39	LEO	VIR	20.00	3
4	LEO	VIR	LIB	16.35	07.14	AQU	08.46	20.10	CAN	LEO	00.31	SCO	4
5	LEO	04.04	23.22	SAG	CAP	00.10	ARI	GEM	14.22	06.19	LIB	SCO	5
6	07.48	LIB	SCO	SAG	14.03	PIS	11.30	GEM	LEO	VIR	13.19	07.57	6
7	VIR	16.46	SCO	01.43	AQU	03.23	TAU	01.12	LEO	18.30	SCO	SAG	7
8	20.38	SCO	10.38	CAP	18.33	ARI	14.33	CAN	00.31	LIB	SCO	18.12	8
9	LIB	SCO	SAG	08.00	PIS	05.29	GEM	08.23	VIR	LIB	01.25	CAP	9
10	LIB	03.19	19.02	AQU	20.44	TAU	18.44	LEO	12.22	07.15	SAG	CAP	10
11	08.55	SAG	CAP	11.07	ARI	07.22	CAN	17.54	LIB	SCO	12.15	02.36	11
12	SCO	10.12	23.45	PIS	21.24	GEM	CAN	VIR	LIB	19.37	CAP	AQU	12
13	18.17	CAP	AQU	11.40	TAU	10.29	01.03	VIR	01.06	SAG	21.10	09.03	13
14	SAG	13.19	AQU	ARI	22.07	CAN	LEO	05.32	SCO	SAG	AQU	PIS	14
15	23.51	AQU	01.10	11.11	GEM	16.22	10.11	LIB	13.28	06.37	AQU	13.21	15
16	CAP	13.54	PIS	TAU	GEM	LEO	VIR	18.15	SAG	CAP	03.21	ARI	16
17	CAP	PIS	00.41	11.41	00.52	LEO	21.55	SCO	23.45	14.53	PIS	15.36	17
18	02.25	13.43	ARI	GEM	CAN	01.47	LIB	SCO	CAP	AQU	06.21	TAU	18
19	AQU	ARI	00.13	15.11	07.14	VIR	LIB	06.07	CAP	19.31	ARI	16.39	19
20	03.33	14.35	TAU	CAN	LEO	13.55	10.33	SAG	06.30	PIS	06.51	GEM	20
21	PIS	TAU	01.47	22.52	17.32	LIB	SCO	15.11	AQU	20.43	TAU	18.03	21
22	04.52	17.58	GEM	LEO	VIR	LIB	21.42	CAP	09.27	ARI	06.27	CAN	22
23	ARI	GEM	06.55	LEO	VIR	02.26	SAG	20.32	PIS	19.55	GEM	21.34	23
24	07.31	GEM	CAN	10.12	06.11	SCO	SAG	AQU	09.37	TAU	07.18	LEO	24
25	TAU	00.34	15.58	VIR	LIB	13.02	05.45	22.43	ARI	19.17	CAN	LEO	25
26	12.11	CAN	LEO	23.09	18.37	SAG	CAP	PIS	08.53	GEM	11.23	04.32	26
27	GEM	10.10	LEO	LIB	SCO	20.46	10.34	23.11	TAU	21.00	LEO	VIR	27
28	19.02	LEO	03.52	LIB	SCO	CAP	AQU	ARI	09.21	CAN	19.37	15.05	28
29	CAN	21.53	VIR	11.35	05.05	CAP	13.11	23.41	GEM	CAN	VIR	LIB	29
30	CAN		16.49	SCO	SAG	02.04	PIS	TAU	12.46	02.38	VIR	LIB	30
31	04.08		LIB		13.14		14.53	TAU		LEO		03.36	31

SUN

mth dy time –> sign

JAN 1   00.00 –> CAP
JAN 20 03.36 –> AQU
FEB 18 17.52 –> PIS
MAR 20 17.03 –> ARI
APR 20 04.19 –> TAU
MAY 21 03.39 –> GEM
JUN 21 11.45 –> CAN
JUL 22 22.40 –> LEO
AUG 23 05.38 –> VIR
SEP 23 03.05 –> LIB
OCT 23 12.13 –> SCO
NOV 22 09.36 –> SAG
DEC 21 22.51 –> CAP

SATURN

mth dy time –> sign

JAN 1   00.00 –> LIB

MERCURY

mth dy time –> sign

JAN 1   00.00 –> CAP
JAN 12 15.48 –> AQU
JAN 31 17.35 –> PIS
FEB 16 08.02 –> AQU
MAR 18 04.33 –> PIS
APR 8   09.11 –> ARI
APR 24 05.31 –> TAU
MAY 8   09.43 –> GEM
MAY 28 17.04 –> CAN
JUN 22 22.51 –> GEM
JUL 12 21.08 –> CAN
AUG 1   18.30 –> LEO
AUG 16 12.47 –> VIR
SEP 2   22.40 –> LIB
SEP 27 11.02 –> SCO
OCT 14 02.09 –> LIB
NOV 9   13.14 –> SCO
NOV 28 20.52 –> SAG
DEC 17 22.21 –> CAP

VENUS

mth dy time –> sign

JAN 1   00.00 –> SAG
JAN 11 06.49 –> CAP
FEB 4   06.08 –> AQU
FEB 28 06.02 –> PIS
MAR 24 07.43 –> ARI
APR 17 12.08 –> TAU
MAY 11 19.45 –> GEM
JUN 5   06.29 –> CAN
JUN 29 20.20 –> LEO
JUL 24 14.04 –> VIR
AUG 18 13.45 –> LIB
SEP 12 22.51 –> SCO
OCT 9   00.04 –> SAG
NOV 5   12.40 –> CAP
DEC 8   20.53 –> AQU

MARS

mth dy time –> sign

JAN 1   00.00 –> AQU
FEB 6   22.48 –> PIS
MAR 17 02.39 –> ARI
APR 25 07.17 –> TAU
JUN 5   05.27 –> GEM
JUL 18 08.54 –> CAN
SEP 2   01.52 –> LEO
OCT 21 01.57 –> VIR
DEC 16 00.15 –> LIB

JUPITER

mth dy time –> sign

JAN 1   00.00 –> LIB
NOV 27 02.20 –> SCO

MOON   MOON

dy	jan	feb	mar	apr	may	jun	jul	aug	sep	oct	nov	dec	dy
1	SCO	10.37	CAP	18.41	06.57	16.48	02.57	18.54	LIB	SCO	12.46	07.09	1
2	15.42	CAP	CAP	PIS	ARI	GEM	CAN	VIR	21.10	16.59	CAP	AQU	2
3	SAG	17.55	03.51	20.25	06.59	16.38	04.47	VIR	SCO	SAG	CAP	17.16	3
4	SAG	AQU	AQU	ARI	TAU	CAN	LEO	02.24	SCO	SAG	00.51	PIS	4
5	01.41	22.21	08.12	20.04	06.01	18.43	09.26	LIB	09.24	05.49	AQU	23.49	5
6	CAP	PIS	PIS	TAU	GEM	LEO	VIR	12.58	SAG	CAP	09.52	ARI	6
7	09.12	PIS	09.48	19.47	06.18	LEO	17.42	SCO	21.48	17.01	PIS	ARI	7
8	AQU	01.01	ARI	GEM	CAN	00.25	LIB	SCO	CAP	AQU	14.38	02.31	8
9	14.42	ARI	10.22	21.34	09.40	VIR	LIB	01.22	CAP	AQU	ARI	TAU	9
10	PIS	03.11	TAU	CAN	LEO	09.55	05.02	SAG	07.58	00.32	15.44	02.30	10
11	18.43	TAU	11.42	CAN	16.55	LIB	SCO	13.20	AQU	PIS	TAU	GEM	11
12	ARI	05.51	GEM	02.36	VIR	21.54	17.35	CAP	14.34	04.01	14.59	01.40	12
13	21.45	GEM	15.06	LEO	VIR	SCO	SAG	22.56	PIS	ARI	GEM	CAN	13
14	TAU	09.43	CAN	10.56	03.24	SCO	SAG	AQU	17.55	04.43	14.37	02.08	14
15	TAU	CAN	21.02	VIR	LIB	10.31	05.19	AQU	ARI	TAU	CAN	LEO	15
16	00.17	15.10	LEO	21.38	15.37	SAG	CAP	05.34	19.30	04.41	16.33	05.38	16
17	GEM	LEO	LEO	LIB	SCO	22.21	15.02	PIS	TAU	GEM	LEO	VIR	17
18	03.08	22.34	05.20	LIB	SCO	CAP	AQU	09.49	20.59	05.52	21.53	12.58	18
19	CAN	VIR	VIR	09.39	04.14	CAP	22.26	ARI	GEM	CAN	VIR	LIB	19
20	07.21	VIR	15.31	SCO	SAG	08.36	PIS	12.43	23.39	09.34	VIR	23.39	20
21	LEO	08.12	LIB	22.50	16.20	AQU	PIS	TAU	CAN	LEO	06.33	SCO	21
22	14.02	LIB	LIB	SAG	CAP	16.44	03.43	15.18	CAN	16.05	LIB	SCO	22
23	VIR	19.54	03.14	SAG	CAP	PIS	ARI	GEM	04.08	VIR	17.36	12.11	23
24	23.45	SCO	SCO	10.31	03.00	22.18	07.18	18.17	LEO	VIR	SCO	SAG	24
25	LIB	SCO	15.51	CAP	AQU	ARI	TAU	CAN	10.29	00.56	SCO	SAG	25
26	LIB	08.29	SAG	20.57	11.05	ARI	09.42	22.10	VIR	LIB	06.00	00.59	26
27	11.49	SAG	SAG	AQU	PIS	01.16	GEM	LEO	18.40	11.38	SAG	CAP	27
28	SCO	19.46	03.52	AQU	15.44	TAU	11.41	LEO	LIB	SCO	18.53	12.53	28
29	SCO		CAP	03.56	ARI	02.21	CAN	03.31	LIB	23.48	CAP	AQU	29
30	00.11		13.15	PIS	17.10	GEM	14.20	VIR	04.53	CAP	CAP	23.01	30
31	SAG		AQU		TAU		LEO	11.02		SAG		PIS	31

1982

SUN
mth dy time –> sign

JAN 1   00.00 –> CAP
JAN 20   09.31 –> AQU
FEB 18   23.47 –> PIS
MAR 20 22.56 –> ARI
APR 20   10.08 –> TAU
MAY 21 09.23 –> GEM
JUN 21   17.23 –> CAN
JUL 23   04.15 –> LEO
AUG 23 11.15 –> VIR
SEP 23   08.46 –> LIB
OCT 23   17.58 –> SCO
NOV 22 15.24 –> SAG
DEC 22   04.39 –> CAP

MERCURY
mth dy time –> sign

JAN 1   00.00 –> CAP
JAN 5   16.49 –> AQU
MAR 13 19.11 –> PIS
MAR 31 20.59 –> ARI
APR 15 18.54 –> TAU
MAY 1   13.29 –> GEM
JUL 9   11.26 –> CAN
JUL 24   08.48 –> LEO
AUG 8   14.07 –> VIR
AUG 28 03.22 –> LIB
NOV 3   01.11 –> SCO
NOV 21 14.28 –> SAG
DEC 10 20.04 –> CAP

VENUS
mth dy time –> sign

JAN 1   00.00 –> AQU
JAN 23   02.56 –> CAP
MAR 2   11.25 –> AQU
APR 6   12.20 –> PIS
MAY 4   12.27 –> ARI
MAY 30 21.02 –> TAU
JUN 25   12.13 –> GEM
JUL 20   16.21 –> CAN
AUG 14 11.09 –> LEO
SEP 7   21.38 –> VIR
OCT 2   01.33 –> LIB
OCT 26   01.19 –> SCO
NOV 18 23.07 –> SAG
DEC 12   20.20 –> CAP

MARS
mth dy time –> sign

JAN 1   00.00 –> LIB
AUG 3   11.46 –> SCO
SEP 20 01.20 –> SAG
OCT 31   23.05 –> CAP
DEC 10 06.17 –> AQU

SATURN
mth dy time –> sign

JAN 1   00.00 –> LIB
NOV 29 10.28 –> SCO

JUPITER
mth dy time –> sign

JAN 1   00.00 –> SCO
DEC 26 01.57 –> SAG

MOON

dy	jan	feb	mar	apr	may	jun	jul	aug	sep	oct	nov	dec	dy
1	PIS	TAU	TAU	CAN	23.45	LIB	SCO	09.36	AQU	PIS	TAU	GEM	1
2	06.33	20.20	01.50	13.36	VIR	21.12	14.25	CAP	16.11	TAU	08.06	10.58	2
3	ARI	GEM	GEM	LEO	VIR	SCO	SAG	22.17	PIS	ARI	00.23	CAN	3
4	11.02	22.28	04.48	18.18	06.32	SCO	SAG	AQU	PIS	13.09	GEM	11.26	4
5	TAU	CAN	CAN	VIR	LIB	08.31	03.15	AQU	00.24	TAU	01.59	LEO	5
6	12.48	23.50	07.50	VIR	15.24	SAG	CAP	09.23	ARI	16.39	CAN	13.32	6
7	GEM	LEO	LEO	00.26	SCO	21.12	16.03	PIS	06.27	GEM	04.10	VIR	7
8	13.01	LEO	11.27	LIB	SCO	CAP	AQU	18.21	TAU	19.39	LEO	18.11	8
9	CAN	02.15	VIR	08.33	02.17	CAP	AQU	ARI	10.57	CAN	07.40	LIB	9
10	13.21	VIR	16.34	SCO	SAG	10.08	03.35	ARI	GEM	22.44	VIR	LIB	10
11	LEO	07.02	LIB	19.07	14.50	AQU	PIS	01.00	14.18	LEO	12.46	01.34	11
12	15.37	LIB	LIB	SAG	CAP	21.44	12.49	TAU	CAN	LEO	LIB	SCO	12
13	VIR	15.16	00.17	SAG	CAP	PIS	ARI	05.22	16.46	02.09	19.42	11.27	13
14	21.17	SCO	SCO	07.41	03.44	PIS	19.00	GEM	LEO	VIR	SCO	SAG	14
15	LIB	SCO	11.03	CAP	AQU	06.20	TAU	07.40	18.57	06.23	SCO	23.15	15
16	LIB	02.45	SAG	20.18	14.46	ARI	22.03	CAN	VIR	LIB	04.52	CAP	16
17	06.46	SAG	23.47	AQU	PIS	11.07	GEM	08.40	22.02	12.21	SAG	CAP	17
18	SCO	15.36	CAP	AQU	22.04	TAU	22.46	LEO	LIB	SCO	16.21	12.12	18
19	19.00	CAP	CAP	06.19	ARI	12.34	CAN	09.40	LIB	21.02	CAP	AQU	19
20	SAG	CAP	11.53	PIS	ARI	GEM	22.35	VIR	03.32	SAG	CAP	AQU	20
21	SAG	03.15	AQU	12.23	01.22	12.13	LEO	12.22	SCO	SAG	05.20	00.56	21
22	07.51	AQU	21.01	ARI	TAU	CAN	23.20	LIB	12.30	08.38	AQU	PIS	22
23	CAP	12.09	PIS	14.59	01.54	11.57	VIR	18.21	SAG	CAP	17.43	11.34	23
24	19.25	PIS	PIS	TAU	GEM	LEO	VIR	SCO	SAG	21.36	PIS	ARI	24
25	AQU	18.17	02.37	15.48	01.38	13.36	02.45	SCO	00.31	AQU	PIS	18.37	25
26	AQU	ARI	ARI	GEM	CAN	VIR	LIB	04.11	CAP	AQU	03.07	TAU	26
27	04.49	22.32	05.39	16.43	02.27	18.30	09.58	SAG	13.21	09.12	ARI	21.49	27
28	PIS	TAU	TAU	CAN	LEO	LIB	SCO	16.42	AQU	PIS	08.31	GEM	28
29	11.58		07.44	19.09	05.43	LIB	20.48	CAP	AQU	17.25	TAU	22.12	29
30	ARI		GEM	LEO	VIR	03.02	SAG	CAP	00.18	ARI	10.36	CAN	30
31	17.03		10.09		12.02		SAG	05.23		22.04		21.33	31

SUN

mth dy time –> sign

JAN 1　00.00 –> CAP
JAN 20　15.17 –> AQU
FEB 19　05.31 –> PIS
MAR 21　04.39 –> ARI
APR 20　15.50 –> TAU
MAY 21　15.07 –> GEM
JUN 21　23.09 –> CAN
JUL 23　10.04 –> LEO
AUG 23　17.08 –> VIR
SEP 23　14.42 –> LIB
OCT 23　23.54 –> SCO
NOV 22　21.18 –> SAG
DEC 22　10.30 –> CAP

MERCURY

mth dy time –> sign

JAN 1　13.33 –> AQU
JAN 12　06.55 –> CAP
FEB 14　09.37 –> AQU
MAR 7　04.24 –> PIS
MAR 23　20.09 –> ARI
APR 7　17.04 –> TAU
JUN 14　08.06 –> GEM
JUL 1　19.18 –> CAN
JUL 15　20.57 –> LEO
AUG 1　10.22 –> VIR
AUG 29　06.08 –> LIB
SEP 6　02.30 –> VIR
OCT 8　23.44 –> LIB
OCT 26　15.47 –> SCO
NOV 14　08.56 –> SAG
DEC 4　11.23 –> CAP

VENUS

mth dy time –> sign

JAN 1　00.00 –> CAP
JAN 5　17.58 –> AQU
JAN 29　17.31 –> PIS
FEB 22　21.35 –> ARI
MAR 19　09.52 –> TAU
APR 13　11.26 –> GEM
MAY 9　10.57 –> CAN
JUN 6　06.04 –> LEO
JUL 10　05.25 –> VIR
AUG 27　11.43 –> LEO
OCT 5　19.35 –> VIR
NOV 9　10.52 –> LIB
DEC 6　16.15 –> SCO

MARS

mth dy time –> sign

JAN 1　00.00 –> AQU
JAN 17　13.10 –> PIS
FEB 25　00.20 –> ARI
APR 5　14.03 –> TAU
MAY 16　21.44 –> GEM
JUN 29　06.54 –> CAN
AUG 13　16.54 –> LEO
SEP 30　00.12 –> VIR
NOV 18　10.26 –> LIB

SATURN

mth dy time –> sign

JAN 1　00.00 –> SCO
MAY 6　19.31 –> LIB
AUG 24　11.52 –> SCO

JUPITER

mth dy time –> sign

JAN 1　00.00 –> SAG

MOON

dy	jan	feb	mar	apr	may	jun	jul	aug	sep	oct	nov	dec	dy
1	LEO	09.47	LIB	16.20	11.01	AQU	PIS	07.37	GEM	12.54	23.31	09.41	1
2	21.49	LIB	23.51	SAG	CAP	19.42	14.47	TAU	02.53	LEO	LIB	SCO	2
3	VIR	14.32	SCO	SAG	23.09	PIS	ARI	14.43	CAN	14.15	LIB	14.56	3
4	VIR	SCO	SCO	02.30	AQU	PIS	ARI	GEM	04.47	VIR	01.53	SAG	4
5	00.44	23.28	07.15	CAP	AQU	06.59	00.05	18.09	LEO	14.42	SCO	22.28	5
6	LIB	SAG	SAG	15.06	11.44	ARI	TAU	CAN	04.36	LIB	06.09	CAP	6
7	07.16	SAG	18.29	AQU	PIS	15.05	05.41	18.37	VIR	16.06	SAG	CAP	7
8	SCO	11.33	CAP	AQU	22.16	TAU	GEM	LEO	04.13	SCO	13.31	08.39	8
9	17.14	CAP	CAP	03.30	ARI	19.37	07.50	17.49	LIB	20.21	CAP	AQU	9
10	SAG	CAP	07.30	PIS	ARI	GEM	CAN	VIR	05.49	SAG	CAP	20.53	10
11	SAG	00.40	AQU	13.37	05.36	21.32	07.54	17.51	SCO	SAG	00.10	PIS	11
12	05.26	AQU	19.47	ARI	TAU	CAN	LEO	LIB	11.08	04.30	AQU	PIS	12
13	CAP	13.02	PIS	20.59	10.03	22.21	07.43	20.44	SAG	CAP	12.41	09.17	13
14	18.26	PIS	PIS	TAU	GEM	LEO	VIR	SCO	20.34	16.00	PIS	ARI	14
15	AQU	23.46	06.00	TAU	12.48	23.38	09.10	SCO	CAP	AQU	PIS	19.33	15
16	AQU	ARI	ARI	02.15	CAN	VIR	LIB	03.33	CAP	AQU	00.36	TAU	16
17	07.02	ARI	14.04	GEM	15.01	VIR	13.38	SAG	08.45	04.41	ARI	TAU	17
18	PIS	08.30	TAU	06.14	LEO	02.36	SCO	13.59	AQU	PIS	10.06	02.23	18
19	18.08	TAU	20.20	CAN	17.37	LIB	21.31	CAP	21.30	16.18	TAU	GEM	19
20	ARI	14.52	GEM	09.26	VIR	07.59	SAG	CAP	PIS	ARI	16.45	06.02	20
21	ARI	GEM	GEM	LEO	21.11	SCO	SAG	02.25	PIS	ARI	GEM	CAN	21
22	02.36	18.31	00.52	12.12	LIB	15.55	08.11	AQU	09.10	01.47	21.10	07.44	22
23	TAU	CAN	CAN	VIR	LIB	SAG	CAP	15.10	ARI	TAU	CAN	LEO	23
24	07.40	19.46	03.43	14.04	02.17	SAG	20.26	PIS	19.12	09.10	CAN	09.01	24
25	GEM	LEO	LEO	LIB	SCO	02.08	AQU	PIS	TAU	GEM	00.19	VIR	25
26	09.28	19.49	05.18	19.04	09.27	CAP	AQU	03.08	TAU	14.47	LEO	11.18	26
27	CAN	VIR	VIR	SCO	SAG	14.07	09.11	ARI	03.24	CAN	03.02	LIB	27
28	09.10	20.30	06.48	SCO	19.07	AQU	PIS	13.38	GEM	18.50	VIR	15.27	28
29	LEO		LIB	01.28	CAP	AQU	21.21	TAU	09.24	LEO	05.57	SCO	29
30	08.35		09.57	SAG	CAP	02.52	ARI	21.49	CAN	21.33	LIB	21.44	30
31	VIR		SCO		07.00		ARI	GEM		VIR		SAG	31

1984

SUN
mth dy time -> sign

JAN 1	00.00	-> CAP
JAN 20	21.05	-> AQU
FEB 19	11.16	-> PIS
MAR 20	10.25	-> ARI
APR 19	21.38	-> TAU
MAY 20	20.58	-> GEM
JUN 21	05.02	-> CAN
JUL 22	15.58	-> LEO
AUG 22	23.00	-> VIR
SEP 22	20.33	-> LIB
OCT 23	05.46	-> SCO
NOV 22	03.11	-> SAG
DEC 21	16.23	-> CAP

MERCURY
mth dy time -> sign

JAN 1	00.00	-> CAP
FEB 9	01.51	-> AQU
FEB 27	18.08	-> PIS
MAR 14	16.27	-> ARI
MAR 31	20.26	-> TAU
APR 25	11.49	-> ARI
MAY 15	12.33	-> TAU
JUN 7	15.45	-> GEM
JUN 22	06.40	-> CAN
JUL 6	18.56	-> LEO
JUL 26	06.49	-> VIR
SEP 30	19.44	-> LIB
OCT 18	03.02	-> SCO
NOV 6	12.09	-> SAG
DEC 1	16.32	-> CAP
DEC 7	20.46	-> SAG

VENUS
mth dy time -> sign

JAN 1	02.00	-> SAG
JAN 25	18.51	-> CAP
FEB 19	04.52	-> AQU
MAR 14	12.35	-> PIS
APR 7	20.13	-> ARI
MAY 2	04.54	-> TAU
MAY 26	14.40	-> GEM
JUN 20	00.49	-> CAN
JUL 14	10.31	-> LEO
AUG 7	19.40	-> VIR
SEP 1	05.07	-> LIB
SEP 25	16.05	-> SCO
OCT 20	05.46	-> SAG
NOV 13	23.54	-> CAP
DEC 9	03.26	-> AQU

MARS
mth dy time -> sign

JAN 1	00.00	-> LIB
JAN 11	03.20	-> SCO
AUG 17	19.51	-> SAG
OCT 5	06.02	-> CAP
NOV 15	18.09	-> AQU
DEC 25	06.38	-> PIS

JUPITER
mth dy time -> sign

JAN 1	00.00	-> SAG
JAN 19	15.05	-> CAP

SATURN
mth dy time -> sign

JAN 1	00.00	-> SCO

MOON

dy	jan	feb	mar	apr	may	jun	jul	aug	sep	oct	nov	dec	dy
1	SAG	AQU	17.29	ARI	TAU	05.53	LEO	04.03	16.30	05.28	AQU	PIS	1
2	06.07	AQU	PIS	23.55	16.02	CAN	19.28	LIB	SAG	CAP	07.50	03.42	2
3	CAP	11.22	PIS	TAU	GEM	10.19	VIR	06.04	22.55	14.03	PIS	ARI	3
4	16.31	PIS	06.07	TAU	23.26	LEO	21.27	SCO	CAP	AQU	20.20	16.20	4
5	AQU	PIS	ARI	10.04	CAN	13.27	LIB	10.30	CAP	AQU	ARI	TAU	5
6	AQU	00.04	18.09	GEM	CAN	VIR	LIB	SAG	08.11	01.19	ARI	TAU	6
7	04.34	ARI	TAU	17.59	04.43	16.03	00.28	17.24	AQU	PIS	08.53	03.24	7
8	PIS	12.05	TAU	CAN	LEO	LIB	SCO	CAP	19.26	13.51	TAU	GEM	8
9	17.15	TAU	04.30	23.01	08.02	18.48	05.03	CAP	PIS	ARI	20.10	11.56	9
10	ARI	21.39	GEM	LEO	VIR	SCO	SAG	02.25	PIS	ARI	GEM	CAN	10
11	ARI	GEM	11.48	LEO	09.54	22.26	11.23	AQU	07.47	02.28	GEM	18.08	11
12	04.36	GEM	CAN	01.11	LIB	SAG	CAP	13.13	ARI	TAU	05.31	LEO	12
13	TAU	03.20	15.21	VIR	11.22	SAG	19.41	PIS	20.33	14.14	CAN	22.35	13
14	12.40	CAN	LEO	01.29	SCO	03.48	AQU	PIS	TAU	GEM	12.34	VIR	14
15	GEM	05.09	15.47	LIB	13.50	CAP	AQU	01.28	TAU	GEM	LEO	VIR	15
16	16.47	LEO	VIR	01.41	SAG	11.41	06.10	ARI	08.26	00.00	17.08	01.52	16
17	CAN	04.32	14.51	SCO	18.43	AQU	PIS	14.13	GEM	CAN	VIR	LIB	17
18	17.49	VIR	LIB	03.44	22.18	CAP	18.26	TAU	17.36	06.41	19.29	04.27	18
19	LEO	03.39	14.49	SAG	CAP	PIS	ARI	TAU	CAN	LEO	LIB	SCO	19
20	17.35	LIB	SCO	09.10	02.55	PIS	ARI	01.31	22.49	09.56	20.30	06.58	20
21	VIR	04.44	17.41	CAP	AQU	10.40	06.52	GEM	LEO	VIR	SCO	SAG	21
22	18.07	SCO	SAG	18.27	14.09	ARI	TAU	09.20	LEO	10.31	21.34	10.21	22
23	LIB	09.22	SAG	AQU	PIS	22.38	17.10	CAN	00.19>VIR	LIB	SAG	CAP	23
24	21.04	SAG	00.36	AQU	PIS	TAU	GEM	13.00	23.41	10.08	SAG	15.47	24
25	SCO	17.49	CAP	06.26	02.39	TAU	23.44	LEO	LIB	SCO	00.17	AQU	25
26	SCO	CAP	11.09	PIS	ARI	08.04	CAN	13.32	23.04	10.43	CAP	AQU	26
27	03.12	CAP	AQU	19.02	14.13	GEM	CAN	VIR	SCO	SAG	06.06	00.18	27
28	SAG	05.02	23.37	ARI	TAU	14.09	02.41	12.57	SCO	14.05	AQU	PIS	28
29	12.12	AQU	PIS	ARI	23.23	CAN	LEO	LIB	00.32	CAP	15.33	11.49	29
30	CAP		PIS	06.30	GEM	17.30	03.29	13.23	SAG	21.13	PIS	ARI	30
31	23.11		12.14		GEM		VIR	SCO		AQU		ARI	31

SUN
mth dy time –> sign

JAN 1 00.00 –> CAP
JAN 20 02.58 –> AQU
FEB 18 17.08 –> PIS
MAR 20 16.14 –> ARI
APR 20 03.26 –> TAU
MAY 21 02.43 –> GEM
JUN 21 10.44 –> CAN
JUL 22 21.36 –> LEO
AUG 23 04.36 –> VIR
SEP 23 02.08 –> LIB
OCT 23 11.22 –> SCO
NOV 22 08.51 –> SAG
DEC 21 22.08 –> CAP

MERCURY
mth dy time –> sign

JAN 1 00.00 –> SAG
JAN 11 18.25 –> CAP
FEB 1 07.44 –> AQU
FEB 18 23.42 –> PIS
MAR 7 00.07 –> ARI
MAY 14 02.10 –> TAU
MAY 30 19.44 –> GEM
JUN 13 16.11 –> CAN
JUN 29 19.34 –> LEO
SEP 6 19.39 –> VIR
SEP 22 23.13 –> LIB
OCT 10 18.50 –> SCO
OCT 31 16.44 –> SAG
DEC 4 19.23 –> SCO
DEC 12 11.04 –> SAG

VENUS
mth dy time –> sign

JAN 1 00.00 –> AQU
JAN 4 06.23 –> PIS
FEB 2 08.29 –> ARI
JUN 6 08.52 –> TAU
JUL 6 08.01 –> GEM
AUG 2 09.10 –> CAN
AUG 28 03.39 –> LEO
SEP 22 02.53 –> VIR
OCT 16 13.04 –> LIB
NOV 9 15.08 –> SCO
DEC 3 13.00 –> SAG
DEC 27 09.18 –> CAP

MARS
mth dy time –> sign

JAN 1 00.00 –> PIS
FEB 2 17.20 –> ARI
MAR 15 05.07 –> TAU
APR 26 09.13 –> GEM
JUN 9 10.41 –> CAN
JUL 25 04.04 –> LEO
SEP 10 01.32 –> VIR
OCT 27 15.16 –> LIB
DEC 14 18.59 –> SCO

SATURN
mth dy time –> sign

JAN 1 00.00 –> SCO
NOV 17 02.09 –> SAG

JUPITER
mth dy time –> sign

JAN 1 00.00 –> CAP
FEB 6 15.35 –> AQU

MOON

dy	jan	feb	mar	apr	may	jun	jul	aug	sep	oct	nov	dec	dy
1	00.36	GEM	15.23	LEO	21.21	SCO	18.22	AQU	05.42	00.35	GEM	CAN	1
2	TAU	05.59	CAN	10.25	LIB	07.33	CAP	12.33	ARI	TAU	08.31	00.59	2
3	12.00	CAN	21.28	VIR	21.17	SAG	21.36	PIS	17.28	13.36	CAN	LEO	3
4	GEM	11.02	LEO	10.54	SCO	08.34	AQU	21.43	TAU	GEM	19.04	09.14	4
5	20.18	LEO	23.43	LIB	20.56	CAP	AQU	ARI	TAU	GEM	LEO	VIR	5
6	CAN	13.09	VIR	10.10	SAG	11.52	03.40	ARI	06.27	GEM	01.59	LEO	6
7	CAN	VIR	23.47	SCO	22.11	AQU	PIS	09.41	GEM	CAN	02.18	LIB	7
8	01.28	14.10	LIB	10.18	CAP	18.47	13.21	TAU	18.10	11.33	VIR	16.56	8
9	LEO	LIB	23.47	SAG	CAP	PIS	ARI	22.31	CAN	LEO	05.52	SCO	9
10	04.40	15.49	SCO	12.57	02.38	PIS	ARI	GEM	CAN	17.09	LIB	17.13	10
11	VIR	SCO	SCO	CAP	AQU	05.24	01.44	GEM	02.27	VIR	06.31	SAG	11
12	07.13	19.09	01.29	19.04	10.56	ARI	TAU	09.28	LEO	19.12	SCO	16.59	12
13	LIB	SAG	SAG	AQU	PIS	18.11	14.23	CAN	06.52	LIB	05.52	CAP	13
14	10.07	SAG	05.55	AQU	22.25	TAU	GEM	16.57	VIR	19.13	SAG	18.15	14
15	SCO	00.27	CAP	04.30	ARI	TAU	GEM	LEO	08.34	SCO	05.53	AQU	15
16	13.48	CAP	13.11	PIS	ARI	06.45	00.54	21.15	LIB	19.06	CAP	22.50	16
17	SAG	07.36	AQU	16.18	11.23	GEM	CAN	VIR	09.17	SAG	08.25	PIS	17
18	18.29	AQU	22.50	ARI	TAU	17.22	08.25	23.44	SCO	20.35	AQU	PIS	18
19	CAP	16.38	PIS	ARI	TAU	CAN	LEO	LIB	10.40	CAP	14.42	07.36	19
20	CAP	PIS	PIS	05.12	00.01	CAN	13.29	LIB	SAG	CAP	PIS	ARI	20
21	00.38	PIS	10.20	TAU	GEM	01.32	VIR	01.51	13.49	00.54	PIS	19.41	21
22	AQU	03.43	ARI	18.01	11.05	LEO	17.10	SCO	CAP	AQU	00.42	TAU	22
23	09.02	ARI	23.06	GEM	CAN	07.32	LIB	04.36	19.11	08.27	ARI	TAU	23
24	PIS	16.27	TAU	GEM	19.54	VIR	20.16	SAG	AQU	PIS	13.07	08.45	24
25	20.05	TAU	TAU	05.26	LEO	11.48	SCO	08.24	AQU	18.47	TAU	GEM	25
26	ARI	TAU	12.02	CAN	LEO	LIB	23.12	CAP	02.50	ARI	TAU	20.44	26
27	ARI	05.11	GEM	14.10	02.06	14.37	SAG	13.31	PIS	ARI	02.08	CAN	27
28	08.53	GEM	23.13	LEO	VIR	SCO	SAG	AQU	12.43	06.59	GEM	CAN	28
29	TAU		CAN	19.24	05.40	16.30	02.21	20.25	ARI	TAU	14.23	06.44	29
30	21.01		CAN	VIR	LIB	SAG	CAP	PIS	ARI	19.59	CAN	LEO	30
31-	GEM		06.51		07.07		06.25	PIS		GEM		14.43	31

1986

SUN
mth dy time –> sign

JAN 1   00.00 –> CAP
JAN 20 08.47 –> AQU
FEB 18 22.58 –> PIS
MAR 20 22.03 –> ARI
APR 20 09.12 –> TAU
MAY 21 08.28 –> GEM
JUN 21 16.30 –> CAN
JUL 23 03.24 –> LEO
AUG 23 10.26 –> VIR
SEP 23 07.59 –> LIB
OCT 23 17.14 –> SCO
NOV 22 14.45 –> SAG
DEC 22 04.02 –> CAP

MERCURY
mth dy time –> sign

JAN 1   00.00 –> SAG
JAN 5   20.42 –> CAP
JAN 25 00.34 –> AQU
FEB 11 05.21 –> PIS
MAR 3   07.22 –> ARI
MAR 11 17.36 –> PIS
APR 17 12.33 –> ARI
MAY 7   12.34 –> TAU
MAY 22 07.26 –> GEM
JUN 5   14.06 –> CAN
JUN 26 14.15 –> LEO
JUL 23 21.50 –> CAN
AUG 11 21.09 –> LEO
AUG 30 03.28 –> VIR
SEP 15 02.28 –> LIB
OCT 4   00.29 –> SCO
DEC 10 00.34 –> SAG
DEC 29 23.10 –> CAP

VENUS
mth dy time –> sign

JAN 1   00.00 –> CAP
JAN 20 05.36 –> AQU
FEB 13 03.11 –> PIS
MAR 9   03.32 –> ARI
APR 2   08.19 –> TAU
APR 26 19.10 –> GEM
MAY 21 13.46 –> CAN
JUN 15 18.52 –> LEO
JUL 11 16.23 –> VIR
AUG 7   20.46 –> LIB
SEP 7   10.15 –> SCO

MARS
mth dy time –> sign

JAN 1   00.00 –> SCO
FEB 2   06.27 –> SAG
MAR 28 03.47 –> CAP
OCT 9   01.01 –> AQU
NOV 26 02.35 –> PIS

SATURN
mth dy time –> sign

JAN 1   00.00 –> SAG

JUPITER
mth dy time –> sign

JAN 1   00.00 –> AQU
FEB 20 16.04 –> PIS

MOON

dy	jan	feb	mar	apr	may	jun	jul	aug	sep	oct	nov	dec	dy
1	VIR	06.19	SCO	CAP	AQU	04.43	TAU	GEM	01.08	VIR	14.19	02.08	1
2	20.45	SCO	14.51	CAP	14.30	ARI	TAU	06.04	LEO	VIR	SCO	SAG	2
3	LIB	09.31	SAG	03.11	PIS	15.45	10.32	CAN	10.06	01.03	15.19	01.28	3
4	LIB	SAG	17.56	AQU	23.01	TAU	GEM	17.26	VIR	LIB	SAG	CAP	4
5	00.44	12.02	CAP	09.03	ARI	TAU	23.19	LEO	16.33	04.35	15.49	01.23	5
6	SCO	CAP	21.42	PIS	ARI	04.26	CAN	LEO	LIB	SCO	CAP	AQU	6
7	02.47	14.35	AQU	17.12	09.59	GEM	CAN	02.44	06.48	17.29	AQU	03.48	7
8	SAG	AQU	AQU	ARI	TAU	17.16	10.56	VIR	SAG	SCO	AQU	PIS	8
9	03.42	18.32	02.48	ARI	22.26	CAN	LEO	10.05	08.52	SCO	21.30	09.49	9
10	CAP	PIS	PIS	03.36	GEM	CAN	20.50	LIB	CAP	PIS	PIS	ARI	10
11	05.01	PIS	10.03	TAU	GEM	05.11	VIR	15.36	SAG	11.45	PIS	19.10	11
12	AQU	01.21	ARI	15.51	11.18	LEO	VIR	SCO	03.28	AQU	04.14	TAU	12
13	08.39	ARI	20.04	GEM	CAN	15.18	04.40	19.17	CAP	16.03	ARI	TAU	13
14	PIS	11.38	TAU	GEM	23.15	VIR	LIB	SAG	06.07	PIS	13.24	06.41	14
15	16.03	TAU	TAU	04.42	LEO	22.38	09.58	21.22	AQU	22.13	TAU	GEM	15
16	ARI	TAU	08.23	CAN	LEO	LIB	SCO	CAP	09.27	ARI	TAU	19.09	16
17	ARI	00.17	GEM	16.10	08.45	LIB	12.34	22.44	PIS	ARI	00.26	CAN	17
18	03.14	GEM	21.04	LEO	VIR	02.36	SAG	AQU	14.33	06.35	GEM	CAN	18
19	TAU	12.39	CAN	LEO	14.41	SCO	13.10	AQU	ARI	TAU	12.46	07.44	19
20	16.12	CAN	CAN	00.24	LIB	03.36	CAP	00.52	22.25	17.15	CAN	LEO	20
21	GEM	22.25	07.38	VIR	17.02	SAG	13.17	PIS	TAU	GEM	CAN	19.30	21
22	GEM	LEO	LEO	04.50	SCO	03.00	AQU	05.27	TAU	GEM	01.25	VIR	22
23	04.14	LEO	14.39	LIB	16.57	CAP	14.59	ARI	09.13	05.37	LEO	VIR	23
24	CAN	04.58	VIR	06.15	SAG	02.50	PIS	13.36	GEM	CAN	12.46	05.05	24
25	13.47	VIR	18.22	SCO	16.15	AQU	20.02	TAU	21.44	18.02	VIR	LIB	25
26	LEO	09.07	LIB	06.16	CAP	05.12	ARI	TAU	CAN	LEO	20.59	11.06	26
27	20.51	LIB	20.05	SAG	17.00	PIS	ARI	01.00	CAN	LEO	LIB	SCO	27
28	VIR	12.06	SCO	06.41	AQU	11.35	05.11	GEM	09.39	04.20	LIB	13.20	28
29	VIR		21.20	CAP	20.54	ARI	TAU	13.40	LEO	VIR	01.13	SAG	29
30	02.10		SAG	09.06	PIS	21.54	17.19	CAN	18.57	11.04	SCO	12.54	30
31	LIB		23.25		PIS		GEM	CAN		LIB		CAP	31

SUN

mth dy	time	-> sign
JAN 1	00.00	CAP
JAN 20	14.41	AQU
FEB 19	04.50	PIS
MAR 21	03.52	ARI
APR 20	14.58	TAU
MAY 21	14.10	GEM
JUN 21	22.11	CAN
JUL 23	09.06	LEO
AUG 23	16.10	VIR
SEP 23	13.45	LIB
OCT 23	23.01	SCO
NOV 22	20.29	SAG
DEC 22	09.46	CAP

MERCURY

mth dy	time	-> sign
JAN 1	00.00	CAP
JAN 17	13.08	AQU
FEB 4	02.31	PIS
MAR 11	21.54	AQU
MAR 13	21.10	PIS
APR 12	20.23	ARI
APR 29	15.39	TAU
MAY 13	17.50	GEM
MAY 30	04.21	CAN
AUG 6	21.20	LEO
AUG 21	21.36	VIR
SEP 7	13.52	LIB
SEP 28	17.21	SCO
NOV 1	01.57	LIB
NOV 11	21.56	SCO
DEC 3	13.33	SAG
DEC 22	17.40	CAP

VENUS

mth dy	time	-> sign
JAN 1	00.00	SCO
JAN 7	10.20	SAG
FEB 5	03.03	CAP
MAR 3	07.55	AQU
MAR 28	16.20	PIS
APR 22	16.07	ARI
MAY 17	11.56	TAU
JUN 11	05.15	GEM
JUL 5	19.50	CAN
JUL 30	06.50	LEO
AUG 23	14.00	VIR
SEP 16	18.12	LIB
OCT 10	20.49	SCO
NOV 3	23.04	SAG
NOV 28	01.51	CAP
DEC 22	06.29	AQU

MARS

mth dy	time	-> sign
JAN 1	00.00	PIS
JAN 8	12.21	ARI
FEB 20	14.44	TAU
APR 5	16.37	GEM
MAY 21	03.01	CAN
JUL 6	16.47	LEO
AUG 22	19.52	VIR
OCT 8	19.27	LIB
NOV 24	03.20	SCO

JUPITER

mth dy	time	-> sign
JAN 1	00.00	PIS
MAR 2	18.40	ARI

SATURN

mth dy	time	-> sign
JAN 1	00.00	SAG

MOON

dy	jan	feb	mar	apr	may	jun	jul	aug	sep	oct	nov	dec	dy
1	11.54	PIS	12.37	TAU	GEM	03.25	VIR	LIB	SAG	CAP	PIS	ARI	1
2	AQU	02.09	ARI	12.16	07.39	LEO	VIR	01.09	17.04	01.51	13.40	01.06	2
3	12.36	ARI	18.11	GEM	CAN	15.56	09.55	SCO	CAP	AQU	ARI	TAU	3
4	PIS	08.53	TAU	23.33	20.06	VIR	LIB	06.47	18.22	03.39	18.02	08.13	4
5	16.51	TAU	TAU	CAN	LEO	VIR	18.03	SAG	AQU	PIS	TAU	GEM	5
6	ARI	19.23	03.26	CAN	LEO	02.24	SCO	08.51	18.37	05.35	TAU	17.20	6
7	ARI	GEM	GEM	12.04	08.07	LIB	22.05	CAP	PIS	ARI	00.16	CAN	7
8	01.13	GEM	15.24	LEO	VIR	09.06	SAG	08.37	19.34	08.57	GEM	CAN	8
9	TAU	07.55	CAN	23.28	17.29	SCO	22.43	AQU	ARI	TAU	09.10	04.40	9
10	12.39	CAN	CAN	VIR	LIB	11.53	CAP	08.01	22.57	15.04	CAN	LEO	10
11	GEM	20.21	03.54	VIR	23.09	SAG	21.49	PIS	TAU	GEM	20.45	17.30	11
12	GEM	LEO	LEO	08.06	SCO	12.05	AQU	09.09	TAU	GEM	LEO	VIR	12
13	01.18	LEO	14.55	LIB	SCO	CAP	21.36	ARI	05.54	00.31	LEO	VIR	13
14	CAN	07.26	VIR	13.41	01.41	11.45	PIS	13.38	GEM	CAN	09.29	05.40	14
15	13.45	VIR	23.34	SCO	SAG	AQU	PIS	TAU	16.22	12.34	VIR	LIB	15
16	LEO	16.44	LIB	17.01	02.37	12.54	00.00	21.59	CAN	LEO	20.48	14.41	16
17	LEO	LIB	LIB	SAG	CAP	PIS	ARI	GEM	CAN	LEO	LIB	SCO	17
18	01.15	LIB	05.57	19.21	03.42	16.56	06.04	GEM	04.50	01.06	LIB	19.33	18
19	VIR	00.04	SCO	CAP	AQU	ARI	TAU	09.19	LEO	VIR	04.47	SAG	19
20	11.09	SCO	10.32	21.45	06.24	ARI	15.33	CAN	17.13	11.50	SCO	21.08	20
21	LIB	05.09	SAG	AQU	PIS	00.09	GEM	21.58	VIR	LIB	09.16	CAP	21
22	18.30	SAG	13.48	AQU	11.23	TAU	GEM	LEO	VIR	19.41	SAG	21.20	22
23	SCO	07.57	CAP	01.02	ARI	09.54	03.13	LEO	03.58	SCO	11.32	AQU	23
24	22.35	CAP	16.18	PIS	18.39	GEM	CAN	10.23	LIB	SCO	CAP	22.10	24
25	SAG	09.08	AQU	05.41	TAU	21.22	15.50	VIR	12.30	00.57	13.13	PIS	25
26	23.42	AQU	18.46	ARI	TAU	CAN	LEO	21.35	SCO	SAG	AQU	PIS	26
27	CAP	10.07	PIS	12.06	03.55	CAN	LEO	LIB	18.49	04.33	15.41	01.05	27
28	23.17	PIS	22.12	TAU	GEM	09.52	04.26	LIB	SAG	CAP	PIS	ARI	28
29	AQU		ARI	20.43	14.59	LEO	VIR	06.49	23.08	07.27	19.36	06.37	29
30	23.24		ARI	GEM	CAN	22.34	15.59	SCO	CAP	AQU	ARI	TAU	30
31	PIS		03.46		CAN		LIB	13.24		10.19		14.29	31

1988

SUN
mth dy time –> sign

JAN 1   00.00 –> CAP
JAN 20 20.25 –> AQU
FEB 19 10.35 –> PIS
MAR 20 09.39 –> ARI
APR 19 20.45 –> TAU
MAY 20 19.57 –> GEM
JUN 21 03.57 –> CAN
JUL 22 14.51 –> LEO
AUG 22 21.54 –> VIR
SEP 22 19.29 –> LIB
OCT 23 04.44 –> SCO
NOV 22 02.12 –> SAG
DEC 21 15.28 –> CAP

MERCURY
mth dy time –> sign

JAN 1   00.00 –> CAP
JAN 10 05.28 –> AQU
MAR 16 10.09 –> PIS
APR 4   22.04 –> ARI
APR 20 06.42 –> TAU
MAY 4   19.40 –> GEM
JUL 12 06.42 –> CAN
JUL 28 21.19 –> LEO
AUG 12 17.29 –> VIR
AUG 30 20.25 –> LIB
NOV 6   14.57 –> SCO
NOV 25 10.04 –> SAG
DEC 14 11.54 –> CAP

VENUS
mth dy time –> sign

JAN 1   00.00 –> AQU
JAN 15 16.04 –> PIS
FEB 9   13.04 –> ARI
MAR 6   10.21 –> TAU
APR 3   17.08 –> GEM
MAY 17 16.26 –> CAN
MAY 27 07.36 –> GEM
AUG 6   23.24 –> CAN
SEP 7   11.38 –> LEO
OCT 4   13.15 –> VIR
OCT 29 23.20 –> LIB
NOV 23 13.34 –> SCO
DEC 17 17.56 –> SAG

MARS
mth dy time –> sign

JAN 1   00.00 –> SCO
JAN 8   15.24 –> SAG
FEB 22 10.15 –> CAP
APR 6   21.44 –> AQU
MAY 22 07.41 –> PIS
JUL 13 20.00 –> ARI
OCT 23 22.04 –> PIS
NOV 1   12.55 –> ARI

SATURN
mth dy time –> sign

JAN 1   00.00 –> SAG
FEB 13 23.50 –> CAP
JUN 10 05.23 –> SAG
NOV 12 09.25 –> CAP

JUPITER
mth dy time –> sign

JAN 1   00.00 –> ARI
MAR 8   15.44 –> TAU
JUL 21 23.59 –> GEM
NOV 30 20.54 –> TAU

MOON

dy	jan	feb	mar	apr	may	jun	jul	aug	sep	oct	nov	dec	dy
1	GEM	18.06	LEO	08.05	01.39	20.58	07.30	17.53	TAU	22.39	LEO	VIR	1
2	GEM	LEO	13.06	LIB	SCO	CAP	AQU	ARI	08.11	CAN	LEO	VIR	2
3	00.17	LEO	VIR	18.26	08.52	23.34	08.33	20.24	GEM	CAN	04.02	00.56	3
4	CAN	06.54	VIR	SCO	SAG	AQU	PIS	TAU	15.37	08.31	VIR	LIB	4
5	11.47	VIR	01.32	SCO	13.54	AQU	10.37	TAU	CAN	LEO	17.04	12.51	5
6	LEO	19.36	LIB	02.29	CAP	02.00	ARI	01.43	CAN	21.01	LIB	SCO	6
7	LEO	LIB	12.27	SAG	17.37	PIS	14.27	GEM	02.14	VIR	LIB	21.55	7
8	00.35	LIB	SCO	08.19	AQU	05.04	TAU	09.52	LEO	VIR	04.46	SAG	8
9	VIR	06.42	20.59	CAP	20.39	ARI	20.16	CAN	14.48	10.03	SCO	SAG	9
10	13.17	SCO	SAG	12.10	PIS	09.02	GEM	20.26	VIR	LIB	14.06	04.07	10
11	LIB	14.36	SAG	AQU	23.23	TAU	GEM	LEO	VIR	21.58	SAG	CAP	11
12	23.39	SAG	02.31	14.24	ARI	14.14	04.08	LEO	SCO	21.12	CAP	08.25	12
13	SCO	18.36	CAP	PIS	ARI	GEM	CAN	08.46	LIB	SCO	CAP	AQU	13
14	SCO	CAP	05.08	15.47	02.22	21.19	14.11	VIR	16.07	07.58	CAP	11.53	14
15	05.58	19.25	AQU	ARI	TAU	CAN	LEO	21.52	SCO	SAG	02.36	PIS	15
16	SAG	AQU	05.42	17.31	06.31	CAN	LEO	LIB	SCO	15.44	AQU	15.03	16
17	08.15	18.44	PIS	TAU	GEM	06.57	02.17	LIB	02.25	CAP	06.34	ARI	17
18	CAP	PIS	05.45	21.10	13.05	LEO	VIR	10.12	SAG	21.05	PIS	18.11	18
19	08.02	18.35	ARI	GEM	CAN	19.03	15.22	SCO	09.45	AQU	09.12	TAU	19
20	AQU	ARI	07.05	GEM	22.51	VIR	LIB	19.55	CAP	23.58	ARI	21.43	20
21	07.27	20.51	TAU	04.04	LEO	VIR	LIB	SAG	13.43	PIS	11.02	GEM	21
22	PIS	TAU	11.21	CAN	LEO	07.57	03.13	SAG	AQU	PIS	TAU	GEM	22
23	08.31	TAU	GEM	14.34	11.12	LIB	SCO	01.49	14.51	00.59	13.12	02.35	23
24	ARI	02.42	19.27	LEO	VIR	18.58	11.42	CAP	PIS	ARI	GEM	CAN	24
25	12.36	GEM	CAN	LEO	23.49	SCO	SAG	04.05	14.29	01.22	17.20	09.57	25
26	TAU	12.12	CAN	03.16	LIB	SCO	16.07	AQU	ARI	TAU	CAN	LEO	26
27	20.02	CAN	06.54	VIR	LIB	02.18	CAP	04.01	14.29	02.55	CAN	20.27	27
28	GEM	CAN	LEO	15.37	10.06	SAG	17.25	PIS	TAU	GEM	00.52	VIR	28
29	GEM	00.12	19.49	LIB	SCO	06.00	AQU	03.29	16.43	07.28	LEO	VIR	29
30	06.11		VIR	LIB	16.57	CAP	17.23	ARI	GEM	CAN	12.00	09.09	30
31	CAN		VIR		SAG		PIS	04.22		16.03		LIB	31

SUN

mth	dy	time	sign
JAN	1	00.00	–> CAP
JAN	20	02.08	–> AQU
FEB	18	16.21	–> PIS
MAR	20	15.29	–> ARI
APR	20	02.39	–> TAU
MAY	21	01.54	–> GEM
JUN	21	09.53	–> CAN
JUL	22	20.45	–> LEO
AUG	23	03.46	–> VIR
SEP	23	01.20	–> LIB
OCT	23	10.35	–> SCO
NOV	22	08.05	–> SAG
DEC	21	21.22	–> CAP

MERCURY

mth	dy	time	sign
JAN	1	00.00	–> CAP
JAN	2	19.42	–> AQU
JAN	29	04.06	–> CAP
FEB	14	18.11	–> AQU
MAR	10	18.08	–> PIS
MAR	28	03.16	–> ARI
APR	11	21.36	–> TAU
APR	29	19.53	–> GEM
MAY	28	22.53	–> TAU
JUN	12	08.55	–> GEM
JUL	6	00.54	–> CAN
JUL	20	09.05	–> LEO
AUG	5	00.55	–> VIR
AUG	26	06.14	–> LIB
SEP	26	15.28	–> VIR
OCT	11	06.10	–> LIB
OCT	30	13.53	–> SCO
NOV	18	03.10	–> SAG
DEC	7	14.30	–> CAP

VENUS

mth	dy	time	sign
JAN	1	00.00	–> SAG
JAN	10	18.08	–> CAP
FEB	3	17.15	–> AQU
FEB	27	16.59	–> PIS
MAR	23	18.32	–> ARI
APR	16	23.53	–> TAU
MAY	11	06.28	–> GEM
JUN	4	17.18	–> CAN
JUN	29	07.21	–> LEO
JUL	24	01.32	–> VIR
AUG	18	01.58	–> LIB
SEP	12	12.23	–> SCO
OCT	8	16.00	–> SAG
NOV	5	10.13	–> CAP
DEC	10	04.55	–> AQU

MARS

mth	dy	time	sign
JAN	1	00.00	–> ARI
JAN	19	08.11	–> TAU
MAR	11	08.52	–> GEM
APR	29	04.38	–> CAN
JUN	16	14.10	–> LEO
AUG	3	13.35	–> VIR
SEP	19	14.38	–> LIB
NOV	4	05.30	–> SCO
DEC	18	04.57	–> SAG

JUPITER

mth	dy	time	sign
JAN	1	00.00	–> TAU
MAR	11	03.26	–> GEM
JUL	30	23.50	–> CAN

SATURN

mth	dy	time	sign
JAN	1	00.00	–> CAP

MOON

dy	jan	feb	mar	apr	may	jun	jul	aug	sep	oct	nov	dec	dy
1	21.34	SAG	SAG	AQU	PIS	TAU	GEM	LEO	VIR	20.53	SAG	CAP	1
2	SCO	23.30	08.58	AQU	11.50	22.02	09.19	LEO	01.47	SCO	SAG	17.42	2
3	SCO	CAP	CAP	01.37	ARI	GEM	CAN	07.19	LIB	SCO	02.47	AQU	3
4	07.11	CAP	13.36	PIS	11.55	GEM	14.37	VIR	14.23	09.29	CAP	AQU	4
5	SAG	02.51	AQU	01.51	TAU	00.17	LEO	18.28	SCO	SAG	12.09	00.48	5
6	13.14	AQU	14.59	ARI	12.03	CAN	23.04	LIB	SCO	20.45	AQU	PIS	6
7	CAP	03.52	PIS	01.07	GEM	05.28	VIR	LIB	02.51	CAP	18.25	05.11	7
8	16.31	PIS	14.36	TAU	14.19	LEO	VIR	07.05	SAG	CAP	PIS	ARI	8
9	AQU	04.18	ARI	01.31	CAN	14.29	10.30	SCO	13.13	05.06	21.08	06.59	9
10	18.31	ARI	14.25	GEM	20.23	VIR	LIB	19.02	CAP	AQU	ARI	TAU	10
11	PIS	05.45	TAU	04.58	LEO	VIR	23.09	SAG	20.02	09.37	21.09	07.15	11
12	20.36	TAU	16.16	CAN	LEO	02.31	SCO	SAG	AQU	PIS	TAU	GEM	12
13	ARI	09.22	GEM	12.31	06.30	LIB	SCO	04.16	23.08	10.41	20.19	07.49	13
14	23.36	GEM	21.27	LEO	VIR	15.11	10.31	CAP	PIS	ARI	GEM	CAN	14
15	TAU	15.40	CAN	23.39	19.07	SCO	SAG	09.59	23.38	09.52	20.51	10.41	15
16	TAU	CAN	CAN	VIR	LIB	SCO	19.01	AQU	ARI	TAU	CAN	LEO	16
17	03.57	CAN	06.13	VIR	LIB	02.12	CAP	12.46	23.22	09.19	CAN	17.19	17
18	GEM	00.33	LEO	12.31	07.48	SAG	CAP	PIS	TAU	GEM	00.45	VIR	18
19	09.57	LEO	17.39	LIB	SCO	10.41	00.35	13.59	TAU	11.09	LEO	VIR	19
20	CAN	11.34	VIR	LIB	18.52	CAP	AQU	ARI	00.16	CAN	08.54	03.45	20
21	18.02	VIR	VIR	01.13	SAG	16.57	04.07	15.10	GEM	16.47	VIR	LIB	21
22	LEO	VIR	06.24	SCO	SAG	AQU	PIS	TAU	03.50	LEO	20.25	16.18	22
23	LEO	00.05	LIB	12.38	03.54	21.36	06.41	17.39	CAN	LEO	LIB	SCO	23
24	04.32	LIB	19.10	SAG	CAP	PIS	ARI	GEM	10.44	02.15	LIB	SCO	24
25	VIR	12.57	SCO	12.15	11.01	PIS	09.10	22.13	LEO	VIR	09.13	04.37	25
26	17.02	SCO	SCO	CAP	AQU	01.06	TAU	CAN	20.32	14.11	SCO	SAG	26
27	LIB	SCO	06.54	CAP	16.13	ARI	12.15	CAN	VIR	LIB	21.30	15.10	27
28	LIB	00.29	SAG	05.33	PIS	03.45	GEM	05.12	VIR	LIB	SAG	CAP	28
29	05.49		SAG	16.26	19.25	TAU	16.32	LEO	08.15	02.56	SAG	23.38	29
30	SCO		CAP	10.03	ARI	06.08	CAN	14.29	LIB	SCO	08.26	AQU	30
31	16.30		22.45		20.59		22.41	VIR		15.23		AQU	31

1990

SUN
mth dy time –> sign

JAN 1	00.00 –>	CAP
JAN 20	08.02 –>	AQU
FEB 18	22.14 –>	PIS
MAR 20	21.20 –>	ARI
APR 20	08.27 –>	TAU
MAY 21	07.37 –>	GEM
JUN 21	15.33 –>	CAN
JUL 23	02.22 –>	LEO
AUG 23	09.21 –>	VIR
SEP 23	06.56 –>	LIB
OCT 23	16.14 –>	SCO
NOV 22	13.47 –>	SAG
DEC 22	03.07 –>	CAP

MERCURY
mth dy time –> sign

JAN 1	00.00 –>	CAP
FEB 12	01.11 –>	AQU
MAR 11	17.15 –>	PIS
MAR 20	00.05 –>	ARI
APR 4	07.36 –>	TAU
JUN 12	00.29 –>	GEM
JUN 27	20.46 –>	CAN
JUL 11	23.49 –>	LEO
JUL 29	11.10 –>	VIR
OCT 5	17.45 –>	LIB
OCT 23	01.46 –>	SCO
NOV 11	00.07 –>	SAG
DEC 2	00.13 –>	CAP
DEC 25	22.57 –>	SAG

VENUS
mth dy time –> sign

JAN 1	00.00 –>	AQU
JAN 16	15.23 –>	CAP
MAR 3	17.51 –>	AQU
APR 6	09.13 –>	PIS
MAY 4	03.52 –>	ARI
MAY 30	10.14 –>	TAU
JUN 25	00.14 –>	GEM
JUL 20	03.41 –>	CAN
AUG 13	22.05 –>	LEO
SEP 7	08.21 –>	VIR
OCT 1	12.13 –>	LIB
OCT 25	12.03 –>	SCO
NOV 18	09.58 –>	SAG
DEC 12	07.18 –>	CAP

MARS
mth dy time –> sign

JAN 1	00.00 –>	SAG
JAN 29	14.11 –>	CAP
MAR 11	15.55 –>	AQU
APR 20	22.09 –>	PIS
MAY 31	07.10 –>	ARI
JUL 12	14.44 –>	TAU
AUG 31	11.40 –>	GEM
DEC 14	07.46 –>	TAU

SATURN
mth dy time –> sign

JAN 1	00.00 –>	CAP

JUPITER
mth dy time –> sign

JAN 1	00.00 –>	CAN
AUG 18	07.30 –>	LEO

MOON

dy	jan	feb	mar	apr	may	jun	jul	aug	sep	oct	nov	dec	dy
1	06.10	19.27	01.43	12.50	00.08	23.31	18.01	SAG	20.51	13.42	ARI	16.23	1
2	PIS	TAU	TAU	CAN	LEO	LIB	SCO	SAG	AQU	PIS	05.31	GEM	2
3	10.56	22.12	03.37	17.50	07.18	LIB	SCO	02.09	AQU	17.42	TAU	15.27	3
4	ARI	GEM	GEM	LEO	VIR	11.21	06.35	CAP	04.06	ARI	05.06	CAN	4
5	14.04	GEM	07.02	LEO	17.28	SCO	SAG	12.19	PIS	19.06	GEM	16.00	5
6	TAU	01.27	CAN	01.42	LIB	23.59	18.39	AQU	08.23	TAU	05.07	LEO	6
7	16.02	CAN	12.24	VIR	LIB	SAG	CAP	19.54	ARI	19.47	CAN	19.39	7
8	GEM	05.51	LEO	11.44	05.22	SAG	CAP	PIS	10.55	GEM	07.24	VIR	8
9	17.52	LEO	19.47	LIB	12.12	CAP	05.07	PIS	TAU	21.29	LEO	VIR	9
10	CAN	12.13	VIR	23.18	17.56	CAP	AQU	01.13	13.05	CAN	12.48	03.00	10
11	21.02	VIR	VIR	SCO	SAG	23.09	13.29	ARI	GEM	CAN	VIR	LIB	11
12	LEO	21.09	05.09	SCO	SAG	AQU	PIS	04.55	15.53	01.16	21.08	13.28	12
13	LEO	LIB	LIB	11.48	06.21	AQU	19.36	TAU	CAN	LEO	LIB	SCO	13
14	02.57	LIB	16.25	SAG	CAP	08.00	ARI	07.41	19.52	07.21	LIB	SCO	14
15	VIR	08.34	SCO	SAG	17.30	PIS	23.29	GEM	LEO	VIR	07.39	01.44	15
16	12.18	SCO	SCO	00.15	AQU	13.55	TAU	10.12	LEO	15.26	SCO	SAG	16
17	LIB	21.07	04.56	CAP	AQU	ARI	TAU	CAN	01.19	LIB	19.39	14.35	17
18	LIB	SAG	SAG	10.53	01.54	16.43	01.32	13.11	VIR	LIB	SAG	CAP	18
19	00.16	SAG	17.01	ARI	PIS	TAU	GEM	LEO	08.34	01.24	SAG	CAP	19
20	SCO	08.30	CAP	17.57	06.31	17.14	02.44	17.33	LIB	SCO	08.32	02.59	20
21	12.44	CAP	CAP	PIS	ARI	GEM	CAN	VIR	18.06	13.09	CAP	AQU	21
22	SAG	16.52	02.31	20.58	07.42	17.10	04.29	VIR	SCO	SAG	21.07	13.48	22
23	23.27	AQU	AQU	ARI	TAU	CAN	LEO	00.17	SCO	SAG	AQU	PIS	23
24	CAP	21.49	08.08	21.03	07.00	18.25	08.17	LIB	05.52	AQU	AQU	21.45	24
25	CAP	PIS	PIS	TAU	GEM	LEO	VIR	09.56	SAG	CAP	07.32	ARI	25
26	07.25	PIS	10.15	20.12	06.34	22.42	15.19	SCO	18.36	14.14	PIS	ARI	26
27	AQU	00.16	ARI	GEM	CAN	VIR	LIB	21.57	CAP	AQU	14.06	02.09	27
28	12.51	ARI	10.26	20.39	08.29	VIR	LIB	SAG	CAP	23.22	ARI	TAU	28
29	PIS		TAU	CAN	LEO	06.47	01.39	SAG	05.54	PIS	16.37	03.26	29
30	16.34		10.42	CAN	14.08	LIB	SCO	10.23	AQU	PIS	TAU	GEM	30
31	ARI		GEM		VIR		14.00	CAP		04.14		03.02	31

MOON

SUN
mth dy time –> sign

JAN 1	00.00 –>	CAP
JAN 20	13.47 –>	AQU
FEB 19	03.58 –>	PIS
MAR 21	03.02 –>	ARI
APR 20	14.09 –>	TAU
MAY 21	13.20 –>	GEM
JUN 21	21.19 –>	CAN
JUL 23	08.11 –>	LEO
AUG 23	15.13 –>	VIR
SEP 23	12.48 –>	LIB
OCT 23	22.05 –>	SCO
NOV 22	19.36 –>	SAG
DEC 22	08.54 –>	CAP

MERCURY
mth dy time –> sign

JAN 1	00.00 –>	SAG
JAN 14	08.02 –>	CAP
FEB 5	22.20 –>	AQU
FEB 24	02.36 –>	PIS
MAR 11	22.40 –>	ARI
MAY 16	22.45 –>	TAU
JUN 5	02.24 –>	GEM
JUN 19	05.40 –>	CAN
JUL 4	06.08 –>	LEO
JUL 26	13.00 –>	VIR
AUG 19	21.40 –>	LEO
SEP 10	17.14 –>	VIR
SEP 28	03.27 –>	LIB
OCT 15	14.01 –>	SCO
NOV 4	10.41 –>	SAG

VENUS
mth dy time –> sign

JAN 1	00.00 –>	CAP
JAN 5	05.03 –>	AQU
JAN 29	04.44 –>	PIS
FEB 22	09.02 –>	ARI
MAR 18	21.45 –>	TAU
APR 13	00.11 –>	GEM
MAY 9	01.29 –>	CAN
JUN 6	01.16 –>	LEO
JUL 11	05.06 –>	VIR
AUG 21	15.06 –>	LEO
OCT 6	21.15 –>	VIR
NOV 9	06.37 –>	LIB
DEC 6	07.21 –>	SCO
DEC 31	15.19 –>	SAG

MARS
mth dy time –> sign

JAN 1	00.00 –>	TAU
JAN 21	01.16 –>	GEM
APR 3	00.49 –>	CAN
MAY 26	12.19 –>	LEO
JUL 15	12.36 –>	VIR
SEP 1	06.38 –>	LIB
OCT 16	19.05 –>	SCO
NOV 29	02.19 –>	SAG

SATURN
mth dy time –> sign

JAN 1	00.00 –>	CAP
FEB 6	18.51 –>	AQU

JUPITER
mth dy time –> sign

JAN 1	00.00 –>	LEO
SEP 12	06.01 –>	VIR

MOON

dy	jan	feb	mar	apr	may	jun	jul	aug	sep	oct	nov	dec	dy
1	CAN	VIR	VIR	SCO	SAG	23.42	17.51	ARI	03.02	CAN	VIR	LIB	1
2	02.54	20.02	06.03	SCO	SAG	AQU	PIS	16.32	GEM	14.58	VIR	16.33	2
3	LEO	LIB	LIB	07.59	03.55	AQU	PIS	TAU	06.19	LEO	04.13	SCO	3
4	04.57	LIB	13.08	SAG	CAP	11.36	03.33	20.54	CAN	17.45	LIB	SCO	4
5	VIR	04.01	SCO	20.20	16.51	PIS	ARI	GEM	08.13	VIR	10.09	01.32	5
6	10.33	SCO	23.35	CAP	AQU	20.25	09.52	22.47	LEO	21.00	SCO	SAG	6
7	LIB	15.23	SAG	CAP	AQU	ARI	TAU	CAN	09.35	LIB	18.21	12.41	7
8	19.59	SAG	SAG	09.00	04.04	ARI	12.42	23.09	VIR	LIB	SAG	CAP	8
9	SCO	SAG	12.14	AQU	PIS	01.13	GEM	LEO	11.52	02.00	SAG	CAP	9
10	SCO	04.16	CAP	19.18	11.34	TAU	13.03	23.35	LIB	SCO	05.16	01.27	10
11	08.06	CAP	CAP	PIS	ARI	02.36	CAN	VIR	16.42	09.58	CAP	AQU	11
12	SAG	16.16	00.31	PIS	15.07	GEM	12.35	VIR	SCO	SAG	18.06	14.19	12
13	21.00	AQU	AQU	01.49	TAU	02.17	LEO	01.52	SCO	21.10	AQU	PIS	13
14	CAP	AQU	10.11	ARI	16.02	CAN	13.12	LIB	01.14	CAP	AQU	PIS	14
15	CAP	01.59	PIS	05.06	GEM	02.10	VIR	07.34	SAG	CAP	06.33	01.06	15
16	09.04	PIS	16.37	TAU	16.14	LEO	16.34	SCO	13.04	10.04	PIS	ARI	16
17	AQU	09.11	ARI	06.41	CAN	04.03	LIB	17.11	CAP	AQU	16.08	08.10	17
18	19.23	ARI	20.40	GEM	17.30	VIR	23.41	SAG	CAP	21.53	ARI	TAU	18
19	PIS	14.24	TAU	08.17	LEO	09.01	SCO	SAG	01.58	PIS	21.49	11.21	19
20	PIS	TAU	23.37	CAN	21.00	LIB	SCO	05.34	AQU	PIS	TAU	GEM	20
21	03.28	18.10	GEM	11.06	VIR	17.18	10.16	CAP	13.20	06.33	TAU	11.55	21
22	ARI	GEM	GEM	LEO	VIR	SCO	SAG	18.27	PIS	ARI	00.22	CAN	22
23	09.01	20.56	02.27	15.29	03.08	SCO	22.55	AQU	21.56	11.55	GEM	11.38	23
24	TAU	CAN	CAN	VIR	LIB	04.16	CAP	AQU	ARI	TAU	01.25	LEO	24
25	12.06	23.13	05.43	21.36	11.41	SAG	CAP	05.51	ARI	15.09	CAN	12.24	25
26	GEM	LEO	LEO	LIB	SCO	16.49	11.49	PIS	03.59	GEM	02.37	VIR	26
27	13.23	LEO	09.41	LIB	22.21	CAP	AQU	15.01	TAU	17.37	LEO	15.37	27
28	CAN	01.50	VIR	05.34	SCO	CAP	23.35	ARI	08.25	CAN	05.12	LIB	28
29	14.03		14.49	SCO	SAG	05.47	PIS	22.00	GEM	20.20	VIR	22.03	29
30	LEO		LIB	15.42	10.40	AQU	PIS	TAU	11.58	LEO	09.47	SCO	30
31	15.44		22.01		CAP		09.20	TAU		23.47		SCO	31

SUN

mth dy	time –> sign
JAN 1	00.00 –> CAP
JAN 20	19.33 –> AQU
FEB 19	09.44 –> PIS
MAR 20	08.48 –> ARI
APR 19	19.57 –> TAU
MAY 20	19.12 –> GEM
JUN 21	03.14 –> CAN
JUL 22	14.09 –> LEO
AUG 22	21.10 –> VIR
SEP 22	18.43 –> LIB
OCT 23	03.57 –> SCO
NOV 22	01.26 –> SAG
DEC 21	14.43 –> CAP

MERCURY

mth dy	time –> sign
JAN 1	00.00 –> SAG
JAN 10	01.46 –> CAP
JAN 29	21.15 –> AQU
FEB 16	07.04 –> PIS
MAR 3	21.46 –> ARI
APR 3	23.53 –> PIS
APR 14	17.35 –> ARI
MAY 11	04.11 –> TAU
MAY 26	21.16 –> GEM
JUN 9	18.27 –> CAN
JUN 27	05.11 –> LEO
SEP 3	08.03 –> VIR
SEP 19	05.41 –> LIB
OCT 7	10.13 –> SCO
OCT 29	17.03 –> SAG
NOV 21	19.44 –> SCO
DEC 12	08.05 –> SAG

VENUS

mth dy	time –> sign
JAN 1	00.00 –> SAG
JAN 25	07.14 –> CAP
FEB 18	16.40 –> AQU
MAR 13	23.57 –> PIS
APR 7	07.16 –> ARI
MAY 1	15.42 –> TAU
MAY 26	01.18 –> GEM
JUN 19	11.23 –> CAN
JUL 13	21.07 –> LEO
AUG 7	06.26 –> VIR
AUG 31	16.09 –> LIB
SEP 25	03.31 –> SCO
OCT 19	17.47 –> SAG
NOV 13	12.48 –> CAP
DEC 8	17.49 –> AQU

MARS

mth dy	time –> sign
JAN 1	00.00 –> SAG
JAN 9	09.47 –> CAP
FEB 18	04.37 –> AQU
MAR 28	02.04 –> PIS
MAY 5	21.35 –> ARI
JUN 14	15.56 –> TAU
JUL 26	18.59 –> GEM
SEP 12	06.05 –> CAN

SATURN

mth dy	time –> sign
JAN 1	00.00 –> AQU

JUPITER

mth dy	time –> sign
JAN 1	00.00 –> VIR
OCT 10	13.26 –> LIB

MOON

dy	jan	feb	mar	apr	may	jun	jul	aug	sep	oct	nov	dec	dy
1	07.30 CAP	AQU	PIS	19.09	GEM	22.15	VIR	SCO	SAG		12.43	09.23	1
2	SAG	14.09	AQU	03.04	TAU	11.58	LEO	08.17	SCO	17.29	AQU	PIS	2
3	19.09	AQU	09.11	ARI	TAU	13.35	CAN	22.37	LIB	00.50 CAP	AQU	21.49	3
4	CAP	AQU	PIS	11.18	00.28	13.35	VIR	11.16	SCO	CAP	01.13	ARI	4
5	CAP	02.51	20.07	TAU	GEM	LEO	VIR	SCO	10.06	04.53	PIS	ARI	5
6	07.59	PIS	ARI	17.33	04.09	15.28	00.27	17.57	CAP	AQU	13.19	08.16	6
7	AQU	14.15	ARI	GEM	CAN	VIR	LIB	SAG	22.08	17.38	ARI	TAU	7
8	20.52	ARI	05.05	22.18	07.07	18.33	04.53	SAG	AQU	PIS	23.19	15.37	8
9	PIS	23.36	TAU	CAN	LEO	LIB	SCO	04.00	AQU	PIS	TAU	GEM	9
10	PIS	TAU	12.03	CAN	09.56	23.27	12.17	CAP	10.56	05.36	TAU	20.05	10
11	08.22	TAU	GEM	01.46	VIR	SCO	SAG	16.06	PIS	ARI	06.49	CAN	11
12	ARI	06.08	16.50	LEO	13.05	SCO	22.16	AQU	23.02	15.48	GEM	22.47	12
13	17.00	GEM	CAN	04.09	LIB	06.29	CAP	AQU	ARI	TAU	12.19	LEO	13
14	TAU	09.31	19.20	VIR	17.15	SAG	CAP	04.51	ARI	TAU	CAN	LEO	14
15	21.55	CAN	LEO	06.10	SCO	15.50	10.03	PIS	09.47	00.08	16.23	00.56	15
16	GEM	10.15	20.13	LIB	23.22	CAP	AQU	17.11	TAU	GEM	LEO	VIR	16
17	23.26	LEO	VIR	09.10	SAG	CAP	22.44	ARI	18.40	06.36	19.28	03.33	17
18	CAN	09.47	20.55	SCO	SAG	03.19	PIS	ARI	GEM	CAN	VIR	LIB	18
19	22.57	VIR	LIB	14.40	08.13	AQU	PIS	04.10	GEM	11.01	22.03	07.20	19
20	LEO	10.05	23.20	SAG	CAP	16.00	11.07	TAU	00.59	LIB	LEO	SCO	20
21	22.22	LIB	SCO	23.40	19.44	PIS	ARI	12.36	CAN	13.27	LIB	12.42	21
22	VIR	13.11	SCO	CAP	AQU	PIS	21.36	GEM	04.19	VIR	00.52	SAG	22
23	23.42	SCO	05.13	CAP	AQU	04.03	TAU	17.36	LEO	14.39	SCO	20.04	23
24	LIB	20.26	SAG	11.38	08.25	08.25	TAU	CAN	05.08	LIB	05.01	CAP	24
25	LIB	SAG	15.09	AQU	PIS	13.28	04.44	19.15	VIR	16.04	SAG	CAP	25
26	04.32	SAG	CAP	AQU	19.52	TAU	GEM	LEO	04.55	SCO	11.38	05.43	26
27	SCO	07.33	CAP	00.20	ARI	19.14	08.08	18.46	LIB	19.29	CAP	AQU	27
28	13.20	CAP	03.44	PIS	ARI	GEM	CAN	VIR	05.44	SAG	21.19	17.28	28
29	SAG	20.34	AQU	11.13	04.16	21.42	08.39	18.11	SCO	SAG	AQU	PIS	29
30	SAG		16.23	ARI	TAU	CAN	LEO	LIB	09.33	02.18	AQU	PIS	30
31	01.07		PIS		09.19		08.01	19.38		CAP		06.07	31

SUN
mth dy time –> sign

JAN 1   00.00 –> CAP
JAN 20 01.23 –> AQU
FEB 18 15.35 –> PIS
MAR 20 14.41 –> ARI
APR 20 01.49 –> TAU
MAY 21 01.02 –> GEM
JUN 21 09.00 –> CAN
JUL 22 19.51 –> LEO
AUG 23 02.50 –> VIR
SEP 23 00.23 –> LIB
OCT 23 09.37 –> SCO
NOV 22 07.07 –> SAG
DEC 21 20.26 –> CAP

MERCURY
mth dy time –> sign

JAN 1   00.00 –> SAG
JAN 2   14.48 –> CAP
JAN 21 11.25 –> AQU
FEB 7   16.20 –> PIS
APR 15 15.18 –> ARI
MAY 3   21.54 –> TAU
MAY 18 06.53 –> GEM
JUN 2   03.54 –> CAN
AUG 10 05.50 –> LEO
AUG 26 07.06 –> VIR
SEP 11 11.18 –> LIB
OCT 1   02.10 –> SCO
DEC 7   01.04 –> SAG
DEC 26 12.47 –> CAP

VENUS
mth dy time –> sign

JAN 1   00.00 –> AQU
JAN 3   23.54 –> PIS
FEB 2   12.37 –> ARI
JUN 6   10.03 –> TAU
JUL 6   00.21 –> GEM
AUG 1   22.38 –> CAN
AUG 27 15.48 –> LEO
SEP 21 14.23 –> VIR
OCT 16 00.13 –> LIB
NOV 9   02.07 –> SCO
DEC 2   23.54 –> SAG
DEC 26 20.09 –> CAP

MARS
mth dy time –> sign

JAN 1   00.00 –> CAN
APR 27 23.41 –> LEO
JUN 23 07.43 –> VIR
AUG 12 01.11 –> LIB
SEP 27 02.15 –> SCO
NOV 9   05.29 –> SAG
DEC 20 00.34 –> CAP

SATURN
mth dy time –> sign

JAN 1   00.00 –> AQU
MAY 21 04.58 –> PIS
JUN 30 08.29 –> AQU

JUPITER
mth dy time –> sign

JAN 1   00.00 –> LIB
NOV 10 08.16 –> SCO

MOON   MOON

dy	jan	feb	mar	apr	may	jun	jul	aug	sep	oct	nov	dec	dy
1	ARI	11.15	GEM	14.21	00.00	10.22	SAG	16.36	PIS	ARI	10.13	02.17	1
2	17.30	GEM	GEM	LEO	VIR	SCO	SAG	AQU	21.21	16.13	GEM	CAN	2
3	TAU	16.56	02.16	16.10	01.20	13.01	01.48	AQU	ARI	TAU	20.25	09.33	3
4	TAU	CAN	CAN	VIR	LIB	SAG	CAP	02.44	ARI	TAU	CAN	LEO	4
5	01.42	18.51	05.40	15.54	01.57	17.26	09.14	PIS	10.09	04.27	CAN	14.43	5
6	GEM	LEO	LEO	LIB	SCO	CAP	AQU	14.39	TAU	GEM	04.06	VIR	6
7	06.10	18.29	05.52	15.32	03.34	CAP	19.10	ARI	22.16	14.42	LEO	18.03	7
8	CAN	VIR	VIR	SCO	SAG	00.39	PIS	ARI	GEM	CAN	08.47	LIB	8
9	07.49	17.58	04.46	17.10	07.51	AQU	PIS	03.22	GEM	21.34	VIR	20.04	9
10	LEO	LIB	LIB	SAG	CAP	10.57	07.11	TAU	07.37	LEO	10.42	SCO	10
11	08.20	19.24	04.40	22.24	15.44	PIS	ARI	14.47	CAN	LEO	LIB	21.39	11
12	VIR	SCO	SCO	CAP	AQU	23.14	19.37	GEM	12.51	00.36	11.00	SAG	12
13	09.30	SCO	07.33	CAP	AQU	ARI	TAU	22.46	LEO	VIR	SCO	SAG	13
14	LIB	00.08	SAG	07.36	02.51	ARI	TAU	CAN	14.20	00.47	11.20	00.06	14
15	12.42	SAG	14.28	AQU	PIS	11.19	06.07	CAN	VIR	LIB	SAG	CAP	15
16	SCO	08.20	CAP	19.33	15.24	TAU	GEM	02.43	13.44	00.01	13.34	04.51	16
17	18.30	CAP	CAP	PIS	ARI	21.12	13.08	LEO	LIB	SCO	CAP	AQU	17
18	SAG	19.05	00.52	PIS	ARI	GEM	CAN	03.41	13.15	00.23	19.08	12.59	18
19	SAG	AQU	AQU	08.14	03.16	GEM	16.47	VIR	SCO	SAG	AQU	PIS	19
20	02.46	AQU	13.11	ARI	TAU	04.05	LEO	03.35	14.53	03.42	AQU	PIS	20
21	CAP	07.12	PIS	20.08	13.07	CAN	18.24	LIB	SAG	CAP	04.27	00.19	21
22	13.00	PIS	PIS	TAU	GEM	08.26	VIR	04.27	19.54	10.49	PIS	ARI	22
23	AQU	19.50	01.51	TAU	20.38	LEO	19.39	SCO	CAP	AQU	16.30	13.05	23
24	AQU	ARI	ARI	06.27	CAN	11.18	LIB	07.45	CAP	21.17	ARI	TAU	24
25	00.47	ARI	13.59	GEM	CAN	VIR	22.00	SAG	04.19	PIS	ARI	TAU	25
26	PIS	08.11	TAU	14.45	02.03	13.46	SCO	13.58	AQU	PIS	05.14	00.46	26
27	13.28	TAU	TAU	CAN	LEO	LIB	SCO	CAP	15.13	09.39	TAU	GEM	27
28	ARI	18.52	00.48	20.39	05.46	16.37	02.13	22.42	PIS	AQU	16.48	09.46	28
29	ARI		GEM	LEO	VIR	SCO	SAG	AQU	PIS	22.20	GEM	CAN	29
30	01.37		09.14	LEO	08.18	20.28	08.27	AQU	03.29	TAU	GEM	15.59	30
31	TAU		CAN		LIB		CAP	09.19		TAU		LEO	31

269

1994

SUN
mth dy time –> sign

JAN 1   00.00 –> CAP
JAN 20 07.08 –> AQU
FEB 18 21.22 –> PIS
MAR 20 20.28 –> ARI
APR 20 07.36 –> TAU
MAY 21 06.49 –> GEM
JUN 21 14.48 –> CAN
JUL 23 01.41 –> LEO
AUG 23 08.44 –> VIR
SEP 23 06.19 –> LIB
OCT 23 15.36 –> SCO
NOV 22 13.06 –> SAG
DEC 22 02.23 –> CAP

MERCURY
mth dy time –> sign

JAN 1   00.00 –> CAP
JAN 14 00.25 –> AQU
FEB 1   10.28 –> PIS
FEB 21 15.16 –> AQU
MAR 18 12.04 –> PIS
APR 9   16.30 –> ARI
APR 25 18.27 –> TAU
MAY 9   21.08 –> GEM
MAY 28 14.52 –> CAN
JUL 2   23.18 –> GEM
JUL 10 12.40 –> CAN
AUG 3   06.09 –> LEO
AUG 18 00.44 –> VIR
SEP 4   04.56 –> LIB
SEP 27 08.51 –> SCO
OCT 19 06.19 –> LIB
NOV 10 12.47 –> SCO
NOV 30 04.39 –> SAG
DEC 19 06.26 –> CAP

VENUS
mth dy time –> sign

JAN 1   00.00 –> CAP
JAN 19 16.28 –> AQU
FEB 12 14.05 –> PIS
MAR 8   14.28 –> ARI
APR 1   19.21 –> TAU
APR 26 06.24 –> GEM
MAY 21 01.27 –> CAN
JUN 15 07.23 –> LEO
JUL 11 06.33 –> VIR
AUG 7   14.37 –> LIB
SEP 7   17.12 –> SCO

MARS
mth dy time –> sign

JAN 1   00.00 –> CAP
JAN 28 04.06 –> AQU
MAR 7   11.02 –> PIS
APR 14 18.02 –> ARI
MAY 23 22.37 –> TAU
JUL 3   22.30 –> GEM
AUG 16 19.15 –> CAN
OCT 4   15.48 –> LEO
DEC 12 11.32 –> VIR

SATURN
mth dy time –> sign

JAN 1   00.00 –> AQU
JAN 28 23.43 –> PIS

JUPITER
mth dy time –> sign

JAN 1   00.00 –> SCO
DEC 9   10.55 –> SAG

MOON

dy	jan	feb	mar	apr	may	jun	jul	aug	sep	oct	nov	dec	dy
1	20.15	LIB	14.43	SAG	16.34	PIS	ARI	11.05	CAN	LEO	LIB	SCO	1
2	VIR	07.49	SCO	03.38	AQU	18.31	14.23	GEM	15.37	06.39	20.19	07.13	2
3	23.31	SCO	16.54	CAP	AQU	ARI	TAU	22.22	LEO	VIR	SCO	SAG	3
4	LIB	11.14	SAG	09.45	00.47	ARI	TAU	CAN	20.33	08.56	19.46	06.43	4
5	LIB	SAG	21.24	AQU	PIS	07.14	03.12	CAN	VIR	LIB	SAG	CAP	5
6	02.29	16.02	CAP	18.51	12.01	TAU	GEM	06.31	22.57	09.22	20.02	07.52	6
7	SCO	CAP	CAP	PIS	ARI	20.03	14.17	LEO	LIB	SCO	CAP	AQU	7
8	05.34	22.16	04.15	PIS	ARI	GEM	CAN	11.42	LIB	09.47	22.48	12.24	8
9	SAG	AQU	AQU	06.09	00.50	GEM	22.43	VIR	00.26	SAG	AQU	PIS	9
10	09.16	AQU	13.09	ARI	TAU	07.22	LEO	15.07	SCO	11.44	AQU	21.03	10
11	CAP	06.23	PIS	18.48	13.43	CAN	LEO	LIB	02.25	CAP	05.04	ARI	11
12	14.25	PIS	23.59	TAU	GEM	16.29	04.48	17.56	SAG	16.09	PIS	ARI	12
13	AQU	16.49	ARI	TAU	GEM	LEO	VIR	SCO	05.44	AQU	14.44	08.56	13
14	22.04	ARI	ARI	04.48	01.27	23.16	09.15	20.53	CAP	23.18	ARI	TAU	14
15	PIS	ARI	12.27	GEM	CAN	VIR	LIB	SAG	10.42	PIS	ARI	22.00	15
16	PIS	05.20	TAU	19.41	10.58	VIR	12.35	SAG	AQU	PIS	02.44	GEM	16
17	08.42	TAU	TAU	CAN	LEO	03.48	SCO	00.18	17.31	08.56	TAU	GEM	17
18	ARI	18.05	01.29	CAN	17.31	LIB	15.09	CAP	PIS	ARI	15.41	10.25	18
19	21.22	GEM	GEM	04.45	VIR	06.20	SAG	04.34	PIS	20.34	GEM	CAN	19
20	TAU	GEM	12.54	LEO	20.54	SCO	17.30	AQU	02.30	TAU	GEM	21.13	20
21	TAU	04.27	CAN	09.58	LIB	07.32	CAP	10.27	ARI	TAU	04.21	LEO	21
22	09.35	CAN	20.39	VIR	21.51	SAG	20.38	PIS	13.47	09.28	CAN	LEO	22
23	GEM	10.48	LEO	11.40	SCO	08.37	AQU	18.55	TAU	15.33	06.01	VIR	23
24	18.55	LEO	LEO	LIB	21.43	CAP	AQU	ARI	TAU	22.15	LEO	12.27	24
25	CAN	13.27	00.14	11.18	SAG	11.10	01.56	ARI	02.41	CAN	LEO	LEO	25
26	CAN	VIR	VIR	SCO	22.17	AQU	PIS	06.13	GEM	CAN	00.09	LIB	26
27	08.38	14.06	00.46	10.48	CAP	16.44	10.31	TAU	15.12	09.05	VIR	16.17	27
28	LEO	LIB	LIB	SAG	CAP	PIS	19.07	TAU	19.07	CAN	LEO	05.22	SCO	28
29	03.39		00.15	12.05	01.19	PIS	22.13	GEM	CAN	16.21	LIB	17.45	29
30	VIR		SCO	CAP	AQU	02.07	TAU	GEM	00.55	VIR	07.21	SAG	30
31	05.34		00.41		08.03		TAU	07.00		19.46		17.57	31